ANNUAL EDITIONS

Adolescent Psychology
Eighth Edition

EDITOR

Fred E. Stickle
Western Kentucky University

Fred E. Stickle received his BS degree from Cedarville University where he majored in Social Science Secondary Education. He completed his graduate study in counseling at Wright State University (MS) and Iowa State University (PhD). He is currently a professor at Western Kentucky University where he teaches adolescent counseling. Dr. Stickle also maintains a private practice where he provides counseling for adolescents and their families.

The McGraw-Hill Companies

Connect
Learn
Succeed™

ANNUAL EDITIONS: ADOLESCENT PSYCHOLOGY, EIGHTH EDITION

1 2 3 4 5 6 7 8 9 0 QDB/QDB 1 0 9 8 7 6 5 4 3 2 1

ISBN 978–0–07–805099–2
MHID 0–07–805099–5
ISSN 1094–2610 (Print)
ISSN 2162–5670 (Online)

Managing Editor: *Larry Loeppke*
Developmental Editor II: *Debra A. Henricks*
Permissions Coordinator: *Shirley Lanners*
Marketing Specialist: *Alice Link*
Project Manager: *Melissa M. Leick*
Design Coordinator: *Margarite Reynolds*
Buyer: *Susan K. Culbertson*
Cover Graphics: *Kristine Jubeck*

Compositor: Laserwords Private Limited
Cover Images: Vicky Kasala/Getty Images (inset); Ryan McVay/Getty Images (background)

www.mhhe.com

Editors/Academic Advisory Board

Members of the Academic Advisory Board are instrumental in the final selection of articles for each edition of ANNUAL EDITIONS. Their review of articles for content, level, and appropriateness provides critical direction to the editors and staff. We think that you will find their careful consideration well reflected in this volume.

ANNUAL EDITIONS: Adolescent Psychology
8th Edition

EDITOR

Fred E. Stickle
Western Kentucky University

ACADEMIC ADVISORY BOARD MEMBERS

Preface

The word *adolescence* is Latin in origin, derived from the verb *adolescere,* which means to grow into adulthood. Growing into maturity involves change. Most would argue that, except for infancy, adolescence is the most change-filled period of life. The traditional definition was based largely on physical growth, as evident in the marked increase in height and weight.

Most researchers define the period of life between age 10 and 20 as adolescence. It is a period of transition in which a person moves from the immaturity of childhood into the maturity of adulthood. There is a growing realization that characteristics of adolescent behaviors do not result simply from the physical changes, but include a variety of psychological and social factors. Environmental settings such as family, peer, and school influence the development and the numerous and dynamic changes that take place.

It is commonplace to hear a discussion concerning adolescence as the story years with new crazes and fads or the problems of teenagers involving crime or sexuality. However, there are many strengths and even advantages to the teenage years.

This anthology of readings will help you understand the bases of the developmental changes young people experience and appropriate aspects of individuals, families, communities, and cultures that give richness to adolescent development. The selection of articles will include opinions of various authors. You may agree with some and disagree with others. Some may even spur classroom debate.

Two new learning features have been added to this edition to aid students in their study and expand critical thinking about each article topic. Located at the beginning of each unit, *Learning Outcomes* outline the key concepts that students should focus on as they are reading the material. *Critical Thinking* questions, located at the end of each article, allow students to test their understanding of the key concepts. A *Topic Guide* assists students in finding other articles on a given subject within this edition, while a list of recommended *Internet References* guides them to the best sources of additional information on a topic.

Fred E. Stickle

Fred E. Stickle
Editor

Contents

UNIT 1
Perspective on Adolescent Development

The concepts in bold italics are developed in the article. For further expansion, please refer to the Topic Guide.

UNIT 2
Developmental Changes of Adolescents: Physical, Cognitive, and Social

The concepts in bold italics are developed in the article. For further expansion, please refer to the Topic Guide.

UNIT 3
Relationships of Adolescents: Family, Peers, Intimacy, and Sexuality

The concepts in bold italics are developed in the article. For further expansion, please refer to the Topic Guide.

UNIT 4
The Contexts of Adolescents in Society: School, Work, and Diversity

The concepts in bold italics are developed in the article. For further expansion, please refer to the Topic Guide.

UNIT 5
Problem Behaviors and Challenges of Adolescents

The concepts in bold italics are developed in the article. For further expansion, please refer to the Topic Guide.

Correlation Guide

The *Annual Editions* series provides students with convenient, inexpensive access to current, carefully selected articles from the public press. **Annual Editions: Adolescent Psychology, 8/e** is an easy-to-use reader that presents articles on important topics such as *development, risk-taking, socialization,* and many more. For more information on *Annual Editions* and other *McGraw-Hill Contemporary Learning Series* titles, visit www.mhhe.com/cls.

This convenient guide matches the units in **Annual Editions: Adolescent Psychology, 8/e** with the corresponding chapters in two of our best-selling McGraw-Hill Psychology textbooks by Santrock and Steinberg.

Annual Editions: Adolescent Psychology, 8/e	Adolescence, 14/e by Santrock	Adolescence, 9/e by Steinberg
Unit 1: Perspective on Adolescent Development	**Chapter 1:** Introduction **Chapter 7:** Moral Development, Values, and Religion	**Introduction:** The Study of Adolescent Development **Chapter 9:** Autonomy
Unit 2: Developmental Changes of Adolescents: Physical, Cognitive, and Social	**Chapter 2:** Puberty, Health, and Biological Foundations **Chapter 3:** The Brain and Cognitive Development **Chapter 4:** The Self, Identity, Emotion, and Personality **Chapter 5:** Gender	**Chapter 1:** Biological Transition **Chapter 2:** Cognitive Transitions **Chapter 3:** Social Transitions **Chapter 8:** Identity
Unit 3: Relationships of Adolescents: Family, Peers, Intimacy, and Sexuality	**Chapter 6:** Sexuality **Chapter 8:** Families **Chapter 9:** Peers, Romantic Relationships, and Life Styles	**Chapter 4:** Families **Chapter 5:** Peer Groups **Chapter 10:** Intimacy **Chapter 11:** Sexuality
Unit 4: The Contexts of Adolescents in Society: School, Work, and Diversity	**Chapter 7:** Moral Development, Values, and Religion **Chapter 10:** Schools **Chapter 11:** Achievement, Work, and Careers **Chapter 12:** Culture	**Chapter 6:** Schools **Chapter 7:** Work, Leisure, and the Mass Media **Chapter 12:** Achievement
Unit 5: Problem Behaviors and Challenges of Adolescents	**Chapter 13:** Problems in Adolescence and Emerging Adulthood	**Chapter 13:** Psychosocial Problems in Adolescence

Topic Guide

This topic guide suggests how the selections in this book relate to the subjects covered in your course. You may want to use the topics listed on these pages to search the Web more easily.

On the following pages a number of websites have been gathered specifically for this book. They are arranged to reflect the units of this Annual Editions reader. You can link to these sites by going to www.mhhe.com/cls

All the articles that relate to each topic are listed below the bold-faced term.

Internet References

The following Internet sites have been selected to support the articles found in this reader. These sites were available at the time of publication. However, because websites often change their structure and content, the information listed may no longer be available. We invite you to visit www.mhhe.com/cls for easy access to these sites.

Annual Editions: Adolescent Psychology

General Sources

ADOL: Adolescence Directory Online
www.education.indiana.edu/cas/adol/adol.html

This website is intended to be a clearinghouse of links to websites related to adolescent issues. Topics range from mental health issues to conflict and violence.

Advocates for Youth
www.adovocatesforyouth.org

The Advocates for Youth website has sections specifically for professionals, policy makers, youth, and parents. Information for professionals covers a diversity of topics, such as "peer education, youth development, and youth adult partnerships."

Questions and Answers about Child and Adolescent Psychiatry
www.aacap.org/about/q&a.htm

The American Academy of Child & Adolescent Psychiatry attempts to answer questions related to feelings and behaviors that cause disruption in the lives of children and young adults and the people around them.

Search Institute
www.search-institute.org

The Search Institute has the mission of providing leadership, knowledge, and resources to promote healthy children, youth, and communities. They are the creators of the "Forty Developmental Assets."

Unit 1: Perspective on Adolescent Development

Adolescent Decision Making: Implications for Prevention Programs Summary of a Workshop
http://aspe.hhs.gov/HSP/adolescent99

In the late 1990s, policy makers, service providers, and researchers convened a workshop to examine adolescent decision making. Together, they explored major research findings and the resulting implications. This website is a result of that workshop.

American Youth Policy Forum
www.aypf.org

The goal of the American Youth Policy Forum is to provide learning opportunities to policymakers, practitioners, and researchers on youth issues. The Forum has three overlapping themes: education, youth development and community involvement, and preparation for careers.

Child Trends
www.childtrends.org

Child Trends is a national research center that studies children and youth at all stages of development. There are number of relevant research reports on this website, including: *What Works for Older Youth During the Transition to Adulthood; Lessons from Experimental Evaluations of Programs and Interventions*

(2010); *Youth Who Are "Disconnected" and Those Who Then Reconnect: Assessing the Influence of Family, Programs, Peers and Communities* (2009); and *A Developmental Perspective on College & Workplace Readiness* (2008).

Facts for Families
www.aacap.org/info_families/index.htm

The American Academy of Child and Adolescent Psychiatry provides concise, up-to-date information on issues that affect teenagers and their families. Fifty-six fact sheets include teenagers' issues such as coping with life, sad feelings, inability to sleep, or not getting along with family and friends.

National Youth Development Information Center
www.nydic.org

The mission of the National Youth Development Information Center is to provide "practice-related information about youth development to national and local youth-serving organizations." This website provides a variety of resources including information about the basics of Positive Youth Development, links to reports by other organizations, funding information, and other resources.

The Network on Transitions to Adulthood
www.transad.pop.upenn.edu

The purpose of The Network on Transitions to Adulthood is to examine the changing nature of early adulthood and the policies, programs, and institutions that support young people as they move into adulthood. Researchers associated with the Network represent a large number of disciplines, which adds to the breadth of the Network's research. An extremely large number of articles, reports, working papers, and other publications are available from this website.

The Opportunity of Adolescence
www.winternet.com/~webpage/adolescencepaper.html

This paper considers adolescence as the turning point in life, after which the future is redirected and confirmed. Discussion on the opportunities and problems of this period to the individual and society using quotations from Erik Erikson, Jean Piaget, and others is presented.

Risky Decision Making in Adolescents
www.human.cornell.edu/che/HD/Outreach_extension/risky-decision-making-in-adolescents.cfm

Valerie Reyna, well-known in the field of decision making, researches human judgment and decision making at Cornell University. This website includes information about her research, such as webcasts of presentations, newspaper articles, reports, and journal articles.

The Urban Institute
www.urban.org

The Urban Institute website has a number of useful reports about the transition to adulthood, including: *Transition to Adulthood: African American Youth and Youth from Low-Income Working Families* (2009); *Vulnerable Youth and the Transition to Adulthood* (2009); and *Coming of Age: Employment Outcomes for Youth Who Age Out of Foster Care Through Their Middle Twenties* (2008).

Internet References

Internet References

Family Violence Prevention Fund
www.endabuse.org

This website is the source of a number of innovative projects to end violence. Coaching Boys into Men (www.endabuse.org/cbim) is a national campaign to prevent violence by teaching youth men to respect women. Building Partnerships Initiative to End Men's Violence (www.endabuse.org/bpi) is a national collaborative to inspire men to take a stand against violence perpetrated by men and to play an active role in promoting healthy, vibrant relationships.

Girls Inc.
www.girlsinc.org

The Girls Inc. website provides information for both teen girls and adults. Fact sheets on this website include information on sexuality; sexual health; HIV, STDs, AIDS; and sexual harassment.

Help for Parents of Teenagers
www.bygpub.com/parents

In addition to discussing the book, *The Teenager's Guide to the Real World,* and how it can help parents, this website lists other book sources and websites for parents and teens.

National Council of Juvenile and Family Court Judges
www.ncifci.org

The Family Violence Department of the National Council of Juvenile and Family Court Judges provides a number of their publications online.

National Dropout Prevention Center/Networking
www.dropoutprevention.org/ndpcdefault.htm

According to their website, the mission of the National Dropout Prevention Center/Network is to increase high school graduation rates through research and evidence-based solutions. The Center has identified 15 strategies that have the most positive impact on the dropout rate, including school-community collaboration.

Stepfamily Association of America
www.stepfam.org

The problems that surround step-parenting and stepchildren are discussed on this website. Click on Facts and Figures and then on FAQs to reach many aspects of adolescent adjustments based on the type of family in which they live.

Talking About Health
www.abouthealth.com/t_talking.htm

This website includes information about sexuality, HIV, and AIDS, peer pressure, and other information to help adolescents.

Unit 4: The Contexts on Adolescents in Society: School, Work, and Diversity

Afterschool Alliance
www.afterschoolalliance.org

The Afterschool Alliance is dedicated to raising awareness of the importance of after school programs.

Decision Making/Reasoning Skills
http://cals-cf.calsnet.arizona.edu/fcs/bpy/content.cfm?
content=decision_making

Written for the National 4H Council, this fact sheet provides an easy-to-read introduction into adolescent decision making and reasoning skills.

National Institute on Out-Of-School Time
www.niost.org

The mission of the National Institute on Out-Of-School Time (NIOST) is to ensure that all youth and families have access to high quality programs, activities, and opportunities during non-school hours.

Public Education Network
www.publiceducation.org

The mission of the Public Education Network is to "build public demand and mobilize resources for quality public education for children through a national constituency of local education funds and individuals."

Public/Private Ventures
www.ppv.org

Public/Private Ventures is a nonprofit research organization committed to improving the effectiveness of social policies, programs and community initiatives, especially those that affect youth and young adults. Their research areas include after-school programs, mentoring, high-risk youth, and education.

What Kids Can Do
www.whatkidscando.org

A national nonprofit organization, What Kids Can Do documents the value of young people working with adults on projects that combine learning with public purpose.

Unit 5: Problem Behaviors and Challenges of Adolescents

Alcohol
National Center on Addiction and Substance Abuse at Columbia University
www.casacolumbia.org

The mission of the National Center on Addiction and Substance Abuse (CASA) is to "inform Americans about the economic and social costs of substance abuse."

Anabolic Steroid Abuse
www.steroidabuse.gov

Created by the federal National Institute on Drug Abuse (NIDA), this website contains information about steroids and steroid abuse, as well as access to the "Game Plan" PSAs, print ads, and downloadable banners featuring athletes from a variety of sports.

Athlete's Substance Use
www.drugfreesport.com/choices

This website provides information on a variety of drugs and their effects on athletes, the psychology of sport, and sport nutrition.

Internet References

Center for Change
www.centerforchange.com

This website includes a number of free resources, mostly in the form of articles written by center staff.

CopeCareDeal: A Mental Health Site for Teens
www.copecaredeal.org

CopeCareDeal is a program by the Annenberg Foundation Trust. This website includes information for teens about how to cope, how to take care of themselves, and how to deal with problems and treatment.

Cornell Research Program on Self-injurious Behavior in Adolescents and Young Adults
www.crpsib.com

This website provides links and resources for information in understanding, detecting, treating, and preventing self-injurious behavior in adolescents and young adults. It includes access to research papers; fact sheets about self-injury (including "Top 15 Misconceptions of Self-injury" and "Information for Parents"); and web-based presentations about therapies that are commonly used to treat self-injury (including Cognitive Behavioral Therapy, Dialectical Behavioral Therapy, and Mindfulness-Based Therapies).

Depression–Children and Adolescents
www.nimh.nih.gov/publicat/depchildmenu.cfnm

This website is a gateway to resources provided by the National Institute of Mental Health.

Focus Adolescent Services: Alcohol and Teen Drinking
www.focusas.com/Alcohol.html

Focus Adolescent Services is an Internet clearinghouse of information and resources to help and support families with troubled and at-risk teens.

Higher Education Center for Alcohol and Other Drug Prevention
www.edc.org/hec

This U.S. Department of Education website has interactive discussion forums as well as a "Just for Students" section.

Justice Information Center (NCJRS): Drug Policy Information
www.ncjrs.org/drgswww.html

National and international websites on drug policy information are provided on this NCJRS site.

Mental Health Risk Factors for Adolescents
http://education.indiana.edu/cas/adol/mental.html

This collection of resources is useful for parents, educators, researchers, health practitioners, and teens. It covers abuse, conduct disorders, stress, and support.

MentalHelp.Net
http://eatingdisorders.mentalhelp.net

This is a very complete list of references on eating disorders, including anorexia, bulimia, and obesity.

National Center for Injury Prevention and Control (NCIPC): Sexual Violence
www.cdc.gov/ncipc/factsheets/svoverview.htm

This section of the NCIPC website provides an overview of sexual violence, including information about the consequences, risk factors for perpetration, and information on prevention.

National Center for Missing and Exploited Children
www.ncmec.org

This website offers a number of important resources on the topic of sexual exploitation of children, including information about child pornography, sex tourism of children, and online enticement of children for sexual acts.

National Clearinghouse for Alcohol and Drug Information
www.health.org

This is an excellent general website for information on drug and alcohol facts that relates to adolescence and the issues of peer pressure and youth culture.

National Sexual Violence Resource Center
www.nsvrc.org

The National Sexual Violence Resource Center collects and disseminates a wide range of resources on sexual violence, including statistics, research, and training curricula, as well as a searchable database of organizations.

National Youth Violence Prevention Resource Center
www.safeyouth.org

The National Youth Violence Prevention Resource Center is sponsored by the Centers for Disease Control and Prevention and the Federal Working Group on Youth Violence.

Partnership for a Drug-free America
www.drugfree.org/playhealthy

This section of the Partnership's website focuses exclusively on performance-enhancing substances. Resources here include access to the Partnership's Public Service Announcements, the "Coaches Corner" blog, and the Parent Talk Kit designed to help parents communicate with their teenage athletes about healthy sport.

RAINN
www.rainn.org

RAINN (Rape, Abuse & Incest National Network) provides crisis information, information about different types of sexual violence, common reactions following sexual violence, and how to assist a friend who has been sexually assaulted.

S.A.F.E. ALTERNATIVES
www.selfinjury.com

S.A.F.E. Alternatives is committed to ending self-injurious behavior through their well-known treatment programs. Resources provided on this website include intervention tips for family, friends, schools, and others and access to research and news articles.

Suicide Awareness: Voices of Education
www.save.org

This popular website provides detailed information on suicide along with material from the organization's many education sessions.

Self-Harm: Recovery, Advice and Support
www.thesite.org/healthandwellbeing/mentalhealth/selfharm

Based in the UK, this website provides information about self-injury. Interesting aspects of this site include videos that feature men who self-injure and such thought-provoking questions as "Should I tell my parents if it's my sister or brother (who self-injures)?" or "What if it's my parents who are self-harming?"

Internet References

Self-injurious Behavior Webcast

www.albany.edu/sph/coned/t2b2injurious.htm

This video interview with Janis Whitlock (Director of the Cornell Research Program on Self-Injurious Behavior in Adolescents and Young Adults) is well produced and informative. Handouts are available and the webcast has been approved for Continuing Education credit. The hour-long webcast was created as part of the Third Thursday Breakfast Broadcast sponsored by the University of Albany, School of Public Health.

Youth Suicide League

www.unicef.org/pon96/insuicid.htm

This UNESCO website provides international suicide rates of young adults in selected countries.

UNIT 1

Perspective on Adolescent Development

Unit Selections

Learning Outcomes

After reading this unit, you should be able to:

- Discuss the reason young people today are transitioning to adulthood later in life than in the 1960s and 1970s.

- Describe the challenges of transitioning later in development for vulnerable youth.

- Explain the living arrangements of unmarried youth from the colonial period to the present.

- Contrast the living arrangements of unmarried from different time periods to the emergence of the independent life stage.

- Compare the engagement in risky behavior of youth with learning to make decisions.

- Identify implications for youth workers who work with youth involved in risky behavior.

- Discuss connectedness of today's adolescents.

- Explain how the Internet contributes to adolescent connectedness.

- Identify the processes youth go through when deciding to take risks.

- Analyze the advantages and disadvantages of reliance on intuitive decision making.

Student Website
www.mhhe.com/cls

Internet References

Adolescent Decision Making: Implications for Prevention Programs Summary of a Workshop
http://aspe.hhs.gov/HSP/adolescent99

American Youth Policy Forum
www.aypf.org

Child Trends
www.childtrends.org

Facts for Families
www.aacap.org/info_families/index.htm

National Youth Development Information Center
www.nydic.org

The Network on Transitions to Adulthood
www.transad.pop.upenn.edu

The Opportunity of Adolescence
www.winternet.com/~webpage/adolescencepaper.html

Risky Decision Making in Adolescents
www.human.cornell.edu/che/HD/Outreach_extension/risky-decision-making-in-adolescents.cfm

The Urban Institute
www.urban.org

Exactly what characterizes adolescence is not clearly established. G. Stanley Hall, who is credited with founding the scientific study of adolescence in the early part of the 1900s, saw adolescence as corresponding roughly with the teen years. He believed individuals of this age had great potential but also experienced extreme mood swings. He labeled adolescence as a period of "storm and stress." Because of their labile emotions, Hall believed that adolescents were typically maladjusted. But what did he believe was the cause of this storm and stress? He essentially believed the cause was biological. Hall's views had a profound effect on the subsequent study of adolescence. Biological factors that underlie adolescence and direct the transition from childhood to adulthood have been repeatedly studied and refined.

Historically, other researchers hold very different views on the causes and characteristics of adolescence. For example, Erik Erikson (1902–1994), a psychologist interested in how people formed normal or abnormal personalities, believed that adolescence was a key period in development. He theorized that during adolescence, individuals develop their identity. Just as Hall did, Erikson believed that there was some biological basis underlying development. Unlike Hall, however, Erikson emphasized the role society plays in the formation of the individual. Erikson proposed that adolescents must confront a number of conflicts (for example, understanding gender roles and understanding oneself as male or female) in order to develop an identity. The form of these conflicts and the problems the adolescent faced coping with them were influenced by the individual's culture. If adolescents were successful in meeting the conflicts, they would develop a healthy identity; if unsuccessful, they would suffer role diffusion or a negative identity. Similar to Hall, Erikson saw adolescence as a period where the individual's sense of self is disrupted, so it was typical for adolescents to be disturbed. Today, Erikson's ideas on identity formation are still influential. The stereotype that all adolescents suffer because of psychological problems has been called into question.

Margaret Mead, an anthropologist who started studying adolescents in the 1920s, presented a perspective on adolescence that differs from both Hall's and Erikson's. She concluded that culture, rather than biology, was the underlying cause of the transitional stage between childhood and adulthood. In cultures that held the same expectations for children as for adults, the transition from childhood to adulthood was smooth; there was no need for a clearly demarcated period where one was neither child nor adult. In addition, adolescence did not have to be a period of storm and stress or of psychological problems. Although some of Mead's work has since been criticized, many of her ideas remain influential. Today's psychologists concur with Mead that adolescence need not be a time of psychological maladjustment. Modern anthropologists agree that biology alone does not define adolescence. Rather, the socio-cultural environment in which an individual is raised affects how adolescence is manifested and characterized.

© BananaStock/PunchStock

A cogent question is, what social and cultural factors lead to the development of adolescence in our society? Modern scholars believe that adolescence as we know it today did not even exist until the end of the 1800s. During the end of the nineteenth century and the beginning of the twentieth century, societal changes caused the stage of adolescence to be "invented." In this period, job opportunities for young people doing either farm labor or apprenticeships in factories were decreasing. For middle-class children, the value of staying in school in order to get a good job was stressed. Since there were fewer job opportunities, young people were less likely to be financially independent and had to rely on their families. By the beginning of the twentieth century, legislation ensuring that adolescents could not assume adult status was passed, child labor laws restricted how much time young people could work, and compulsory education laws required adolescents to stay in school. In the 1930s, for the first time in this country's history, the majority of high school age individuals were enrolled in school. The teenagers were physically mature people who were dependent on their parents; they were neither children nor adults.

The articles in Unit 1 focus on the perspective of adolescent development. Transition to adulthood is reported from a historical perspective. Included in the historical view is the study of teen emergence of independence. One very important developmental task is making decisions. How risky behaviors effect these decisions is examined. Critical to the development of effective intervention is an understanding of the processes teens go through when deciding to take risks. One author believes that teens are more connected than ever with the help of the Internet, which helps in their development.

Passage to Adulthood

It is no longer the case that when adolescence ends, adulthood begins.

FRANK F. FURSTENBERG, PhD

It seems that few demographic trends have attracted as much attention from the mass media as the change in the timing of adult transitions. A half a century ago, adulthood came early: most male youth finished school and entered the labor force by their late teens; the majority of women married and had their first child by their early twenties, with men not far behind. In 1960, most men and women navigated the passage to adulthood—as measured by completing school, leaving home, entering full-time employment, marriage, and parenthood—by age 25. Today, only a minority completes these transitions by age 30 (see Figure 1) (Furstenberg et al., 2004). Why has this change occurred, and what does it mean for young adults, their families, and the larger society? In particular, how is this pattern of a later coming of age affecting the less privileged? This article will first discuss the transition to adulthood from a historical perspective. Then, the challenges of this transition for vulnerable youth will be explored. Finally, a few of the many policy changes which can support these youth will be examined.

Historical Perspective

A later timing of adulthood per se is neither ominous nor reassuring. Youth came of age much later at the beginning of the previous century than they did at mid-century during the postwar era. As overviewed by Fussell and Furstenberg (2005), in the early decades of the twentieth century, it took a long time to come of age because many youth could not afford to strike out on their own, and others were staying home to help support their natal families and preparing to support a family of their own in the future. Economic and social conditions changed abruptly after the Great Depression and World War II. During this time, the economy grew rapidly, absorbing young people into the labor force at a faster pace and it was possible to get a good job even without a high school diploma. At the same time, the prospect that Social Security would provide for elderly parents freed young adults to set out on their own earlier than their parents had. For 20 years, from the mid-1940s to the mid-1960s, teenagers left home and married early as a way of establishing independence; many of these couples were also pregnant, which created a powerful pressure to wed (Fussell &

Furstenberg, 2005; Rosenfield, 2007; Settersten, Furstenberg, & Rumbaut, 2005).

The pattern of early adulthood established from the mid-40s to mid-60s is now considered by many to be "the traditional family," and is the standard against which current trends are compared. However, the economy changed in the 1970s as jobs began to leave the U.S. and the price of oil skyrocketed, creating an economic recession and a period of slow growth that extended for more than a decade. The restructuring of the economy into one that relied less on manufacturing and more on skills and technology, was in part responsible for the end of early adulthood. It now takes much longer to get started because a successful start requires more education (Levy, 1999).

As a result, today a far higher proportion of young people are enrolled in school in their late teens than was true in 1970. For example, according to the U.S. Census, college enrollment among 18–19 year olds increased from 37% in 1970 to 49% in 2008 (Current Population Survey Data, Data File). However, despite this increased enrollment, college completion has barely grown in the past two decades, hovering from 20–24% for all adults over age 25 (Bauman & Graf, 2003). Increasing the rate of graduation among those who enter college remains an urgent national priority (Obama, 2009), as many more young adults are struggling to find a foothold in the labor force in their early 20s, and far fewer today have settled into full-time employment (Danziger & Rouse, 2007).

This slower passage into full-time employment has no doubt been a factor in the delay of other transitions, such as marriage and parenthood (see Table 1). Today, most couples prefer to cohabit before marrying. Gradually, teens and young adults are becoming more adept at preventing premarital births (Guttmacher, 2006), and when a premarital birth does occur, young people no longer regard it as reason to immediately wed (Furstenberg, 2007; Wu & Wolfe, 2001). Thus, both economic and cultural changes encourage, if not require, young adults in their late teens and 20s to take more time to settle into work and family roles.

This pattern of a later transition to adulthood has been greeted with some misgivings, particularly in the popular press. Young people are seen as lacking ambition, dependent, and coddled by their parents. Although some young adults

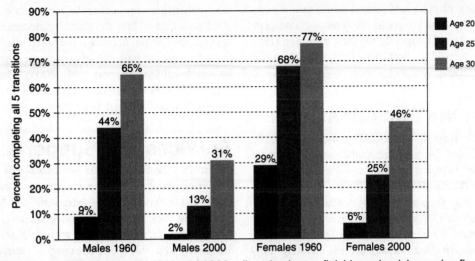

Figure 1 Completing the Adult Transition in 1960 and 2000   (Leaving home, finishing school, becoming financially independent, getting married, and having a child)

Notes: Data are from the Integrated Public Use Microdata Series extracts (IPUMS) of the 1960 and 2000 U.S. Censuses. Men are defined as financially independent if they are in the labor force, women are defined as financially independent if they have completed all transitions except employment in the labor force.

Table reprinted, with permission, from: Furstenberg, F.F., Kennedy, S., McLoyd, V.C., Rumbaut, R.G., & Settersten, R.A. (2003). *Between Adolescence and Adulthood: Expectations about the Timing of Adulthood.* (Working Paper No. 1). Philadelphia, PA: Network on Transitions to Adulthood

Table 1   Median Age at First Marriage

	Men	Women
2009	28.1	25.9
1970	23.2	20.8
1920	24.6	21.2

Data from the U.S. Census Bureau, Current Population Survey, March and Annual Social and Economic Supplements, 2009 and Earlier. Retrieved January 21, 2010 from: www.census.gov/population/socdemo/hh-fam/ms2.xls

surely fit this profile, the vast majority do not. Most who live at home do so while working or attending school, with few youth doing neither, and they rapidly enter work and family roles by their late 20s, indicating only a later, not a more problematic, entrance to adulthood (Fussell & Furstenberg, 2005). Indeed, there are distinct benefits to the delay, particularly for those youth who are gaining educational credentials. True, while many youth rely on their family for partial or even total support during this extended period of training, there is little evidence that well-educated youth are eschewing adult responsibilities. Most work while in college or graduate school, and most eventually marry and begin families of their own. The delay, it could be argued, enhances their prospects of a successful work career and appears to be linked to more stable unions. Among college graduates, who generally marry in their mid-20s or later, divorce rates have actually diminished over the past several decades (Ellwood & Jencks, 2005; Goldstein & Kenney, 2001).

Far less is known about the circumstances of youth who do not complete a four-year college degree. They are an extremely heterogeneous population, ranging from those youth who obtain an associate's degree at a community college, to those who enter but then eventually leave college, or to those who move directly into the labor force.

Family Support during the Transition to Adulthood

Family support is often essential in making a successful transition to adulthood. Families can serve as role models, provide important connections to employment, pay for schooling or other training, supply housing, and give financial support (Schoeni & Ross, 2005). The absence of family support may be linked to early departure from higher education (Luster & McAdoo, 1996). The need for material assistance during the third decade of a child's life is often a huge burden on parents with modest means, who must begin saving for their own retirement. It is unclear how these families manage to lend support to adolescent aged children transitioning to adulthood or whether these children reciprocate this material support later in life. A pattern of later transitions to adulthood may be imposing greater hardship on middle-income families than is currently recognized by policymakers, reducing children's prospects of intergenerational mobility and creating burdens for families with modest means to manage successful retirement (Berlin, Furstenberg, & Waters, in press).

For youth from families who fall just above or below the poverty line, a later transition to adulthood is the most problematic. Most families in the bottom third of the income distribution are frequently ill-equipped to provide much support to their young adult children. They often lack the material resources (income and housing), human capital (information), and social capital (connections) to help their children move into higher education or find stable employment. Not by chance, longitudinal data indicate that youth from disadvantaged families are at high risk of not making a successful transition to adulthood (finding work, forming a family, and becoming integrated into the community) (Settersten, Furstenberg, & Rumbaut, 2005). A sizable proportion of young adults who grow up in poor or near poor families have physical and mental health disabilities, come out of special education programs, experience encounters with the legal system, have children during their teens and early 20s, or merely find themselves both out of school and out of work (Osgood et al., 2005).

Stranded In the Transition

The percentage of so-called "disconnected" youth (those youth between the ages 16 and 24, who are neither working nor in school) has fluctuated between an estimated 4% and 7% during the past 20 years (Fernandes & Gabe, 2009). However, this figure excludes the rising proportion of youth who are incarcerated or those not captured by government surveys, and is, no doubt, an underestimate. Researchers at Child Trends estimate that 15% of youth age 16–24 are disconnected, meaning they are neither employed nor in school (Hair et al., 2009). Most disconnected youth in this age group are discouraged workers (i.e., unable to find a job), disabled, or caring for a child or another family member. A sizable fraction will eventually find their way into the labor force, but most are likely to remain marginally employed throughout their early adult years (Osgood et al., 2005).

There are a number of reasons why youth are vulnerable to becoming disconnected during the transition to adulthood. They may be challenged with physical or mental problems, may not have the social and family support necessary to make a successful transition, or may have been relying on government support programs (foster care, public assistance, the mental health system, among others) during their youth. Additionally, they may have dropped out of school, may lack the skills necessary to acquire a job, or lack the skills and maturity necessary to cope with adult life (Osgood et al., 2005). These vulnerable youth are disproportionately racial or ethnic minorities or from disadvantaged immigrant groups, and frequently grow up in households where a parent or parents have had mental, physical, or social problems. In a certain sense, early adulthood constitutes a last chance to provide assistance to individuals who are either off track or dealing with prior problems in school or in the criminal justice system, limited human capital, or particular disabilities.

Among the most difficult populations to serve are those who have grown up in foster care or have been incarcerated as juveniles or, worse yet, in the adult criminal justice system. Physical and mental health problems, poor social skills, behavioral problems, lack of education, cognitive disabilities, and limited familial support are common issues for youth who have been removed from their families because of neglect or abuse. Previously incarcerated youth have the added disadvantage of stigma when entering the labor market. Many, if not most, youth in these troubled circumstances face formidable challenges to self-sufficiency, forming stable and lasting emotional ties, and caring for their children when they become parents (see Foster & Gifford, 2005).

Although policymakers are aware of these disconnected and vulnerable youth, they have done little to develop comprehensive approaches to incorporate these young people into society. Over the past decade, researchers and policy makers have begun to think more about what can and should be done for youth at high risk of making an unsuccessful transition to adulthood (see Osgood et al., 2005). The costs of ignoring vulnerable youth or failing to take action to improve their prospects of succeeding will be enormous.

Services and Supports for Youth

A growing body of literature shows that older adolescents and young adults in their early 20s have the highest levels of many risk behaviors, have extraordinarily high levels of poverty when they are residing independently, and often require physical health, mental health, and social services that may not be readily available (see for example, Harris et al., 2006; Park et al., 2006). Most programs designed to provide services to older children and adolescents end around age 18 or, at most, 21. At this age youth are assumed to be prepared to enter the adult world or eligible to enter the adult service system. Whether such an assumption was true or not at times in the past, it is not viable today. This is the inevitable consequence of economic and social changes described earlier.

As a consequence, policymakers must reconsider the structure of economic and welfare support for young adults who are likely to linger in a stage of semi-autonomy for a lengthy period as they navigate the transition to adulthood. For example, improving the prospects of youth exiting foster care can be greatly enhanced by extending the age of care from 18 to 21. A recent study revealed sizable positive social outcomes (such as college attendance, work, and staying out of trouble) when foster youth were supported into their early 20s by their foster families (Osgood, Foster, & Courtney, in press). Interventions for youth exiting from the juvenile justice system are underway, but as yet we lack careful evaluations of the outcomes of these programs and policies. Far more attention must be devoted to this problem. Urgently needed are programs and services designed to divert youth who are exhibiting minor behavior problems from incarceration and into services that provide training, counseling, and other forms of assistance. As yet, we do not have an effective public system of remediation for youth at risk of failing to make a successful transition to adulthood. Government support for the development and evaluation of model programs, particularly those that combine housing, training, and social services, are a high priority.

Increasing College Completion

Of course, we have long recognized the need to provide a better link between secondary and postsecondary education for vulnerable youth and, more broadly, for those who are from low-income families, in particular those who are not college bound. Part of the problem stems from the weakness of the secondary educational systems, especially those serving disadvantaged minorities in urban areas. Improving these schools will ultimately increase the flow of students prepared for and motivated to attend college.

At the same time, the price of higher education leaves many youth far short of the resources required to complete college. Additionally, many colleges do not provide adequate support for first-generation college students. Therefore, there is much that can be done to increase the rate of college completion among students who enter higher education in the United States. While the rate of college completion in this country has stagnated, other nations have succeeded in increasing their numbers of college graduates. The United States, which once had the highest rate of college graduates, has slipped down to the middle among nations with advanced economies (Conference Board of Canada, 2010). Financial support will help, but we must improve the preparation for college among disadvantaged youth and also further develop transition programs designed to help youth remain in school once they enter higher education.

Youth Not College Bound

That said, about one-half of all young adults will never attend college, or they will start but never finish more than a course or two for credit. Two decades ago, an influential publication, *The Forgotten Half: Non-College Youth in America,* argued for an expansion of training programs and social services for youth not heading for college (William T. Grant Foundation, 1988). Since its publication, we have achieved little headway in improving the prospects for this population. The Obama administration's current emphasis on expanding the role of community colleges and vocational training may help to reinvigorate attempts to improve the human capital of disadvantaged and vulnerable youth. Community colleges are one of the few institutions that can take on this task, but they have been woefully underfunded.

The armed forces also play a constructive role in training youth who do not have a college education, but the all-volunteer military has drastically reduced the size of the population who go into the service. Moreover, the military has become more selective, usually requiring youth to have completed high school. There may well be room for increasing the role of programs that target high school dropouts, preparing them for the military, the workforce, or entrance to community colleges. One notable program, Youth ChalleNGe (www.ngycp.org), is run by the National Guard and appears to have great success in working with potential high school dropouts (Bloom, Gardenhire-Crooks, & Mandsager, 2009).

There is also room for experimentation in the area of youth development through civic engagement and public service. Although experts agree that such programs may be helpful in providing a range of skills to young adults in addition to gaining resources for postsecondary training, the current approaches need refinement, resources, and careful evaluation if they are to be expanded and made more universal (see Settersten, 2005). This is an area where we might well draw on some of the lessons of the military in training and supporting young adults for extended periods of time.

Conclusion

Only in the past decade have Americans awakened to the challenge of providing more help to young people in making a successful transition to adult roles. It is no longer the case that when adolescence ends, adulthood begins. The new schedule of growing up has introduced a stage of semi-autonomy in life when youth are receiving training and education, entering the labor market and finding a secure job, and, more broadly, learning about life by living as young adults. For those whose families can provide support during this period, this extension may not be problematic. Many families and young adults, particularly those headed for college degrees and perhaps graduate training, can and will succeed—and perhaps benefit from this new timetable.

Only in the past decade have Americans awakened to the challenge of providing more help to young people in making a successful transition to adult roles.

However, the extended passage to adulthood created by the need for a longer period of education and training has proved problematic for a substantial and growing number of youth and their families. These families lack the resources and often the know-how to manage a longer and more complex passage to adulthood. Policymakers have sometimes embraced the unrealistic vision that if early childhood programs succeeded, development in middle childhood, adolescence, and early adulthood would more or less follow automatically. We are beginning now to recognize that even if we succeed in improving the early lives of children from low-income families, many are bound to experience problems once they enter school. There is growing pressure to improve the school system and increase learning opportunities for youth during middle childhood as well as adolescence.

A serious challenge lies in bolstering the prospects of youth who are not college-bound and are from families who are ill-equipped to assist them in this lengthier and more hazardous transition to work and future family life. These youth cannot afford merely to mark time during this new period of life. Without training, support, counseling, and perhaps housing, they are likely to drop out, and not just from school or the labor force, but from family and civic life. As such, many will ultimately become charges of the state and their cost to taxpayers will only mount with time. By providing support and services to those youth as they transition to adulthood, we can hopefully divert them from lives of dependency and set them on a path to self-sufficiency.

References

Bauman, K.J., & Graf, N.L. (2003) Educational Attainment: 2000. *Census 2000 Brief.* US Census Bureau. Accessed January 19, 2010 from www.census.gov/prod/2003/pubs/c2kbr-24.pdf.

Berlin, G., Furstenberg, F.F., & Waters, M. (In press). *The Future of Children: Transition to Adulthood, 20,* 1.

Bloom. D., Gardenhire-Crooks, A., & Mandsager. C. (2009). Reengaging high school dropouts: Early results of the National Guard Youth Challenge program evaluation. Available at www.mdrc.org/publications/512/overview.html.

Conference Board of Canada (2010). Retrieved January 22, 2010 from www.Conferenceboard.ca/hcp/details/education/college-completion.aspx.

Current Population Survey Data, Bureau of the Census [Data file]. "Table A-5b. The Population 18 and 19 Years Old by School Enrollment Status, Sex, Race, and Hispanic Origin: October 1967 to 2008." Available online at www.census.gov/population/www/socdemo/school.html. Accessed January 19, 2010.

Danziger, S., Rouse, C.E. (Eds.). (2007). *The Price of Independence; The Economics of Early Adulthood,* New York: Russell Sage Foundation.

Ellwood, D.T., & Jencks, C. (2005). The spread of single-parent families in the United States since 1960. In D.P. Moynihan, T. Smeeding, & L. Rainwater (Eds.) *The Future of the Family* (pp. 25–65). New York; Russell Sage Foundation.

Fernandes, A.L.,& Gabe, T. (2009). *Disconnected youth: A look of 16- to 24-year olds who are not working or in school.* Congressional Research Service Report 7-5700, R40535. U.S. Department of State.

Foster, E.M. & Gifford, E.J. (2005). The transition to adulthood for youth leaving public systems; Challenges to policies and research. In R.A. Settersten, Jr., F.F. Furstenberg, Jr., & R.G. Rumbaut (Eds.) *On the Frontier of Adulthood: Theory, Research, and Public Policy* (pp. 501–533). Chicago, IL: University of Chicago Press.

Furstenberg, F.F. (2007). *Destinies of the Disadvantaged: The Politics of Teenage Childbearing.* New York: Russell Sage Foundation.

Furstenberg, F.F., Kennedy, S., McLoyd, V., Rumbaut, R.G., & Settersten, P. (2004). Growing up is harder to do. *Contexts, 3*(3), 42–47.

Fussell, E., & Furstenberg, F.F. (2005). The transition to adulthood during the twentieth century: Race, nativity, and gender. In R.A. Settersten, Jr., F.F. Furstenberg, Jr., & R.G. Rumbaut (Eds.) *On the Frontier of Adulthood: Theory Research, and Public Policy* (pp. 29–75). Chicago, IL: University of Chicago Press.

Goldstein, J.R., & Kenney, C.T. (2001). Marriage delayed or marriage forgone? New cohort forecasts of first marriage for U.S. women. *American Sociological Review, 66,* 506–519.

Guttmacher Institute (2006). *U.S. Teenage Pregnancy Statistics National and State Trends and Trends by Race and Ethnicity.* Author. Retrieved January 20, 2010 from www.guttmacher.org/pubs/2006/09/12/USTPstats.pdf

Hair, E.C., Moore, K.A., Ling, T.J., McPhee-Baker, C, & Brown, B.V. (2009). *Youth who are "disconnected" and those who then reconnect: Assessing the influence of family, programs, peers and communities.* Child Trends, Inc., research brief #2009–37. Washington, D.C.; Child Trends, Inc.

Harris, K.M., Gordon-Larsen, P., Chantala, K., & Udry, R. (2006). Longitudinal trends in race/ethnic disparities in leading health indicators from adolescence to young adulthood. *Archives of Pediatric and Adolescent Medicine, 160,* 74–81.

Levy, F. (1999). *Dollars and Dreams: American Incomes and Economic Change.* New York. Russell Sage Foundation.

Luster, T., & McAdoo, H.P. (1996). Family and child influences on educational attainment: A secondary analysis of the High/Scope Perry Preschool data. *Developmental Psychology, 32,* 26–39.

Obama, B. (2009, February 24). *Remarks of President Barack Obama: Address to Joint Session of Congress.* Retrieved January 20, 2010 from www.whitehouse.gov/the_press_office/remarks-of-president-barack-obama-address-to-joint-session-of-congress

Osgood, D.W., Foster, E.M., & Courtney, M.E. (In press). Vulnerable populations and the transition to adulthood. *The Future of Children, 20,* 1.

Osgood, D.W., Foster, E.M., Flanagan, C.,& Ruth, G.R. (2005). *On Your Own Without a Net: The Transition to Adulthood for Vulnerable Populations.* Chicago; University of Chicago Press.

Park, M.J., Mulye, T.P., Adams, S.H., Brindis, C.D., Irwin, C.E. (2006). The health status of young adults in the United States. *Journal of Adolescent Health, 39,* 305–317.

Rosenfield, M.J. (2007). *The Age of Independence: Interracial Unions, Same-Sex Unions, and the Changing American Family.* Cambridge, Mass: Harvard University Press.

Schoeni, R.F., & Ross, K.E. (2005). Material assistance from families during the transition to adulthood. in R.A. Settersten, Jr., F.F. Furstenberg, Jr., & R.G. Rumbaut (Eds.) *On the Frontier of Adulthood: Theory, Research, and Public Policy* (pp. 396–416). Chicago, IL. University of Chicago Press.

Settersten, R.A. (2005). Social policy and the transition to adulthood: Toward stronger institutions and individual capacities. In R.A. Settersten, Jr., F.F. Furstenberg, Jr., & R.G. Rumbaut (Eds), *On the Frontier of Adulthood: Theory, Research, and Public Policy* (pp. 534–560). Chicago: University of Chicago Press.

Settersten, R.A., Furstenberg, F.F., & Rumbaut, R.G. (Eds,) (2005). *On the Frontier of Adulthood: Theory, Research, and Public Policy.* Chicago: University of Chicago Press.

U.S. Census Bureau (2001). *Population Profile of the United States: 2000.* Author. Accessed online at www.census.gov/population/www/pop-profile/files/2000/profile2000.pdf on January 21, 2010.

William T. Grant Foundation. (1938). *The Forgotten Half: Non-college Youth in America.* Washington, D.C.: Youth and America's Future: The William T. Grant Foundation Commission on Work, Family and Citizenship.

Wu, L.L., & Wolfe, B. (Eds.) (2001). *Out of Wedlock: Causes and Consequences of Non-marital Fertility.* New York: Russell Sage Foundation.

Critical Thinking

1. What is the effect of young people transitioning later in life to adulthood than in the early 1960s and 1970s?

2. Why are youth transitioning later in life to adulthood than they did 50 years ago?

3. What challenges does a later transitioning offer for vulnerable youth?

4. What policy changes support these vulnerable youth?

FRANK F. FURSTENBERG, PhD, is the Zellerbach Family Professor of Sociology and Research Associate in the Population Studies Center at the University of Pennsylvania. He is a member of the MacArthur Foundation Research Network on Transitions to Adulthood (www.transad.pop.upenn.edu/). Dr. Furstenberg's interest in the American family began at Columbia University where he received his PhD in 1967. His recent books include *Destinies of the Disadvantaged:* *The Politics of Teenage Childbearing* (2007); *On the Frontier of Adulthood: Theory, Research, and Public Policy* edited with Richard Settersten and Rubén Rumbaut (2005); *Looking at Lives: American Longitudinal Studies of the 20th Century* edited with Erin Phelps and Anne Colby (2002); and *Managing to Make It: Urban Families in High-Risk Neighborhoods* with Thomas Cook, Jacquelynne Eccles, Glen Elder, and Arnold Sameroff (1999).

The Independence of Young Adults, in Historical Perspective

Americans have always had an image of themselves as ruggedly independent. Legends and heroes include a great number of loners, of single-minded inventors, of young people striking out on their own, of Western cowboys with no family ties. While we have always celebrated individuality, the reality of family life was usually quite different from the legend. For most of American history, young people were tightly tied to their families. It used to be the case, for instance, that unmarried young Americans usually lived with their parents. For some Americans in past eras, getting married was the only way they could move out of their parents' home.

MICHAEL J. ROSENFELD, PHD

In the 17 and 18th centuries, in some of the American colonies, it was illegal for unmarried people to live on their own (Morgan [1944] 1966). The reason colonial leaders did not tolerate people living on their own was that they wanted everyone to be part of a family so that each citizen would have at least one other co-resident citizen looking after them. Colonial leaders called this system of mutual supervision "family government." Family government ensured that rules and norms were followed, that drunkenness and revelry were held in check, that young adults were raised according to local standards, and that young peoples' marriages were made according to custom and community approval.

From colonial times until about 1940, unmarried young adults usually lived with their parents, or with relatives, or sometimes with other families. In the 17th and 18th centuries, many families sent their children away to be servants or apprentices. Beginning around World War II, this historical pattern of family government began to change. Young adults began to live on their own, and to postpone marriage. A new life stage for young adults began emerging after 1960, the Independent Life Stage (Rosenfeld 2007). The Independent Life Stage usually includes travel away from home to college, living apart from parents, moving to the city, traveling abroad, and exposure to a variety of cultures.

Figure 1 shows the percentage of unmarried young adults who lived with their parents. The data in the figure come from the decennial U.S. Census, the American Community Survey of 2005, and the Current Population Surveys of January 2008–November, 2009. From 1880 to 1940, the percentage of young unmarried women who lived with their parents was always higher than 65 percent. Young men were traditionally allowed more independence, so the percentage of young men who lived with their parents was slightly lower. In the post-1960 world,

this gender disparity has been reversed. Now it is the young women who are more likely to live apart from their parents. Feminism, birth control, the delay of marriage, and women's labor force participation are just a few of the dramatic changes that have transformed young women's lives.

In some ways, Figure 1 understates the historical change to the family system that has taken place in the last 70 years. In the 19th and early 20th centuries, many of the young adults who did not live with their parents could not have done so because their parents were already deceased. As life expectancy increased, and as parents lived longer, the opportunity to live with one's parents has increased. Yet the percentage of unmarried young adults who live with their parents declined to an all-time low in 2000.

Between 2000 and 2009, the percentage of unmarried young women living with parents has crept up a little bit, from a low of 36.2 percent in 2000, to 38.6 percent in 2005, to a range of 40–42 percent during the 2008-09. You will sometimes see stories in the popular press about the "boomerang effect," of young people increasingly returning to the parental nest (Buss 2005; Ellin 2002; Lewin 2003), but in fact the percentage of young adults who live with their parents remains near an all-time low. The popular press loves stories about young adults moving back in with their parents. In reality, young adults in their 20s seem to prefer to live on their own.

Independence of Young Adults during Economic Recession

During the deep economic recession we experienced in the U.S. starting in the fall of 2008, millions of people lost their jobs and almost a million homes were seized by banks because

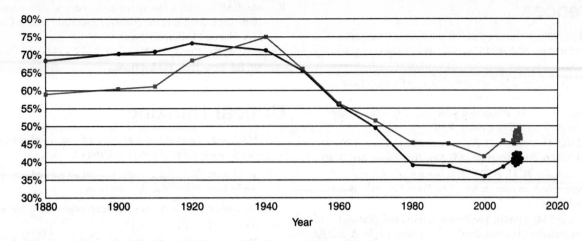

Figure 1   Percent of Young Unmarried Americans Who Live with Their Parents

Source: US Census microdata via IPUMS, 1880-2000; American Community Survey 2005; Current Population Survey data for each month Jan 2008–November 2009, via NBER. All Individuals are US born, age 20–29, never married. Percentages are weighted by household weights. "Living with Parents" means living with either or both parents.

of foreclosure. In this kind of economic environment, young people fresh out of school have had a difficult time finding jobs. You might expect that the recession would cause young people in great numbers to move back in with their parents, but the data from 2008 and 2009 do not show much of this. The cloud of points at the end of Figure 1 shows monthly data on the percentage of young adults who lived with their parents for each month from January, 2008 to November, 2009 (the most recent public data we have). These little data clouds reflect some seasonal variation and some random noise, but they do not show much of an upward spike in the percentage of young adults living with their parents during the Great Recession of 2008–2009. At most, the recession seems to have increased by a percentage point or two the proportion of unmarried young adults who live with their parents. Even in tough times, it seems that most American young adults prefer to live independently.

Independence and Parenting

Evidence suggests that middle-class and upper-middle class parents in the U.S. have been moving toward more child-centered parenting in the past 50 or 60 years. Benjamin Spock's *Baby and Child Care* has been through 8 editions and more than 50 million copies since its introduction in 1946 (and Spock's book continues to be updated and to sell even after Spock's own death, see Spock and Needlman, 2004). I remember my mother had a copy of Spock's book on the shelf and consulted it often.

Before Dr. Spock, parents were usually advised to be strict, direct, and unyielding with children. The old authoritarian parenting style was well suited to prepare children to be obedient, to grow up and to work in factories or to work on the family farm. In the post–World War II era, middle-class American parents have realized that they need to prepare their children to make it on their own someplace beyond the boundaries of immediate parental influence. Therefore, children had better be taught how to think for themselves, and how to be tolerant of others who may be different from themselves. Comparisons of the classic 1924 study by the Lynds of Muncie, Indiana, and

later follow-up studies of Muncie showed a dramatic drop in authoritarian parenting over the course of the 20th century, and a rise in parenting styles that taught children to be tolerant and to think for themselves (Alwin 1988; Lynd and Lynd 1929; Rosenfeld 2007).

Independence and Loneliness and Depression

The independence of young adults from their families has some important potential benefits. For instance, young adults are better able to choose mates without undue interference from their families. This has resulted in a rise of interracial and same-sex couples in the last few decades. The greater freedom of young people to select their own mates may be experienced as a benefit of modernity by young people; their parents may have mixed emotions about this kind of freedom.

In addition to some beneficiaries, there are also certain to be some casualties of the new Independent Life Stage. Not all young people are well suited to independence, and even young people who have plenty of independent spirit can get in to trouble. Without family close by, i.e., without family government, small problems can grow into more serious problems. Some therapists and scholars believe that our independence from our families of origin makes us more vulnerable to anxiety and depression (Olds & Schwartz 2009).

Social scientists have been complaining about the loss of community for as long as social science has existed. In the modern era, they may have a point. The long-term trends suggest that Americans are less involved in political and social life, and that Americans seem to have fewer friends (Putnam, 2000). Modern life can be lonely and disorienting, especially for young people who are only beginning to figure out where they are headed. Even when the young adults have a strong idea of where they are headed, the path to full adulthood can be full of twists and turns. Parents will inevitably worry about their young adult children, even as their young adult children exercise the very independence that the parents taught them to have.

References

Alwin, D. F., (1988). From obedience to autonomy: Changes in traits desired in children, 1924–1978. *Public Opinion Quarterly* 52:33–52.

Buss, D. (2005, January 23). Sure, come back to the nest. Here are the rules. *The New York Times,* Sec 3: P.8.

Ellin, A. (2002, June 16). You earned your wings, so return to the nest. *The New York Times,* Sec 3: P.10.

Lewin, T. (2003, December 22). For more people in 20s and 30s, home is where the parents are. *The New York Times,* Sec B: P.1.

Lynd, R. S., & Lynd, H. M. (1929). *Middletown, a study in contemporary American culture.* New York: Harcourt, Brace and Company.

Morgan, E. S. [1944]. (1966). The Puritan family: Religion and domestic relations in seventeenth century New England. 2nd Ed. New York: Harper.

Olds, J., & Schwartz, R. S. (2009). *The lonely American: Drifting apart in the twenty-first century.* Boston: Beacon Press.

Putnam, R. D. (2000). *Bowling alone: The collapse and revival of American community.* New York: Simon & Schuster.

Rosenfeld, M. J. (2007). *The age of independence: Interracial unions, same-sex unions, and the changing American family.* Cambridge, MA: Harvard University Press.

Spock, B., & Needlman, R. (2004). *Dr. Spock's baby and child care,* 8th Ed. New York: Pocket Books.

Critical Thinking

1. What were the living arrangements of unmarried young adults in the colonial period of history?

2. What were the living arrangements of unmarried young adults from World War II to the present?

3. How did the emergence of the independent life stage begin the 1960s?

4. How does the author account for the change in living arrangements over history?

MICHAEL J. ROSENFELD, PhD, is associate professor in the Department of Sociology at Stanford University, Palo Alto, CA.

From *Family Therapy Magazine,* May/June 2010, pp. 17–19. Copyright © 2010 by American Association for Marriage and Family Therapy—AAMFT. Reprinted by permission via Copyright Clearance Center.

Adolescent Decision Making

An Overview

Adolescence is a time of great changes that result in desire for autonomy in decision making, and by mid to late adolescence, most individuals have the cognitive abilities to understand and judge risks. Nevertheless, adolescents may lack the psychosocial traits required to consistently make and act upon mature decisions.

BONNIE HALPERN-FELSHER

Adolescence is a time of great and rapid cognitive, psychological, social, emotional, and physical changes. These changes result in a more adult-like appearance, an increased ability to think abstractly, greater need for autonomy and independence, increased social and peer comparison, and greater peer affiliation. These changes typically translate into adolescents' desire to participate in, and eventually lead, their decision making. Learning to make decisions, experiencing related positive and negative consequences, and learning from these outcomes is an important developmental task.

In general, with some cultural variation, adolescents are afforded opportunities to make decisions in a wide range of areas such as friendship, academics, extracurricular involvement, and consumer choices. Simultaneously, their ability to make competent decisions is sometimes called into question because adolescence is also often a time of engagement in risky behaviors, such as using alcohol, tobacco and other drugs, or engaging in risky sexual activity. Often these behaviors represent simple adolescent experimentation, while for a few adolescents these early behaviors represent the first in a line of more harmful behaviors.

This article will provide an overview of adolescent decision making, including definitions of competent decision making, descriptions of decision-making models, and the physical, cognitive, social and emotional influences on adolescent decision making. This article will also discuss implications of adolescent decision making that are relevant to health educators, healthcare providers, policy makers, and adolescent researchers.

Definitions of Competent Decision Making

Definitions of what constitutes a competent decision vary widely. It is important to note that competent decision making refers to the *process* of *how* the decision was made. Competent decision making is *not* determined by the actual behavior or outcome. For example, while adults might disagree with an adolescent's decision to have sex, an adolescent can still demonstrate decision-making competence by showing that he or she has considered and weighed all of the options (e.g., have sex, not have sex, just kiss), risks (e.g., getting pregnant, feeling guilty), benefits (e.g., pleasure), and other key components involved in the decision-making process, as described next.

Since adults are generally considered competent in the eyes of the law, many have used adults as the gold standard against which to compare adolescents. Other definitions of decision-making competence employ a model against which to compare individuals. For example, the legal standards of informed consent stipulate that decisions must be made knowingly; that one must understand all procedures, related risks, and alternative courses of action; and that a person's choice must be made without substantial input or control from others (e.g., Gittler, Quigley-Rick, & Saks, 1990; Poythress, Lexcen, Grisso, & Steinberg, 2006).

Models of Decision Making

Normative models of decision making are commonly used in theory, empirical investigation, and policy to describe competent decision making. These models describe the most common steps that one should take in order to make the most rational decision for the individual. As noted above, competent decision making is defined as the process, not the ultimate decision. Normative models encompass elements similar to the legal definition, with the components articulated in terms of five general processes: 1) identifying all possible decision options; 2) identifying the possible consequences of each option, including all possible related risks and benefits; 3) evaluating the desirability of each consequence; 4) assessing the probability or likelihood that each particular consequence will actually occur, should that course of action be adopted; and 5) combining all information using a decision rule, resulting in the identification of the best option or action. It is important to note that in this decision-making process, it is expected that one not only consider engaging in a particular action, but that one also considers the consequences associated with *not* choosing an event or behavior. This is especially important for adolescents, for whom often the choice is between engaging or not engaging in a risky behavior, both of which have positive and negative outcomes for youth (Beyth-Marom, Austin, et al., 1993; Beyth-Marom & Fischhoff, 1997).

These models of decision making have been typically used to explain engagement in health-compromising or health-promoting behavior, such as tobacco use, alcohol use, sexual behavior, seatbelt use, and so on. Many theories of health behavior have incorporated elements of these normative decision-making models, including the Theory of Reasoned Action (Ajzen, 1985), Theory of Planned Behavior (e.g., Fishbein & Ajzen, 1975), and the Health Belief Model (e.g., Rosenstock, 1974). While specific model components vary across theories, in general these theories assume that adoption of health promoting and health compromising behaviors are the result of a deliberative, rational, and analytical process, with the outcome of this process leading to increased or decreased likelihood of performing the behavior. Specifically, as shown in Figure 1, intentions to engage and actual engagement in health-related behavior is determined by an individual's:

1. assessment concerning both the potential positive and negative consequences of their actions or inactions, such as feeling more relaxed after smoking a cigarette or getting into an accident if driving drunk;
2. perceptions of their vulnerability to those consequences, such as the perceived percent chance that one would get pregnant after having unprotected sex;
3. desire to engage in the behavior despite potential consequences (e.g., I know that I can get an STD from having sex, but it is more important to me to keep my relationship); and
4. perceptions of the extent to which similar others are engaging in the behavior (e.g., most of my friends are using marijuana, so why can't I?).

While these decision-making models have been extremely useful in predicting a number of behaviors, the application of these models is limited when used to explain behaviors involving more irrational, impulsive, or socially undesirable behavior, such as tobacco use. Importantly, when placed within a developmental framework, decision making must be defined as much more than a series of complex cognitive, analytic, and rational processes. Instead, for an adolescent, the process of decision making must be immersed within the set of psychosocial, contextual, emotional, and experiential changes that define adolescence (e.g., Cauffman & Steinberg, 2000). These rational decision-making models are also less applicable to adolescents and some young adults for whom the ability to analytically process information is not yet fully formed (Gibbons et al., in press; Michels, Kropp, Eyre, & Halpern-Felsher, 2005; Reyna & Farley, 2006).

Dual-Process Models

To address the less deliberate and more social, emotional, and reactive process often employed by adolescents, it is useful to consider dual-process models that reflect multiple paths to decision making. One important path reflects the more analytic, rational processing discussed above. In this path, decision making includes deliberate, cognitive processing such as consideration of consequences and perceptions of risks and benefits; attitudes about the behaviors and related outcomes; and injunctive social norms such as what one believes others expect them to do and not do. These factors are expected to predict intentions to behave, with intentions being the most immediate predictor of actual behavior. This path also includes additional decision-making criteria (e.g., Gibbons et al., in press; Reyna & Farley, 2006), such as:

- the willingness to make a decision;
- the capacity to make autonomous decisions;
- searching for, recognizing, and incorporating new information relevant to the decision;
- the ability to judge the value of advice from other sources;
- the willingness to change one's decisions;
- the ability to implement and carry out one's decisions;
- the ability to evaluate and learn from one's decisions;
- the ability to reach decisions one is satisfied with; and
- the ability to make decisions that are consistent with one's goals.

Their ability to make competent decisions is sometimes called into question because adolescence is also often a time of engagement in risky behaviors.

The second path represents the less planned and more experience-based, reactive, and affective path often employed by adolescents. This path includes descriptive social norms such as personal perceptions and misperceptions about the extent to which peers and other important groups are engaging in a behavior as well as images or perceptions regarding others who have engaged or are engaging in a behavior. For example, adolescents are less likely to smoke if they hold negative images that smokers are dirty, wrinkled, and have yellow teeth.

This path also includes variation in adolescents' psychosocial maturity to make decisions (Cauffman & Steinberg, 2000), including the following:

- acknowledgement that adolescents' decisions are often impulsive rather than planned;
- ability to recognize and acknowledge when advice is needed;
- social perspective taking, or the ability to recognize that other people may have a different point of view or set of knowledge from one's own;
- future perspective taking, including the ability to project into the future, to consider possible outcomes associated with various choices, and to plan for the future.

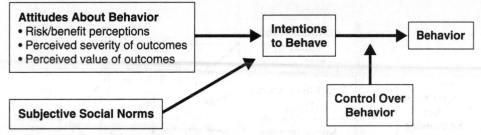

Figure 1 General model of health-related decision making.

These variables are expected to predict willingness to consider a behavior. Willingness to engage is differentiated from the planful notion of intentions. While one may not have an active plan in mind to smoke or have unprotected sex, it is often the case that adolescents find themselves in situations in which they would consider engaging in the behavior even though they were originally committed to avoiding it. Figure 2 depicts these processes.

Adolescents' decisions are often impulsive rather than planned.

A particular focus within all of these models of decision making, especially as they pertain to adolescents, has been the notion of risk perceptions or risk judgments. Individuals' beliefs about the degree to which they are vulnerable to specific negative outcomes are viewed as crucial factors in individuals' decisions concerning health-damaging and health-promoting behaviors. More specifically, theory and research indicates that individuals take risks in part because they believe they are invulnerable to harm, or less likely to experience harm compared to others (e.g., Song et al., in press). More recently, research suggests that in addition to health risks (e.g., lung cancer, pregnancy), adolescents view perceptions of and knowledge about social risks as critical in their decision making. This makes sense when one realizes that adolescence is a time when peers and other social factors play a large role in adolescent development, and therefore their decisions. It has also been recognized that an emphasis on perceived risk alone may be inadequate to predict or change behavior because risk is only part of the behavioral decision-making equation. Adolescents' perceptions of benefits have also been shown to factor into their decision-making equations, and may explain why adolescents engage in particular behaviors despite known risks (e.g., Goldberg, Halpern-Felsher, & Millstein, 2002; Millstein & Halpern-Felsher, 2002; Song et al., in press).

Factors Influencing Adolescent Decision Making
Gender Differences in Decision Making

Adolescent boys and girls do differ in their perceptions of and concerns over health-related risks and benefits. For example, girls are more likely to believe that they can get pregnant from having unprotected sex, get lung cancer from smoking, and have an accident while driving drunk. In contrast, boys perceive that they are more likely to experience positive outcomes, such as experiencing pleasure from sex. Despite these differences in perceptions, studies have not determined whether the actual decision-making process differs between adolescent boys and girls. The few studies that have examined gender differences in decision making have generally found that the process is remarkably similar (e.g., Michels et al., 2005).

Age Differences in Decision Making

Given the importance of understanding age differences in competent decision making, there are surprisingly few studies that have compared adolescents' and adults' decision making, or examined age differences in decision-making competence within the adolescent years. A review of the small literature base paints a mixed picture regarding adolescent decision-making competency, with some studies suggesting no or few age differences between adolescents and adults, and others showing significant age differences, with younger adolescents demonstrating less competence than older adolescents and/or adults. The age differences reported by these studies suggest that competence continues to increase throughout adolescence and into young adulthood. Furthermore, many of the attributes that are thought to be essential for competent decision making, such as resistance to peer pressure, self-reliance, perspective taking, future time perspective, and impulse control, also increase with age and over time (see, for example, Halpern-Felsher & Cauffman, 2001; Steinberg & Monahan, 2007).

Cultural Variation in Decision Making

Unfortunately, few studies have examined cultural variation in adolescent decision-making competence or decision-making processing.[1] However, there is racial, ethnic, and cultural variation in certain areas of psychosocial development known to influence decision-making capacities, such as autonomy, orientation to the future, and values for academic achievement. Research has also documented that approaches to decision making itself vary. For example, in some cultures (such as some Native American or Asian cultures), decision making is a group dynamic, with much input and directive from the family or other adults. In these decisions, not only is the individual considered, but the impact that the decision and potential outcomes have on family members and others is put into the decision-making equation. In contrast, in other cultures such as in Northern Europe, decision making is more of an individual

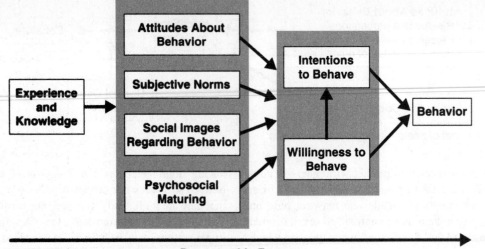

Figure 2 Dual-process model of adolescent decision making: cognitive, psychosocial, and experiential factors.

process, and the impact of the decision on the family is less likely to enter into the decision process. Clearly, in order to successfully understand and encourage competent adolescent decision making, one must have sufficient understanding of the relevant cultural systems that underlie decision making.

The Role of Experience and Knowledge

Adolescents simply have less experience with and knowledge about making decisions than do adults. Thus, adolescents have fewer opportunities to receive feedback, whether positive or negative, for the choices they have made. Experience with and knowledge about choices and obtaining feedback from decisions is especially important when one considers that perceptions of risks and benefits play a critical role in decision making. To the extent that adolescents have less experience with and less knowledge about making decisions, as well as less experience with decision outcomes, they might believe that they are less likely to experience harm and therefore discount harm in the future. Adolescents are also less aware of the cumulative nature of their behaviors as they have received so little feedback (Jacobs, 2004).

The Role of Social/Peer Affiliation

In addition to the vast number of individual-level physical, social, and emotional transformations occurring, adolescence is also defined as a time in which the social environment is also greatly changing. Compared to children, adolescents are less likely to be in structured and supervised settings, and they are more likely to affiliate with similar-aged peers rather than adults. Such environmental and social changes certainly lead to increased opportunities to make decisions and receive feedback. These decisions are also influenced by the normative behavior of adolescents' peers as well as by their perceived norms—that is, the extent to which they believe their peers are engaging in certain behaviors or making decisions. Simultaneous to adolescents' greater peer affiliation, they are also struggling with learning to make more

autonomous decisions, which requires the ability to resist undue influence from others (e.g., Gibbons et al., in press).

> **In order to successfully understand and encourage competent adolescent decision making, one must have sufficient understanding of the relevant cultural systems that underlie decision making.**

Brain Development

There are four lobes in the brain: parietal lobe, occipital lobe, temporal lobe, and the frontal lobe. The frontal lobe is the largest part of the brain, and contains the prefrontal cortex, which is located in front of the brain, behind the forehead. The prefrontal cortex is responsible for executive functions, including cognition, thought, imagination, abstract thinking, planning, and impulse control. In short, the prefrontal cortex oversees critical abilities for decision making. Research has shown that gray matter, or the tissue in the frontal lobe responsible for our ability to think, is reduced or "shed" during the adolescent and young adult years. Simultaneously, a process of myelination occurs, where the white matter in the brain matures to work more efficiently. These processes have been shown to continue through age 25. As such, the aspects of the brain responsible for decision making and impulse control are not fully developed until young adulthood, with males developing even slower than females (see for example, Giedd, 2008).

> **Adolescents' perceptions of benefits have also been shown to factor into their decision-making equations, and may explain why adolescents engage in particular behaviors despite known risks.**

Implications and Importance of Adolescent Decision Making

The questions of how adolescents make decisions and the extent to which adolescents can and do make informed choices have been of great interest to researchers and practitioners in diverse areas including the behavioral sciences, medicine, social work, law, and social policy. A number of compelling forces have motivated this interest. The primary motivator has been the desire to understand and prevent adolescents' engagement in risky behavior. Adolescents' decisions to engage in risky behaviors have led many to conclude that adolescents take risks because they perceive low likelihood of experiencing negative consequences, perceive themselves to be invulnerable to harm, and have poorly developed decision-making skills. Others have interpreted adolescents' risky behavior as evidence of their impulsive nature and that they are easily persuaded by others. As such, intervention and prevention programs focus on enhancing decision-making competence through various knowledge and skill-building efforts. For example, extensive efforts have been made to provide adolescents with information about risks, particularly health risks, to reduce their engagement in risky behavior. Program curricula have also focused on developing adolescents' skills, such as skills to resist peer pressure.

More recently, it has been recognized that rather than solely focusing efforts on disseminating information about the health implications of risky behavior, we need to broaden our discussions to include aspects of decision making most relevant and immediate to youth. For example, we need to acknowledge potential benefits of various risky behaviors, and provide youth with safer ways of obtaining similar benefits or learning how to delay the need or acknowledge and defer the desire for such benefits. We also need to include in the discussion social consequences that adolescents highly value in their decision-making process. For example, studies have shown that adolescents care greatly about whether they are popular or look more grown up, and such desires to gain positive social feedback and avoid negative social consequences influences their decisions (e.g., Ott, Millstein, Ofner, & Halpern-Felsher, 2006). Finally, we need to encourage youth to make conscious decisions and help them set meaningful boundaries for themselves that encompass their goals, relationship desires, and other developmental needs.

Concern over adolescents' decision-making competence is also relevant to adolescents' rights to make certain decisions, such as whether to participate in research studies, obtain medical treatment, or refuse medical treatment. Given results demonstrating adolescents' relative lack of maturity, many of these rights have been greatly restricted by federal, state, and local laws. Such presumptions about the inherent immaturity of adolescents are pervasive within the law. For example, the age of majority is 18 years in all but three states (Alaska, Nebraska, and Wyoming, where the age is 19). Individuals below age 18 are neither expected nor permitted to be responsible for their own welfare. Similarly, research showing that adolescents' decision making is less competent compared to adults or compared to standards set forth in normative decision-making models has led to justifying raising the age at which adolescents accused of violent crimes may be tried as adults (Gittler et al., 1990; Grisso et al., 2003; Poythress et al., 2006).

Summary

In summary, there is great interest and importance in understanding the extent to which adolescents are able to make competent decisions. Adolescence is a time of great changes that result in desire for autonomy in decision making, and by mid to late adolescence, most individuals have the cognitive abilities to understand and judge risks. Nevertheless, adolescents may lack the psychosocial traits required to consistently make and act upon mature decisions. It is thus imperative that we protect adolescents from serious harm while simultaneously providing them with appropriately risky opportunities to practice and grow their decision-making skills.

Note

1. Culture in this case encompasses a broad definition, including race, ethnicity, country of origin, acculturation, language use, economic status, and social status.

References

Ajzen, I. (1985). From intentions to actions. In J. Kuhl & J. Beckman (Eds.), *Action Control from Cognition to Behavior.* New York: Springer-Verlag.

Beyth-Marom, R., Austin, L., Fischhoff, B., Palmgren, C., & Jacobs-Quadrel, M. (1993). Perceived consequences of risky behaviors: Adults and adolescents. *Developmental Psychology, 29,* 549–563.

Beyth-Marom, R., & Fischhoff, B. (1997). Adolescents' decisions about risks: A cognitive perspective. In J. Schulenberg, J.L. Maggs, & K. Hurrelmann (Eds.) *Health risks and developmental transition during adolescence* (pp. 110–135). Cambridge, UK: Cambridge University Press.

Cauffman, E., & Steinberg, L. (2000). (Im)maturity of Judgment in Adolescence: Why adolescents may be less culpable than adults. *Behavioral Sciences & the Law, 18,* 741–764.

Fishbein. M., & Ajzen, I. (1975). *Beliefs, attitudes, intention, and behavior: An introduction to theory and research.* Reading, MA: Addison-Wesley.

Gibbons, F.X., Houlihan A.E., & Gerrard, M. (In Press). Reason and reaction: The utility of a dual-focus, dual-processing perspective on promotion and prevention of adolescent health risk behavior. *British Journal of Health Psychology.*

Giedd, J.N. (2008). The teen brain: Insights from neuroimaging. *Journal of Adolescent Health, 42,* 335–343.

Gittler, J., Quigley-Rick, M., & Saks, M.J. (1990). *Adolescent health care decision making: The law and public policy.* Washington, DC: Carnegie Council on Adolescent Development.

Goldberg, J.H., Halpern-Felsher, B.L., & Millstein, S.G. (2002). Beyond invulnerability: The importance of benefits in adolescents' decision to drink alcohol. *Health Psychology, 21,* 477–484.

Grisso, T., Steinberg, L., Woolard, J., Cauffman, E., Scott, E., Graham, S., et al. (2003). Juveniles' competence to stand trial: A comparison of adolescents' and adults' capacities as trial defendants. *Law and Human Behavior, 27,* 333–63.

Halpern-Felsher, B.L., & Cauffman, E. (2001). Costs and benefits of a decision: Decision-making competence in adolescents and adults. *Journal of Applied Developmental Psychology, 22,* 257–273.

Jacobs, J. (2004). Perceptions of risk and social judgments: Biases and motivational factors. In R.J. Bonnie & M.E. O'Connell (Eds.), *Reducing underage drinking: A collective responsibility* (pp.417–436). Washington, DC: The National Academies Press.

Michels, T.M., Kropp, R.Y., Eyre, S.L., & Halpern-Felsher, B.L. (2005). Initiating sexual experiences: How do young adolescents make decisions regarding early sexual activity? *Journal of Research on Adolescence, 15,* 583–607.

Millstein, S.G., & Halpern-Felsher, B.L. (2002) Perceptions of risk and vulnerability. *Journal of Adolescent Health, 315,* 10–27.

Ott, M.A, Millstein, S.G., Ofner, S., Halpern-Felsher, B.L. (2006). Greater expectations: Adolescents' positive motivations for sex. *Perspectives on Sexual and Reproductive Health. 38,* 84–89.

Poythress, N., Lexcen, F.J., Grisso, T., & Steinberg, L. (2006). The competence-related abilities of adolescent defendants in criminal court. *Law and Human Behavior, 30,* 75–92.

Reyna, V.F., (2006) & Farley, F. Risk and rationality in adolescent decision making. Implications for theory, practice, and public policy. *Psychological Science in the Public Interest 7,* 1–44.

Rosenstock, I.M. (1974). Historical origins of the health belief model. In M.H. Becker (Ed.)1, *The health belief model and personal health behavior* (pp. 1–8). Thorofare, NJ: Charles B. Sclack.

Song, A.V., Morrell, H., Cornell, J.L., Ramos, M.E., Biehl, M., Kropp, R.Y., & Halpern-Felsher, B.L. (in press). Perceptions of tobacco-related high risk and low benefit predict adolescent tobacco initiation. *American Journal of Public Health.*

Steinberg L., & Monahan, K.C. (2007). Age differences in resistance to peer influence. *Developmental Psychology, 43,* 1,531–1,543.

Critical Thinking

1. What important developmental tasks during adolescence does the author discuss?
2. How does the author explain positive and negative consequences?
3. Why is teenagers' ability to make competent decisions often called into question?
4. What do youth workers need to know concerning youth decision making?

DR. BONNIE HALPERN-FELSHER (HalpernFelsherB@peds.ucsf.edu) is an Associate Professor in the Division of Adolescent Medicine, Department of Pediatrics, University of California, San Francisco. She is also the Associate Director of the General Pediatrics Fellowships, and is a faculty member at UCSF's Psychology and Medicine Postdoctoral Program, The Center for Health and Community, the Center for Tobacco Control Research and Education, the Comprehensive Cancer Center, and the Robert Wood Johnson Scholars Program. **DR. HALPERN-FELSHER** is a developmental psychologist whose research has focused on cognitive and psychosocial factors involved in health-related decision making, perceptions of risk and vulnerability, health communication, and risk behavior; and she has published in each of these areas.

From *The Prevention Researcher,* April 2009, pp. 3–7. Copyright © 2009 by Integrated Research Services, Inc. Reprinted by permission.

Something to Talk About

Humans, by nature, are social beings. Teenagers, by nature, are social machines.

ASHLEY JONES

The advent of online social networking giants Facebook and MySpace—among others—has reshaped the face of a mainstay within teenage culture: socializing. A new study released by the Pew Internet & American Life Project, "Teens and Social Media," shows that teens today are more connected than ever, and with the help of the web, they will become even more intertwined.

During my teenage years, my friends and I communicated with one another the old-fashioned ways: face-to-face and via a landline phone. Content creation and sharing came in the form of writing and passing notes to each other in class. It wasn't even that common for teens to own a personal cell phone—and this was the mid-to-late '90s.

Nowadays, teenagers are creating and sharing content and posting comments online at incredibly high rates. This study, the most recent in a string of teen-focused reports conducted by Pew, focuses on the difference in teens' online participation compared to that of adults. Mary Madden, a senior research specialist at Pew and one of the writers of this report, says, "We decided to focus on social media in this survey because we saw a really big difference in teens' online participation compared to adults."

That discrepancy is obvious when you look at the numbers. As the 90:9:1 adage goes, a whopping 90% of online adults are merely lurkers, and only 10% actually contribute to the Web 2.0 movement. In contrast, according to the report's findings, 64% of online teens have participated in a content-creating activity on the Internet, up from 57% of online teens in 2004.

Most of the content creation among teens today occurs on social networking websites like the aforementioned Facebook or MySpace. In fact, according to the study, 55% of online teens ages 12–17 have a profile on a social networking site. Madden says, "This survey discusses the conversational portion of social media. We found that teens want feedback, and they can get that feedback on social networking sites."

When it comes to social networking sites, feedback comes in many forms. Wall posts, photo albums, comments, blogging, and video posts are among the most popular, and the report from Pew finds that not only are teens in general using social networking sites to interact, but the type of online interaction varies depending on gender.

The study indicates that teenage girls as a whole are more likely to be content creators than are teenage boys (55 % and 45%, respectively). In this case, Pew defines content creators as "online teens who have created or worked on a blog or webpage, shared original creative content, or remixed content they found online into a new creation." The differences continue as methods of content creation are broken down.

For instance, teenage girls are blogging. The study states that 35% of all online teen girls blog, compared to only 20% of teen boys, and that "virtually all of the growth in teen blogging between 2004 and 2006 is due to the increased activity of girls." Furthermore, older teen girls are more likely to blog than older teen boys (38% versus 18%), but younger teen girls are now outpacing older teen boys in the blogosphere: 32% of girls ages 12–14 blog compared to 18% of boys ages 15–17. Madden says, "Girls have always demonstrated a more aggressive adoption of online messaging in general. Prior to Web 2.0, it was instant messaging, and now it is seen in the forms of writing on friends' walls and blogging. It seems that girls are more focused on verbal expression."

In contrast, teenage boys are posting video files more readily than girls. While the study states that 57% of all online teens watch videos online, teenage boys are twice as likely as girls to post video files (19% versus 10%). "There is a fascination with visual media, especially among boys, today," says Madden.

It also appears that all online teenagers have a comment about something: 89% of teens who post photos online say that people comment at least "sometimes" about the photos they post, and 37% of those teenagers say that their audience comments on their photos "most of the time." Further, 72% of teen video posters report receiving comments "sometimes," and 24% say that people comment "most of the time."

What all of these numbers seem to suggest is that teenagers today are super-connected communicators. A huge aspect of adolescence is socialization, the need to feel like a part of a larger group, and social networking sites make achieving that sense of belonging easier. "I think teens are more open to exploring and trying out these new tools," posits Madden.

"They just want to feel connected, maintain ties, and receive feedback from friends."

Critical Thinking

1. Why are teenagers today more connected?
2. How does the Internet play a role in teenage connectedness?
3. What does the author believe is the future of teenage connectedness?
4. How was the study done that provided the results the author presented?

Intuitive Risk Taking during Adolescence

JAMES D. HOLLAND, M. A. AND PAUL A. KLACZYNSKI, PHD

Laypersons, policy makers, and researchers are generally aware that adolescents take more risks than children or adults (Steinberg, 2007). For decades, theorists believed that adolescents engaged in risky behaviors because they perceived immunity from harm. For example, an adolescent might think, "Although other girls have unprotected sex and get pregnant, it won't happen to me." However, most adolescents *do not* perceive themselves as invulnerable. Rather, quite the opposite: Adolescents typically *overestimate* the probability of harm resulting from risky activities (e.g., of unprotected sex resulting in STDs and pregnancy). These findings are both counter to conventional wisdom and paradoxical. Adolescents are clearly prone to risk-taking behaviors, yet they believe that the possibility of negative consequences is higher than true rates warrant (Reyna & Farley, 2006). For instance, after unprotected sex with an infected partner, adolescents believe that the risk of contracting HIV ranges from 53% to 66% (Millstein & Halpern-Felsher, 2002). The actual probability is considerably lower, roughly around 10% (Downs & De Vincenzi, 1996). Foremost among the numerous questions these findings raise is, how can this paradox be resolved?

Adolescents typically *overestimate* the probability of harm resulting from risky activities.

To address this question, we first discuss evidence pertinent to Elkind's (1967) theory of the adolescent "personal fable." Next, we review research on the link between risk perceptions and actual behavior. In discussing this research, we also introduce an important component of dual-process theories of risk taking. Specifically, we note that previous research on risk perception probably elicited a form of information processing that is primarily "analytic" rather than intuitive (see Klaczynski, 2009; Stanovich, 1999). Finally, in the third section, we argue that when most adolescents make decisions to take risks,

particularly in emotionally laden and fast-paced situations, they often rely on intuitive information processing. Our goal for this article is thus to provide a brief overview of dual-process theories of everyday cognition and, in so doing, tentatively answer questions about adolescent risk taking that cannot be answered by more traditional theories of adolescent cognition.

The Personal Fable

Many misconceptions of adolescent risk taking are based on Elkind's (1967) theory of the adolescent "personal fable." For decades, this theory was used to explain why adolescents take numerous risks and make a variety of poor decisions. In Elkind's view, as adolescents transition into Piaget's stage of abstract, scientific thinking (formal operations), their evolving self-conceptions come to include notions of omnipotence, invulnerability, and distinctiveness (e.g., "I am so unique that others can neither understand nor appreciate my thoughts and actions"). Despite its appeal to textbook writers, most of the basic premises underlying Elkind's theory have been disproved. First, as discussed previously, adolescents are prone to risk taking, but *do not* believe they are invulnerable. Second, personal fable ideations are unrelated to formal reasoning abilities (O'Connor & Nikolic, 1990). Third, egocentrism does not decline from early to middle adolescence and, indeed, remains a component of adult thinking (Frankenberger, 2000). In general, research has provided little support for the theoretical assumptions underlying Elkind's theory (Lapsley & Murphy, 1985). This empirical evidence has led most researchers to abandon Elkind's conception of the personal fable as an explanation of adolescent risk taking. However, *some* adolescents *do* develop personal fables. Relative to other adolescents, these adolescents deal better with stress and are less prone to depression. These same "invulnerable" adolescents, however, tend to score high on measures of narcissism and risk taking (Aalsma, Lapsley, & Flannery, 2006). It thus appears that, even if perceptions of invulnerability sometimes have adaptive value, other qualities associated with the personal fable undermine that value.

Risk Perceptions, Risk Taking, and Analytic Processing

It is now clear that we need alternative theories to explain adolescents' propensities to take risks. Recent research sheds some light on the difficulties inherent in explaining the link between adolescents' risk perceptions and their actual risk taking behavior. Some research indicates that adolescents who overestimate the dangers linked to various risks do, in fact, take fewer risks than adolescents whose "danger estimates" are more realistic. Other research shows the opposite: Adolescents who overestimate the dangers of risk behaviors take *more* risks than adolescents with more realistic risk appraisals (see Reyna & Farley, 2006). Although the notion is intuitively appealing, the evidence that risk overestimation prevents adolescents from risk taking is not especially strong.

This does not mean that adolescents' perceptions of the consequences of risky activities are without value. Rather, the perceived *benefits* of risk taking predict risk taking better than the perceived harmful consequences (Goldberg, Halpern-Felsher, & Millstein, 2002). The perceived benefits or rewards of risk taking (such as peer approval, "highs") are more immediate than the perceived costs (such as lung cancer, STDs). If, as behavior decision theorists argue, decision competence is the ability to choose actions that increase the probability that subjectively valued goals will be achieved (see Fischhoff, 2008), then adolescents' decisions to take risks might be considered rational. To be more precise, adolescents often engage in a type of "analytic processing" that involves weighing the potential risks against potential rewards of engaging in a behavior. If an adolescent determines that, overall, the rewards outweigh the risk, then the risk is taken. When one considers that the true rates of negative consequences are much lower than adolescents realize, this approach is not entirely irrational: Adolescents often achieve their goals and thus are reinforced for taking risks because they are not only recipients of perceived benefits, but also have likely not suffered negative consequences.

Intuitive Risk Taking

Traditionally, theorists interested in the development of decision making have focused on changes in analytic reasoning abilities, such as those required to conduct cost/benefit analyses. A common assumption in these traditional theories is that decisions are largely based on conscious reasoning and deliberation. A critical feature that distinguishes dual-process theories from traditional developmental theories is the assumption that, although most decisions are based on the confluence of analytic and intuitive processing, *intuitive processing dominates* most everyday thinking. Indeed, even adults fall prey to numerous logical fallacies, over-rely on simple heuristics ("quick and easy" cognitive rules of thumb), and make judgments based on biased representations (Stanovich, 1999). Because these cognitive faux pas occur on a variety of computationally simple problems, the poor decision making that characterizes much of adult thinking cannot be attributed to a lack of intellectual ability. Instead, decisions are often made

rapidly, typically without considering whether more analytically based thinking would produce decisions more likely to meet the decision makers' goals.

This intuitive decision making is based on different processes than the analytic process of weighing perceived costs against perceived rewards, described previously. Numerous characteristics separate intuitive or "experiential" processing from analytic processing (Evans, 2008). For this discussion, we note six important characteristics of intuitive processing. Intuitive processing (1) requires few cognitive resources and little cognitive effort, (2) is unrelated to intellectual ability, (3) is minimally conscious, (4) activates general beliefs, biases, and heuristics that are neither precise nor computational in nature, (5) elicits "gut feelings" of "correctness" that are not accompanied by analyses of the reasons for these feelings, and (6) depends on previous experiences, especially experiences related to the present situation and people.

If intuitive processing is the default processing system among adults, how do the two systems—intuitive/experiential and analytic—change from childhood through adolescence? The answer to this question is not simple; however, existing data point to three conclusions. First, a variety of evidence indicates age-related increases in reliance on heuristics and other cognitive biases (Klaczynski, 2009). These data suggest that, at least under some conditions, intuitive processing becomes increasingly predominant with age. Second, the research cited above, in addition to other research, involved different tasks that activated different heuristics and biases. For example, when told that John is a friend of Sam, and Sam is a friend of Robert, older children are more likely to judge that "John and Robert are friends" than younger children (Markovits & Dumas, 1999); that is, they use a non-logical "friends of friends are friends" heuristics. The argument can then be made that repertoires of heuristics become increasingly diverse and are employed in more situations with development. Third, the acquisition of most heuristics depends on experience. Initially, these heuristics are invoked deliberately and consciously. For instance, young children have acquired some knowledge of a "cheerleader" stereotype. When they encounter a girl whose physical and social characteristics align with the stereotype, they do not automatically judge her a cheerleader. Instead, because the "cheerleader" prototype is still accessible to consciousness, they engage in an explicit comparison between the girl's features and the prototype. By contrast, in adolescents and adults, the "cheerleader" prototype is activated automatically by the girl's features (Jacobs & Potenza, 1991). Implicit activation of the prototype leads them to designate the girl as a cheerleader automatically, without deliberating alternative possibilities. Thus, "practice" or repeated use of a heuristic facilitates the process of converting a once-explicit judgment tactic into an "intuitive" method of judging.

At first glance, decisions based predominantly on intuition may appear both socially destructive and personally misleading. Indeed, judgments and decisions based on intuition rely on a form of processing that is the exact opposite of critical thinking. However, intuitive decisions are not without adaptive value. Specifically, experiential processing is fast and requires little cognitive effort. Theoretically, decisions based on intuition save time and cognitive energy and can lead to accurate solutions. The caveat here is that such processing is most likely to prove adaptive when adolescents are confronted with multiple processing demands and tasks do not require precise solutions. Even if intuitive processing does not yield optimal decisions, the negative consequences are often negligible; indeed, in making some decisions, reliance on intuitive processing often makes more sense than reliance on analytic processing. For instance, a hungry adolescent could spend 15 minutes weighing the pros and cons of driving to different pizza parlors. These computations may well lead the adolescent to the best decision—one that takes into account her hunger, her preferences, driving distance, likely traffic, and so forth. However, reliance on intuition, such as "go to the closest place," takes only moments and may result in a satisfactory outcome (perhaps not the best pizza, but pizza that is "close enough," satisfies the girl's hunger, time, and driving constraints).

Theoretically, decisions based on intuition save time and cognitive energy and can lead to accurate solutions.

A related benefit concerns "cognitive economy." Intuitive decisions are often automatic. Consequently, reliance on intuition achieves two implicit goals. First, it conserves effort and, as such, does not result in cognitive fatigue. Second, intuitive processing frees working memory for tasks that require conscious attention. For instance, learning to drive is computationally complex and requires extensive working memory resources to coordinate verbal instructions with eye, hand, and foot movements. Once this coordination is automatic, then the basic cognitive demands of driving diminish, which allows working memory to perform other tasks, such as planning routes, and attending to and avoiding dangerous conditions.

Experts and Non-Experts: Two Forms of Intuitive Decision Making

It is, however, important to recognize that not all intuitive decisions are produced equally. Reyna and Lloyd (2006) make an important distinction between relatively expert and relatively novice intuitive processing. In medicine, for instance, expert diagnosticians process information more quickly and rely on less information, and yet make more accurate risk assessments (e.g., for cardiac arrest), than non-experts (Reyna & Lloyd, 2006). Adolescents are typically non-experts, particularly in their risk perceptions. To illustrate, high-risk adolescents, who had been expelled from public schools and lived in high-crime neighborhoods, indicated the probability that various behaviors (such as, smoking or using illicit drugs) would result in serious personal and interpersonal harm. Critically, half the adolescents were presented hypothetical base rate information (i.e., regarding

the "actual" likelihood of harm resulting from various risky activities). Adolescents who received this information adjusted their probability estimates, such that risk perceptions were *more* realistic, and consequently believed that potentially health-compromising behaviors were *less* likely to have negative effects than adolescents not given base rate information (Welsh, Klaczynski, & Gorman, 2009). This suggests that the domain of risky beliefs is somewhat unique. In most domains, adolescents resist changing their beliefs, even when presented evidence that contradicts those beliefs (see Klaczynski, 2009). The ease with which risk perceptions were altered therefore distinguishes this domain from other belief domains. The findings of Welsh and colleagues further suggest that adolescents' beliefs about the consequences of risky activities are not consolidated. That is, unlike expert diagnosticians, adolescents are non-experts in this domain and *recognize* their non-expert stature. It follows that adolescents *do not* consciously reflect on their beliefs when they make risky decisions. Instead, they likely rely on quick, economical, and *non-expert* heuristics (e.g., "everyone's doing it") that "feel right" at the moment.

This form of intuitive decision-making has adaptive advantages similar to those of expert intuition; in both cases, decisions are automatic, fast, and accompanied by feelings of "rightness." However, whereas experts' intuitive decisions have a foundation in implicit and explicit knowledge, those of non-experts lack a firm knowledge base. The foregoing discussion of the malleability of adolescents' base rate beliefs clearly supports this claim. In the case of non-experts, intuitive decisions are based on neither clear knowledge nor reflection and deliberation. Decisions instead depend on situational cues (e.g., peer pressure), emotions, stereotypes, vivid memories, heuristics, dispositions to shun tasks that appear cognitively difficult, goal-planning abilities, the abilities to inhibit automatic responses, and impulse control. The different basis for non-expert intuitive decisions means that these decisions are more prone to error and negative consequences than the intuitive decisions of experts.

If the decisions and heuristics activated by intuitive processing do not have some adaptive functions, why are they used more often with increasing age? As debates surrounding definitions of rationality reveal, there exist multiple levels and meanings of the term "adaptive." Decisions may be considered adaptive if they allow adolescents to attain their goals or, at least, avoid harm. The same decision may, of course, be maladaptive and irrational. Like adults, tasks that appear cognitively difficult, goal-planning abilities, adolescents have both implicit and explicit goal structures. If an adolescent's immediate goals are hedonic, then impulsive, "it feels right" decisions may be made without consideration of the impact of those decisions on more important, but temporarily subverted, long-term goals. For example, an adolescent may have a long-term goal of going to college. However, at a party, the adolescent may encounter an attractive peer who is willing to have unprotected sex with them. Obviously, unprotected sex could impact the college goal, either by contracting a serious STD or by the financial burdens that accompany having a child. However, *in the moment*, the decision to have sex "feels right." The potential long-term impacts of unprotected sex simply do not enter into the adolescent's mind or affect the adolescent only at a peripheral level, perhaps leading to momentary hesitation.

If an adolescent's immediate goals are hedonic, then impulsive, "it feels right" decisions may be made without consideration of the impact of those decisions on more important, but temporarily subverted, long-term goals.

Metacognitive Intercession and Development

In most situations, intuitive processing precedes analytic processing (Evans, 2008). Subsequent processing may proceed in parallel and may involve interactions between the two processing systems. Awareness of one's own thought processes, "metacognitive intercession," is a function of analytic processing. Using metacognitive intercession may lead adolescents to scrutinize intuitive decisions and override intuitive processing with analytic processing (Klaczynski, 2009). However, if initial processing is indeed sequential, and if a "feeling of rightness"—the essence of intuition—arises from the initial situation, then spur of the moment decisions may win the day.

This analysis may appear to apply equally to adolescents and adults. Adults, however, differ from adolescents in three important ways. First, they are relatively more expert in numerous (but not all) domains; hence, their intuitions are likely more reliable than those of adolescents. Second, both behavioral and neurological evidence indicates that goal planning is better developed in adults. Even if intuitive processing triggers similar decisions in adolescents and adults, adults are more likely to resist acting on these decisions, because they have superior metacognitive intercession abilities. Third, impulsivity and emotional reactivity increase during the adolescent years but then decline during early adulthood.

In addition to the cognitive demands of engaging in metacognitive intercession, more effort is required of adolescents if they are to control impulses to make non-reflective, intuitive decisions. Adolescents are far less likely to reflect on the quality of their intuitions than adults for a number of reasons: (a) the emotional and cognitive effort required, (b) that most intuitive decisions, even if not particularly beneficial, at least cause no harm, (c) the preconscious sources from which intuitive decisions arise, (d) the "it feels right" nature of many intuitively-based decisions, (e) peer norms and expectations that often seem to "require" thoughtless actions, and (f) the rapid changes in location and pace that constitute adolescents' daily lives. As an example, adolescents' estimates of the probability of contracting STDs from unprotected sex are generally higher than those of adults. Although these estimates may sometimes serve as protective factors, they are likely to do so only when adolescents can process their estimates analytically; that is, in situations free of the peer pressures and impulses to act that are part and parcel of realistic situations. Put another way, factual statistics may decrease the likelihood of an adolescent taking risk in contrived laboratory situations. However, that same factual information may have little impact on an adolescent's decision at a party. In situations that call for immediate decisions, these estimates are unlikely to play any role in determining adolescents' behavior because intuitive processing is not only predominant but also difficult to override.

Conclusion

Developmental research on intuitive processing is in its infamy. Theorists and interventionists have generally assumed that, if analytic processing can be fostered, adolescents' tendencies to make risky decisions will decrease. However, traditional educational programs have done little to reduce unhealthy risk taking: Almost all adolescents have received sex, driving, and drug education, yet many continue to take unnecessary risks (Steinberg, 2007). In an overview of sex education programs, the majority of programs had no significant impact in delaying the onset of sexual activity or decreasing the frequency of sex or the number of partners (Kirby, 2008). Of the programs that have successfully increased condom use, the more successful programs focused specifically on HIV. These programs may sometimes be successful because HIV and the health outcomes associated with HIV are highly salient. Salience is an important activator of general heuristics, such as, "better safe than sorry." Because they are based on intuitive processing and are cognitively simple, heuristics are remembered more easily and more easily brought into play than more complex "lessons." The same may be true in other areas involving risky behaviors. For instance, interventions that reduce impulsivity and increase intuitive thinking have successfully reduced cravings in substance abusers (e.g., Motto, Strolin, & Magro-Wilson, 2008).

Despite these successes, adolescents live in worlds that are less stable, faster-paced, and more rapidly changing than those of adults. In those adolescent worlds, neither overriding intuitive processing with analytic processing nor becoming relatively expert in intuitive risk assessment is easily achieved. Even if they possessed the metacognitive and emotion regulation abilities of adults, many adolescents' decisions are made in confusing social and emotionally-laden contexts. Before effective interventions can be constructed, researchers must first acquire a more complete understanding of adolescent decision making. Although achieving this will undoubtedly be difficult, we believe that it may well be a necessary goal before realistic steps can be taken to improve adolescents' decisions.

References

Aalsma, M.C., Lapsley, D.K., & Flannery, D.J. (2006). Personal fables, narcissism, and adolescent adjustment. *Psychology in the Schools, 43*, 481–491.

Downs, A.M., & De Vincenzi, I. (1996). Probability of heterosexual transmission of HIV: relationship to the number of unprotected sexual contacts. European Study Group in Heterosexual Transmission of HIV. *Journal of Acquired Immune Deficiency Syndromes and Human Retrovirology, 11*, 388–395.

Elkind, D. (1967). Egocentrism in adolescence. *Child Development, 38,* 1,025–1,033.

Evans, J. St. B.T. (2008). Dual-process accounts of reasoning judgment, and social cognition. *Annual Review of Psychology, 59,* 255–278.

Fischhoff, B. (2008). Assessing adolescent decision-making competence. *Developmental Review, 28,* 12–28.

Frankenberger, K.D. (2000). Adolescent egocentrism: A comparison among adolescents and adults. *Journal of Adolescence, 23,* 343–354.

Goldberg, J.H., Halpern-Felsher, B.L., & Millstein, S.G. (2002). Beyond invulnerability: The importance of benefits in adolescents' decision to drink alcohol. *Health Psychology, 21,* 477–484.

Jacobs, J.E., & Potenza, M. (1991). The use of judgment heuristics to make social and object decisions: A developmental perspective. *Child Development, 62,* 166–178.

Kirby, D. (2008). Effective approaches to reducing adolescent unprotected sex, pregnancy, and childbearing. *The Journal of Sex Research, 39(1),* 51–57.

Klaczynski, P.A. (2009). Cognitive and social cognitive development: Dual-process research and theory. J. St. B.T. Evans & K. Frankish (Eds.), *In Two Minds: Psychological and Philosophical Theories of Dual Processing* (pp.265–292). Oxford, UK: Oxford University Press.

Lapsley, D.K., & Murphy, M.N. (1985). Another look at the theoretical assumptions of adolescent egocentrism. *Developmental Review, 5,* 201–217.

Markovits, H., & Dumas, C. (1949). Developmental patterns of understanding social and physical transitivity. *Journal of Experimental Child Psychology, 73,* 95–114.

Matto, H.C., Strolin, J.S., & Mogro-Wilson, C. (2008). A pilot study of a dual processing substance user treatment intervention with adults. *Substance Abuse & Misuse, 43(3),* 285–294.

Millstein, S. G., & Halpern-Felsher, B. L. (2002). Judgments about risk and perceived invulnerability in adolescents and young adults. *Journal of Research on Adolescence, 12,* 399–422.

O'Connor, B.P., & Nikolic, J. (1990). Identity development and formal operations as sources of adolescent egocentrism. *Journal of Youth and Adolescence, 19,* 149–158.

Reyna, V.F., & Farley, F. (2006). Risk and rationality in adolescent decision making: Implications for theory, practice, and public policy. *Psychological Science in the Public Interest, 7,* 1–44.

Reyna, V.F., & Lloyd, F.J. (2006). Physician decision making and cardiac risk: Effects of knowledge, risk perception, risk tolerance, and fuzzy processing. *Journal of Experimental Psychology: Applied, 12,* 179–195.

Stanovich, K.E. (1999). *Who is Rational? Studies of Individual Differences in Reasoning.* Erlbaum: Mahwah, NJ.

Steinberg, L. (2007). Risk taking in adolescence: New perspectives from brain and behavioral science. *Current Directions in Psychological Science, 16,* 55–59.

Welsh, M., Klaczynski, P.A., & Gorman, P.B. (2009, April). *An Experimental Examination of the Effects of Hypothetical Base Rates on Adolescents' Perceptions of Risky Behaviors.* Society for Research on Child Development. Denver, CO.

Critical Thinking

1. What is the process that adolescents go through when deciding to take risks?

2. Contrast the two information processing systems youth go through when choosing risky behavior?

3. What are the advantages and disadvantages of reliance on intuition decision making?

4. What are the difficulties adolescents must overcome in overriding intuition processing with analytic processing?

JAMES D. HOLLAND (jimdholland@yahoo.com) is a PhD student in Northern Colorado University's graduate program in educational psychology. His interests are in adolescent risk taking, aggression, and executive control. **PAUL A. KLACYNSKI** (paul.klaczynski@unco.edu) is an Associate Professor of Psychological Science at Northern Colorado University. Formerly a program officer at the National Science Foundation, his interests include risk taking, decision making, biases in social reasoning, and obesity stereotypes.

UNIT 2

Developmental Changes of Adolescents: Physical, Cognitive, and Social

Unit Selections

Learning Outcomes

After reading this unit, you should be able to:

- Contrast the links between student health and academic performance.

- Outline the Health Education Assessment Project.

- Describe the mental health issues that challenge college applicants.

- Discuss the worries college admission offices have concerning college applicants with mental health issues.

- Explain the factors that increase the risk for body dissatisfaction.

- Analyze the role of body dissatisfaction in relationship to predictors of the development of body dissatisfaction.

- Explain the trend of women and girls in sexual media depiction.

- Describe how pop culture images are targeting young girls and the psychological damage that follows.

- Explain how the brain may be the key to why adolescents sleep in, take risks, and won't listen to reason.

- Describe what the teenage brain can master.

- Explain how stressful life events account for increased rates of psychological problems.

- Describe how the role of stressors in the development of mental health problems for adolescents.

- Analyze the author's suggestion that parents control sleep of preteen girls.

- Explain why the preteen years may be the last period of time parents may be able to control sleeping.

Student Website
www.mhhe.com/cls

The physical changes accompanying the onset of puberty are usually the first clear indicators that a child is entering the period of adolescence. The changes can be a source of both pride and humiliation for the developing adolescent. These physiological changes are regulated by a structure in the brain known as the hypothalamus. The hypothalamus is responsible for stimulating increased production of hormones that control development of the primary and secondary sex characteristics. Primary sex characteristics include physical changes in the reproductive system. Examples include growth of the ovaries and testicles. Secondary sex characteristics are physical changes not directly involved in reproduction. Examples include voice changes, height increases, growth of facial hair in males and breast development in females.

The hypothalamus signals the pituitary gland which in turn stimulates the gonads to produce hormones (androgens and estrogens). The hypothalamus then detects the level of sex hormones present in the bloodstream and will either call for more or less hormone production. During childhood the hypothalamus is very sensitive to sex hormones and keeps production at a low level. For some reason that is not yet completely known, the hypothalamus changes its sensitivity to the sex hormones in adolescence. As a result, significantly greater quantities of sex hormones are needed before the hypothalamus signals the pituitary gland to shutdown production. The thyroid and adrenal glands also play a role in the development of secondary sex characteristics.

The physiological changes themselves occur over a 5 to 6 year span. Girls generally start to under go puberty 18 to 24 months before boys, with the typical on set at 10 or 11. The earliest pubertal changes in girls are breast budding, height spurt, and sparse pubic hair. Experiencing a first menstrual cycle is a mid-pubertal event, with the average age of menarche in the United States currently being 12 years old. For boys, initial signs of puberty are that the testicles begin to increase in size and the height spurt begins. Facial hair, deepening voice, and first ejaculation occur later.

The sequence of pubertal change is fairly constant across individuals; however, the timing of puberty varies greatly from one person to the next. Some adolescents are out of step with their peers because they mature early, whereas others are late-maturers. The advantages and disadvantages of early versus late maturation have been the subject of much research, so a few readings touch on this topic. One conclusion is that early maturation is correlated with earlier involvement in risk-taking behaviors like

© PhotoAlto/Veer

alcohol use and sexual activity. In extreme cases, biological disorders result in delayed or precocious puberty, but there are new medications for treating these conditions.

The onset of puberty is affected by diet, exercise, and genetic history. Largely due to improved nutrition and to better control of illnesses, pubertyoccurs3 to 4 years earlier in the twenty-first century than it did 150 years ago. Adolescents today also grow several inches taller and weigh more. A visit to historical homes will show that the doorways and beds were much smaller in previous centuries. This trend toward earlier maturation is a worldwide phenomenon that has presumably reached a leveling off point. Adolescents experience psychological and social challenges related to puberty. For example, sexual arousal increases and the teenager must learn how to handle sexual situations. Likewise, gender-typical behavior is more expected by others observing the youth. The adolescent must also incorporate bodily changes into his or her self-image. Concerns about physical appearance become a major preoccupation and play a significant role in self-esteem at this time. These issues are addressed in this unit. In particular, the readings examine the body image concerns adolescents experience. This contributes to adolescents' anxiety about their bodies and how "normal" they are. On the other hand, other cultures employ rites of passage to mark entrance into manhood or womanhood. Many such rites of passage involve physical markings on the adolescent, such as circumcision or body tattooing.

Adolescence entails changes in cognitive capacities that are just as monumental as the biological changes.

Whereas children tend to be more literal, more tied to reality and to the familiar; adolescents are more abstract, systematic, and logical. Adolescents can appreciate metaphors and sarcasm, they can easily think about things that do not exist, they can test abstract ideas against reality, and they can readily conceive of multiple possibilities. Many of these improvements in thinking ability contribute to conflicts with adults as adolescents become better able to argue a point or take a stand. They are better at planning out their case and anticipating counter arguments. They are also more likely to question the way things are because they now conceive of alternate possibilities.

The study of cognitive changes that occur in adolescence has largely been based on the work of the Swiss psychologist, Jean Piaget, and his colleague Barbel Inhelder. Piaget and Inhelder described the adolescent as reasoning at the formal operational stage. Children from the approximate ages of 7 to 11 years old were described as being in the "concrete operational" stage. Not all researchers agree with Piaget and Inhelder that changes in adolescent cognitive abilities represent true stage-related changes. They do, however, agree that adolescent thought is characteristically more logical, abstract, and hypothetical than that of children. Recognize, though, that having certain mental capacities does not mean that adolescents, or even adults for that matter, will always reason at their rational best!

Piaget's views on cognitive development have been very influential, particularly in the field of education. Awareness of the cognitive abilities and shortcomings of adolescents can make their behaviors more comprehensible to parents, teachers, counselors, and other professionals who work with them. Similarly, as Piaget suggested, schools need to take the developmental abilities and needs of adolescents into account in planning programs and designing curricula. In addition, Piaget's general philosophy was that learning must be active. Others in the field of education, however, caution that there are other important issues left un-addressed by Piaget. For example, the U.S. has an elevated school drop-out rate, so we need to find alternatives for keeping the nation's youth in school.

Building on the work of Piaget and Inhelder, David Elkind has argued that the newly emerging formal operational cognitive abilities of adolescents lead to some troublesome consequences. For one thing, adolescents tend to over intellectualize. They often make things too complex and fail to see the obvious, a phenomenon that Elkind calls pseudostupidity. Teachers often bear the brunt of this phenomenon as adolescents overanalyze every word of a multiple-choice question. Elkind also maintains that much of the extreme self-consciousness of adolescents occurs because of the construct of an imaginary audience. Formal operations make it possible for adolescents to think about other people's thoughts. Adolescents lose perspective and think that others are constantly watching them and thinking about them. A related mistake is that adolescents are likely to believe that everyone shares their concerns and knows their thoughts. This belief, that one is at the center of attention, further leads to the development of what Elkind calls the personal fable. Namely, if everyone is paying so much attention to me. I must be special and invulnerable. Bad things won't happen to me. I won't get in a car crash. I won't get pregnant. The phenomena-pseudostupidity, the imaginary audience, and the personal fable diminish as adolescents' cognitive abilities mature and as they develop friendships in which intimacies are shared. Peer interaction helps adolescents see that they are not as unique as they thought, nor are they the focus of everyone else's attention.

Each age period is associated with developmental tasks. A major aspect of psychosocial development for adolescents is the formation of a coherent personal identity. Erik Erikson referred to this as the adolescent identity crisis. Identity formation is a normative event, but it represents a turning point in human development that has consequences for later psychosocial skills.

Children's identities often represent an identification with parents and significant others. Adolescents reflect on their identity and come to some sense of who they are and who they are not. Identity formation involves an examination of personal likes and dislikes; political, religious, and moral values; occupational interests, as well as gender roles and sexual behaviors. Adolescents must also form an integrated sense of their own personality across the various roles they engage in (e.g., son or daughter, student, boyfriend or girlfriend, part-time worker, etc.).

The first article in this unit discusses discoveries in brain science that explains a teen's inclination to make rush decisions. Next, Eddy Ramirez explains the challenges that mental health issues pose to college applicants.

An understanding of factors that increase the risk for body dissatisfaction is presented by Presnell, Bearman and Madeley, and Stacy Weiner describes the troubling trend of women and girls sexual media depiction. She explains that Pop Culture images are targeting younger girls, which often leads to eating disorders, lower self-esteem, and depression.

Nora Underwood reports that the teen brain may be the key to why adolescents sleep in, take risks, and won't listen. Next, Kathryn Grant discusses the evidence that increased stress may account for the increased rates of psychological problems in teens. Finally, the unit concludes with Dr. Schoumacher suggesting that parents control the amount of sleep that their pre-teen receives.

Internet References

ADOL: Adolescence Directory On-Line
http://education.indiana.edu/cas/adol/adol.html

At-Risk Children and Youth
www.ncrel.org/sdrs/areas/at0cont.htm

Biological Changes in Adolescence
http://inside.bard.edu/academic/specialproj/darling/adolesce.htm

Center for Adolescent Health: Confronting Teen Stress
www.jhsph.edu/bin/q/j/Teen_Stress_Guide.pdf

Eating Disorders Coalition
www.eating disorderscoalition.org

Educational Forum on Adolescent Health: Youth Bullying
www.ama-assn.org/ama1/pub/upload/mm/39/youthbullying.pdf

Finding Balance
www.findingbalance.com

National Eating Disorders Association (NEDA)
www.nationaleatingdisorders.org

The Renfrew Center Foundation
www.renfrew.org

Something Fishy Website on Eating Disorders
www.something-fishy.org

Teens Health
www.teenshealth.org

Teens in Distress Series: Adolescent Stress and Depression
www.extension.umn.edu/distribution/youthdevelopment/DA3083.html

Women's Health.Gov: Loving Your Body Inside and Out
www.4women.gov/bodyimage

Healthier Students, Better Learners

The Health Education Assessment Project helps teachers provide the skills-based, standards-based health instruction that students need.

BETH PATEMAN

When we think back on health classes from our school days, many of us have only vague memories. We may recall some discussion of food groups, a film about puberty, or a lecture on dental hygiene conducted when the weather was too rainy to go outside for physical education. Few of us remember our K-12 health education experiences as being relevant to our lives outside the classroom.

Fortunately, that picture is changing. Asserting that "healthy students make better learners, and better learners make healthy communities," the Council of Chief State School Officers (CCSSO) and the Association of State and Territorial Health Officials (ASTHO) (2002) have summarized compelling research evidence that students' health significantly affects their school achievement. Even if their schools have the most outstanding academic curriculum and instruction, students who are ill or injured, hungry or depressed, abusing drugs or experiencing violence, are unlikely to learn as well as they should (Kolbe, 2002).

Effective health education programs have a vital role to play in enhancing students' health and thus in raising academic achievement. Kolbe's 2002 review of the research found that modern school health programs can improve students' health knowledge, attitudes, skills, and behaviors and enhance social and academic outcomes. How do these modern health programs differ from those that most of us remember from our school days? Thanks to growing knowledge about how to prevent unhealthy and unsafe behaviors among young people, today's exemplary health education combines *skills-based* and *standards-based* approaches.

Focus on Skills

The Centers for Disease Control and Prevention have identified six types of behavior that cause the most serious health problems in the United States among people over 5 years old: alcohol and other drug use, high-risk sexual behaviors, tobacco use, poor dietary choices, physical inactivity, and behaviors that result in intentional or unintentional injury. Stressing the importance of education efforts, the Centers state that

these behaviors usually are established during youth; persist into adulthood; are interrelated; and are preventable. In

addition to causing serious health problems, these behaviors contribute to many of the educational and social problems that confront the nation, including failure to complete high school, unemployment, and crime. (n.d.)

> ## Effective health education programs have a vital role to play in enhancing students' health and thus in raising academic achievement.

In response to the Centers' focus on these major health-risk behaviors, education researchers have worked to identify educational approaches that positively affect health-related behaviors among young people. Many research studies have established the effectiveness of skills-based school health education in promoting healthy behavior and academic achievement (ASTHO & Society of State Directors of Health, Physical Education, and Recreation, 2002; Collins et al., 2002; Kirby, 2001). Lohrmann and Wooley (1998) determined that effective programs

- Focus on helping young people develop and practice personal and social skills, such as communication and decision making, to deal effectively with health-risk situations;
- Provide healthy alternatives to specific high-risk behaviors;
- Use interactive approaches that engage students;
- Are research-based and theory-driven;
- Address social and media influences on student behaviors;
- Strengthen individual and group norms that support healthy behavior;
- Are of sufficient duration to enable students to gain the knowledge and skills that they need; and
- Include teacher preparation and support.

Health Education Standards

- *Standard 1: Students will comprehend concepts related to health promotion and disease prevention.* For example, students will be able to identify what good health is, recognize health problems, and be aware of ways in which lifestyle, the environment, and public policies can promote health.
- *Standard 2: Students will demonstrate the ability to access valid health information and health-promoting products and services.* For example, students will be able to evaluate advertisements, options for health insurance and treatment, and food labels.
- *Standard 3: Students will demonstrate the ability to practice health-enhancing behaviors and reduce health risks.* For example, students will know how to identify responsible and harmful behaviors, develop strategies for good health, and manage stress.
- *Standard 4: Students will analyze the influence of culture, media, technology, and other factors on health.* For example, students will be able to describe and analyze how cultural background and messages from the media, technology, and friends influence health choices.
- *Standard 5: Students will demonstrate the ability to use interpersonal communication skills to enhance health.* For example, students will learn refusal and negotiation skills and conflict resolution strategies.
- *Standard 6: Students will demonstrate the ability to use goal-setting and decision-making skills to enhance health.* For example, students will set reasonable and attainable goals—such as losing a given amount of weight or increasing physical activity—and develop positive decision-making skills.
- *Standard 7: Students will demonstrate the ability to advocate for personal, family, and community health.* For example, students will identify community resources, accurately communicate health information and ideas, and work cooperatively to promote health.

Source: Joint Committee on National Health Education Standards. (1995).

New Standards for a Skills-Based Approach

In 1995, the American Cancer Society sponsored the development of national health education standards that use a skills-based approach to learning (Joint committee on National Health Education Standards, 1995). The standards, summarized below, advocate health literacy that enhances individuals' capacities to obtain, interpret, and understand basic health information and services and their competence to use such information and services in health-enhancing ways (Summerfield, 1995).

Together with the Centers for Disease Control and Prevention's priority health-risk behaviors, the national health education standards provide an important new framework for moving from an information-based school health curriculum to a skills-based curriculum. Skills-based health education engages students and provides a safe environment for students to practice working through health-risk situations that they are likely to encounter as adolescents.

An information-based approach to tobacco use prevention might require students to memorize facts about the health consequences of tobacco use, such as lung cancer, heart disease, and emphysema. In contrast, a skills-based approach ensures that students demonstrate the ability to locate valid information on the effects of tobacco use. Students learn and practice a variety of skills: For example, they use analysis to identify the influences of family, peers, and media on decisions about tobacco use and they use interpersonal communication skills to refuse tobacco use.

The skills-based approach outlined in the national health education standards helps students answer questions and address issues that are important in their lives. For example, young children need to learn how to make friends and deal with bullies. Older children need to practice a variety of strategies to resist pressures to engage in risky health behaviors while maintaining friendships. Early adolescents need to learn how to obtain reliable, straightforward information about the physical, emotional, and social changes of puberty. High school students need to learn to weigh their health-related decisions in terms of their life plans and goals. All students need to learn how to respond to stress, deal with strong feelings in health-enhancing ways, and build a reliable support group of peers and adults.

The Health Education Assessment Project

Standards-based health education requires a new approach to planning, assessment, and instruction. Although many educators are excited about the prospect of standards-based teaching in health education, they may lack a clear picture of what standards-based performance would look like in their classrooms. To address this need, the Council of Chief State School Officers' State Collaborative on Assessment and Student Standards initiated the Health Education Assessment Project in 1993 (see www.ccsso.org/scass).

The Health Education Assessment Project develops standards-based health resources through a collaborative process. Funding for the project comes from the Centers for Disease Control and Prevention and the membership fees of 24 state and local education agencies. During its first decade, the project has built a foundation for a health education assessment system, created an assessment framework, developed and tested a pool of assessment items, and provided professional development and supporting materials to help teachers implement the assessment system and framework.

A skills-based approach to tobacco use prevention ensures that students demonstrate the ability to locate valid information on the effects of tobacco use.

Sample Performance Task: Advocacy for Mental Health

Student Challenge

Your challenge is to select and examine a mental health problem, such as anxiety, depression, eating disorders, suicide ideation, bipolar disorder, or schizophrenia. Your tasks are to

- Locate and analyze valid information sources to determine the causes and symptoms of the problem.
- Explore treatment options and health-enhancing ways of managing the problem.
- Recommend helpful tips for talking with friends or family members who might be experiencing the problem.
- Provide a list of helpful community resources.
- Design a computer-generated brochure or presentation targeted to high school students that includes a summary of your information on causes, symptoms, and management/treatment; tips for talking with others; and a list of community resources.

Assessment Criteria for a Great Presentation

Your work will be assessed using the following criteria. You will be required to

- Provide accurate and in-depth information and draw conclusions about relationships between behaviors and health.
- Cite your information sources accurately and explain why your sources are appropriate.
- Provide specific recommendations for health-enhancing ways of managing stress and ways of talking with others about the problem.
- Demonstrate awareness of your target audience (high school students) and persuade others to make healthy choices.

Additional criteria may be determined by class members.

The project helps educators translate theory into practice. It provides educators with a wide range of assessment items developed in a variety of formats, including selected response, constructed response, and performance tasks (see the sample below). The project provides teacher and student rubrics for assessing performance and examples of student papers for scoring practice. Perhaps the greatest benefit to educators has been the hands-on professional development opportunities to practice aligning standards, assessment, and instruction for their own classrooms (CCSSO, 2003).

Classrooms in which students are evaluated by health education standards and criteria are substantially different from classrooms in which many teachers have taught and been taught. Teachers need hands-on preparation and experience with planning, implementing, and evaluating curriculum and instruction aligned with standards and assessment. The Health Education Assessment Project can improve the health of students by providing teachers with the tools they need to meet the important health needs of today's youth.

References

Association of State and Territorial Health Officials & Society of State Directors of Health, Physical Education, and Recreation. (2002).*Making the connection: Health and student achievement* (CDROM). Washington, DC: Authors.

Centers for Disease Control and Prevention, Division of Adolescent and School Health. (n.d.). *Health topics* [Online]. Available: www.cdc.gov/nccdphp/dash/risk.htm

Collins, J., Robin, L., Wooley, S., Fenley, D., Hunt, P., Taylor, J., Haber, D., & Kolbe, L. (2002). Programs that work: CDC's guide to effective programs that reduce health risk behavior of youth. *Journal of School Health, 72*(3), 93–99.

Council of Chief State School Officers. (2003). *Improving teaching and learning through the CCSSO-SCASS Health Education Assessment Project.* Washington, DC: Author.

Council of Chief State School Officers & Association of State and Territorial Health Officials. (2002). *Why support a coordinated approach to school health?* Washington, DC: Authors.

Joint Committee on National Health Education Standards. (1995). *National health education standards: Achieving health literacy.* Reston, VA: Association for the Advancement of Health Education.

Kirby, D. (2001). *Emerging answers: Research findings on programs to reduce teen pregnancy.* Washington, DC: The National Campaign to Prevent Teen Pregnancy.

Kolbe, L. J. (2002). Education reform and the goals of modern school health programs. *The State Education Standard, 3*(4), 4–11.

Lohrmann, D. K., & Wooley, S. F. (1998). Comprehensive school health education. In E. Marx & S. F. Wooley (Eds.), *Health is academic: A guide to coordinated school health programs* (pp. 43–66). New York: Teachers College Press.

Summerfield, L. M. (1995). *National standards for health education* (ERIC Digest No. ED 387 483). Washington, DC: ERIC Clearinghouse on Teaching and Teacher Education. Available: www.ericfacility.net/databases/ERIC_Digests/ed387483.html

Critical Thinking

1. What is the Health Education Assessment Project?
2. What is the link between student health and academic performance?
3. Which cites does the author provide to encourage development of state education programs in the schools?
4. What two organizations encourage this development?

BETH PATEMAN is an associate professor at the Institute for Teacher Education, University of Hawaii at Manoa, Honolulu, HI 96822; (808) 956-3885; mpateman@hawaii.edu.

Mental Assessment Test

Eddy Ramirez

Colleges Scrutinize Applications from Troubled Students More Closely

Growing up in New York City, Emily Isaac studied Hebrew, performed in school musicals, and played soccer. She fantasized about going to a prestigious university like Harvard and becoming a lawyer for Hollywood celebrities. But her drive and ambition faded when she reached high school. She ignored homework assignments and argued with teachers. Her grades dropped to mostly C's and D's. She was so difficult that she was asked to leave three private schools in two years. Emily says she was angry and depressed over a family member's drug use. At age 17 last fall, she was applying to colleges and had a tough decision to make: How to present herself to admissions officers increasingly wary of troubled students?

Concerned about liability and campus safety in the wake of shootings at Northern Illinois University and Virginia Tech, more colleges and universities are scrutinizing the character of applicants. They want to know about students' past behavior, and, if there is any doubt, they will call high school counselors for answers. Admissions officers say "youthful indiscretions" like a schoolyard brawl or an unpaid traffic ticket aren't likely to result in denial letters. But a pattern of troubling behavior could cost someone an admission.

"We're not only admitting students for intellectual reasons but for community reasons," says Debra Shaver, director of admissions at Smith College, a private women's liberal arts school in Massachusetts. "We want to make sure they will be good community members." Smith and other schools acknowledge that making judgments about character is sometimes a messy process. It doesn't involve precise measures like SAT scores or grade-point average. "In some cases, you say, 'This makes me nervous,' and maybe it is an intuition and some reasonable people would disagree, but it goes with the territory," says Bruce Poch, dean of admissions at Pomona College in Claremont, Calif.

Full disclosure. It's not surprising, then, that students like Emily agonize over the decision to disclose personal and academic problems. "We finally hired an independent counselor," says Lisa Kaufman, Emily's mother.

Not all counselors agree on what advice to give families. Some discourage students from bringing up mental illnesses and emotional problems altogether. Others say full disclosure helps when a student's records show poor grades or other inconsistencies that are likely to make colleges suspicious. Shirley Bloomquist, an independent college counselor in Great Falls, Va., says she once called a liberal arts college in Massachusetts to say she was disappointed by its decision to reject an applicant who had written about overcoming a drug addiction. The student had completed a drug rehabilitation program and had been clean for a year. "Colleges are more concerned than ever about student emotional stability," Bloomquist says. "I think it is imperative that the student, the parent, and the high school counselor discuss the situation and decide what should or should not be revealed."

Sally Rubenstone, senior counselor with collegeconfidential .com and coauthor of *Panicked Parents' Guide to College Admission*, says being forthright about past behavior or mental health problems doesn't mean "The Jerry Springerization of the College Admissions Essay." "Sometimes I have to implore [students] to stay mum," she says. "There are clearly times when personal problems are too personal—or inappropriate—to include in a college essay."

Emily's problems, however, needed airing—but not all of them. For example, she didn't disclose her troubles in middle school because colleges asked only (via the Common Application) about academic and behavioral misconduct in high school. She says she was asked to leave one high school after a confrontation with another student, but the offense was never recorded in her file, so she didn't volunteer that information either. On the advice of her counselor, Emily wrote cover letters and an essay focusing instead on the reasons for her documented troubles in school and how she had grown from those experiences.

Although colleges would know from her transcripts that she had been at a boarding school for troubled teens, Emily didn't explicitly mention depression in her essay. Rubenstone, who served as Emily's counselor in the admissions process, says, "Colleges can run scared when they hear the word depression." Emily, who got treatment, hoped colleges would pay attention to her improvement instead. "I thought I was taking a risk, but I had faith that people would understand," she says. In one of her cover letters, Emily wrote: "What I am trying to say is that my past no longer dictates my future and that I am a far more capable, hard-working, mature student than depicted in my forms."

Colleges cannot legally deny admission specifically on the basis of mental illness, but it's hard to account for how that characteristic figures into the calculus of who gets in and who doesn't. Admissions officers undoubtedly are aware that the shooters at Virginia Tech and Northern Illinois had troubled histories before they applied to school: Indeed, the graduate student responsible for the NIU attack had written about his emotional struggles in adolescence in his admission application. Admissions officers, ever mindful of the diversity on campus, also are aware that reports of depressed college students are on the rise.

Not all colleges offer students a second chance. One high school senior in Tucson, Ariz., with an impressive academic record was rejected by a selective liberal arts college after his counselor says he told the school that the student had been disciplined for smoking marijuana on a field trip. The counselor says he helped the student with his essay, believing that if it struck the right tone and offered a sincere apology and a pledge from the student that he would not make the same mistake again, the essay would persuade the college to admit him. It didn't. "This particular school was trying very hard to diminish its reputation as being 'kind of tolerant of druggies'—the very words used by the college representative," the counselor says.

Barmak Nassirian of the American Association of Collegiate Registrars and Admissions Officers says too much pressure is being put on college admission officers who lack the expertise to evaluate the seriousness of an offense or an applicant's emotional well-being. In the absence of clear guidelines, Nassirian says, colleges should stop asking about past behavior altogether. "It's very tempting for colleges to say we're excluding the next Jack the Ripper from sitting next to your son or daughter," he says. "But it's really your son or daughter who is getting nabbed and getting nabbed for having done something stupid in high school."

Common Application

That may be the reason that many high schools don't disclose information about a student's disciplinary history. A recent survey of 2,306 public and private high schools found that only 23 percent of schools said they allowed for the disclosure of such information to colleges, 39 percent said they disclose sometimes, and 38 percent said they never do. The results refer to questions asked by about 340 colleges that use the Common Application, which inquires if students have ever been convicted of a crime or been severely disciplined in high school. This year, 347,837 high school students used the Common Application. Of those, only 2 percent said they had a serious discipline problem in high school, and 0.22 percent said they were convicted of a misdemeanor or felony.

It's not clear how many students refuse to answer the questions or conceal their past troubles. In what one admissions counselor sees as a separate, disturbing trend, high schools that once suspended or expelled students for offenses such as academic dishonesty now strike deals with parents and students that result in less severe consequences and no record of the student's indiscretion. One New York student who has been accepted to several competitive schools says he caught a lucky break when the private high school he attended his freshman year decided that rather than expel him, it would let him quietly transfer to another school after he was caught stealing a biology exam. The school told him it would not notify colleges about the incident. At his new high school, the student was suspended for insulting another student. And again he was able to cut a deal with the principal at that school. The student, who requested anonymity, says he was able to "work off" the suspension from his record by performing community service. He says his guidance counselor discouraged him from bringing up either incident on his college applications. "It's not that I wanted to lie," he says. "I just didn't want to lose everything that I've worked so hard for."

If an applicant's school records raise suspicion, colleges say they will make every effort to verify the information. Some, for instance, will turn to Google, Facebook, or another source on the Internet. But it's not clear how thorough most colleges are when high schools don't cooperate. It is often the case, some say, that an anonymous tipster or an upset parent of a child who was not admitted to the school will come forward. Colleges say a high school's refusal to share information could damage the school's relationship with the college, especially in the event that the applicant is admitted and later commits a crime.

Marlyn McGrath Lewis, director of admissions at Harvard, says high schools that knowingly withhold troubling information about applicants will be held responsible. "We're not a detective agency," she says. "We operate on the assumption that schools are behaving honorably." If administrators learn that an applicant has lied, colleges can rescind offers of admission. That's what happened in 1995 when Harvard administrators found out that an admitted applicant had killed her mother when she was 14. The applicant, a straight-A student, had not disclosed the incident in her Harvard application on the advice of her lawyer.

Seth Allen, dean of admissions at Grinnell College, a liberal arts school in Iowa, says colleges expect that students will answer questions about their past behavior truthfully and completely. "We want to understand if you slipped up why it happened," he says. "If we understand that there is a death in the family or a personal crisis that would help us say, 'This is not a normal pattern of behavior,' we can forgive you." Sometimes, he adds, an honest and thoughtful response can make a candidate more appealing.

Earlier this year, Emily was offered admission to six schools; she has decided to attend Simmons College in Boston. She was turned down by four other schools. "I'm grateful because I feel people are willing to take a chance on me," she says. "It just makes me hopeful that the world is moving away from fear and towards acceptance of those of us who haven't had the easiest times."

Critical Thinking

1. What challenges are found by college applicants with mental health issues?
2. What are the worries of college admissions offices?
3. How would you compare the challenges and worries of the prospective students and admissions offices?
4. What are the possible answers to this serious problem?

Body Dissatisfaction in Adolescent Females and Males: Risk and Resilience

Katherine Presnell, PhD, Sarah Kate Bearman, PhD, and Mary Clare Madeley, BA

One of the most remarkable and consistent research findings is the overwhelming prevalence of weight and shape-related concerns among adolescents. Estimates from community samples of adolescents suggest that as many as 46% of girls and 26% of boys report significant distress about their body size and shape, while only 12% of girls and 17% of boys indicate that they are satisfied with their body shape (Neumark-Sztainer, Story, Hannan, Perry, & Irving, 2002; Ricciardelli & McCabe, 2001). In fact, body dissatisfaction has become so commonplace in Western culture that it has been termed a "normative discontent" (Rodin, Silberstein, & Striegel-Moore, 1985). This is especially troubling because, at the upper end of the continuum, body dissatisfaction is associated with high levels of subjective distress, unhealthy weight control behaviors, and extreme methods of altering appearance, such as cosmetic surgery and steroid use (Neumark-Sztainer, Paxton, Hannan, Haines, & Story, 2006).

> **As many as 46% of girls and 26% of boys report significant distress about their body size and shape.**

Body image is a broad term comprised of an individual's internal perceptions, thoughts, and evaluation of their outward physical appearance. Body dissatisfaction is one component of body image, and refers to the subjective negative evaluation of some aspect of one's physical appearance (Thompson, Heinberg, Altabe, & Tantleff-Dunn, 1999). Body dissatisfaction has been consistently shown to place adolescents at increased risk for the development and maintenance of disordered eating (Stice & Shaw, 2002), because strategies such as extreme dietary restriction or compensatory measures may be used in an attempt to alter weight and shape. Moreover, body image concerns are often resistant to change during treatment for eating disorders, and persistent body image disturbances are associated with relapse in anorexia and bulimia nervosa (Keel, Dorer, Franko, Jackson, & Herzog, 2005). Body dissatisfaction is also a strong predictor of depressed mood and low self-esteem among adolescents (Paxton, Neumark-Sztainer, Hannan, & Eisenberg, 2006). The negative impact of body dissatisfaction on a range of psychological problems underscores the need to explore factors that contribute to its development. Recent research also suggests that reducing body dissatisfaction may be successful in preventing the onset of depression and eating pathology (Bearman, Stice, & Chase, 2003).

Adolescence is a critical developmental period, bringing numerous physical changes, social challenges, and role transitions that increase vulnerability to body dissatisfaction. Theories of the development of body dissatisfaction highlight multiple contributing factors, including individual, familial, peer, and sociocultural influences. This article will highlight factors that influence the development of body dissatisfaction during adolescence, and consider protective factors that may decrease adolescents' risk of body image concerns. Understanding the mechanisms that link these factors to body dissatisfaction can help guide the development of effective prevention interventions.

Sociocultural Influences
Ideal-body Internalization

Beauty standards that are sanctioned by an individual's culture are hypothesized to influence how individuals perceive and evaluate their bodies. Western culture currently endorses an ultra-thin figure for women and a lean, muscular one for men. Pressure to conform to these ideals is evident in messages from the media, parents, and peers. As these ideals become increasingly difficult to attain, a sense of dissatisfaction often develops in those who place high importance on achieving them. Historically, there has been greater sociocultural emphasis on appearance and thinness for females, and research indicates consistently higher rates of body dissatisfaction among females in relation to males (Thompson et al., 1999). However, body dissatisfaction is also a substantial concern among adolescent boys. Adolescent boys are more likely than girls to engage in behaviors to increase weight and musculature, and there is evidence that boys are divided between those who desire to lose weight and those who wish to gain weight and musculature (e.g., Neumark-Sztainer et al., 1999). Thus, there may be two pathways to body dissatisfaction among boys—weight concerns and muscularity concerns—whereas girls consistently report a desire to be thinner. Regardless of gender, however, failure to attain a highly-valued ideal has been shown to lead to body dissatisfaction (Jones, 2004).

Differences in Ideals across Cultures

There is some evidence that beauty ideals and body dissatisfaction vary among cultural or ethnic groups. Ethnic groups that place greater emphasis on thinness tend to have higher levels of body dissatisfaction, particularly as obesity rates rise. For example, African American girls generally endorse a larger body ideal and report greater body satisfaction than Caucasian girls (Perez & Joiner, 2003). However, recent research indicates that this gap in body dissatisfaction may be decreasing, and that the most pronounced disparity occurs during the college-age years (Roberts, Cash, Feingold, & Johnson, 2006). Other research also suggests few differences in body dissatisfaction among African American, Asian American, and Hispanic women (Grabe & Hyde, 2006). Moreover, ethnic status failed to moderate the relation between body dissatisfaction and depression for girls, suggesting that regardless of ethnic identity, dissatisfaction with one's body increases the risk of depression (Siegel, 2002).

Media Influences

Use of media that conveys messages about body ideals is consistently associated with greater body dissatisfaction, and experimental exposure to images portraying the thin-ideal result in moderate decreases in self-esteem and increases in body dissatisfaction among females (e.g., Stice & Shaw, 1994). Some evidence suggests that media and peer influences are more influential during adolescence than parental influences for girls (Shroff &

Thompson, 2006), but that the effect of media may be less pronounced among boys (McCabe & Ricciardelli, 2001).

Parent and Peer Influences

Although societal norms regarding ideal body shape and weight are transmitted in a variety of ways, messages from one's immediate subculture may be particularly salient in communicating these values. These may be transmitted through parental modeling of eating and body-related attitudes and behaviors, as well as through direct comments about weight and encouragement of weight loss. Adolescent girls perceive greater feedback from their mothers to lose weight and increase muscle tone than do boys, and this perception is greater for girls who are heavier (McCabe & Ricciardelli, 2001). Direct messages from parents encouraging their children to lose weight predict higher drive for thinness and body dissatisfaction among daughters, and appear to have a greater influence than parental modeling of dieting behaviors (Wertheim, Martin, Prior, Sanson, & Smart, 2002).

Relatedly, criticism and teasing about appearance have been associated with greater body dissatisfaction, although this may differ by gender. Boys tend to receive more messages from family and friends regarding increasing muscles and these messages decrease over time, whereas girls receive more messages regarding weight loss, and these messages increase over time (McCabe & Ricciardelli, 2005). For both adolescent boys and girls, messages from their parents and closest same-sex friend resulted in attempts to change physical size and shape.

In addition to direct pressure, lack of social support or support that is perceived as conditional on meeting appearance expectations, may promote body dissatisfaction. Indeed, deficits in social support from parents and peers predicted body dissatisfaction for both adolescent girls and boys (Bearman, Presnell, Martinez, & Stice, 2006).

Biological Factors
Body Mass and Pubertal Status

Biological factors may play a role in the development of body dissatisfaction when they deviate from culturally-sanctioned attractiveness ideals. Pubertal changes, including increased body fat, move girls farther from the thin-ideal. Increasing body mass is consistently associated with greater body dissatisfaction among girls, although dissatisfaction is not always associated with being objectively overweight, as many normal-weight females also express displeasure with their bodies (Presnell, Bearman, & Stice, 2004). Boys, however, may have a more complex relationship between body mass and body dissatisfaction. Overweight boys report lower self-esteem and greater self-consciousness than normal-weight boys, yet adolescent boys report nearly equal rates of wanting to lose versus gain weight, suggesting the optimal weight range may fall in the middle (Blyth et al., 1981). Indeed, research suggests that body dissatisfaction is greatest for boys who are over-or underweight, with those of average weight being the most satisfied with their appearance (Presnell, Bearman, & Stice, 2004). Both types of concerns have been associated with elevated body dissatisfaction among boys, although they may employ different strategies to achieve this ideal weight, including dieting to reduce body mass, or excessive exercise and steroid use to increase size and muscularity (Ricciardelli & McCabe, 2003).

Pubertal timing may also be associated with body dissatisfaction. McCabe and Ricciardelli (2004) noted that early-maturing and on-time girls reported higher levels of body dissatisfaction than girls whose pubertal development was delayed relative to peers. Again, this may be because pubertal increases in body size move girls farther from the ideal. In contrast, boys who physically matured earlier than their same-sex peers had the highest levels of body satisfaction. However, other research suggests that pubertal status may interact with other variables, such as initiating dating, to place adolescents at risk for body dissatisfaction (Cauffman & Steinberg, 1996).

Individual Risk Factors
Negative Mood
Mood disturbances have also been implicated in the development of body dissatisfaction because depressed mood induces selective attention to negative information about oneself and the world. This may result in a focus on displeasing aspects of one's body and foster negative comparisons to others. Experimental studies indicate that temporary increases in negative mood result in temporary increases in body dissatisfaction in girls, suggesting at least a short-term relation (Baker, Williamson, & Sylve, 1995). However, prospective studies have failed to demonstrate this relationship, perhaps because the experimental studies may not represent the types of mood disturbances experienced outside of the laboratory. There is some evidence that this relation may differ by gender, with boys showing a stronger relation between negative affect and body dissatisfaction than girls (Presnell et al., 2004). Additionally, negative affect also predicted body change strategies in a sample of adolescent boys (Ricciardelli & McCabe, 2003).

Dieting
Adolescents who believe that being thin will result in psychosocial benefits may turn to dieting as a means of altering their physique. Adolescent girls in particular may

attempt to counter pubertal weight gain by restricting their caloric intake. However, research suggests that self-reported attempts to restrict caloric intake predict weight gain, rather than weight loss (Stice et al., 1999). Thus, dieting may increase frustration and reduce feelings of self-efficacy for producing weight change. Indeed, self-reported dieting attempts predict increases in body dissatisfaction among both girls and boys (Bearman et al., 2006). Despite the suggestion that boys may be more likely to strive to achieve bulk in the form of muscle rather than to lose weight, boys who express concern about weight loss and dieting are also more likely to express body dissatisfaction (Jones & Crawford, 2005). Additionally, boys with lower levels of body satisfaction are more likely to diet, and less likely to engage in activities that might increase muscle, such as physical activity (Neumark-Sztainer et al., 2006)

> **Self-reported attempts to restrict caloric intake predict weight gain, rather than weight loss.**

Potential Protective Factors
Few studies have identified factors that either enhance body image or buffer the negative effects of risk factors for body dissatisfaction. To date, this work has primarily focused on positive parental relationships. Feeling supported by one's immediate social network may serve as a protective factor from the myriad pressures that are hypothesized to foster body dissatisfaction. One prospective study found that a supportive maternal relationship was associated with increased body satisfaction (Barker & Galambos, 2003). Another found that feeling close to either parent was associated with fewer concurrent weight and eating concerns among girls, but the prospective association between parental closeness and weight concerns was not significant (Swarr & Richards, 1996). Several studies have demonstrated no impact of parental relationships or acceptance on body dissatisfaction for boys (e.g. Barker & Galambos, 2003).

It will be important for future research to consider other variables that may mitigate the impact of body dissatisfaction. Theoretically, cognitive factors such as attributional style or perceived control, which have been linked to disorders such as depression and anxiety, may be associated with body dissatisfaction. Control-related beliefs play a role in the impact of life stressors on depressed mood and perceived helplessness regarding the future (Weisz, Southam-Gerow & McCarty, 2001). It is possible that individuals who have control-related beliefs regarding their weight and shape may face less risk of body dissatisfaction because they believe they are capable of changing their appearance or adapting to those displeasing aspects. Higher levels of perceived control have been shown to act as protective factors for depression among youth (Weisz, Sweeney, Proffitt, & Carr, 1993); future research should examine the role control related beliefs play in the development of body dissatisfaction, as well as other potential buffering factors that have been implicated in research of other related disorders.

Conclusions

Body dissatisfaction has been identified as one of the most potent and consistent risk factors for eating disorders, and contributes significantly to poor self-esteem and depression among adolescents. An understanding of the factors that increase the risk for body dissatisfaction can help guide prevention efforts for these outcomes. This article has highlighted internalization of socially-prescribed body ideals, body mass, media influences, and messages from parents and peers as key risk factors for the development of body dissatisfaction, whereas others have received less consistent support. Given the complexity of the development of body image concerns, interventions aimed at reducing body dissatisfaction will likely need to target multiple factors, including individual, familial, and sociocultural factors. Interventions that reduce sociocultural pressures to be thin and educate adolescents to more critically evaluate messages from the media hold promise in reducing body dissatisfaction. Unfortunately, there is relatively little research on protective factors that may aid youth in developing a positive body image. Additional research is needed to determine how best to foster greater body satisfaction or mitigate the effects of established risk factors.

References

Baker, J.D., Williamson, D.A., & Sylve, C. (1995). Body image disturbance, memory bias, and body dysphoria: Effects of negative mood induction. *Behavior Therapy, 26,* 747–759.

Barker, E.T., & Galambos, N.L. (2003). Body dissatisfaction of adolescent girls and boys: Risk and resource factors. *Journal of Early Adolescence, 23,* 141–165.

Bearman, S.K., Presnell, K., Martinez, E., & Stice, E. (2006). The skinny on body dissatisfaction: A longitudinal study of adolescent girls and boys. *Journal of Youth and Adolescence, 35,* 229–241.

Bearman, S.K., Stice, E., & Chase, A. (2003). Evaluation of an intervention targeting both depressive and bulimic pathology: A randomized prevention trial. *Behavior Therapy, 34*(3), 277–293.

Blyth, D.A., Simmons, R.G., Bulcroft, R., Felt, D., Van Cleave, E.F., & Bush, D.M. (1981). The effects of physical development in self-image and satisfaction with body image for early adolescent males. *Research in Community and Mental Health, 2,* 43–73.

Cauffman, E., & Steinberg, L. (1996). Interactive effects of menarcheal status and dating on dieting and disordered eating among adolescent girls. *Developmental Psychology, 32,* 631–635.

Grabe, S. & Hyde, J.S. (2006). Ethnicity and body dissatisfaction among women in the United States: A meta-analysis. *Psychological Bulletin, 132*(4), 622–640.

Jones, D.C. (2004). Body image among adolescent girls and boys: A longitudinal study. *Developmental Psychology, 40,* 823–835.

Jones, D.C., & Crawford, J.K. (2005). Adolescent boys and body image: Weight and muscularity concerns as dual pathways to body dissatisfaction. *Journal of Youth and Adolescence, 34*(6), 629–636.

Keel, P.K., Dorer, D.J., Franko, D.L., Jackson, S.C., & Herzog, D.B. (2005). Postremission predictors of relapse in women with eating disorders. *American Journal of Psychiatry, 162,* 2,263–2,268.

McCabe, M.P., & Ricciardelli, L.A. (2001). Parent, peer, and media influences on body image and strategies to both increase and decrease body size among adolescent boys and girls. *Adolescence, 36,* 225–240.

McCabe, M.P., & Ricciardelli, L.A. (2004). A longitudinal study of pubertal timing and extreme body change behaviors among adolescent boys and girls. Adolescence, 39, 145–166.

McCabe, M.P., & Ricciardelli, L.A., (2005). A prospective study of pressures from parents, peers, and the media on extreme weight change behaviors among adolescent boys and girls. *Behaviour Research and Therapy, 43,* 653–668.

Neumark-Sztainer, D., Paxton, S.J., Hannan, P.J., Haines, J., & Story, M. (2006). Does body satisfaction matter? Five-year longitudinal associations between body satisfaction and health behaviors in adolescent females and males. *Journal of Adolescent Health, 39,* 244–251.

Neumark-Sztainer, D., Story, M., Falkner, N.H., Beuhring, T., & Resnick, M.D. (1999). Sociodemographic and personal characteristics of adolescents engaged in weight loss and weight/muscle gain behaviors: Who is doing what? *Preventive Medicine, 28,* 40–50.

Neumark-Sztainer, D., Story, M., Hannan, P.J., Perry, C.L., & Irving, L.M. (2002). Weight-related concerns and behaviors among overweight and nonoverweight adolescents: Implications for preventing weight-related disorders. *Archives of Pediatric Adolescent Medicine, 156,* 171–178.

Paxton, S.J., Neumark-Sztainer, D., Hannan, P.J., & Eisenberg, M.E. (2006). Body dissatisfaction prospectively predicts depressive mood and low self-esteem in adolescent girls and boys. *Journal of Clinical Child and Adolescent Psychology, 35,* 539–549.

Perez, M., & Joiner, T.E. (2003). Body image dissatisfaction and disordered eating in black and white women. *International Journal of Eating Disorders, 33,* 342–350.

Presnell, K., Bearman, S.K., & Stice, E. (2004). Risk factors for body dissatisfaction in adolescent boys and girls: A prospective study. *International Journal of Eating Disorders, 36,* 389–401.

Ricciardelli, L.A., & McCabe, M.P. (2001). Dietary restraint and negative affect as mediators of body dissatisfaction and bulimic behavior in adolescent girls and boys. *Behaviour Research and Therapy, 39,* 1,317–1,328.

Ricciardelli, L.A., & McCabe, M.P. (2003). Sociocultural influences on body image and body changes among adolescent boys and girls. *Journal of Social Psychology, 143,* 5–26.

Roberts, A., Cash, T.F., Feingold, A., & Johnson, B.T. (2006). Are black-white differences in females' body dissatisfaction decreasing? A meta-analytic review. *Journal of Consulting and Clinical Psychology, 74,* 1,121–1,131.

Rodin, J., Silberstein, L., & Striegel-Moore, R. (1985). Women and Weight: A Normative Discontent. Nebraska Symposium on Motivation, Lincoln, Nebraska: University of Nebraska Press, 267–307.

Shroff, H., & Thompson, J.K. (2006). The tripartite influence model of body image and eating disturbance: A replication with adolescent girls. *Body Image, 3,* 17–23.

Siegel, J.M. (2002). Body image change and adolescent depressive symptoms. *Journal of Adolescent Research, 17,* 27–41.

Stice, E., Cameron, R.P., Killen, J.D., & Taylor, C.B. (1999). Naturalistic weight-reduction efforts prospectively predict growth in relative weight and onset of obesity among female adolescents. *Journal of Consulting & Clinical Psychology, 67,* 967–974.

Stice, E., & Shaw, H.E. (1994). Adverse effects of the media portrayed thin-ideal on women and linkages to bulimic symptomatology. *Journal of Social and Clinical Psychology, 13,* 288–308.

Stice, E., & Shaw, H.E. (2002). Role of body dissatisfaction in the onset and maintenance of eating pathology: A synthesis of research findings. *Journal of Psychosomatic Research, 53,* 985–993.

Swarr, A.E., & Richards, M.H. (1996). Longitudinal effects of adolescent girls' pubertal development, perceptions of pubertal timing, and parental relations on eating problems. *Developmental Psychology, 32,* 636–646.

Thompson, J.K., Heinberg, L.J., Altabe, M., & Tantleff-Dunn, S. (1999) *Exacting Beauty: Theory, Assessment, and Treatment of Body Image Disturbance.* Washington, D.C.: American Psychological Association.

Weisz, J.R., Sweeney, L., Proffitt, V., & Carr, T. (1993). Control-related beliefs and self-reported depressive symptoms in late childhood. *Journal of Abnormal Psychology, 102,* 411–418.

Weisz, J., Southam-Gerow, M.A., & McCarty, C.A. (2001). Control-related beliefs and depressive symptoms in clinic-referred children and adolescents: Developmental differences and model specificity. *Journal of Abnormal Psychology, 110,* 97–109.

Wertheim, E.H., Martin, G., Prior, M., Sanson, A., & Smart, D. (2002). Parent influences in the transmission of eating and weight-related values and behaviors. *Eating Disorders, 10,* 321–334.

Critical Thinking

1. How can understanding the factors that increases the risk for body dissatisfaction help guide prevention efforts?
2. What is the prevalence of body dissatisfaction?
3. Compare body dissatisfaction of girls and boys.
4. What are several predictors of the development of body dissatisfaction?

Katherine Resnell, PhD, is an Assistant Professor in the Department of Psychology at Southern Methodist University (SMU) and Director of the Weight and Eating Disorders Research Program at SMU. Her research focuses on understanding sociocultural, psychological, and behavioral risk factors that contribute to eating disorders and obesity, as well as developing effective prevention interventions for these disorders. **Sarah Kate Bearman, PhD,** is a postdoctoral fellow at the Judge Baker Children's Center, Harvard Medical School. Her research interests include the etiology and prevention of youth depression and body image concerns, as well as the effectiveness of evidence-based interventions for children in real-world settings. **Mary Clare Madeley, BA,** is a graduate student in the Department of Psychology at Southern Methodist University. Her research interests focus on risk factors for eating disorders.

Goodbye to Girlhood

As pop culture targets ever younger girls, psychologists worry about a premature focus on sex and appearance.

STACY WEINER

Ten-year-old girls can slide their low-cut jeans over "eye-candy" panties. French maid costumes, garter belt included, are available in preteen sizes. Barbie now comes in a "bling-bling" style, replete with halter top and go-go boots. And it's not unusual for girls under 12 to sing, "Don't cha wish your girlfriend was hot like me?"

American girls, say experts, are increasingly being fed a cultural catnip of products and images that promote looking and acting sexy.

"Throughout U.S. culture, and particularly in mainstream media, women and girls are depicted in a sexualizing manner," declares the American Psychological Association's Task Force on the Sexualization of Girls, in a report issued Monday. The report authors, who reviewed dozens of studies, say such images are found in virtually every medium, from TV shows to magazines and from music videos to the Internet.

While little research to date has documented the effect of sexualized images specifically on *young* girls, the APA authors argue it is reasonable to infer harm similar to that shown for those 18 and older; for them, sexualization has been linked to "three of the most common mental health problems of girls and women: eating disorders, low self-esteem and depression."

Said report contributor and psychologist Sharon Lamb: "I don't think because we don't have the research yet on the younger girls that we can ignore that [sexualization is] of harm to them. Common sense would say that, and part of the reason we wrote the report is so we can get funding to prove that."

Boys, too, face sexualization, the authors acknowledge. Pubescent-looking males have posed provocatively in Calvin Klein ads, for example, and boys with impossibly sculpted abs hawk teen fashion lines. But the authors say they focused on girls because females are objectified more often. According to a 1997 study in the journal Sexual Abuse, 85 percent of ads that sexualized children depicted girls.

Even influences that are less explicitly erotic often tell girls who they are equals how they look and that beauty commands power and attention, contends Lamb, co-author of "Packaging Girlhood: Rescuing Our Daughters from Marketers' Schemes" (St. Martin's, 2006). One indicator that these influences are reaching girls earlier, she and others say: The average age for adoring the impossibly proportioned Barbie has slid from preteen to preschool.

When do little girls start wanting to look good for others? "A few years ago, it was 6 or 7," says Deborah Roffman, a Baltimore-based sex educator. "I think it begins by 4 now."

While some might argue that today's belly-baring tops are no more risque than hip huggers were in the '70s, Roffman disagrees. "Kids have always emulated adult things," she says. "But [years ago] it was, 'That's who I'm supposed to be as an adult.' It's very different today. The message to children is, 'You're already like an adult. It's okay for you to be interested in sex. It's okay for you to dress and act sexy, right now.' That's an entirely different frame of reference."

It's not just kids' exposure to sexuality that worries some experts; it's the kind of sexuality they're seeing. "The issue is that the way marketers and media present sexuality is in a very narrow way," says Lamb. "Being a sexual person isn't about being a pole dancer," she chides. "This is a sort of sex education girls are getting, and it's a misleading one."

Clothes Encounters

Liz Guay says she has trouble finding clothes she considers appropriate for her daughter Tanya, age 8. Often, they're too body-hugging. Or too low-cut. Or too short. Or too spangly.

Then there are the shoes: Guay says last time she visited six stores before finding a practical, basic flat. And don't get her started on earrings.

"Tanya would love to wear dangly earrings. She sees them on TV, she sees other girls at school wearing them, she sees them in the stores all the time. . . . I just say, 'You're too young.'"

"It's not so much a feminist thing," explains Guay, a Gaithersburg medical transcriptionist. "It's more that I want her to be comfortable with who she is and to make decisions based on what's right for her, not what everybody else is doing. I want her to develop the strength that when she gets to a point where kids are offering her alcohol or drugs, that she's got enough self-esteem to say, 'I don't want that.'"

Some stats back up Guay's sense of fashion's shrinking modesty. For example, in 2003, tweens—that highly coveted marketing segment ranging from 7 to 12—spent $1.6 million on thong underwear, Time magazine reported. But even more-innocent-seeming togs, toys and activities—like tiny "Beauty Queen" T-shirts, Hello Kitty press-on nails or preteen make-overs at Club Libby Lu—can be problematic, claim psychologists. The reason: They may lure young girls into an unhealthy focus on appearance.

Studies suggest that female college students distracted by concerns about their appearance score less well on tests than do others. Plus, some experts say, "looking good" is almost culturally inseparable for girls from looking sexy: Once a girl's bought in, she's hopped onto a consumer conveyor belt in which marketers move females from pastel tiaras to hot-pink push-up bras.

Where did this girly-girl consumerism start? Diane Levin, an education professor at Wheelock College in Boston who is writing an upcoming book, "So Sexy So Soon," traces much of it to the deregulation of children's television in the mid-1980s. With the rules loosened, kids' shows suddenly could feature characters who moonlighted as products (think Power Rangers, Care Bears, My Little Pony). "There became a real awareness," says Levin, "of how to use gender and appearance and, increasingly, sex to market to children."

Kids are more vulnerable than adults to such messages, she argues.

The APA report echoes Levin's concern. It points to a 2004 study of adolescent girls in rural Fiji, linking their budding concerns about body image and weight control to the introduction of television there.

In the United States, TV's influence is incontestable. According to the Kaiser Family Foundation, for example, nearly half of American kids age 4 to 6 have a TV in their bedroom. Nearly a quarter of teens say televised sexual content affects their own behavior.

And that content is growing: In 2005, 77 percent of prime-time shows on the major broadcast networks included sexual material, according to Kaiser, up from 67 percent in 1998. In a separate Kaiser study of shows popular with teenage girls, women and girls were twice as likely as men and boys to have their appearance discussed. They also were three times more likely to appear in sleepwear or underwear than their male counterparts.

Preteen Preening

It can be tough for a parent to stanch the flood of media influences.

Ellen Goldstein calls her daughter Maya, a Rockville fifth-grader, a teen-mag maniac. "She has a year's worth" of Girls' Life magazine, says Goldstein. "When her friends come over, they pore over this magazine." What's Maya reading? There's "Get Gorgeous Skin by Tonight," "Crush Confidential: Seal the Deal with the Guy You Dig," and one of her mom's least faves: "Get a Fierce Body Fast."

"Why do you want to tell a kid to get a fierce body fast when they're 10? They're just developing," complains Goldstein. She also bemoans the magazines' photos, which Maya has plastered on her ceiling.

"These are very glamorous-looking teenagers. They're wearing lots of makeup. They all have very glossy lips," she says. "They're generally wearing very slinky outfits. . . . I don't think those are the best role models," Goldstein says. "When so much emphasis is placed on the outside, it minimizes the importance of the person inside."

So why not just say no?

"She loves fashion," explains Goldstein. "I don't want to take away her joy from these magazines. It enhances her creative spirit. [Fashion] comes naturally to her. I want her to feel good about that. We just have to find a balance."

Experts say her concern is warranted. Pre-adolescents' propensity to try on different identities can make them particularly susceptible to media messages, notes the APA report. And for some girls, thinking about how one's body stacks up can be a real downer.

In a 2002 study, for example, seventh-grade girls who viewed idealized magazine images of women reported a drop in body satisfaction and a rise in depression.

Such results are disturbing, say observers, since eating disorders seem to strike younger today. A decade ago, new eating disorder patients at Children's National Medical Center tended to be around age 15, says Adelaide Robb, director of inpatient psychiatry. Today kids come in as young as 5 or 6.

Mirror Images

Not everyone is convinced of the uglier side of beauty messages.

Eight-year-old Maya Williams owns four bracelets, eight necklaces, about 20 pairs of earrings and six rings, an assortment of which she sprinkles on every day. "Sometimes, she'll stand in front of the mirror and ask, "Are these pretty, Mommy?"

Her mom, Gaithersburg tutor Leah Haworth, is fine with Maya's budding interest in beauty. In fact, when Maya "wasn't sure" about getting her ears pierced, says Haworth, "I talked her into it by showing her all the pretty earrings she could wear."

What about all these sexualization allegations? "I don't equate looking good with attracting the opposite sex," Haworth says. Besides, "Maya knows her worth is based on her personality. She knows we love her for who she is."

"Looking good just shows that you care about yourself, care about how you present yourself to the world. People are judged by their appearance. People get better service and are treated better when they look better. That's just the way it is," she says. "I think discouraging children from paying attention to their appearance does them a disservice."

Magazine editor Karen Bokram also adheres to the beauty school of thought. "Research has shown that having skin issues at [her readers'] age is traumatic for girls' self-esteem," says Bokram, founder of Girls' Life. "Do we think girls need to be gorgeous in order to be worthy? No. Do we think girls' feeling good about how they look has positive effects in other areas of their lives, meaning that they make positive choices academically, socially and in romantic relationships? Absolutely."

Some skeptics of the sexualization notion also argue that kids today are hardier and savvier than critics think. Isaac Larian, whose company makes the large-eyed, pouty-lipped Bratz dolls, says, "Kids are very smart and know right from wrong." What's more, his testing indicates that girls want Bratz "because they are fun, beautiful and inspirational," he wrote in an e-mail. "Not once have we ever heard one of our consumers call Bratz 'sexy.'" Some adults "have a twisted sense of what they see in the product," Larian says.

"It is the parents' responsibility to educate their children," he adds. "If you don't like something, don't buy it."

But Genevieve McGahey, 16, isn't buying marketers' messages. The National Cathedral School junior recalls that her first real focus on appearance began in fourth grade. That's when classmates taught her: To be cool, you needed ribbons. To be cool, you needed lip gloss.

Starting around sixth grade, though, "it took on a more sinister character," she says. "People would start wearing really short skirts and lower tops and putting on more makeup. There's a strong pressure to grow up at this point."

"It's a little scary being a young girl," McGahey says. "The image of sexuality has been a lot more trumpeted in this era. . . . If you're not interested in [sexuality] in middle school, it seems a little intimidating." And unrealistic body ideals pile on extra pressure, McGahey says. At a time when their bodies and their body images are still developing, "girls are not really seeing people [in the media] who are beautiful but aren't stick-thin," she notes. "That really has an effect."

Today, though, McGahey feels good about her body and her style.

For this, she credits her mom, who is "very secure with herself and with being smart and being a woman." She also points to a wellness course at school that made her conscious of how women were depicted. "Seeing a culture of degrading women really influenced me to look at things in a new way and to think how we as high school girls react to that," she says.

"A lot of girls still hold onto that media ideal. I think I've gotten past it. As I've gotten more comfortable with myself and my body, I'm happy not to be trashy," McGahey says. "But most girls are still not completely or even semi-comfortable with themselves physically. You definitely still feel the pressure of those images."

Critical Thinking

1. What is the troubling trend of women and girls in sexual media depiction?

2. How is pop culture targeting younger girls?

3. What are the psychological damages in the sexual media depictions?

4. How do eating disorders, lower self-esteem, and depression relate to sexual media depiction?

STACY WEINER writes frequently for Health about families and relationships. Comments: health@washpost.com.

The Teenage Brain

Why Adolescents Sleep in, Take Risks, and Won't Listen to Reason

Nora Underwood

You don't have to suffer to suffer to be a poet. Adolescence is enough suffering for anyone.

—American poet John Ciardi, 1962.

In his speech at the launch of the 1997 I Am Your Child campaign, director and actor Rob Reiner stated that "by the age of ten, your brain is cooked." And until recently, most child experts, including Dr. Spock, would have agreed. They considered the first few years of a child's life to be the most important—and the experiences a child had during those years to play a crucial role in defining the kind of person he or she would ultimately become. That understanding also helped create a whole generation of obsessively child-focused parents, who, with the best of intentions, have tried to cram a lifetime of "educating" into a few short years, subjecting their unwitting fetuses to a diet of *Eine kleine Nachtmusik* and their pre-verbal toddlers to basic arithmetic and multiple viewings of *Baby Einstein* DVDs. (A wise elementary-school principal once noted, "I very much doubt Einstein was doing any of this when *he* was young.")

Somewhere along the line, or so many of us believed, the window of opportunity would close. The foundations of the adult-to-be would be laid, and the worst damage would be done. The majority of brain development does, in fact, take place in the early years, when billions of synaptic circuits that will last the child's lifetime are forming. But growth and change don't end there. Important developmental changes, scientists are discovering, are still taking place in a big way through the adolescent years—and into the mid-twenties. Perhaps this helps to explain the growing phenomenon of adult children who linger on under the parental roof; their growing may not be over, despite their arrival at "adulthood."

In recent years, researchers have finally been able to get real insight into the workings of the brain thanks to magnetic resonance imaging (MRI), using the technology to map blood flow to the areas of the brain that are activated by exposure to various stimuli. By scanning the same group of adolescents over a period of years or by comparing the brain responses of teenagers to those of adults, researchers are putting together a portrait of adolescence that confirms what many parents have always suspected: adolescents might as well be a whole different species. They are, as one neuroscientist puts it, a "work-in-progress."

Over the past decade, scientists have started to grasp exactly how distinctive the adolescent brain is and how crucial the years between ten and twenty-five are in terms of its development. And their discoveries have implications not only for parents, educators, and the medical community but also for policymakers. "I wouldn't disagree with Rob Reiner that the first three years are important," says Jay Giedd, chief of brain imaging in the child-psychiatry branch of the National Institute of Mental Health in Bethesda, Maryland. "I would just say that so are the next three and the next three and the next three, up to twenty-five and perhaps even beyond."

This news may not come as a surprise to the mother who still lies awake at 3 A.M., waiting for her basement-dwelling, twenty-two-year-old post-grad son to come home. What science suggests is that "adulthood" as we have defined it doesn't necessarily signal the end of childhood development—or of parental worries.

If the media is to be believed, the stereotypical teen is a selfish, volatile, rude, rebellious hormone-head, capable of little more than taking outrageous risks, ingesting too many harmful substances (legal and otherwise), committing crimes, crashing parties, trashing houses, and generally being a layabout. Of course, this is a gross misrepresentation: many teenagers pass through adolescence smoothly and happily, without becoming parents themselves, dropping out of school, or acquiring a criminal record instead of a degree. Still, there's a stubborn tendency in the culture to ascribe every negative teen moment to "hormones." Recent brain research, however, relieves hormones of much of the blame for this period of "storm and stress," as psychologist G. Stanley Hall, father of adolescent research, called it.

The full extent to which hormones actually influence adolescent behaviour remains unknown. So is what role they play in brain development. Hormones are certainly responsible for the most obvious hallmarks of puberty; at some mysterious point in a child's life, a protein called kisspeptin causes the hypothalamus—an area in the brain that orchestrates certain autonomic nervous-system functions—to secrete the gonadotropin-releasing hormone, which sets the pubertal changes in motion. Ultimately, estrogen and testosterone are responsible for the physical transformations—breast and genital development, body-hair growth, deepening of the voice, and so on—but by no means all the behavioural changes of adolescence. Hormones may have nothing to do with the fact that your daughter can't bear your singing voice, for instance; it's a safe bet, however, that a teenager's fixation on sex and social standing is pretty much hormone related.

But puberty does have an impact on how they think. For instance, as Giedd points out, boys fairly predictably base their decisions on the question "Will this lead to sex?" Giedd adds: "They may not say it in that way or it may not be that blatant, but if you just sort of go with that model it works pretty well." When girls make decisions, he adds, they are more likely to keep the social group, and their place in it, in mind. But Giedd feels that puberty's influence doesn't extend much outside that realm. "Your ability to do a logic problem or to do geometry or to do other things seems to be more [related to] age itself." Researchers have also found that the onslaught of testosterone in both male and female adolescents at puberty literally swells the amygdala—the brain centre associated with the emotions. Perhaps we can blame the amygdala for the slammed doors and sudden tears that overcome previously sunny children when they hit adolescence.

So hormones are not the only players in the changes that characterize adolescence. And while it is difficult to tease out the varying roles played by chromosomes, hormones, and other factors in teen behaviour, the insights that MRI reveals are nothing short of astounding.

Jay Giedd has been using MRI since 1991 to understand how the brain develops from childhood through adolescence and into early adulthood. He has scanned the brains of about 1,800 children, teenagers, and young adults every two years and interviewed them about their lives and feelings. As it turns out, Dr. Spock was not entirely wrong: by the time a child reaches the age of six, the brain is 90 to 95 percent of its adult size. But massive changes continue to take place for at least another fifteen years. They involve not just the familiar "grey matter," but a substance known as "white matter," the nerve tissue through which brain cells communicate—literally the medium that delivers the messages. White matter develops continuously from birth onward, with a slight increase during puberty. In contrast, grey matter—the part of the brain responsible for processing information, or the "thinking" part—develops quickly during childhood and slows in adolescence, with the frontal and temporal lobes the last to mature.

And this is the crux: the frontal lobe, or more precisely the prefrontal cortex, is the home of the so-called "executive functions": planning, organization, judgment, impulse control, and reasoning. The part that should be telling the sixteen-year-old not to dive off the thirty-foot cliff into unknown water. The seat of civilization.

What Giedd has witnessed via MRI is a constant push and pull in the grey matter. Certain forces cause a process known as arborization, during which grey matter gets bushier and grows new dendrites. Balancing that is a regressive pull, a competition for survival of sorts, in which some branches of the grey matter thrive while others are sacrificed. Both processes are continuous; as some new pathways grow, others are being pruned back. The quantity of grey matter peaks in girls around the age of eleven and in boys around thirteen, after which the amount of white matter increases. As grey matter decreases, there is also an increase in myelination, a process during which neurons, or nerve fibres, are insulated to enhance their performance.

In the end, though, the amount of grey matter isn't really the issue. "It's much more related to quality than quantity," explains Giedd. "This pruning process is normal and natural and healthy in terms of optimizing the brain for different environments. Our brains are built to be very adaptable during the teen years"—just the time when children start to figure out how to make it in the world. "The brain is incredibly plastic, which allows us to make it at the North Pole or the equator, to use a computer versus hunting with a stick. The teen brain is able to make changes depending on the demands of the environment." (This might explain a thirteen-year-old's ability to easily master new technology while parents struggle with the TV remote.)

What determines the fate of a cell is whether it has made a meaningful connection with other cells. This is a real use-it-or-lose-it process. As some scientists have noted, if an adolescent forgoes reading in favour of lying around on the couch playing video games, those unused synapses will be pruned. Nobel Prize-winning scientist Gerald Edelman has called this "neural Darwinism"—the survival of the fittest synapses. So scientists know that different activities—playing sports, speaking a second language, drinking, smoking, and so on—influence how the adolescent's brain will ultimately be wired, though they aren't clear what the implications are: Is the pianist going to do better in life than the crossword-puzzle fiend? Will the jock have a leg up, brain-wise, on the geek? "Can you actually see changes in the brain of someone doing music? The answer to that is yes," says Giedd. "But is that a good thing particularly? Is it just that our brains will become specialized in whatever we spend our time doing or is there a more general benefit?"

A father compliments his thirteen-year-old daughter on her new dress, only to have her swivel around, glare at him, and hiss, "What's *that* supposed to mean?" Nervous parents can rarely tell when an adolescent is going to fly off the handle. Why do they often have such hair-trigger responses? Two different MRI studies indicate that teenagers do not process emotion the same way adults do. In fact, one study shows that the adolescent brain actually reads emotion through a different area of the brain. Dr. Deborah Yurgelun-Todd, director of neuropsychology and cognitive neuroimaging at McLean Hospital in Belmont, Massachusetts, has scanned both adults and teenagers as they were shown images of faces that are clearly expressing fear. All the adults correctly identified the emotion; many of the teens got it wrong (about half labelled the expression one of "shock," "sadness," or "confusion"). Yurgelun-Todd found that during the scan of the adults, both the limbic area of the brain—the area especially connected to emotions—and the prefrontal cortex lit up. When teens were seeing the same pictures, the limbic area was bright but there was almost no activity in the prefrontal cortex. They were having an emotional response essentially unmediated by judgment and reasoning.

In another brain-imaging study, Daniel Pine, a researcher at the National Institute of Mental Health, tried to determine how the brain was able to stay focused on a task while the subject was being exposed to faces that were registering strong emotion. The result: activity in the frontal cortex of the adults was steadier, indicating they were better able to stay on task than teenagers. The emotional faces seemed to activate key areas in the brains of both age groups but only the adults were able to mute that activity so they could stay focused. Teenagers are more at the mercy of their feelings.

There is another fascinating phenomenon that plays havoc with the family of a teen: the adolescent sleep pattern. Suddenly, the kid who always woke you up at sunrise, when you were desperate to sleep, turns thirteen or fourteen and can neither be dragged from bed in the morning nor forced into it at night. Making matters worse, this change invariably occurs as the sleep needs of the middle-aged parents are flipping around the other way. It may seem like just another case of teenage passive aggression, but it's just biology; the circadian rhythm of the brain has changed and teenagers simply don't want to—or can't—go to bed before 12 or 1 A.M.

Why this happens has been the focus of some interest. Researchers at Brown University and Bradley Hospital in Providence, Rhode Island, measured the amount of melatonin, the hormone that helps regulate the sleep-wake cycle, in teenagers' saliva over the course of the day. They discovered that the levels of the hormone increased later in the day and decreased later in the morning in teenagers than in adults and children. A separate study indicated that the biological trigger for sleep—called the sleep pressure rate—slowed down during adolescence.

So if teenagers appear to be cycling through the day at a different pace from the rest of the world, it's because they are. In fact, because they are waking up when the world dictates—rather than when their bodies tell them to—teenagers are chronically sleep-deprived, which can have consequences ranging from superficial to severe. For starters, as Carlyle Smith, a psychology professor at Trent University in Peterborough, Ontario, who has studied how the adolescent brain processes information during sleep, notes, "They're just sleepy." They go to school tired, unfocused, and—because nobody likes to eat breakfast when they'd rather be sleeping—typically unfed. And as many teachers can attest, teenagers are also generally less able to absorb information in the morning. But by later in the afternoon, as the rest of the world is struggling not to nod off at their desks, teenagers begin to fire on all cylinders. "[As an adult], your temperature is at its high point shortly after lunch," explains Smith, "and then it starts its way down and drops all night until 3 or 4 A.M., when it starts to go up again. Theirs doesn't reach its height until later in the day." As a result, teenagers are just starting to focus and become more verbally adept as the rest of the world is crashing. By midnight, while the rest of the family is doing its best to fall asleep, teenagers are wide awake and instant-messaging away.

What is the fallout from a world that runs against the adolescent clock? There are four non-REM stages of sleep, and stages three and four, the deepest, which occur during the first third to first half of the night, are particularly useful to adolescents, who still have those frontal lobes to myelinate and lots of overall growing left to do (growth hormone is released during deep sleep). But because teenagers are so often deprived of REM sleep, which occurs during the last part of the night, their memories can suffer; they lose out on the stage of sleep that sees the information they've absorbed throughout the day replayed and consolidated. "Kids should be getting over nine hours of sleep," says Smith. "Most are getting one to two hours less than they should. They're missing quite a chunk of REM sleep and that's important for understanding new things. If you don't get much REM sleep, you're not going to learn as fast as people who do."

In one study, Smith set his subjects, who ranged in age from eighteen to twenty-two, to learning a logic task and then deprived them of the last half of the night of sleep. A week later, after the participants had recovered, the researchers tested them again. All had forgotten between 20 and 30 percent of what they'd learned. Once in a while, this kind of sleep loss is no problem. People can catch up. But when sleep deprivation becomes chronic, the consequences are compounded. "You're forgetting 20 percent, but 20 percent every day," says Smith. "And that goes on for months and months and months. That's an inefficient system."

Chronic sleep deprivation also increases the risk of developing depression (though, paradoxically, if someone is already depressed, sleep deprivation tends to help them feel better). This is a particularly serious issue for adolescents, as certain mental-health disorders tend to manifest themselves during these years. "There's so much confusion over this," Smith admits, "but one of the worries is if you just keep on with the sleep deprivation, eventually [that person] will become depressed. And we're seeing a lot more depressed kids around now."

But it's not easy to fight nature; perhaps the best parents can do is to encourage a slowdown of activity at a reasonable time in the evening, keep technology out of the bedroom and caffeine out of the fridge, and let their kids catch up on weekends.

Most adults know what they're up against because they remember their own night-owl days. They may have dabbled in rule-breaking, underage drinking, and general wildness as teenagers and now they shudder at the thought of their own children doing the same or worse. They were lucky, but will their kids inherit their luck? (The bad news for former hellraisers: some research suggests a person's tendency to take risks is partly genetic.)

In fact, there's some indication that cultivating unhealthy habits through this whole tumultuous period of development can have serious long-term effects. Those who start smoking during adolescence, for example, will likely have a much harder time quitting later in life than those who take up smoking in their twenties; the addiction, according to researchers at Duke University in Durham, North Carolina, appears to get hard-wired during the teen years.

Evidence from some studies also suggests that alcohol is more likely to damage memory and learning ability in the hippocampus of the evolving adolescent brain. At the same time, adolescent rats—whose brains are relatively similar to those of adolescent humans—suffer less from some of alcohol's other effects, including sedation. That sounds like a good thing, but if it is indeed true for adolescents (and for obvious ethical reasons researchers don't put adolescents through alcohol-related trials), it means they can drink more, and for longer periods—and therefore run a greater risk of long-term damage. Repeated alcohol use during these years may also lead to lasting memory and learning impairment—not to mention the fact that young binge drinkers are more likely to set themselves up with a lifetime alcohol-abuse problem.

This is one area where brain-research findings have affected how Giedd, the father of four, behaves as a parent. "In terms of substance abuse and alcohol, I'm a lot less hip now," he says. "I wouldn't have the mentality of, 'Oh it's better to have them do it at home.' [Adolescence is] a very vulnerable time in brain development to be exposed to these other substances." Giedd is surprised by how many parents say that their kids are going to drink and take drugs anyway, so they might as well do it at home, in a safe environment. "Biologically, it's a time when the cement is setting. If people cannot do these things until the age of nineteen, the odds of them not having trouble as adults go up enormously."

But experimenting, taking risks, and searching for good times are, it would seem, all part of the adolescent picture. As difficult as it is for parents to grasp, adolescents don't always make poor choices just to get their goats, or because they're suddenly gripped by temporary insanity. This sort of behaviour appears to be a predictable part of the identity-formation process, which begins in the early years but dramatically accelerates during adolescence. That's when children begin playing different roles, trying on different hats, figuring out if they're gay, straight, or bisexual, whether they're a geek, a jock, or cool. At the same time, their frontal lobes aren't fully developed, which means that the appetite for experimentation doesn't necessarily go along with the capacity to make sound judgments or to see into the not-so-distant future. In other words, by their very nature, teenagers are not especially focused on, or equipped to assess, the consequences of their actions.

A 2004 MRI study suggested that adolescent brains are less active than those of adults in regions that motivate reward-based behaviour. James Bjork, a neuroscientist at the National Institute on Alcohol Abuse and Alcoholism, and his colleagues conducted a brain scan on twelve adolescents between the ages of twelve and seventeen and a dozen adults aged twenty-two to twenty-eight. During the scan, the participants responded to targets on a screen by pressing a button; the object was to win (or avoid losing) varying amounts of money. The researchers found that areas of the brain associated with seeking gain lit up in both age groups. But in the adolescents, there was less activity. Adults, says Bjork, may have developed circuitry that enables them to motivate themselves to earn relatively modest rewards—the satisfaction felt after volunteering at church, say, or walking through a ravine. Adolescents, on the other hand, "may need activities that either have a very high thrill payoff or reduced effort requirement or a combination of the two." Examples, he adds, would be "sitting on the couch playing violent video games or sitting on the couch and pounding alcohol."

Even if, in quiet conversation, teenagers understand the risks of certain actions—drinking and driving, sex without protection, jumping off cliffs—when the moment of truth actually arrives, reason can be shot to hell. In the heat of the moment, the limbic area of the brain lights up like a pinball machine while the prefrontal cortex, the good angel that tamps down intense feeling and helps us navigate through emotional situations, is essentially asleep. In addition, experts have found that teenagers have a higher level of dopamine, a neurotransmitter connected to pleasure, movement, and sexual desire, which may increase the need for extra stimulation through risk-taking.

Some teenagers slide through adolescence unscathed. But there's no doubt that adolescents in the throes of hormone surges and brain development are extremely vulnerable—to making poor choices, to mental-health problems, to death and injury. A quick look at the statistics paints a troubling picture. According to Statistics Canada, adolescents between fourteen and nineteen

are more likely to commit property crimes and violent offences than any other age group; 25 percent of teenagers reported binge drinking at least once a month in 2000–2001, a rate second only to the twenty- to thirty-four-year-olds. During that same period, the pregnancy rate for girls between fifteen and nineteen was thirty-six out of 1,000. Most discouraging is the suicide rate for teenagers: currently about eighteen for every 100,000, with the highest rate occurring among teenaged boys (although girls are hospitalized for attempted suicide at a far greater rate than boys).

In fact, the three leading causes of death for teenagers in North America are accidents, suicide, and homicide. Unsurprisingly, the majority of accidents involve motor vehicles; in 2004, in the United States, about 20 percent of accidents that resulted in fatalities were due to a driver who had a high blood-alcohol level. According to the Insurance Institute for Highway Safety, injuries suffered by teenagers in car crashes have become a pressing public-health problem. Sixty-two percent of teenage passenger deaths in 2004 occurred when another teenager was driving. And teenage drivers are more likely to be at fault in crashes.

All of which is not going to make parents sleep any better—if indeed they can get to sleep in the first place.

Teenage speeding, irresponsibility, and status-seeking are not the only explanations for the statistics (though teenagers have been shown to take greater risks behind the wheel when their friends are with them). In fact, they also appear to be at a disadvantage because they have not refined the ability to multitask—driving while drinking a beverage, listening to music, talking on a cellphone, or even chatting with a passenger. One sensible response to this, according to many scientists and policy-makers, is graduated licensing, which is already in place everywhere in Canada except Nunavut. In 1996, many American states started to introduce some aspects of graduated licensing, and according to a 2003 report in the *Journal of Safety Research,* they have seen a decrease in crash rates.

So if adolescents are a work-in-progress in terms of judgment, should they be held accountable for their crimes in the same way adults are? Recent adolescent brain-development research was used in arguments against the juvenile death penalty in the United States. If adolescents aren't yet fully capable of controlling their emotional responses or understanding the consequences of their actions, groups like the International Justice Project said, then they should not be punishable by death. In March 2005, when the U.S. Supreme Court finally abolished the juvenile death penalty, there were seventy-three people on death rows across the United States for crimes they had committed before the age of eighteen. Many brain researchers believe that science should be part of the debate. But, Giedd adds, "it becomes a very slippery slope: the same data that might support abolishing the juvenile death penalty could be used to take away teenagers' ability to make their own reproductive-rights decisions."

Despite these new findings, has brain science told us anything we don't already know? Bjork's answer: "As Jay Giedd says, a lot of what we're finding out in brain research is the neuroanatomical, neurometabolic correlate of what grandma always told you." Indeed, brain mapping has provided proof of a neurological and biological basis for what sometimes ails the still-forming adult (and the adults who love and live with them).

Of great urgency for Giedd and others now is why certain disorders—anxiety and eating disorders, substance abuse, schizophrenia—develop during adolescence, but not autism, ADHD, Alzheimer's, and others. "Many of the things that plague adults really do happen during the teen years," says Giedd, "so identifying them early, treating them early, when the brain is more plastic, would seem to make more sense in terms of really having a life-long impact." Parents are wise not to assume that misery and anxiety are just part of the teenage rite of passage; it may be that serious unhappiness in adolescence is an early-warning sign of adult disorders.

Another task for scientists is to determine which things in a teenager's environment and experience will, for better or worse, influence brain development. "So many things have already been put forward—music, education in general, learning a second language, bacteria, viruses, video games, diet, sleep, exercise," says Giedd, "and all of them are probably true to some extent."

But what the general culture has to offer to teenagers is only one part of the equation. The brain has always been built for learning by example and experience—which experiences lead to pain, which lead to good outcomes. And for Giedd, that facility is what will give adolescents the best chance to grow up well—the ability to learn from the people around them. "It's the little things, the day-to-day things that we say in the car or when we're solving problems, how we handle relationships, emotions, our work ethic," he says. "They will believe much more what we *do* than what we tell them."

In fact, if there is anything parents can take away from all the scientific research into adolescent brain development, it's that their influence, patience, understanding, and guidance are very necessary—even when the teenager or young adult shrinks away from affection, grunts, slams doors, blasts music, rolls eyes, breaks house rules, and seems incapable of following simple instructions. Developing brains often can't handle organizational problems; they have more trouble making social, political, and moral judgments; they have to be reminded of potential consequences and carefully directed toward risks that aren't quite so, well, risky. Developing adults need appropriate amounts of independence, freedom, and responsibility.

"I would say with a clear conscience that the teen brain is different than the adult brain," says Giedd. "Just as I would feel comfortable saying men are taller than women." We ignore those differences at our peril, he adds. Teenagers may drive the family car, move away from home, go to college, and spend their early twenties wrestling with life decisions, all of which are a normal part of growing up. But as Giedd says, just because adolescents have left childhood behind, "parents shouldn't say, 'My work is done.'"

Critical Thinking

1. Why might the brain be the key to the reasons teenagers sleep in?
2. Why do teens take risks?
3. What does the teenage brain easily master?
4. How should teens react having learned the principles discussed?

NORA UNDERWOOD is a senior editor at The Walrus.

Adolescent Stress

The Relationship between Stress and Mental Health Problems

KATHRYN E. GRANT, PhD, ET AL.

Although exposure to some negative events is considered a normal part of development, stressful life experiences can threaten the well-being and healthy development of children and adolescents. Adolescents, in particular, are exposed to high rates of stressful life experiences (e.g., romantic break-ups, community violence, date rape), and there is some evidence that increases in stressors account, at least in part, for the increased rates of psychological problems adolescents experience (e.g., depression, conduct disorder, substance abuse) (Arnett, 1999).

This article will summarize recent research on the relation between stressful life experiences and mental health problems in adolescents. It will provide a definition of stress, present a conceptual model of the ways in which stressors affect adolescent mental health, and summarize research that has tested each of the basic tenets of the conceptual model. To clarify theory and research findings, illustrations based on the authors' own research with adolescents living in urban poverty will be provided.

Defining Stress

Few constructs in mental health have been as important, yet as difficult to define, as the concept of stress. The common theme across all prevailing definitions of stress is a focus on environmental events or conditions that threaten, challenge, exceed, or harm the psychological or biological capacities of the individual (Cohen, Kessler, & Gordon, 1995).

In recent decades, the most widely accepted definition of stress has been the transactional definition offered by Lazarus and Folkman (1984): "Psychological stress involves a particular relationship between the person and the environment that is *appraised* by the person as taxing or exceeding his or her resources and endangering his or her well being" (p. 19, emphasis added).

Recently, however, researchers have begun to question the appropriateness of a definition that relies on cognitive appraisals for children and adolescents. Results of research on stress during infancy indicate there are clear negative effects of maternal separation, abuse, and neglect on infants (Field, 1995). These negative effects occur, presumably, without the cognitive appraisal component that is central to the transactional definition. In addition, preliminary research indicates that cognitive appraisal processes that play a significant role later in development do not play the same role among younger children exposed to stressors (e.g., Turner & Cole, 1994). During adolescence, the brain continues to develop, and it is not clear when or to what extent cognitive appraisals influence the effects of stress.

Also, in recent years, theoretical models of the ways in which stressful experiences lead to mental health problems in adolescents have become more sophisticated, and there is greater emphasis on processes that influence or explain the relation between stressors and mental health problems (Cicchetti & Cohen, 1995). A model of stress that "lumps" potential intervening processes (i.e., processes that influence or explain the association between stressors and mental health problems), such as cognitive appraisal, in with stressors is conceptually unclear and poses problems for examining each of these factors individually (Reiss & Oliveri, 1991). To fully understand how stressful experiences and intervening processes relate to one another in the prediction of mental health problems, it is important to define and measure each of these variables, explicitly. This is particularly true in adolescent research, as the role of specific intervening processes is likely to shift across development.

Stressful life experiences can threaten the well-being and healthy development of children and adolescents.

For these reasons, we have proposed that stress be defined as *environmental events or chronic conditions that objectively threaten the physical and/or psychological health or well-being of individuals of a particular age in a particular society* (Grant,

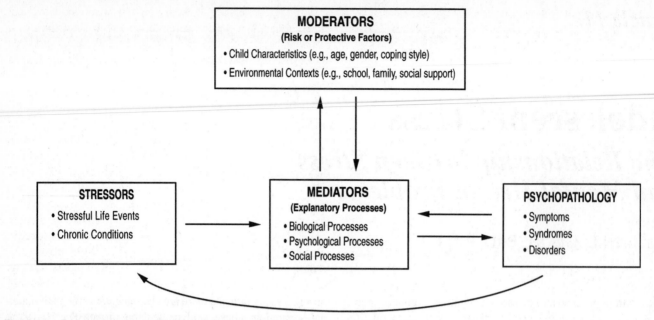

Figure 1 General conceptual model of the role of stressors in the development of mental health problems in adolescents.

Compas, Stuhlmacher, et al., 2003). Such a definition is consistent with traditional "stimulus-based" definitions of stress (Holmes & Rahe, 1967) and more recent definitions of "stressors" (Rice, 1999) and "objective stress" (Brown & Harris, 1989).

Relationship between Stress and Mental Health Problems

We (Grant et al., 2003) have proposed a general conceptual model of the role of stressors in the development of mental health problems for adolescents. This model builds on previously proposed specific models of psychopathology (e.g., Albano, Chorpita, & Barlow, 2001; Hammen & Rudolph, 2001) and includes five central hypotheses: 1) stressors lead to psychopathology; 2) moderators influence the relation between stressors and psychopathology; 3) mediators explain the relation between stressors and psychopathology; 4) there is specificity in the relations among particular stressors, moderators, mediators, and types of psychopathology; and 5) relations among stressors, moderators, mediators, and psychopathology are reciprocal and dynamic (See Figure 1). Each of these central hypotheses are described in detail below.

Stressors Lead to Psychopathology

The first hypothesis, that stressors lead to psychopathology, provides the conceptual basis for all studies of the relation between stressors and psychological problems in adolescents. Our recent review of longitudinal studies (Grant, Compas, et al., 2004) revealed consistent evidence that stressful life experiences predict psychological problems in adolescents over time. Likewise, there is growing evidence that youth who are exposed to high rates of stressful life experiences are at heightened risk for mental health problems.

For example, poverty sets the stage for an extraordinary number of stressful life experiences ranging from major life events (e.g., increased levels of child abuse), to chronic interpersonal stressors (e.g., marital conflict), to community violence, to the daily hassles associated with "trying to make ends meet" (Guerra et al., 1995). Extant research on psychological symptoms in low-income, urban youth has indicated that these youth are at heightened risk for a range of psychological problems including anxiety/depression, aggression, delinquency, social problems, withdrawal, and somatic complaints (Grant, Katz, et al., 2004). These findings provide further evidence of the most basic relation between stressors and psychopathology.

Influence of Moderators

The second tenet of the model is that moderators influence the relation between stressors and psychopathology. Moderators may be conceptualized as risk or protective factors, as they represent pre-existing characteristics (in existence prior to exposure to the stressor) that increase or decrease the likelihood that stressors will lead to psychopathology. Potential moderating variables include age, gender, social support, and coping styles. Moderating variables may be the result of genetic vulnerabilities (or protective factors), non-stressor environmental influences (e.g., parenting/peer influences), or, in some cases, stressful experiences. For example, exposure to severe and chronic stressors may lead to changes in the way adolescents view the world (e.g., they may develop a more pessimistic, less trusting perspective) and these changes in thinking may actually make adolescents more vulnerable to psychological symptoms when they are exposed to future stress (Grant et al., 2003).

Our recent review of the literature on moderators of the association between stressors and psychological problems in young people revealed few consistent findings (Grant, Compas, et al., 2005). One possible reason for the lack of consistency is that researchers have not focused on a particular risk or protective factor and examined it systematically across a number of studies. Unfortunately, this means that we know very little about factors that can break the connection between stressors and mental health problems in young people. Some individual studies have found evidence of particular protective effects and there is mounting evidence that having a cluster of protective factors is most beneficial (Beam, Gil-Rivas, Greenberger, & Chen, 2002; Meschke & Patterson, 2003). There is also some disconcerting evidence that youth exposed to the most pervasive and severe stressors (e.g., low-income urban youth of color) may be least likely to benefit from any particular protective factor (Gerard & Buehler, 2004; Luthar, 1991; Seidman, Lambert, Allen, & Aber, 2003). For example, in our own work with low-income urban youth, we have found preliminary evidence that youth who rely on particular individually-based coping strategies without broader supports may actually do more poorly over time than youth who report they don't have any protective factors at all (Grant, 2005).

Mediators

Although some factors may serve either a moderating or mediating function (e.g., cognitive attributions, coping), mediators are conceptually distinct from moderators in that they are "activated" or "caused by" the current stressful experience and serve to, conceptually and statistically, account for the relation between stressors and psychopathology (Baron & Kenny, 1986). Whereas moderators are characteristics of the child or his/her social network prior to the stressor, mediators become characteristics of the child or his/her social network in response to the stressor. Mediators may include variables such as coping styles, cognitive perceptions, and family processes (Grant et al., 2003).

Our recent review of the literature on mediators of the relation between stressors and psychological problems in young people (Grant et al., 2005) revealed that significant progress has been made in this area. The most frequently examined and empirically supported conceptual model has been one in which negative parenting mediates the relation between poverty (or economic stressors) and adolescent psychopathology (Grant et al., 2005). In particular, research suggests that, as parents experience economic pressures associated with poverty, they become less nurturant and more hostile toward their children, which leads to adolescent psychological problems (Conger, 2001). In our own work with low-income urban youth, we have seen evidence of similar patterns (Grant, McCormick, et al., in press).

Specificity

The fourth hypothesis is that there is specificity in relations among particular stressors, moderators, mediators, and psychological outcomes. According to this proposition, a particular type of stressor (e.g., urban poverty) is linked with a particular type of psychological problem (e.g., somatic complaints) through a particular mediator (e.g., a belief that expressions of anxiety or depression will make one look weak and leave one more vulnerable to victimization by others) in the context of a particular moderator (e.g., being a female adolescent). Analysis of full specificity models such as this one have yet to be reported in the literature.

There have been a large number of studies testing for specificity between particular stressors and particular psychological outcomes in young people, but these studies have yielded inconsistent results (McMahon et al., 2003). Nonetheless, some individual studies have found interesting evidence of specificity. For example, in our own work, we have found that particular types of psychological symptoms appear to be particularly common in the context of urban poverty. Somatic complaints is the internalizing symptom most frequently reported in our sample (Grant, Katz, et al., 2004). We have speculated that somatic complaints may be especially adaptive in a hostile urban environment. More stereotypically internalizing symptoms, such as anxiety or depression, may leave adolescents more vulnerable to victimization, but somatic complaints (like a stomach ache or headache) may allow them to avoid dangerous situations while still "saving face." Somatic complaints may also allow low-income urban youth to garner the most possible support from a network that may already be taxed with stressors of its own (Grant, Katz, et al., 2004).

Relations Are Reciprocal & Dynamic

The final hypothesis that relations among stressors, moderators, mediators, and psychopathology are reciprocal and dynamic broadly encompasses the following specific hypotheses: 1) each variable in the model influences the other (with some exceptions, for example, fixed moderators such as age will not be influenced by other variables); 2) the role of specific variables within the model may vary across specific stressors and shift over time (e.g., a mediator that developed in response to a particular stressor may become a fixed pattern of responding and, thus, interact as a moderator with subsequent stressors); 3) reciprocal and dynamic relations among stressors, moderators, and mediators will predict not only the onset of psychological problems, but also the exacerbation of symptoms and the movement along a continuum from low-level symptoms to the development of a clinically diagnosable disorder.

Of the basic tenets of our proposed conceptual model, this last hypothesis has received the least research attention. That is notable given that examination of this hypothesis, in particular, is essential for understanding the ways in which stressors influence adolescents, as it addresses the shifting nature of relations among variables across development. So far, the only consistent evidence for this proposition is that a number of studies have found that stressors not only predict psychological symptoms, but symptoms, in turn, predict exposure to additional stressful experiences (Grant, Compas, et al., 2004). In our own work with urban youth, we too have found evidence that psychological symptoms place youth at greater risk for exposure to additional stressors over time (Grant, Thomas, et al., 2005). This finding suggests that some youth are caught in a vicious cycle. Exposure to heightened rates of stressors places them at heightened risk for psychological symptoms, which, in turn, place them at risk for exposure to even more stressors, which place them at heightened risk for even more psychological distress (Grant, Thomas, et al., 2005).

Summary and Implications for Prevention

Recent research in the area of stressors and mental health problems in adolescents has led to the following conclusions:

1. Stress should be defined as *environmental events or chronic conditions that objectively threaten the physical and/or psychological health or well-being of individuals of a particular age in a particular society.*
2. There is strong evidence that stressful life experiences are predictive of mental health problems in adolescents. Adolescents exposed to high rates of stressful life experiences are at increased risk for a range of mental health problems.
3. The relation between stressors and mental health problems is thought to be affected by moderating variables. However, there is little consistent evidence of particular moderating effects. Additional research on protective factors is especially needed.
4. There is strong evidence that mediators explain the relation between stressors and mental health problems in adolescents. For example, the effects of poverty on adolescent mental health appear to be mediated by poverty's effects on family processes.
5. The relations among stressful life experiences, moderating and mediating processes, and psychopathology are thought to be specific, such that particular types of stressors are linked with particular types of mental health problems through particular intervening processes. There has been little systematic investigation of this hypothesis; consequently, little consistent evidence has been found for full specificity models.
6. The relations among stressful life experiences, moderating and mediating processes, and psychopathology are thought to be reciprocal and dynamic. This hypothesis has received little research attention, but there is growing evidence that stressors not only predict psychopathology, but psychopathology also predicts additional exposure to stress.

Implications

Given the risks associated with stressors, efforts to reduce adolescents' exposure to stressful life events are needed. These might include efforts at the individual family level to reduce marital conflict and domestic violence or to prevent child abuse. They might also include development of programs at the school or neighborhood level designed to reduce the effects of stressors associated with poverty, such as programs that provide affordable child care and job training. Most important are advocacy efforts at the sociopolitical level to address the inequities of our society that contribute to high poverty rates and childhood exposure to community violence in economically disadvantaged urban settings.

In addition, more research is needed to understand what variables (if any) are actually capable of breaking the connection between stressful life events and mental health problems in young people. These protective factors could then be promoted through educational curricula, after-school programming, parent trainings, and other prevention efforts. Until stronger evidence is found for particular protective factors, it will be important to help young people develop protective contexts which facilitate development of a number of particular protective factors. For example, adolescents should be involved in at least one protective structure (e.g., family, school, church, after-school program), which facilitates the development of strong interpersonal relationships, which provide modeling, encouragement, and advice, which, in turn, facilitate the development of a positive value system or world view and healthy coping strategies (Grant, 2005). A constellation of protective factors, such as these, are likely to contribute to positive adolescent mental health.

References

Albano, A. M., Chorpita, B. F., & Barlow, D. H. (2001). Childhood anxiety disorders. In E. J. Mash & R. A. Barkley (Eds.), *Child Psychopathology. Second Edition.* New York, NY: Guilford Press.

Arnett, J. J. (1999). Adolescent storm and stress, reconsidered. *American Psychologist, 54,* 317–326.

Baron, R. M., & Kenny, D. A. (1986). The moderator-mediator variable distinction in social psychology research: Conceptual, strategic, and statistical considerations. *Journal of Personality and Social Psychology, 51,* 1,173–1,182.

Beam, M. R., Gil-Rivas, V., Greenberger, E., & Chen, C. (2002). Adolescent problem behavior and depressed mood: Risk and protection within and across social contexts. *Journal of Youth and Adolescence, 31,* 343–357.

Brown, G., & Harris, T. O. (1989). Depression. In G.W. Brown & T. O. Harris (Eds.), *Life Events and Illness* (pp. 49–93). New York: Guilford Press.

Cicchetti, D., & Cohen, D. (1995). Perspectives on developmental psychopathology. In D. Cicchetti, & D. Cohen, (Eds.), *Developmental Psychopathology Vol 1: Theory and Methods. Wiley Series on Personality Processes* (pp. 3–20). New York: John Wiley & Sons.

Cohen, S., Kessler, R. C., & Gordon, L. U. (1995). *Measuring Stress.* New York: Oxford University Press.

Conger, R. D. (2001). Understanding child and adolescent response to caregiver conflict: Some observations on context, process, and method. In A. Booth & A. C. Crouter (Eds.), *Couples in Conflict* (pp. 161–172). Mahwah, NJ: Lawrence Erlbaum Associates.

Field, T. (1995). Infants of depressed mothers. *Infant Behavior and Development, 18*(1), 1–13.

Gerard, J. M., & Buehler, C. (2004). Cumulative environmental risk and youth maladjustment: The role of youth attributes. *Child Development, 75,* 1,832–1,849.

Grant, K. E. (June, 2005). *Stressors and Adolescent Mental Health: Protective Factors in the Lives of Urban Youth.* Paper presented at the annual meeting of the William T. Grant Foundation Scholars' program, Jackson, WY.

Grant, K. E., Compas, B. E., Stuhlmacher, A., Thurm, A. E., McMahon, S., & Halpert, J. (2003). Stressors and child/

adolescent psychopathology: Moving from markers to mechanisms of risk. *Psychological Bulletin, 129,* 447–466.

Grant, K. E., Compas, B. E., Thurm, A.E., McMahon, S. D., & Gipson, P. Y. (2004). Stressors and child and adolescent psychopathology: Measurement issues and prospective effects. *Journal of Clinical Child and Adolescent Psychology, 33*(2), 412–425.

Grant, K. E., Compas, B. E., Thurm, A. E., McMahon, S. D., Gipson, P., Campbell, A. J., & Krochock, K. (2005). *Moderating and Mediating Processes in the Relation Between Stressors and Child/Adolescent Psychopathology. Manuscript submitted for publication.*

Grant, K. E., Katz, B. N., Thomas, K. J., O'Koon, J. H., Meza, C. M., DiPasquale, A. M., Rodríguez, V. O., & Bergen, C. (2004). Psychological symptoms affecting low-income urban youth. *Journal of Adolescent Research, 19*(6), 613–634.

Grant, K. E., McCormick, A., Poindexter, L., Simpkins, T., Janda, C. M., Thomas, K. J., Campbell, A., Carleton, R., & Taylor, J. (in press). Family and neighborhood processes in the relation between poverty and psychological symptoms in urban African American adolescents. *Journal of Adolescence.*

Grant, K. E., Thomas, K. J., Apling, G. C., Gipson, P. Y., Mance, G. A., Carleton, R. A., Ford, R. E., Taylor, J. J., & Sajous-Brady, D. L. (2005). *Stressors and Psychological Symptoms in Urban Youth: A Test of a Conceptual Model.* Manuscript submitted for publication.

Guerra, N. G., Huesmann, L. R., Tolan, P. H., Van Acker, R., & Eron, L. D. (1995). Stressful events and individual beliefs as correlates of economic disadvantage and aggression among urban children. Special Section: Prediction and prevention of child and adolescent antisocial behavior. *Journal of Consulting & Clinical Psychology, 63*(4), 518–528.

Hammen, C., & Rudolph, K. D. (2001). Childhood depression. In E. J. Mash & R. A. Barkley (Eds.), *Child Psychopathology. Second Edition* New York, NY: Guilford Press.

Holmes, T. H., & Raye, R. H. (1967). The Social Readjustment Rating Scale, *Journal of Psychosomatic Research, 11,* 213–218.

Lazarus, R. S., & Folkman, S. (1984). *Stress, Appraisal, and Coping.* New York: Springer.

Luthar, S. S. (1991). Vulnerability and resilience: A study of high-risk adolescents. *Child Development, 62,* 600–616.

McMahon, S. D., Grant, K. E., Compas, B. E., Thurm, A. E., & Ey, S. (2003). Stress and psychopathology in children and adolescents: Is there evidence of specificity? *Journal of Child Psychology and Psychiatry and Allied Disciplines: Annual Research Review, 44,* 107–133.

Meschke, L. L., & Patterson, J. M. (2003). Resilience as a theoretical basis for substance abuse prevention, *The Journal of Primary Prevention, 23,* 483–514.

Reiss, D., & Oliveri, M. (1991). The family's conception of accountability and competence: A new approach to the conceptualization and assessment of family stress. *Family Process, 30,* 193–214.

Rice, P. L. (1999). *Stress and Health.* New York: Brooks/Cole Publishing Company.

Seidman, E., Lambert, L. E., Allen, L., & Aber, J. L. (2003). Urban adolescents' transition to junior high school and protective family transactions. *Journal of Early Adolescence, 23,* 166–193.

Turner, Jr., J. E., & Cole, D. A. (1994). Developmental differences in cognitive diatheses for child depression. *Journal of Abnormal Child Psychology, 22,* 15–32.

Critical Thinking

1. How do stressful life events account for increased rates of psychological problems?

2. What is the author's conceptual model of the role of stressors in development?

3. How does stress relate to mental health problems?

4. How should a teenager better handle stress?

KATHRYN E. GRANT, PhD, is a licensed Clinical Psychologist, Associate Professor, and Director of Clinical Training at DePaul University. She and her research team are currently conducting a longitudinal study of stress and its effects on urban adolescents. Steven Behling, BS, is a doctoral student at DePaul University. His research interests include prevention of family violence and child maltreatment. Polly Y. Gipson, MA, is a doctoral student at DePaul University. She recently completed her thesis on stress and anxiety in urban adolescents. Rebecca E. Ford, MA, is a doctoral student at DePaul University. She recently defended her dissertation on the effects of acculturation on Latino adolescent mental health.

I'm Just Tired

How Sleep Affects Your Preteen

TERI BROWN

What is happening to your preteen? Your once active child has suddenly become as much of a couch fixture as the cushions are. They ooze around the house as slow as pudding, yawning and stretching, as if they hadn't just woke from a marathon snooze an hour ago. Everyone knows that teenagers are famous sleepers, but preteens?

Too Much Too Soon Too Early

Oftentimes the culprit is their schedule. Candice Haaga's 12-year-old son has become more and more sluggish as the school year wore on.

"I think the ridiculously early start time for school is partly to blame," says Haaga, mother of two from Rockville, Md. "He has to get up at 6:20 A.M. daily to catch his 7:15 A.M. bus to start school at 8 A.M. Sometimes I think he's upset or mad about something, and it turns out he's just tired."

Being overtired can cause attitude problems as well as difficulties with focus and concentration at school. "When overtired from too little sleep, my 12-year-old son acts apathetic, doesn't smile and speaks more slowly," says Haaga. "He is more cranky, gets upset more easily, talks less and is generally less responsive."

Haaga's son is not alone in having a tight schedule that doesn't allow a preteenager to get the sleep they need. It seems as if it is almost epidemic. According to a national study conducted by the Survey Research Center at the University of Michigan, from 1981 to 1997, children's free time declined by 12 hours per week. Free time is often down time, helping your child unwind, which in turn leads to better quality sleep.

Early Puberty May Be to Blame

While early school mornings and overscheduling can lead to a sleepy preteen, oftentimes there are very real physiological reasons your 9- to 13-year-old seems to be exhausted. Dr. Kyle Johnson, associate director of the Oregon Health & Science University's Sleep Medicine Program, believes that while the vast majority of preteens are not getting enough sleep because of increasing social and academic pressures, there are those who seem to be at the mercy of an early adolescence.

"Research demonstrates that children delay their sleep schedules as they proceed through puberty," says Dr. Johnson. "This delay in sleep schedules seems to be biologically driven and influenced by sociocultural changes. Some preteens mature sooner than others, and these kids may be proceeding through puberty at this age."

Potential Sleep Problems

Numerous sleep disorders can present at this age including obstructive sleep apnea, restless leg syndrome, narcolepsy, insomnia and circadian rhythm disorders such as delayed sleep phase disorder.

"Parents need to ask themselves if the sleepiness is interfering with daytime functioning or causing mood problems on a continuing basis," says Dr. Johnson. "Parents should seek consultation with a physician experienced in pediatric sleep problems if a child is excessively sleepy and is snoring or gasping for breath while sleeping, since these are risk factors for obstructive sleep apnea."

Restless leg syndrome may be present if a child has trouble initiating sleep and is complaining of leg cramps or "creepy crawly" feelings in their legs, especially if there is a family history of restless leg syndrome. This syndrome is generally felt at night and may contribute to your preteen's ability to get quality sleep.

Adults who suffer from delayed sleep phase disorder are frequently called night owls, as they often aren't ready to sleep until 2 A.M. or so, but this disorder can affect the preteen, as well. The primary symptoms of delayed sleep phase syndrome are an extreme difficulty falling asleep at normal hours and not being able to wake easily the next morning. This can be extremely hard for an adult with a morning job, let alone a child who must get up for school.

The best way to judge if your preteen has any of these problems is to observe their waking and sleep patterns. If you suspect their sleepiness is caused by something other than poor sleep habits, it may be time to contact your physician.

Teaching Good Sleep Habits

Pediatric pulmonologist Dr. Robert Schoumacher is the director of the Pediatric and Adolescent Sleep Center at Le Bonheur Children's Medical Center in Memphis, Tenn. He is passionate about teaching your children good sleep patterns.

Dr. Schoumacher believes a healthy preteen who is getting enough sleep and is not going through early adolescence is not tired. "In research on patients of this age, they have been described as the most alert humans on the planet," he says. "There may have been some gradual erosion of bedtime standards. It seems clear to me that many children in our society are not getting as much sleep as they need and are not getting as much sleep as their parents did at the same age."

Dr. Schoumacher suggests that while there are a number of societal factors, there are also some physiologic factors that come into play. For example, TV, computer use and video games are increasingly popular, but they are a very poor form of activity in the hour or so before bedtime.

"They provide too much light directly into the child's eyes, which can interfere with the body's natural circadian rhythm," says Dr. Schoumacher. "They are also too stimulating to permit the child to wind down and get ready for sleep. Strenuous physical activity such as roughhousing or pillow fights also interferes with the body's preparations for sleep. Reading, bath time, some kinds of music and family time are much more appropriate in the crucial 30 to 60 minutes before bed."

It turns out that it is up to parents to make sure their children are getting enough sleep at this age. Telling them it's time for bed at age 12 is still OK to do.

"It is the last age where we parents have enough control to set these limits, and it is very important that we do so," says Dr. Schoumacher. "Our children are not likely to learn good sleep habits as teenagers if we don't show that we take this matter seriously when they are preteens. We should set a reasonable bedtime for them and enforce it, we should prohibit activities that interfere with quality sleep right before bedtime, and we should make sure their sleep environment is restful."

The average 9- to 12-year-old child needs 10 hours of sleep per night. The amount of sleep that your child needs may be an hour or so more or less than that without being in any way abnormal. The correct amount of sleep for a given child is the amount that allows him to be maximally alert during the subsequent day.

"One good way to know that the amount of sleep is adequate is that the child gets out of bed easily and doesn't require any extra sleep time on the weekends," says Dr. Schoumacher.

The importance of an adequate amount of sleep is incalculable for your preteen. Sleep is just as important and integral to a healthy lifestyle as are diet and exercise.

"No child (or adult!) can be at their best when they are sleepy," says Dr. Schoumacher. "It is bound to affect school performance, social development and general health and happiness. So help them get more and better sleep."

Critical Thinking

1. Why does Dr. Schoumacher suggest that parents control the sleep of preteens?
2. Why does this need to be done early on?
3. How do you think a parent could control the sleep of preteens?
4. Explain your views on parents controlling sleep of preteens.

UNIT 3

Relationships of Adolescents: Family, Peers, Intimacy, and Sexuality

Unit Selections

Learning Outcomes

After reading this unit, you should be able to:

- Describe the stresses placed on military service members and their families.
- Explain the ways that youth development professionals can support youth.
- Analyze parents' concerns over computer and video games.
- Describe computer and video addictions of teenagers.
- Explain adolescent dating aggression.
- Outline warning signs and methods of prevention of adolescent dating aggression.
- Identify evidence for the conclusion that some parents are being held liable for their teen's drinking.
- Describe teen drinking parties.
- Explain how adolescents' attitudes regarding sexual behaviors are a key to understanding teen sexual behavior.
- Analyze environmental differences that shape adolescents' sexual attitudes.
- Explain how youth use the new media to learn about sex.
- Outline how the new media can be employed to promote healthier sexual behaviors.
- Describe the use of pornography of youth.
- Explain how to talk to teens about the topic of pornography.

Student Website

www.mhhe.com/cls

The family is the most important and most intimate social context for adolescents. Families are vitally involved in providing the skills to become functioning adults in society. They pass along the attitudes, skills, and values needed in society. Families promote survival and offer comfort for adolescents. A family is indeed a complex system that responds to its members. When a teenager is included in the family system, changes occur that affect other members and their relationships. Both the functions of the family and the expectations of the family change. At times it may be less stable and predictable. Teens often expect greater autonomy, which may cause frictions with parents.

American teens spend much more time with their peers than they do with their parents or siblings. The shift from family to peers is influenced by the trends toward smaller families, more dual-earner families, and access to increased number of peers. Many adolescents look to their peers as a group to provide information about what is normal and expected. The peer group offers a baseline for judging their performance and serves as a knowledgeable audience. Teens have a need to belong and the need to satisfied with their peer group.

Adolescents are without a doubt more peer-oriented than any other age group. But it is simplistic to assume that peer influence is always negative and that it outweighs parental influence. Research demonstrates that the nature of the parent–child relationship is consistently the best predictor of adolescent psychological health and well-being. Adolescents who have poor relationships with their parents are precisely the adolescents who are most susceptible to negative peer influences. Poor parent–adolescent relationships are not the norm during the pubertal years, but, rather, conflicted relationships more likely represent a continuation of poor family relationships from childhood.

Research also indicates that most adolescents feel close to and respect their parents. Most adolescents share their parents' values, especially when it comes to moral, religious, political, and educational values. The school the adolescent attends, the kind of neighborhood the parents live in, whether the parents attend religious services, and what parents do for a living all influence their children. Parental choices such as these have a definite impact on their children for the network of friends they select.

Several factors have contributed to the misconception that adolescents reject their parents in favor of peers. First, peers play a greater role in the adolescent's day-to-day activities, style of dress, and musical tastes than do parents. Second, parents often confuse the adolescent's struggle for autonomy with rebellion. G. Stanley Hall's views of adolescence as a biologically necessary time of "storm and stress" contributed to this confusion as well. Similarly, Anna Freud, arguing from her father's psychoanalytic tradition and her own experience with troubled adolescents, maintained that the adolescent–parent relationship is highly laden with conflicts causing adolescents to turn to their peers. According to Anna Freud, such conflicts ensure a successful resolution of the Oedipus/Electra complex. This model of intense parent–adolescent conflict has not been

© Blend Images/Getty Images

empirically supported and can be detrimental if parents fail to seek help because they believe intense conflict is "normal" during adolescence.

Another myth about peer influence during adolescence is that it is primarily negative. As Thomas Berndt discusses in his research, peer influence is mutual and has both positive and negative effects. Peer pressure is rarely coercive, as is popularly envisaged. It is a more subtle process where adolescents influence their friends and the friends influence them. Just as adults do, adolescents choose friends who already have similar interests, attitudes, and beliefs.

Another misconception about peer relations is that teen culture is a unified culture with a single way of thinking and acting. A visit to any secondary school today will reveal the variety of teen cultures that exist. The formation of peer groups and adolescent crowds is partly a function of a school structure and school activities. As in past decades, one can find jocks, populars, brains, delinquents, and nerds. One would also encounter members of today's grunge and body-piercing crowds. Media attention is often drawn toward bizarre or antisocial groups further contributing to the myth that peer influence is primarily negative.

Music is very much a part of youth culture, although there is no universal type of music liked by all adolescents. One way adolescents have always tried to differentiate themselves from adults has been through music. On the other hand, today, adults are concerned that music, movies, and television have gone too far in the quest for ever more shocking and explicit sexual and violent content. Widespread and easy access to the Internet has also compounded concerns about the types of material today's adolescents are exposed to.

Like other aspects of psychological development, sexuality is not an entirely new issue that surfaces for the first time during adolescents. Children are known to be curious about their bodies at a very early age. And of course, sexual interest and development continues after adolescence. Most would argue that adolescence is a fundamentally important time for the development of sexuality.

During adolescence there is an increase in the sex drive as a result of hormonal changes. During puberty individuals become capable of sexual reproduction. Individuals also develop the secondary sex characteristics that serve as a basis for sexual attraction and as dramatic indicators that the young person is no longer physically a child.

The nature and extent of adolescent sexuality clearly has changed in recent years. Several different patterns of sexual behavior characterize contemporary adolescents. Many of the patterns include engagement in sexual behaviors that place the young person at risk of experiencing health, psychological, and social problems.

In much of American culture, the link between marriage and sexual activity has practically disappeared. This means that there is no particular age for sanctioning the initiation of sexual activity. Largely as a result of such changes, sexual activity is initiated at earlier ages than in the past, by increasing proportions of adolescents.

Attitudes toward sex became more liberal from the late 1960s through the 1970s. The changed attitude, which was generally more liberal, has had a major impact on several major implications for youth's attitude today toward sex. First, there has been a greater openness in our society in sexual matters. Both the printed page and media openly discuss such topics as abortion, rape, and sexual abuse. Just a generation ago, such topics were not discussed as openly as today. The natural consequence is that youth today, who have been brought up in this atmosphere, are much more open and often feel more comfortable discussing sexual issues openly and honestly with both peers and adults. A second attitude change is that more adults and teens than a generation ago consider sexual intercourse outside of marriage as acceptable. No longer do many consider legal marriage as a required sanction for sex. Many believe that sex is acceptable within a "relationship," and some youth have adopted the liberal attitude that casual sex or sex for primarily personal pleasure regardless of whether a relationship exists is acceptable.

Many adolescents are initiating sexual intercourse at an earlier age than in the previous generation. Gender attitudes continue to demonstrate a difference in belief systems. Young women are much more likely than men to desire a strong relationship or even marriage before engaging in sexual intercourse.

Many of the problems associated with teenage sexual activity have increased with more teens' sexual involvement. American teenagers have one of the highest rates of premarital pregnancies in the world. Although more teenagers are now using contraceptives than in the past, there is still a large number who use no method of birth control or fail to use it properly. Legal abortion is an option that has become increasingly available even though it continues to be highly controversial. Because youth often delay making a decision to abort the baby, more complications persist. In addition, mental agony and guilt accompany making such a major decision.

Increased sexual activity also corresponds to a rise in sexually transmitted diseases. The most common among youth are gonorrhea, chlamydia, and herpes. Although some of the sexually transmitted diseases (STDs) may continue in the body for the rest of the life span and affect reproduction, the AIDS disease often results in an early, painful death. In an attempt to prevent a nationwide epidemic, educational programs about sex, diseases, and how to prevent the spread of these are taught around the country. Although not accepted by many, abstinence is the only true method to prevent sexually transmitted diseases.

Donna Fennessy, presents in the first reading in Unit 3, advice for improving parent–teen relationships. Next, Melissa Mucron offers suggestions on how teenage girls should maintain their relationships with their fathers. Many parents are wondering how much is too much computer and video games. Jennifer Wagner attempts to answer the question and explain that many teens become addicted. In many teen romantic relationships, youth act out aggressively toward each other. The next article reviews adolescent dating aggression, focusing on warning signs and methods of prevention. Emma Schwartz explains that parents are being held criminally liable for their teen's drinking parties.

The last three articles in the unit cover teenage sexuality. The first one focuses on understanding teens' attitudes regarding sexual behavior, while the second one addresses the influence the media has on teen sexual behavior. The last article discusses porn sites and explains how to talk to teens about the topic.

Internet References

Advocates for Youth
www.youthresource.com

American Sexual Behavior
www.norc.uchicago.edu/Publications/
American+Sexual+Behavior+2006.htm

CDC National AIDS Clearinghouse
www.cdcnpin.org

CYFERNET: Cooperative Extension System's Children, Youth, and Family Information Service
www.cyfernet.org

ETR Associates
www.etr.org

Family Violence Prevention Fund
www.endabuse.org

Girls Inc.
www.girlsinc.org

Help for Parents of Teenagers
www.bygpub.com/parents

National Council of Juvenile and Family Court Judges
www.ncjfci.org

National Dropout Prevention Center/Networking
www.dropoutprevention.org/ndpcdefault.htm

Stepfamily Association of America
www.stepfam.org

Talking About Health
www.abouthealth.com/t_talking.htm

Supporting Youth during Parental Deployment

Strategies for Professionals and Families

Angela J. Huebner, PhD, and Jay A. Mancini, PhD

The Global War on Terrorism has heightened our awareness of the sacrifices of military service members and their families. Over half (55%) of active military members are married and about 43% have children (40% of whom are under the age of 5 years, 32% between the ages of 6 and 11, and 24% between the ages of 12 and 18) (Office of the Deputy Under Secretary of Defense, 2005). There are currently about 263,000 service members deployed overseas, with the vast majority located in Iraq and Afghanistan (Glod, 2008). Their service has often included multiple deployments—meaning that they have been in war zones for 12–15 months, back in the U.S. for 12 months, then deployed again (Morse, 2006). The experience of being deployed is obviously a stressful situation for both the military service member and his or her family. There are particular and significant ways youth development professionals can provide support to youth and to their families. These strategies are briefly described below. Quotes from youth who participated in our focus groups are included to highlight some of the deployment-related issues they face.

The Deployment Cycle and Families' Adjustment

Deployment is the assignment of military personnel to temporary, unaccompanied (meaning no family) tours of duty. It is usually divided into three phases: (1) Pre-Deployment/Preparation, (2) Deployment/Separation, and (3) Post-Deployment/Reunion. Each phase of the deployment cycle has unique associated family Stressors (Morse, 2006).

Pre-deployment usually includes "mobilization." During mobilization, service members prepare for war or other national emergencies by organizing their resources. Although service members are not necessarily sent overseas during mobilization, they may be required to relocate to a military installation to complete their tasks. Mobilization begins the process of family separation and the associated Stressors, including loss (Huebner, Mancini, Wilcox, Grass, & Grass, 2007). Mobilization raises family concerns about financial constraints, employment changes, increased childcare needs, and social support. Depending on the family structure, plans may be made for the military connected youth to go live with relatives or other guardians. In our investigations (e.g. Huebner & Mancini, 2005) we often find that grandparents assume a pivotal role in providing various kinds of support for youth and their families. If the relatives are not nearby, this may mean changing schools and leaving friends. These are important issues families must consider before the military member leaves.

Deployment occurs when the service member is actually assigned a tour of duty. During this phase of the cycle, the service member usually becomes geographically separated from his or her family. Regardless of whether or not the family has to relocate, the absence of the service member is stressful for the family. However, in some families, the absence relieves family tension. The service member's spouse is now acting as a single parent. He or she likely has sole responsibility for maintaining the household and raising the children. The family financial situation may necessitate the parent take on a new job or change jobs. If the deployed parent was a single parent to begin with, these problems are intensified.

If youth are unable to communicate with their deployed parent they may feel isolated. They worry about their parent's safety, particularly due to the massive media coverage of conflicts. Because of the changed family structure, youth may be experiencing inconsistent parenting, or changes in the family schedule, responsibilities, and rules. These changes may be particularly acute for National Guard and Reserve members who have traditionally had part-time commitments. They and their families may have never defined themselves as military families and thus never accessed military support systems.

> "The first day after he [dad] left, it was like no one wanted to do anything. We just wanted to sit in the house and stare at the walls. . ."
>
> —Teen Male

Post-Deployment refers to the time when the service member returns home. Although this is a potentially joyful time, it is also stressful due to struggles over family reorganization. Depending on the length of the deployment, the family may have functioned without the military member for several months or even years. Usually the family has adapted to the new structure and roles. When the military member returns, it may upset the balance that had been achieved. Roles need to be renegotiated, not just between adults in the family but also between adults and youth. Returning military members may feel like they are no longer needed in their families and youth may be hesitant to give up newly acquired responsibilities. In addition, very pragmatic issues are faced, including concerns about the service member's civilian employment status.

When the military member returns . . . roles need to be renegotiated, not just between adults in the family but also between adults and youth.

Deployment Impacts on Families

Families experience the impacts of military deployments in various ways. Although deployment is a stressful situation for all families, families vary in their degree of resilience in coping with the situation. Several factors have been shown to influence the effect of deployments on families. These include the quality of pre-deployment family relationships; the age, sex, and maturity of children; the meaning of the absence to the family; the extent of danger to which the military member is exposed; and how the remaining spouse deals with the absence, including her or his coping skills and mental health status (Huebner & Mancini, 2005; Huebner & Powell, 2007; Jensen & Shaw, 1996).

Researchers have linked parental deployment (usually defined as father deployment) to several youth outcomes. These include depression, acting out or negative behavioral adjustment, poor academic performance, and increased irritability and impulsiveness (Hiew, 1992; Hillenbrand, 1976; Huebner & Mancini, 2005; Jensen, Martin, & Watanabe, 1996; Levai, Kaplan, Ackerman, & Hammock, 1995; Yeatman, 1981). Research conducted with military families also demonstrates that the mental health of the at-home parent (usually the mother) is very influential in determining child adjustment (Huebner & Powell, 2007; Jensen et al., 1996).

Research conducted with military families demonstrates that the mental health of the at-home parent is very influential in determining child adjustment.

> "When my dad left, I stayed separate from the family. I would really keep to myself. . . . I was taking on more and more responsibilities and I was taking charge so I tried to hide my feelings because my mom and my sister were constantly crying and stuff so I was always trying to comfort them. And I couldn't show any emotion for that because I had to be the strong one. I was hiding my emotions at certain times then always lashing out at certain people that maybe I shouldn't have been."
>
> —Teen Female

Providing Support

In the summer of 2004, early in the deployments for the Global War on Terrorism, we conducted focus groups with youth who were currently experiencing parental deployment to an active war zone (Huebner et al., 2007; see Huebner & Mancini, 2005 for the full report). For those affiliated with the National Guard or Reserve force, this marked the first time for such a separation; it also marked the first time these youth even considered themselves part of the military system. The primary purpose of this study was to explore the many dimensions of the deployment experiences of teens in military families, so that military and civilian program professionals could be more intentional and directed regarding developing support programs for young people.

Youth were identified via their attendance in one of several camps sponsored by the National Military Family Association designed for those with deployed military parents. Study participants were 107 ethnically diverse adolescent boys and girls ranging in age from 12 to 18 years. Active duty service representation included 39% Army, 3% Navy, 10% Air Force, and 4% Marines; 23% of participants had parents in the National Guard (all services), and 13% in the Reserves (all services). The vast majority of youth in this study stated that they had a father deployed.

As part of the process, youth were asked about their support networks. Youth's responses clustered around 1) informal supports, 2) formal supports, and 3) support processes.

Informal support received from family members, friends, and others not connected with a support service or program are invaluable for providing opportunities for youth to deal with concerns associated with a parent's deployment. Informal support is evidenced in talking about worries, or merely by having others to spend time with in enjoyable activities. Youth mentioned a number of sources that were supportive to them, including parents and grandparents, friends who are also in military families, as well as friends who are not. They reported that others often gave them a chance to release tensions by talking. Having others to engage with in activities diverted their attention from deployment worries.

It is important to note that some reported they did *not* seek out people with whom to talk about deployment-related worries—they spoke about times when informal support was *not* helpful. For example, some teens said they felt others almost over-reacted when hearing about their concerns on deployment, or felt that people were just being polite by listening to them.

"I've got one friend that will actually talk about it because she has a brother being deployed soon. But all the rest of my friends don't, it sort of makes them uncomfortable for me to talk about it, and that makes me uncomfortable, too."

—Teen Female

We associate formal support as that originating within agencies and organizations, including churches, civic groups, as well as military youth serving agencies (Mancini, Bowen, & Martin, 2005). Within these formal organizations, relationships among participants often develop, so that formal support and informal support become interrelated. Formal support personnel include teachers, counselors and therapists, and youth workers. Regardless of formal support source, most teens are open to formal support services if the teens feel like those services are relevant and that the adults offering those services can empathize with teens because of their own similar experiences with deployment.

"I feel like my teachers are more understanding and you know, more apt to give me an extension on my homework because they know about my family. Because I had this one teacher whose dad was deployed and he died while he was over there. And you know, she just took me under her wing and was like my counselor throughout the rest of the year."

—Teen Female

Within both formal and informal support are a set of processes, called support functions, which teens find helpful. Usually these functions are associated with what individual people say or do. These processes can be instrumental or practical, or more emotional or psychological. Youth told us about a wide variety of support processes they used. Support processes that youth say are helpful include listening, understanding, and providing assurance. They also mentioned that sometimes being "distracted" with other activities was helpful because it provided them a break from thinking about deployment. Interestingly, teens were also quick to point out displeasure with those who provided "fake" support or whose support faltered over time.

"At first when my dad got deployed, there was a lot of support as in like people calling, people giving us, you know, food and stuff. But then as time went on, it just kind of died down and nobody really cared that he was deployed."

—Teen Male

"I don't want to talk about it 24/7. I want to go out, have fun, get together, eat, you know? I don't want to just talk about it, you know, deployment and stuff because there's other things happening in our lives, you know."

—Teen Female

Implications for Program Professionals
Support for Youth
Findings from the study point to several ways youth development professionals can be supportive to youth in military families. Support for youth fall into one of three categories: (1) increasing knowledge/awareness of deployment-related issues; (2) increasing knowledge of and vigilance around depression and stress symptoms in youth; and (3) increasing opportunities for connection and support of these youth.

Increasing Knowledge and Awareness about Deployment Related Issues
Youth-serving professionals and other support personnel can support youth during parental deployment by;

- understanding the unique situation of teens with deployed parents. Because a broad array of formal support organizations come in contact with teens in military families, all could benefit from receiving information about families and deployment.

- developing public awareness campaigns to educate local communities about issues facing military families.
- learning about the significance of the deployment cycle and how teens' reactions vary depending on the specific stage, as well as on their own age.

Increasing Knowledge of and Vigilance around Depression and Stress Symptoms in Youth

This can be accomplished by:

- recognizing signs and symptoms of depression and other mental health issues in teens. Very often it is assumed that the natural resilience of youth will carry them through difficult times, yet our data show otherwise.
- recognizing that a range of emotions are experienced by teens when a parent is deployed and tailoring intervention efforts to deal with these complexities, rather than assume a narrow range of emotional responses by teens.

Increasing Opportunities for connection and Support

Increasing support and connection can be accomplished by:

- making a special effort to connect with teens that have a deployed parent. Many youth will be reluctant to express their concerns about a deployed parent, but will respond to others who show concern for them.
- helping teens to develop social networks with other teens who have deployed parents. These could occur in school, community, or religious organizational settings.
- supporting the informal networks of teens by intentionally developing networking skills among teens that include how to communicate feelings, and how to develop bonds with other military teens. This may include developing social support or mentoring programs led by young adults who have themselves experienced the deployment of a parent.
- providing ongoing, accessible social activities for teens so that they have distraction opportunities. Youth can only focus on worries connected with the welfare of a deployed parent for so long without experiencing extreme fatigue. This type of support may involve partnering with other youth serving organizations to increase the number of available program options. Try to recruit teens to participate in programs that include recreation as well as life skills development.
- ensuring appropriate support systems for the at-home parent. The at-home parent is the linchpin in the well-being of the adolescent.

Support for Parents

Our research findings also point to implications about how to support those parents experiencing spousal deployment in supporting their own children. Program professionals can help support parents by providing educational information in three areas: (1) recognizing reactions to deployment related stress; (2) becoming intentional about providing consistency in family routines and rituals; and (3) providing and accessing informal support systems.

Recognizing Reactions to Deployment Related Stress

Content areas should include:

- the importance of parents taking a developmentally appropriate and intentional approach to discussing deployment and subsequent family changes with teens. We discovered many adults were over-informing younger youth, and adding unnecessary strains in their lives. Parents need to learn how to make developmentally appropriate disclosures about family issues and war information.
- the awareness that teens often do not have adequate ways to discuss their worries about parental deployment, and that some teens are not speaking with anyone about their concerns.
- the importance of recognizing that teens' behaviors and emotions may vary with different stages of the deployment cycle and with different developmental levels, each requiring attention from parents. Deployment-related adjustment is ongoing, and it is a mistake to assume youth fears are resolved in the short-term.
- signs and symptoms of depression and other mental health issues for teens. Parents must be better equipped to monitor how well their children are dealing with ongoing deployment-related worries and changes. They should also be aware of the range of emotions teens may experience and ways to teach them to express these emotions in a healthy manner.
- how parents can model appropriate self-care and stress reduction, so that teens do not feel responsible for parental emotional well-being. Certain parents forget that their own condition has dramatic effects on the well-being of their children.

Teens often do not have adequate ways to discuss their worries about parental deployment, and . . . some teens are not speaking with anyone about their concerns.

Becoming Intentional about Providing Consistency in Family Routines and Rituals

Educational information for parents about family routines and rituals should include:

- the importance of maintaining consistent expectations about school, work, and family responsibilities. Young people need consistency and predictability in environments. This is one area in which they may feel like they have some control over their lives. Information for parents should also highlight the importance of doing pleasurable things together as a family, as a way of building family rapport and supporting family adjustment to deployment.
- the importance of maintaining family rituals and creating new ones to support family identity and continuity. Families need intentional ways of connecting with each other, and of acknowledging that their living situation and family life has changed. This may include ideas for documenting events and rituals the deployed member may miss.

Providing and Accessing Informal Support Systems

Content for parents in this area include:

- the importance of getting teens involved in social support networks and information on potential opportunities for youth involvement.
- teaching parents to encourage teens to gain new life skills in areas such as stress management, cooking, budgeting, car maintenance, and lawn care, that can prepare them to successfully take on more responsibilities at home.

Deployment-related adjustment is ongoing, and it is a mistake to assume youth fears are resolved in the short-term.

Supporting Youth, Supporting Families: Conclusions

For the most part, youth in military families are underserved by both military support systems and community support systems. In addition to the normative and usual developmental challenges, youth in military families are faced with unique challenges stemming from the deployment of one or both parents. While most military-affiliated youth have the raw materials for resilience, they require supports that enable them to mobilize their abilities while their family situations change. Support for youth can be best accomplished by supporting the adults in the family, insuring that those adults have the necessary skills, characteristics, and personal efficacy to guide, support, and protect their children.

". . . Like when they come home is that like awkward bonding phase all over again, like you're starting from scratch. And then like they've missed out on so much stuff and it's like hard to catch them up with it. Like some of the stuff you just had to be there and they weren't. And it's not like you can be mad at them for it, like inside you're going to be a little bit mad, but you know it's not their fault."

—Teen Female

References

Glod, M. (2008, July 17), Coping with their parents' war. *The Washington Post*, pp. Al, A9,

Hiew, C.C, (1992), Separated by their work: Families with fathers living apart. *Environment and Behavior, 24*, 206–225.

Hillenbrand, E.D. (1976). Father absence in military families. *The Family Coordinator, 25*, 251–258.

Huebner, A. J., & Mancini, J.A. (June 2005). *Adjustment Among Adolescents in Military Families When a Parent is Deployed: A final report submitted to the Military Family Research Institute and the Department of Defense Quality of Life Office.* Falls Church, Virginia: Virginia Tech, Department of Human Development. Available online at www.cfs,purdue.edu/mfri/pages/research/Adjustments_in_adolescents.pdf

Huebner, A., Mancini, J., Wilcox, R., Grass, S., & Grass, G. (2007). Parental deployment and youth in military families: Exploring uncertainty and ambiguous loss. *Family Relations, 56*(2), 112–122.

Huebner, A., & Powell, C. (2007, November). *Exploring Attachment and Family Adjustment During Deployment: "When Momma ain't Happy, ain't Nobody Happy"*. Paper presented at the 67th National Council on Family Relations Annual Conference, Minneapolis, MN.

Jensen, P.S., Martin, D., & Watanabe, H, (1996), Children's response to separation during Operation Desert Storm. *Journal of the American Academy of Child and Adolescent Psychiatry, 35*, 433–441.

Jensen, P., & Shaw, J. (1996). The effects of war and parental deployment upon children and teens. In R. Ursano & A. Norwood (Eds.), *Emotional Aftermath of the Persian GulfWar: Veterans. Families, Communities, and Nations* (pp.83–109). Washington, DC: American Psychiatric Press.

Levai, M., Kaplan, S., Ackerman, R., & Hammock, M. (1995). The effect of father absence on the psychiatric hospitalization of Navy children. *Military Medicine, 160*, 103–106.

Mancini, J.A., Bowen, G.L., & Martin, J.A. (2005). Community social organization: A conceptual linchpin in examining families in the context of communities. *Family Relations: Interdisciplinary Journal of Applied Family Studies, 54*, 570–582.

Morse, J, (2006), *The New Emotional Cycle of Deployment.* Retrieved June 28, 2007 http://deploymenthealthlibrary.fhp.osd.mil/products/Emotional%20Cycles%20of%20Deployment%20(241).pdf

Office of the Deputy Under Secretary of Defense (2005). *2005 Demographics Report.* Retrieved October 25, 2007, from Purdue University, Military Family Research Institute Web site: www.cfs.purdue.edu/mfri/pages/military/2005_Demographics_Report.pdf

Yeatman, G.W. (1981). Parental separation and the military child. *Military Medicine, 146*, 320–322.

Critical Thinking

1. How have recent wars affected military members and their families?

2. In what ways are youth professionals able to support families through this difficult time?

3. What are the various phases a military family goes through during deployment?

4. How can youth of military families be helped during military deployment?

ANGELA J. HUEBNER, PhD, (ahuebner@vt.edu) is an Associate Professor in the Department of Human Development, in the Marriage and Family Therapy Program at Virginia Tech in Fails Church; Virginia. Her research focuses on issues of positive youth development, and adjustment and adaptation among youth. JAY A. MANCINI, PhD, is a Professor in the Department of Human Development, and a Senior Research Fellow with the institute for Society, Culture, and Environment at Virginia Tech, His research focuses on the lifespan, vulnerable populations, and building community capacity and resilience. He is a Fellow of the National Council on Family Relations, and a Fellow of the World Demographic Association.

From *The Prevention Researcher,* December 2008. Copyright © 2008 by Integrated Research Services, Inc. Reprinted by permission.

When Play Turns to Trouble

Many Parents Are Now Wondering: How Much Is Too Much?

JENNIFER SETER WAGNER

Ollie Morelli, 7, logs on to the family laptop before sunup to make sure his pet lion, Cedric, is set for the day. The character in the online game Webkinz would appear to be: His house, furnished by Ollie, boasts a football-shaped refrigerator, a football-helmet coffee table, a couch, and a flat-screen TV. Cedric requires hours of after-school attention, too—and sometimes inspires an outburst when Mom and Dad say, "Enough!" Like many parents these days, Ollie's have wondered uneasily where childish pastime begins to edge toward obsession. "The issue is not the amount of time," says Brian Morelli. "We can control that. It's the fact that he gets up before everyone else and sneaks onto the computer. It's like he sets his internal clock so he can play Webkinz."

Concern is spreading among parents and mental-health professionals that the exploding popularity of computer and video games has a deeper dark side than simple couch-potatohood. Software sales jumped 28 percent last year to $9.5 billion; an average of nine games were sold every second of the year, according to the Entertainment Software Association. Studies show that 92 percent of children under age 18 play regularly. According to the Media Research Lab at Iowa State University, about 8.5 percent of 8-to-18-year-old gamers can be considered pathologically addicted, and nearly one quarter of young people—more males than females—admit they've felt addicted. Little wonder: In February, a team at Stanford University School of Medicine showed that areas of the brain responsible for generating feelings of addiction and reward are activated during game play. "We are seeing it over and over again," says Liz Woolley, founder of On-Line Gamers Anonymous (www.olganonboard.org), a virtual 12-step program for gaming addicts. "We're losing [kids] into the games, and it's turning their brains to mush."

Software sales hit $9.5 billion last year, an average of nine games sold each second.

Saying when. How can parents know when a lot is too much? Media experts are quick to point out that computer and video games are not inherently bad for kids; indeed, most players find a balance, says David Walsh, founder of the National Institute on Media and the Family in Minneapolis: "They play their video games; they do their homework; they keep up with their responsibilities and have other interests. No problem."

But when the other areas of a child's life begin to suffer, parents may have cause to take corrective action. Kimberly Young, director of the Center for Internet Addiction Recovery in Bradford, Pa., points to several common warning signs of pathological behavior: fantasizing or talking about game characters or missions when offline; lying about or hiding how much time is spent playing or disobeying parental limits; losing interest in sports and hobbies; choosing the game over time with friends; and continuing to play despite plummeting grades, loss of a scholarship, a breakup with a partner. An addicted gamer's physical appearance may also change as he loses sleep, neglects to shower, and skips meals.

Team first. The games most apt to be overplayed are what people in the industry call MMORPGs, or "massively multiplayer online role-playing games." Games of this type—World of Warcraft and Call of Duty are two popular examples—connect players in cyberspace who then form "guilds" or "clans" that participate in raids against opposing squads. Generally, each player is represented by an avatar—usually a three-dimensional character that either the game or the player creates—and has a role to play, such as defender or strategist. Guild members may be from all over the world, and the missions can go on for days. "Let's say I'm a ninth grader, with teammates in Japan and Bulgaria, and Mom says it's time to do homework," says Walsh. "I E-mail my teammates I need to stop, and their response is: 'Are you nuts?' The membership on the teams becomes very important to these kids. Dropping out of a mission is not OK." The longer you play, says Young, "the more you begin to identify with this make-believe world."

One mother and physician in the Midwest, who asked for anonymity to protect her son, is all too familiar with the siren call of the game. Her son, now 21, started playing computer games as a young child, graduated to World of Warcraft in high school, and spent so much time online as a college freshman that he got mostly F's and was forced to withdraw. His mom says that the progression from great kid and student to self-destructive abuser stupefied the family. "I didn't understand this was a whole different thing," she says of the game. "I'd call him to dinner, and he couldn't come," she says. " 'We're in the middle of a raid!' he'd say. 'They need me!'"

Once he left college, he had to make a choice: either find somewhere else to live and play the game, at his expense, or quit the game, start working, and go back to school part time. He chose the latter and is now finishing up an associate's degree. "We determined there would be no computer games allowed in our house when we saw how destructive they could be," says his mother. The family even locked up the computers. "The longer he spends away from this, the more he'll realize how destructive and what a fantasy world it was," she says. "But I don't know what will happen when he goes out on his own."

Therapy wasn't an option, since the young man was an adult and refused to go. But even when age or willingness isn't an issue, finding effective professional help can be a challenge. For now, game addiction is not recognized by the American Psychiatric Association, which means that there are no national guidelines for what therapy should entail. Whether this will change in 2012, the date a new APA handbook on mental disorders is scheduled to come out, is still up for discussion. Pathological video and computer game play would now be considered one of a broad group of "behavioral addictions" that also includes compulsive shopping and addiction to online pornography, for example. The only behavioral addiction now specifically listed in the handbook is pathological gambling. To treat these disorders, cognitive behavioral therapy is often used to identify the thought processes that lead to the compulsion and to change the destructive thinking. Families seeking help may need to pay out of their own pockets, because insurance typically doesn't cover addictions that don't officially exist. That said, many young gamers are

---

Resources for Parents

A few places for worried families to look for guidance:

On-Line Gamers Anonymous (www.olganonboard.org). A virtual 12-step program aimed at helping gamers and their families battle game addiction.

Center for Internet Addiction Recovery (www.netaddiction.com). Educational information about Internet addictions, online support group, quiz for those who suspect an online gaming addiction.

Aspen Education Group (www.aspeneducationgroup.com/gameaddiction/suws.asp). Information about how wilderness therapy may help the gaming addict.

Smith & Jones Center (www.smithandjones.nl/eng/index.html). Video game residential addiction treatment center in Amsterdam.

---

diagnosed with other conditions such as depression or obsessive-compulsive disorder.

Elsewhere in the world, the problem is recognized as huge. Governments in China and South Korea have helped fund treatment centers and hotlines for electronic game addicts. Keith Bakker, director of the Smith and Jones Center in Amsterdam, a residential detox center that treats video game addicts from around the world, compares their poison to crack cocaine. But "it's easier to treat a coke addict than it is a gamer," he says. "The gamer's denial is so great, and it's compounded by family and community," he says. "Who in the world thinks gaming is a problem?" At first, the center kept gamers physically apart from other addicts, but results were much better when the kids took group therapy with residents troubled by eating disorders, marijuana, or cocaine. "They began to see the similarities between themselves," Bakker says. After they stop denying they have an addiction and the damage it's causing, he notes, many young people never pick up a game again.

Outside help. In this country, some families are turning to wilderness therapy. The Aspen Education Group, a California-based organization that treats underachievers from around the country, provides young people ages 11 to 18 with a back-to-nature approach to ending their gaming obsessions. "At home when they have frustrations, they go to their video games," says therapist Aaron Shaw. "Here they have cold weather, hiking." By being away from their screens for seven to nine weeks, he says, "they learn some healthier coping mechanisms." Shaw first tries to discover kids' reasons for playing; often, he finds, it's to find freedom and fun and out of a need for greater acceptance from their parents. (If Mom is always nagging that games are a waste of time, notes Shaw, "they say: 'Screw you, my friends online love me, and I'll hang out with them.'")

To that point, Young advises parents who want to head off serious trouble to find ways to limit play without blaming or criticizing. Better to set—and enforce—time restrictions, as the Morellis do, put electronics in a well-trafficked area, and make it easy for a child to choose clubs or sports. Games should never be a child's main focus, cautions Woolley. Her wisdom is hard won. Several years ago, Woolley's son committed suicide in front of his computer with his favorite game on the screen.

Critical Thinking

1. What are parents' thoughts on how much time a teen should spend on the computer and on video games?
2. At what point does play turn to trouble when it comes to computer use and video games?
3. What is a good definition of teen addiction to computer and video games?
4. What can parents do about video and computer addiction?

From *U.S. News & World Report*, May 19, 2008, pp. 51–53. Copyright © 2008 by U.S. News & World Report, LP. Reprinted by permission via Wright's Media.

Aggression in Adolescent Dating Relationships: Predictors and Prevention

JENNIFER CONNOLLY, PHD, AND WENDY JOSEPHSON, PHD

The emergence of romantic relationships is one of the most striking features of adolescence. By the late adolescent years, most teenagers have been in a romantic relationship at least once and roughly half of teens are dating currently. Alarmingly though, in many of these relationships adolescents act aggressively toward each other and this behavior appears almost as early as relationships emerge (Connolly, Pepler, Craig, & Taradash, 2000). Aggression in adolescent dating relationships is of high concern. There are negative psychological consequences as well as the risk of physical injury. Moreover, use of aggression in dating relationships may set in motion a pattern of interpersonal violence that continues into adulthood. On the bright side, adolescence is a period of transition and opportunity. Preventing dating aggression at this developmental stage may reap significant positive outcomes later in life. In this article, we provide a review of adolescent dating aggression, focusing on warning signs and methods of prevention.

Prevalence and Impact

Adolescence is a period of heightened risk for aggression between dating partners (see Table 1 for definitions). Recent estimates indicate that between 20% and 50% of adolescents have been in an aggressive relationship. Very few studies have focused on dating aggression in gay and lesbian relationships, but the available information suggests that the rates are similar to those reported in heterosexual relationships (Johnson, 2006). In heterosexual adolescent couples, dating aggression occurs for both genders. Both boys and girls report perpetration of aggression as well as victimization and these roles frequently occur within the same relationship. In one study, 66% of adolescent dating aggression was bi-directional (Gray & Foshee, 1997). It may, though, occur for different reasons. Boys more often

Table 1 Definitions of Dating Violence and Dating Aggression

Dating aggression is now the term researchers commonly use to refer to actual or threatened harm between adolescent dating partners. Often it is these milder forms of aggression (e.g., pushing, slapping, or shoving) that occur between young dating partners.

Dating violence is actual or threatened harm between current or former partners.

Physical violence is the intentional use of physical force that could cause harm to another person. It includes mildly *aggressive* behaviors such as scratching, pushing, and shoving, as well as more severely *violent* behaviors such as biting, choking, shaking, slapping, punching, burning, or use of a weapon.

Psychological or emotional violence involves verbally abusive and coercive tactics intended to control, embarrass, humiliate, or isolate the partner from friends and family; it often precedes physical violence.

report dating aggression because of anger and girls more often report aggression in self-defense (O'Keefe, 2005). It is also important to keep in mind that, in heterosexual relationships, girls' aggression is far less physically injurious than that of boys. While boys almost always report being unhurt by their girlfriends' aggression, very few girls reported being unhurt.

Dating aggression is not a trivial occurrence, limited to a single relationship or a single episode. Rather repeated aggression within a relationship is a risk for at least some adolescents who remain in a relationship even though there have been acts of aggression. And equally worrying, there are some adolescents who appear to be prone to aggression in their relationships as they report aggression later on in a new romantic relationship.

Although understudied in comparison to research on adult intimate violence, it is now becoming clear that adolescent dating aggression has a serious negative impact on the victims' health and well-being. In a study of high school girls, Jay Silverman and colleagues (2001) found that girls who reported being hurt by their boyfriends were more likely to report substance use, disordered eating, risky sexual behaviors, and suicidal thoughts. Although less is known about this, it does appear that the negative impact extends to boys and that both genders report fear, anxiety, and emotional disturbance in association with dating aggression as well as an increased probability of running away from home and dropping out of school.

Risk Factors and Warning Signs

So, what are the warning signs for dating violence? A complex array of factors, such as family violence, attitudes, peers, problem behavior, and couple hostility increase the risk for dating aggression. To understand how these multiple risk factors might be linked, psychologists distinguish between two types of risk factors. The first of these are **"background"** factors, so-called because they provide powerful models that can lead an adolescent to use aggression as a response to interpersonal problems generally. Particularly significant background factors are violence in the family of origin, prior use of aggression with peers, a peer group that tolerates romantic aggression, and an attitude of accepting the use of aggression to solve romantic problems. These background factors form the social context in which the adolescent grows up and learns about relationships. They predispose the adolescent to respond with aggression in future interactions with a dating partner. Then **"situation"** factors take over. These are specific features of the dating relationship that lead an adolescent to respond aggressively with that particular romantic partner. Some of the most significant of these are the quality of the relationship, the use of psychological or verbal aggression, partner aggression, and poor interpersonal skills. These factors play a pivotal role in that they are the developmental outcome of aggression-tolerant family or peer contexts and also most directly lead to aggression towards a dating partner.

Background Risk Factors
Aggression in the Family of Origin

Researchers have been very interested in the long-term effects of growing up in a home in which there is violence between the parents or from the parent to the child. It is a reasonable hypothesis that adolescents who have witnessed aggression between their parents or who have experienced very harsh parenting might carry these patterns forward into their own intimate relationships. However, the research support is mixed. As summarized recently by O'Keefe (2005), some studies identify these links, especially for boys, while other studies do not find the link. Focusing on high-risk youth though, the findings are clearer that child maltreatment is a significant risk factor for later dating violence. Wolfe and his colleagues (2004) studied dating violence among adolescents in child protection and found a significant link between child abuse and dating aggression in adolescence. Families from which a child is removed for safety experience high levels of stress and disruption, in addition to maltreatment, and these factors collectively contribute to the adolescent's increased risk for perpetrating dating aggression.

Aggression with Peers

In contrast to the mixed findings for direct family influences, there is growing evidence that peer relationships are formative for dating aggression. These influences are both direct and indirect. For example, adolescent boys who fight and are aggressive with their peers also show these same behaviors with a romantic partner. Equally though, the aggressive behavior of adolescents' friends can influence dating aggression. Adolescent boys who talk together about girls in hostile or disrespectful ways are equally at risk for dating aggression (Capaldi et al., 2001). Adolescents who believe that their friends would be aggressive to a romantic partner are also more likely to act with aggression toward their own dating partner.

Recently, bullying peers has been identified as a significant risk behavior for dating aggression (Connolly et al., 2000; Pepler et al., 2006). Bullying refers to aggressive behaviors, either physical or psychological, that youth use to exert their power over other young people who are less able to defend themselves. Over half of young people are involved in bullying at some point during their elementary or high school years and perhaps 10% of adolescents bully others frequently and persistently. While in the past bullying was often dismissed as a passing problem of childhood, there is now substantial evidence that it can set a young person on a pathway to using aggression to get his or her way in a wide range of relationships, including those with a romantic partner. During the transition to adolescence, as romantic relationships emerge and sexuality becomes a sensitive issue for young people, youngsters who bully frequently appear to transfer their power-asserting aggression to dating relationships. Both sexual harassment of peers and aggression towards a romantic partner are common behaviors of both boys and girls who bully.

Aggression-Tolerant Attitudes

Most adolescents have very disapproving attitudes toward dating aggression, especially physical or sexual aggression by boys against girls (Josephson & Proulx, in press). Some are more tolerant of dating aggression under particularly provocative circumstances, such as infidelity or the other person hitting first. The more teens think that dating aggression is justified in a variety of situations, the more likely they are to be aggressive to their own dating partners.

Situational Risk Factors
Quality of the Relationship

Dating relationships characterized by high levels of conflict and low levels of intimacy and satisfaction are at risk for dating aggression (O'Keefe, 1997). Adolescents with a history of bullying their peers are more likely to be involved in the low quality relationships that are vulnerable to dating aggression. Although their dating relationships are very important to them, adolescents who bully their peers have romantic relationships that are less affectionate, intimate, committed, and equitable than the romantic relationships experienced by their peers (Connolly et al., 2000).

Psychological Aggression to Romantic Partner

Psychological aggression typically precedes physical aggression and can be a warning sign of violence to come (O'Leary & Slep, 2003). It is also very common. Most studies of verbal aggression in dating relationships report that it occurs in at least 80% of romantic couples. Psychological and emotional aggression can seriously undermine the recipient's self-esteem. Illogically, some aspects of psychological aggression, the controlling behaviors and jealousy-related verbal rages, are sometimes interpreted by the recipient as originating from love, which may lead to a paradoxical intensifying of commitment to the relationship following aggression. However, the verbally abusive and humiliating aspects of psychological aggression are not subject to this kind of mis-attribution, and appear to have a stronger negative effect on self-esteem than being subjected to physical dating aggression. Consequently, psychological and emotional aggression may be a stronger impetus for ending a physically aggressive relationship than is the severity of the physical aggression.

Partner Aggression

Adolescent dating aggression is primarily bi-directional (Gray & Foshee, 1997). In fact, a dating partner's aggression is often the strongest predictor of an adolescent's own dating aggression. Gray and Foshee found that adolescents in mutually aggressive relationships perpetrated more aggression, and sustained more injuries, than those in relationships for which aggression was one-sided. This may be because of the tendency for aggressive adolescents to form romantic relationships with others who are similarly aggressive and so partners provoke each other and learn aggressive tactics from each other. This is one very important way in which adolescent dating aggression differs from the patterns found in long-term adult relationships. Aggression is more likely to be mutual in adolescent dating relationships than in the relationships of adults. Probably this is because control is

usually distributed more evenly in adolescents' dating relationships although when there is unequal power it presents a risk factor for young women's victimization from physical aggression (Johnson, 2006).

Aggression is more likely to be mutual in adolescent dating relationships than in the relationships of adults.

Poor Interpersonal Skills

Poor conflict resolution tactics are associated with psychological and emotional aggression. One recent study (Josephson & Proulx, in press) found that failure to use reasoning and negotiation effectively to resolve conflicts was associated with an escalating pattern of resorting to psychological aggression and, ultimately, physical aggression.

Prevention of Dating Aggression

Taking this profile of risk factors into consideration, there is quite a strong consensus about the features that are necessary for effective prevention of dating aggression:

- **A comprehensive approach:** Prevention programs work better if they reach more of the levels (individual, family, peer group, couple) at which adolescents may be put at risk for dating aggression. Comprehensiveness includes taking a holistic approach to the adolescent as a whole person, providing a variety of different activities. For example, the *Healthy Relationships* curriculum (Men for Change, 1994) provides 53 activities intended to help adolescents build knowledge, change attitudes, and develop skills to positively affect the cognitive, emotional, and behavioral aspects of relationships with friends, family, dating partners, and others in their school and community.
- **Peer involvement:** Because of the critical role of peers in adolescents' lives, as role models, norm enforcers, and preferred providers of advice and support, it is especially important to engage young people themselves in prevention activities. For example, the RISE program (*Respect in Schools Everywhere,* Weiser & Moran, 2006) trains high school volunteers for 12 weeks about bullying, dating violence, and healthy relationships, then provides them with coaching and support to give two workshops on these topics to every classroom in their own schools and nearby middle schools. The "upside" of the strong role of peers in the development of

dating aggression is that they are a powerful force to prevent it, if their influence is positive. For this reason, universal programs are recommended over targeted interventions with just those who are at risk, even though additional supports may need to be put in place for high risk adolescents.

- **Appropriate goals for change:** Prevention efforts that address the real pattern of mutual and less severe dating aggression in adolescent relationships will be more effective than those based on the one-sided "intimate terrorism" model that better fits intensive interventions for perpetrators of domestic violence (Johnson, 2006). For instance, the BRIGHT program (*Building Relationships in Greater Harmony Together,* Cascardi & Avery-Leaf, 1998) was designed to take a gender-neutral focus on dating aggression. Program developers believe that this will avoid having prevention efforts undermined by the resistance that they anticipated if they appeared to be unfairly stereotyping men and presenting a version of dating aggression that did not correspond to the experiences of adolescents. Because many young people will receive a prevention program before they even begin dating, and many dating relationships have no physical dating aggression at all, prevention programs should focus on changing those factors that put young people at risk for physical dating aggression: psychological and emotional aggression, tolerant attitudes toward dating aggression, and poor interpersonal skills.

- **Emphasis on building skills:** In their focus group study on dating aggression, Heather Sears and colleagues (2006) found that high school students wanted assistance to develop skills for maintaining healthy relationships and dealing with relationship conflict. Prevention programs should provide a chance for adolescents to build strong skills for promoting healthy relationships. For example, the *Fourth R* program (Townsley et al., 2005) provides role play activities and scenarios to help young people learn general communication and conflict management skills, problem solving, social perspective taking, assertiveness, and frustration tolerance. Skill-building activities are best begun as early as possible, with opportunities for practice, such as role playing activities, and taking on more challenging situations as skills develop.

Conclusion

Adolescent dating aggression is a serious problem for many teenagers. Yet like other forms of aggression, warning signs are often present that a young couple may be at risk. By understanding these precursors we can help adolescents avoid problematic situations and instead develop healthy dating relationships that will set in place a solid foundation for satisfying relationships throughout life.

References

Capaldi, D.M., Dishion, T.J., Stoolmiller, M., & Yoerger, K. (2001). Aggression toward female partners by at-risk young men: The contribution of male adolescent friendships. *Developmental Psychology, 37,* 61–73.

Cascardi, M., & Avery-Leaf, S. (1998). *Building Relationships in Greater Harmony Together (BRIGHT) Program.* Glen Ridge, NJ: DVPP, Inc.

Connolly, J., Pepler, D., Craig, W., & Taradash, A. (2000). Dating experiences of bullies in early adolescence. *Child Maltreatment, 5,* 299–310.

Gray, H.M., & Foshee, V. (1997). Adolescent dating violence: Differences between one-sided and mutually violent profiles. *Journal of Interpersonal Violence, 12,* 126–141.

Johnson, M.P. (2006). Violence and abuse in personal relationships: Conflict, terror and resistance in intimate relationships. In A.L. Vangelisti & D. Perlman (Eds.), *The Cambridge Handbook of Personal Relationships* (pp. 557–576). New York: Cambridge University Press.

Josephson, W.L., & Proulx, J.B. (in press). Violence in young adolescents' relationships: A path model. *Journal of Interpersonal Violence.*

Men for Change (1994). *Healthy Relationships: A violence-prevention curriculum* (Second ed.). Halifax, NS: Author.

O'Keefe, M. (1997). Predictors of dating violence among high school students. *Journal of Interpersonal Violence, 12,* 546–568.

O'Keefe, M. (2005). Teen dating violence: A review of risk factors and prevention efforts. *Applied Research Forum,* 1–13.

O'Leary, K.D., & Slep, A.M.S. (2003). A dyadic longitudinal model of adolescent dating aggression. *Journal of Clinical Child and Adolescent Psychology, 32,* 314–327.

Pepler, D., Craig, W., Connolly, J., Yuile, A., McMaster, L., & Jiang, D. (2006). A developmental perspective on bullying. *Aggressive Behaviour, 32,* 376–384.

Sears, H.A., Byers, E.S., Whelan, J.J., Saint-Pierre, M., & the Dating Violence Research Team (2006). "If it hurts you, then it is not a joke": Adolescents' ideas about girls' and boys' use and experience of abusive behavior in dating relationships. *Journal of Interpersonal Violence, 21,* 1,191–1,207.

Silverman, J.G., Raj, A., Mucci, L.A., & Hathaway, J.E. (2001). Dating violence against adolescent girls and associated substance use, unhealthy weight control, sexual risk behavior, pregnancy, and suicidality. *Journal of the American Medical Association, 286,* 572–579.

Townsley, D., Crooks, C., Hughes, R., & Wolfe, D.A. (2005). *The Fourth R: Relationship-Based Violence Prevention.* London, ON: CAMH Centre for Prevention Science.

Weiser, J., & Moran, M. (2006). *RISE Manual: How to Engage Youth in Violence Prevention Strategies.* Toronto, ON: East Metro Youth Services.

Wolfe, D., Wekerle, C., Scott, K., Straatman, A., & Grasley, C. (2004). Predicting abuse in adolescent dating relationships over one year: The role of child maltreatment and trauma. *Journal of Abnormal Psychology, 113,* 406–415.

Critical Thinking

1. What is considered dating aggression?
2. What are the warning signs of dating aggression?
3. What methods of prevention could help in dating aggression?
4. Why do youth get involved in dating aggression?

Dr. Jennifer Connolly is a Professor of Clinical-Developmental Psychology at York University in Toronto, Canada and is the Director of the LaMarsh Centre for Research on Violence and Conflict Resolution. With Dr. Josephson, she is currently examining the use of peer-led interventions to prevent dating aggression in middle/high schools. **Dr. Wendy Josephson** is a Professor of Social Psychology at the University of Winnipeg, in Winnipeg, Canada. Her research is primarily in the areas of aggression and violence reduction, including media effects on aggression, prevention of dating violence, and the effects of youth engagement in violence prevention.

A Host of Trouble

More Parents Are Being Held Criminally Liable for Their Teens' Drinking Parties.

EMMA SCHWARTZ

The day had gone just as Les Foster had planned. More than 100 friends had gathered at his private dirt track for an annual day of car racing in Gardner, Kan., where Foster's team won the prized traveling trophy. By sunset, he had retired happily to his house down the road. The peace did not last. A few hours later, Foster, who runs an auto repair shop, was jolted awake by a knock on the door. It was the police, and they wanted to know what Foster could tell them about a 17-year-old boy who had been killed on the racetrack when his intoxicated teenage friend ran over him.

With that tragic episode began a two-year legal nightmare. Foster, 43, was convicted in 2006 of allowing underage drinking on his property, even though he says he did not know that the teens had returned to the track. He was sentenced to a year's probation and ordered to deliver six speeches about underage drinking to high school students. Then the victim's family filed a civil suit against him, demanding he pay them $2.5 million. His insurance company settled for $452,000.

Foster's is an experience that more and more adults—especially parents—may encounter as a growing number of states pass laws increasing parental liability for teenage drinking. Twenty-three states have now passed "social host" laws targeting adults who allow underage drinking in their homes. And 33 states have some form of civil liability laws. "Homeowners and parents are at risk now because they don't appreciate what their kids are doing in the backyard," says Suzanne Bass, a Florida attorney who has handled these suits.

Binge drinking

Although teen drinking rates have declined significantly over the past few decades, they remain disturbingly high: More than 40 percent of college students say they binge drink. And at more than 5,000 a year, alcohol-related fatalities remain the leading cause of death among teens.

The key statistic behind the new laws, however, is that two thirds of teens get their booze from adults. Some parents provide it deliberately, believing that if they condone it in moderation, their children will be less likely to abuse it. Stanton Peele, a psychologist and addiction expert, says research bears that theory out. "It's accurate to say that *not* drinking at home with parents is a significant risk factor," says Peele.

But advocates of the new laws take just the opposite view. Stricter parental liability, they say, can reverse society's tacit acceptance of underage drinking just as tougher laws have changed the public's attitude toward drunk driving. "We have to get adults to understand the ways in which [they] contribute to this problem," says Richard Bonnie, a law professor at the University of Virginia and coeditor of a 2003 study by the National Academy of Sciences that called for increased enforcement against parents. "We're not going to change social norms among kids if we don't change social norms among parents."

Heightened parental liability raises thorny questions about where the balance of responsibility and punishment should lie. Should parents be jailed for allowing teens to drink? Can the law hold adults liable if they're not even aware of the drinking? Does a zero-tolerance policy encourage worse drinking habits among teens?

Critics say this prohibitionist tack will never eliminate teen drinking and is likely to push thoughtful discussion out of the public arena. "How much more do we need to spend in order to achieve enforcement that constitutes success?" asks John McCardell, the former president of Middlebury College who is leading a national campaign to lower the drinking age to 18.

Jail sentence

There is no research on whether social host laws are effective, and most adults arrested under them are siblings or friends in their 20s. Still, it is clear the penalties are falling harder on parents. In June, Elisa Kelly of Charlottesville, Va., was sentenced to 27 months in jail for hosting a drinking party for her teenage son. She bought the alcohol and thought she was protecting the kids by taking their car keys for the night. And an Illinois couple, Jeffrey and Sara Hutsell, were convicted for allowing their son to host a drinking party after which two teens died in a car crash. A judge last week sentenced Sara to probation and her husband to 14 days in jail, with time off to go to work.

How You Can Protect Yourself

If you have a teen and own your home, you are at risk

The good news for parents is that so-called social host cases can be difficult to litigate, and they are likely only in the event of a catastrophic injury or death resulting from underage drinking. But that doesn't mean you're free from risk.

Homeowners face the greatest threat from these types of lawsuits since a home is insured and it's a financial asset that a plaintiff can try to tap. Liability laws differ from state to state. Minnesota, for instance, says a liable host knowingly provides a minor with alcohol, while in California, a host is liable only if he provides alcohol to "an obviously intoxicated person."

Regardless of the law, homeowners who are sued may face resistance from their insurers. "The insurance company's first reaction will be to try to find a way to disprove coverage," says Richard Campbell, an attorney who handles social host liability cases in Massachusetts.

The insurance company's first reaction may be to deny coverage.

Lawyers suggest parents check their homeowners policies to see what is covered. Most policies will cover some form of legal liability, but some may have exceptions for underage drinking and may not protect against a steep judgment. Homeowners insurance may or may not cover legal fees, which can mount quickly.

In short, there is only one sure way to avoid legal trouble, lawyers say. Make sure there is never underage drinking on your property—period.

—E.S.

Barrington, R.I., is an affluent seaside community where two teens died in drunk-driving accidents in 2005. Police there observed that more parents were allowing their children to drink at home. But they had trouble charging parents because they couldn't always prove that the parents had bought the alcohol for the teens.

It was a dilemma faced by other Rhode Island towns. So in 2006, the General Assembly passed a law allowing police to charge parents criminally for permitting underage drinking even if they didn't provide the booze. It allows for religious exemptions (such as drinking wine on the Jewish Sabbath) but is otherwise among the nation's stiffest. The penalty is a minimum $350 fine and up to six months behind bars.

The college town of Salisbury, Md., doesn't have a social host law. But single mother Janet Lane found herself in legal trouble last year when the police broke up a party thrown by her two sons while she was at a business conference. Responding to a tip from another parent, police found music blaring, beer bottles strewn on the lawn, and one teen gagging on his own vomit. Breathalyzer tests showed that 11 of the 24 teens—although not Lane's sons—had been drinking. Lane, a paralegal, says she knew nothing of the ruckus, but police slapped her with more than a dozen charges of allowing minors to drink.

The evidence—largely based on partygoers who were themselves intoxicated—was shaky, and a neighbor was eventually convicted of buying the booze. Eventually, though, Lane pleaded guilty to having a disorderly house, and the police dropped the other charges. But the experience left Lane with $3,000 in legal bills and a bitter taste. "They had a good reason for trying to understand who did it," she says. "But how they went about it was wrong."

In California, meanwhile, officials have taken a different approach to teen drinking: steep fines. The state does not have a criminal social host ordinance, but individual counties have targeted parents with civil laws that allow police to fine them—in some cases up to $2,500—for allowing underage drinking. Officials in Marin County, a liberal enclave north of San Francisco, worried that criminalizing parental involvement would send the wrong message; the goal wasn't to punish people but to deter bad behavior. So the county passed a civil fine ordinance under which police have cited four people, including one 19-year-old who called the police herself when a party got out of hand.

A Threat to Teen Brains

Alcohol's harms are worse for young people

Everyone knows the deleterious effects of heavy drinking. But the effects are far more pronounced for young people. That's because research shows that the brain doesn't fully develop until the mid-20s.

The areas that show the most change between the teens and mid-20s are the brain's frontal lobes, which are central to planning, decision making, impulse control, and language. This physiological transformation helps explain why even level-headed teens are prone to riskier behavior, a tendency only aggravated by alcohol.

The consequences are both short- and long-term. Young drinkers are more likely to drive drunk, get into fights, or engage in unprotected or unwanted sex. And alcohol-related incidents remain the leading cause of death among teens, from car accidents (38 percent), homicides (32 percent), and suicides (6 percent).

Over the long haul, early alcohol consumption can hurt brain development. And the earlier youths begin drinking, the more likely they are to have chronic alcohol and other health problems.

Teenagers who start drinking before age 15 are four times as likely to become alcoholics as those who wait until they are 21. And those who drink at a young age are more likely to have other substance abuse problems as well.

—E.S.

One of the two parents fined under the ordinance was Mill Valley businesswoman Deborah Walters. She had allowed her 17-year-old son to host some friends for a barbecue and explicitly forbade drinking. She was in the house when the police came (in answer to a neighbor's complaint) and found the boys drinking beer outside. Walters was fined $750, a penalty she is making her son pay back at $100 a month. "He knows that if he does it again," she says, "he doesn't have a place to live."

In some jurisdictions, proposed liability laws have encountered challenges. Davette Baker, director of a substance abuse project in Harrodsburg, Ky., successfully pushed through a social host ordinance in her town. But when she took the proposal to nearby Burgin, she struck out. The police chief argued that state laws already on the books, such as one concerning an unlawful transaction with a minor, gave him the ability to charge adults.

Fatal crash

In other cases, prosecutions have failed. Rebekah Perrin of Warren, Mass., lost her 19-year-old daughter, Abbigayle, in a drunk-driving accident just after Christmas in 2005. Abbigayle, a vivacious athlete and recent high school graduate, hadn't been drinking. But she had left a house party after midnight in a car with a friend who had. The friend crashed into a guardrail, and Abbigayle was killed almost instantly.

Prosecutors charged the friend, then went after Marc Holly, the father of the teen who held the party, alleging that he not only allowed the drinking party but joined the youths in a game of beer pong. During his trial on a misdemeanor charge, Holly denied condoning the drinking and said he found out only when he returned from an evening out. (Jurors also didn't know he had been incarcerated for coming to court high on cocaine.)

Although some party-goers testified against him, Holly was acquitted. Says an angry Perrin: "It should have been this man who paid the price." Trying to make him do just that, Perrin has filed a civil suit against Holly's wife, who owns their home. Holly's lawyer, Michael Erlich, says his client is not responsible. "It can get to a point where [the law is] not reasonable anymore," he says. "We have to hold teens to some standard that *they* can take responsibility."

Few would disagree with that sentiment, but the pressure is on public officials to fight teen drinking on all fronts. That's why Tucson, Ariz., which has also passed a social host ordinance, is focusing on landlords. In 2001, Tucson alerted landlords that they could be in legal trouble if they didn't take action against underage revelers. So Ricardo Fernandez, who manages a 300-unit apartment complex near the University of Arizona, declared that renters would be evicted if they violated the city's underage drinking laws. Other landlords followed suit. The result: Citywide arrest rates for minors caught with alcohol have dropped almost 20 percent since 2004.

Likewise, the city of Long Beach, N.Y., has taken a broader approach by extending the limits of its ban on outdoor drinking. "Social host is not a silver bullet," says Lt. John Radin of the Long Beach Police Department. "It's got to be part of a systematic strategy."

Critical Thinking

1. What is the extent of teen drinking parties?
2. How can a parent be held liable for his or her teen's drinking?
3. How does the knowledge that a parent can be held liable for his or her teen's drinking affect the parent's concerns?
4. What methods will help curb the problem of teen drinking parties?

From *U.S. News & World Report*, 10/8/2007. Copyright © 2007 by U.S. News & World Report, LP. Reprinted by permission via Wright's Media.

Adolescent Sexual Attitudes and Behaviors

A Developmental Perspective

Understanding how, why, and when an adolescent decides to initiate sex, or abstain from sex, and why a particular type of sexual behavior will be chosen, is critical for the development of more effective public health campaigns aimed at delaying or preventing adolescent sexual behavior.

BONNIE L. HALPERN-FELSHER, PHD AND YANA REZNIK

Bridging childhood and adulthood, adolescence is a fundamental and exciting time of life. It describes a colorful and unique spectrum of development that is marked by rapid and extreme biological, social, cognitive, and emotional changes. One of the hallmarks of adolescent development is sexual maturation, as pubertal development and hormonal changes result in the development of secondary sexual characteristics, including breasts, pubic hair, and menses. These newfound physical characteristics often result in the adolescent looking more mature and occur around the same time as the desire for more autonomy and decision-making opportunities develop, including in the area of sexual behavior. Adolescents' physical development and increases in their need for autonomy, coupled with new social influences, yield important new attitudes toward sexual behavior and sexuality.

In this review, we will first briefly describe adolescent sexual behavior, including the broad spectrum of sexual behaviors experienced during adolescence, as well as both positive and negative outcomes experienced after engaging in sexual behavior. Then we discuss adolescent sexual attitudes, including definitions of sexual attitudes and how such attitudes vary by gender, age, race/ethnicity, and type of sexual behavior. Finally, we briefly describe the multitude of social and environmental influences that shape, either directly or indirectly, adolescent sexual attitudes.

Adolescent Sexual Behavior

Adolescent sexual behaviors are broadly defined, typically beginning with self-stimulation (masturbation) and then extending to behaviors involving another person. These partnered sexual behaviors include kissing, touching, mutual masturbation, oral sex, anal sex, and vaginal sex. The timing of when these behaviors emerge varies greatly by gender, race/ethnicity, and type of sexual behavior.

Approximately 47% of all high school students reported having had sexual intercourse at some point during high school, ranging from 34% of 9th graders to 63% of 12th graders. A greater percentage of males report onset of sexual intercourse during high school than do female adolescents (NAHIC, 2007).

Evidence is mounting that adolescents are more likely to initiate and engage in oral sex than vaginal sex. At least 20% of adolescents have had oral sex by the end of ninth grade, and over 50% of high school students report having had oral sex at some point. Among adolescents between the ages of 15 and 19, 55% of males and 54% of females have had oral sex with members of the opposite sex (Mosher, Chandra, & Jones, 2005). Additionally, between 14% and 50% of adolescents had oral sex prior to vaginal sex, and both sexual behaviors are more prevalent than anal sex. As discussed further below, it appears that the trend toward oral rather than vaginal sex is based in part on sexual attitudes, namely the desire to avoid risk while still experiencing pleasure (Cornell & Halpern-Felsher, 2006; Halpern-Felsher et al., 2005).

Rates of sexual behavior vary by race and ethnicity. Data from the 2007 Youth Risk Behavior Surveillance Survey (YRBS) showed the overall prevalence rate of ever having had sexual intercourse to be higher among black (67%) and Hispanic (52%) adolescents, compared to white adolescents (44%) (Eaton et al., 2008). A pooled analysis of four years of data from the YRBS found that Asian adolescents were less likely than other adolescents to have engaged in sexual intercourse (Grunbaum et al., 2000). The limited research available on racial/ethnic disparities in oral sex behaviors suggests that white adolescents are more likely to engage in oral sex compared to black and Hispanic adolescents (Lindberg, Jones, & Santelli, 2008), and that Asian adolescents have the lowest rates of oral sex compared to other racial/ethnic groups (Schuster et al., 1998).

Unfortunately, rates of sexual behavior among gay and lesbian youth are much more difficult to find, in part because researchers fail to ask the question, or more often the venues from which data are being collected do not allow these questions to be posed to adolescents. Further, there is debate over how one should define gay and lesbian sexual behavior. Some argue it is important to determine adolescents' stated sexual identity, while others focus more on whether and the extent to which an adolescent has engaged in same-sex sexual behaviors. A recent national study of adolescents showed that approximately 1.1% of males and 2% of females report having same-sex relations (Knopf et al., 2007).

Adolescents' Sexual Experiences

Understanding the outcomes adolescents experience following sexual behavior is important. These outcomes are likely to be shaped by previous sexual perceptions, and also help mold subsequent sexual attitudes. As such, it is critical not only to explore negative consequences but positive outcomes that adolescents experience during and following sexual engagement. To our knowledge, however, no study has examined adolescents' experiences following kissing, touching, or masturbation. However, one study did examine adolescents' stated experiences following initiation of oral and/or vaginal sex. Brady and Halpern-Felsher (2007) found that adolescents report both positive and negative outcomes associated with engagement in sexual behavior, with 61% of the adolescents reporting at least one positive outcome from having oral sex, and 86% reporting at least one positive experience from vaginal sex. Specific positive outcomes

included experiencing pleasure, becoming popular, having their relationship improve, and feeling good about oneself. Interestingly, compared to the reported positive outcomes, fewer adolescents reported negative outcomes from oral sex (31%) or vaginal sex (58%). These negative consequences included getting into trouble with parents, having a bad reputation, relationship worsening, feeling guilty, having regret, feeling used, becoming pregnant, or contracting a sexually transmitted infection (STI).

Attitudes Toward Sexual Behavior

Understanding adolescents' attitudes regarding sexual behavior is key to understanding why they choose to engage or not engage in sex, which sexual behavior(s) they initiate and continue, and the outcomes experienced during and following sexual behavior. There is no one definition of adolescent sexual attitudes. Most often, sexual attitudes are measured by perceptions of the positive and negative outcomes one experiences from engaging in or abstaining from sex. Others have measured sexual attitudes in terms of the perceptions of the prevalence of sexual behaviors (i.e., social norms). We will review several areas of sexual attitudes, then follow with a discussion of the origins of some of these attitudes.

Many models explaining adolescent risk behavior, including sexual behavior, propose that adolescents' perceptions of potential consequences (risks and benefits) play an important role in adolescents' behavioral decision making (e.g., Beyth-Marom & Fischhoff, 1997; Fishbein & Ajzen, 1975; Reyna & Farley, 2006). Research examining the relationship between sexual behavior and sex-related positive and negative perceptions generally support these models, showing that adolescents are more likely to have sex if they believe sex will result in positive outcomes, and they are less likely to have sex if they perceive great chance of risk (Millstein & Halpern-Felsher, 2002). Data examining onset of sexual intercourse among female adolescents found that ambivalent (mixed positive and negative) perceptions of social and emotional risks and benefits predicted delayed intercourse among non-depressed females (Rink, Tricker, & Harvey, 2007). Two other studies found that perceptions of greater social and emotional risks and less social and emotional benefits predicted less likelihood of sexual debut among adolescents (Meier, 2003; Rostosky, Regnerus, & Wright, 2003). Some gender differences have been noted, with studies typically showing that adolescent females perceive higher sexual risks compared to their male counterparts, and males perceiving greater benefits than do adolescent females.

Sexual behavior is also largely influenced by positive motivations.

Sexual behavior is also largely influenced by positive motivations, including desires for physical pleasure or excitement, intimate personal relationships, peer approval or peer respect, and self-confidence and exploration. Ott and colleagues (2006) went a step beyond just examining perceptions of benefits to identify attitudinal factors that actually explain why an adolescent chooses to have sex. Specifically, they examined goals associated with sexual behavior, whether adolescents believed these goals would be met, and whether there were differences in goals and expectations by gender and sexual experience. In this study, adolescents first valued the goal of intimacy, followed by social status, and then sexual pleasure, although they expected that sex would most likely lead to pleasure, followed by intimacy, and then social status. Significant and important gender differences were found: adolescent females valued the goal of intimacy more than did males, whereas males valued pleasure more.

Adolescents perceive oral sex as significantly less risky than vaginal sex.

Adolescents' sexual attitudes clearly vary by the type of sexual behavior. For example, comparing perceptions associated with oral and vaginal sex, Halpern-Felsher and colleagues (2005) showed that adolescents perceive oral sex as significantly less risky than vaginal sex. These attitudinal differences were greater among adolescents who reported intentions to have oral sex in the next six months: for these adolescents, the differentiation between perceived risk for oral sex and vaginal sex is even greater. That is, they perceive that vaginal sex is much more likely to result in negative outcomes than will oral sex. Other attitudinal variables have also been explored. For example, Halpern-Felsher and colleagues (2005) showed that adolescents largely believed that it was not okay to have vaginal or oral sex with someone they are not dating, but they did agree that it was okay to have sex with someone they were dating or with whom they were in love. These attitudes did vary by type of sexual behavior, with adolescents believing it was more acceptable to have oral than vaginal sex, and that oral sex was less against their moral values than was vaginal sex.

Few studies have examined racial/ethnic differences in sex-related perceptions, or whether such differences in perceptions might account for observed racial/ethnic differences in rates of sexual behavior. Cuffee et al. (2007) examined racial differences in perceived sex-related social and emotional risks and benefits among white and African American adolescents. This study found that African American males perceived less sex-related shame and guilt than white males. There were no racial/ethnic differences in perceived benefits of sex. The authors also found that higher perceived benefits of sex predicted higher likelihood of sexual initiation among African American females, and higher perceived risks decreased the likelihood of sexual initiation for white males and females. Dzung and colleagues (2009) expanded this line of research to examine differences in health-related risks of vaginal sex, risk and benefit perceptions of oral sex, or differences in perceptions between white, Latino, and Asian adolescents. They found that, compared to white adolescents, Asian and to a lesser extent Latino adolescents generally perceived a greater chance of risks and a lower chance of benefits associated with either vaginal or oral sex. In general, adolescents who had engaged in vaginal and oral sex perceived lower risks and higher benefits from these behaviors, compared to adolescents who had not engaged. However, analyses did not reveal racial/ethnic differences in the relationship between sex-related risk and benefit perceptions and sexual behaviors.

It is important to note that adolescents also develop attitudes concerning not having sex. For example, Brady and Halpern-Felsher (2008) reported that adolescents' perceived consequences from not having sex included positive consequences such as having a good reputation, having friends proud, and feeling responsible. Negative perceived outcomes from not having sex included partner becoming angry, having a bad reputation, feeling regret or left out, and feeling like you let your partner down (Brady & Halpern-Felsher, 2008). In a recent article, Ott and Pfeiffer (2009) conducted a qualitative study to examine early adolescents' views of abstinence. Adolescent participants were between the ages of 11 and 14. Their answers fell into three main categories. Younger adolescents, especially the 11 year olds, viewed sex as "nasty" and not open for discussion with their peers. They thus viewed abstinence positively. These "nasty" attitudes were largely shaped by their beliefs that they would get into trouble if they had sex. A second category was "curiosity" about sex and the facts surrounding sexual behavior. These youth felt that abstinence was good, believing that sex should be limited until marriage or within the context of a monogamous relationship.

Finally, adolescents (all age 14) felt that sex was a normative part of development and recognized that they too would have sex at some point.

Factors Influencing Adolescents' Sexual Attitudes

While there are many studies identifying psychosocial and environmental influences on adolescent sexual behavior, few studies have examined factors that specifically influence adolescents' sexual attitudes. In this section, we review the limited literature on the role of parents, school, media, and religiosity. Although studies have not examined well the role of parental sexual attitudes on adolescents' sexual attitudes, a few studies have examined the role of parental sexual attitudes on adolescents' sexual behavior. For example, Dittus and Jaccard (2000) found that adolescents were less likely to have sexual intercourse if they believed their mothers disapproved of adolescent sexual behavior. Others have found that adolescents, especially younger adolescents, have more negative attitudes toward sex in part because of fear that they would get into trouble if they have sex (Ott & Pfeiffer, 2009), or if they believed their parents would disapprove of sex (Jaccard & Dittus, 2000).

Adolescents are constantly exposed to mixed messages about sexuality. On the one hand, adolescents see sex in the media portrayed in a very positive light, with sexual behavior often portrayed as a normal part of adolescent and adult life. It is not surprising then that adolescents' exposure to sex through various media outlets (including television and the Internet) has also been shown to shape adolescents' sexual attitudes. Braun-Courville and Rojas (2009), for example, found that adolescents exposed to sexually explicit Web sites had more permissive sexual attitudes than did youth with less exposure to these Web sites. It is thus not surprising that messages aimed at reducing or delaying adolescent sexuality are met with frustration, as the positive images of sex often drown out the health risk warnings.

Religiosity is another important factor shaping adolescent sexual attitudes and behavior, although again most studies examine the extent to which religion reduces sexual behavior rather than its impact on attitudes. As discussed by Uecker and colleagues (2008), adolescents who describe themselves as more religious and indicate that religion is an important part of their lives, are less likely to engage in any form of sexual behavior. This pattern is particularly strong among adolescents who actually attend religious services on a frequent basis (deVisser et al., 2007; see also Cotton et al., 2006; Rew & Wong, 2006).

Adolescents' bonding with school and relationships with peers also shapes their sexual attitudes. Bersamin and colleagues (2006) showed that adolescents who were more bonded to school were less likely to have vaginal or oral sex. Adolescents are also more likely to have favorable attitudes toward sex if they believe their friends are accepting of sexual behavior and if they believe more of their friends are having sex.

Summary

Adolescent sexual behavior varies greatly, ranging from kissing and petting, to non-coital behaviors such as oral sex and anal sex, to vaginal intercourse. Although rates of initiation and patterns of engagement in sexual activity depends on age, gender, race/ethnicity and type of sexual behavior, clearly the high school years mark the onset of sexual behavior for many youth. Understanding how, why, and when an adolescent decides to initiate sex, or abstain from sex, and why a particular type of sexual behavior will be chosen, is critical for the development of more effective public health campaigns aimed at delaying or preventing adolescent sexual behavior. An understanding of adolescents' sexual attitudes is likely to get us a step closer to understanding sexual behavior.

Many studies examining adolescents' sexual attitudes have been within the context of decision-making models. These models posit that engagement in any behavior, including sexual behavior, entails the weighing of perceived positive and negative outcomes, both of which are expected to predict behavior. These models have been largely supported, with data showing that not only does fear of risk reduce likelihood of engagement in sexual activity, but perceptions of benefits predict greater engagement. Adolescents' attitudes toward not having sex (abstinence) are also important to consider. While studies do show that adolescents have positive beliefs about delaying sexual activity, they also believe that abstinence entails some risk, including both social and personal risk.

Identifying factors that shape adolescents' sexual attitudes is more challenging, as studies typically examine the role of psychosocial and contextual variables directly on behavior and not necessarily moderated through attitudes. However, studies do show that factors such as parental attitudes toward adolescent sex, religiosity, the media, school bonding, and perceived peer social norms influence sexual attitudes.

The studies summarized within this article show the importance of considering the broad array of sexual attitudes that adolescents consider. Clearly it is not enough to deter adolescents away from sexual behavior by simple encouraging negative sexual attitudes. As adolescents develop and mature physically, cognitively, socially, and emotionally, they need information that helps them shape and weigh both positive and negative perceptions of having, as well as abstaining from sex, so that they can make the best decision possible.

References

Bersamin, M.M., Walker, S., Fisher, D.A., & Grube, J.W. (2006). Correlates of oral sex and vaginal intercourse in early and middle adolescence. *Journal of Research on Adolescence, 16,* 59–68.

Beyth-Marom, R., & Fischhoff, B. (1997). Adolescents' decisions about risks: A cognitive perspective. In J. Schulenberg, J.L. Maggs, & K. Hurrelmann (Eds.) *Health Risks and Developmental Transitions During Adolescence* (pp. 110–136). Cambridge University Press.

Brady, S.S., & Halpern-Felsher, B.L. (2007). Adolescents' reported consequences of having oral sex versus vaginal sex. *Pediatrics, 119,* 229–236.

Brady, S.S, & Halpern-Felsher, B.L. (2008). Social and emotional consequences of refraining from sexual activity among sexually experienced and inexperienced youths in California. *American Journal of Public Health, 98,* 162–168.

Braun-Courville, D.K., & Rohas, M. (2009). Exposure to sexually explicit Web sites and adolescent sexual attitudes and behavior. *Journal of Adolescent Health, 45,* 156–162.

Cornell, J.L., & Halpern-Felsher, B.L. (2006). Adolescents tell us why teens have oral sex. *Journal of Adolescent Health, 38,* 299–301.

Cotton, S., Zebracki, K., Rosenthal, S.L., Tsevat, J., & Drotar, D. (2006). Religion/spirituality and adolescent health outcomes: a review. *Journal of Adolescent Health, 38,* 472–480.

Cuffee, J.J., Hallfors, D.D., & Waller, M.W. (2007). Racial and gender differences in adolescent sexual attitudes and longitudinal associations with coital debut. *Journal of Adolescent Health, 41,* 19–26.

deVisser, R.O., Smith, A.M. Richters, J., & Rissel, C.E. (2007). Associations between religiosity and sexuality in a representative sample of Australian adults. *Archives of Sexual Behavior, 36,* 33–46.

Dittus, P.J., & Jaccard, J. (2000). Adolescents' perceptions of maternal disapproval of sex: relationship to sexual outcomes. *Journal of Adolescent Health, 26,* 268–278.

Dzung, V.X., Song, A.V., & Halpern-Felsher, B.L. (2009). Role of race/ethnicity on adolescents' perceptions of sex-related risks and benefits [abstract]. *Journal of Adolescent Health, 44,* S2.

Eaton, D.K., Kann, L., Kinchen, S., Shanklin, S., Ross, J., Hawkins, J., et al. (2008). Youth risk behavior surveillance—United States, 2007. *Morbidity and Mortality Weekly Report Surveillance Summary, 57,* 1–131.

Fishbein, M., & Ajzen, I. (1975). *Beliefs, Attitudes, Intention, and Behavior: An Introduction to Theory and Research.* Reading, MA: Addison-Wesley.

Grunbaum, J.A., Lowry, R., Kann, L., & Pateman, B. (2000). Prevalence of health risk behaviors among Asian American/ Pacific Islander high school students. *Journal of Adolescent Health, 27,* 322–330.

Halpern-Felsher, B.L., Cornell, J.L., Kropp, R.Y., & Tschann, J.M. (2005). Oral versus vaginal sex among adolescents: perceptions, attitudes, and behavior. *Pediatrics, 115,* 845–851.

Jaccard, J., & Dittus, P.J. (2000). Adolescent perceptions of maternal approval of birth control and sexual risk behavior. *American Journal of Public Health, 90,* 1,426–1,430.

Knopf, D.K., Park, J.M., Brindis, C.D., Mulye, T.P., & Irwin, C.E. (2007). What gets measured gets done: assessing data availability for adolescent populations. *Maternal and Child Health Journal, 11,* 335–345.

Lindberg, L.D., Jones, R., & Santelli, J.S. (2008). Noncoital sexual activities among adolescents. *Journal of Adolescent Health, 43,* 231–238.

Meier, A.M. (2003). Adolescents' transitions to first intercourse, religiosity, and attitudes about sex. *Social Forces, 81,* 1,031–1,052.

Millstein, S.G., & Halpern-Felsher, B.L. (2002). Perceptions of risk and vulnerability. *Journal of Adolescent Health, 31,* 10–27.

Mosher, W.D., Chandra, A., & Jones, J. (2005). Sexual behavior and selected health measures: Men and women 15–44 years of age, United States, 2002. Advance data from vital and health statistics; No 362. Hyattsville, MD: National Center for Health Statistics.

National Adolescent Health Information Center, University of California, San Francisco. (2007). *Fact Sheet on Reproductive Health: Adolescents and Young Adults.* Retrieved September 9, 2009, from http://nahic.ucsf.edu/downloads/ReproHlth2007.pdf.

Ott M.A., Millstein, S.G., Ofner, S., & Halpern-Felsher, B.L. (2006). Greater expectations: adolescents' positive motivations for sex. *Perspectives in Sexual Reproductive Health, 38,* 84–89.

Ott, M.A., & Pfeiffer, E.J. (2009). "That's nasty" to curiosity: early adolescent cognitions about sexual abstinence. *Journal of Adolescent Health, 44,* 575–581.

Rew, L., & Wong, J.Y. (2006). A systematic review of associations among religiosity/spirituality and adolescent health attitudes and behaviors. *Journal of Adolescent Health, 38,* 433–442.

Reyna, V.F., & Farley, F. (2006). Risk and rationality in adolescent decision making. Implications for theory, practice, and public policy. *Psychological Science in the Public Interest, 7,* 1–44.

Rink, E., Tricker, R., & Harvey, S.M. (2007). Onset of sexual intercourse among female adolescents: the influence of perceptions, depression, and ecological factors. *Journal of Adolescent Health, 41,* 398–406.

Rostosky S.S., Regnerus M.D., & Wright M.L. (2003). Coital debut: the role of religiosity and sex attitudes in the Add Health Survey. *Journal of Sex Research, 40,* 358–367.

Schuster, M.A., Bell, R.M., Nakajima, G.A., & Kanouse, D.E. (1998). The sexual practices of Asian and Pacific Islander high school students. *Journal of Adolescent Health, 23,* 221–31.

Uecker, J.E., Angotti, N., & Regnerus, M.D. (2008). Going most of the way: "technical virginity" among American adolescents. *Social Science Research, 37,* 1,200–1,215.

Critical Thinking

1. Why is the understanding of teens' attitudes regarding sexual behaviors a key to understanding why they choose to engage or not engage in sex?

2. What sexual behaviors do most teens initiate and continue?

3. What are the negative and positive outcomes experienced by adolescent sexual behavior?

4. How do environmental influences help shape adolescent's sexual attitudes?

Dr. Bonnie Halpern-Felsher (bonnie.halpernfelsher@ucsf.edu) is an Associate Professor in the Division of Adolescent Medicine, Department of Pediatrics, University of California, San Francisco. She is also the Associate Director of the General Pediatrics Fellowships, and is a faculty member at UCSF's Psychology and Medicine Post-doctoral Program, The Center for Health and Community, the Center for Tobacco Control Research and Education, the Comprehensive Cancer Center, and the Robert Wood Johnson Scholars Program. Dr. Halpern-Felsher is a developmental psychologist whose research has focused on cognitive and psychosocial factors involved in health-related decision making, perceptions of risk and vulnerability, health communication, and risk behavior; and she has published in each of these areas. **Yana Reznik** is a college student at the University of San Francisco. She is also a Research Assistant for the University of San Francisco California Department of Pediatrics, Division of Adolescent Medicine Research and Policy Center for Childhood and Adolescence. She has also published in the Permanente Journal focusing on Adolescent Sexual Health. Yana Reznik is an full-time undergraduate Pre-Medical Student with a Biology and Neuroscience Major.

From *The Prevention Researcher,* November 2009, pp. 3–6. Copyright © 2009 by Integrated Research Services, Inc. Reprinted by permission.

Sex, Sexuality, Sexting, and SexEd

Adolescents and the Media

Jane D. Brown, PhD, Sarah Keller, PhD, and Susannah Stern, PhD

Adolescents in the United States spend six to seven hours a day with some form of media, including television, music, movies, magazines, the Internet, and smart cell phones (Roberts, Foehr, & Rideout, 2005). These media have become important sex educators as they include frequent discussion and portrayals of sexual behavior that affect adolescents' conceptions of sexual attractiveness, romantic relationships, and sexual behavior. Here we summarize briefly what is known about the use, content and effects of sexual media among adolescents, consider how new media forms such as the Internet and cell phones are being used, and finally, discuss how the media can also be used to promote healthy sexual behavior.

Traditional Media Use, Content, and Effects

As can be seen in Table 1, adolescents still spend a great deal of time each day using what we might call the "traditional" media—television, radio, movies, magazines. Much of the content in each of these media contains discussion and depictions of some aspect of sexuality and/or sexual behavior, although little of the content includes any mention or depiction of the possible risks or responsibilities of early, unprotected sexual behavior (Hust et al., 2008). Exposure to such content is related to sexual outcomes, ranging from body dissatisfaction, to earlier sexual intercourse, less contraceptive use, and even pregnancy (for a comprehensive review see Brown & Strasburger, 2007).

Media use and effects on sexuality vary dramatically by a number of factors, including sexual maturity, gender, and race. Studies have shown, for example, that earlier maturing girls are more likely to be interested in sexual content in the media than their less physically mature agemates (Brown, Halpern, & L'Engle, 2005). One study found that of 150 television programs frequently viewed by early adolescents, only four were watched by more than one-third of both black and white adolescents. Girls and boys also differed dramatically in their most frequently watched television programs, with girls preferring more relationship-oriented shows and boys preferring sports and action-adventure (Brown & Pardun, 2004).

The wide array of media available to teens provides the opportunity for choosing different kinds of content. Some apparently seek sexual content while others would rather not see it. L'Engle and colleagues (2007) identified four patterns of sexual media use among early adolescents (12 to 14 years old) which suggested that some teens also will be more susceptible to what they see about sex in the media than others, given their motivations and prior sexual experience. The teens they called "Virgin Valedictorians," for example, were the least interested in sexual media content and were focusing on doing well in school, while the "Sexual Sophisticates" preferred sexual content, including pornography, and were the most likely to have had sexual relationships.

Today most traditional media content is accessible on the Internet, and soon will be widely available 24/7 on handheld devices. Research on how teens are using such new media forms for learning about sex is just getting started, but some recent studies provide insight about trends.

New Media Use, Content, and Effects

The new media, also sometimes called digital media, include text messaging on cell phones, MP3 players (e.g., iPods), blogs or chat rooms on Web sites, and Internet social networking sites (SNS) such as Facebook or MySpace, where many users can simultaneously create and communicate on the same Web pages.

As can be seen in Table 2, adolescents are already using the new media to engage in activities relevant to sex and sexuality. However, those who speak sweepingly of the "dangers" or "promise" of the new media, oversimplify a dynamic and complex set of practices and potential effects.

Initial research suggests that adolescents, especially boys, are using pornography on the Internet. According to surveys of Dutch adolescents (12 to 17 years old) and young U.S. teens (12 to 14 years old), about 30% of females and 50 to 70% of males have viewed sexually explicit images online. Longitudinal studies have found that such exposure predicts less progressive gender role attitudes and perpetration of sexual harassment

Table 1 Traditional Media: Illustrative Findings of Adolescents' Use and the Effects of Sexual Content

Medium/Channels	Use by Adolescents (12–17 years old)	Sexual Content	Sexual Attitudes/Behavior Implications
Television	• Average 12 hours per week • Males average about 1.5 hours more per week than females (Ypulse.com, 2009)	• 70% top teen programs include sex • 10% mention risk/responsibility of sexual behavior (Kunkel et al., 2005)	Frequent exposure to sexual TV content hastens sexual initiation and early pregnancy (Chandra et al., 2008; Collins et al., 2004).
Radio/Music	• Average 16 hours per week • 86% have CD/MP3 player in bedroom • 52% listen to online radio (NPD Group, 2009)	• 37% popular songs refer to sexual activity • 2/3 (most commonly Rap) include degrading sex (Primack et al., 2008)	Frequent exposure to sexually degrading music is associated with earlier sexual intercourse (Primack et al., 2009).
Movies	• Average 2 movies per month in theater • Prefer action-adventure, comedies (Ypulse.com, 2009)	• 25% of teen movie characters engage in sexual intercourse, often as way to achieve specific ends • Contraception rarely portrayed (Stern, 2005)	Exposure to X-rated movies linked to more sexual partners and less contraceptive use among black adolescent urban females (Wingood et al., 2001).
Magazines	• 63% of teens read a magazine for fun in last month (Chartier, 2008) • Boys prefer sports, activity magazines; girls prefer fashion, celebrity magazines	• Teen girl magazines portray girls as obsessed with guys, and their own appearance (Wray & Steele, 2002) • Teen boys' magazines are more visually suggestive, all males heterosexual (Batchelor, Kitzinger, et al., 2004)	Reading fashion, sports, and health/fitness magazines related to body image and eating disturbances for both adolescent boys and girls (Botta, 2003).

for males, and sexual uncertainty, uncommitted sexual exploration (i.e., one-night stands, hooking up), earlier oral sex and sexual intercourse for both males and females (Brown & L'Engle, 2009; Peter & Valkenburg, 2006, 2008a, b).

Adolescents also now have greater opportunity than ever before to present themselves publicly to a geographically disparate audience. Many young people choose to display information about their sexuality and sexual lives, such as by indicating their sexual orientations on their SNS profiles, posting stories and poems about sexual desire and experience on blogs, sharing naked or semi-naked pictures and videos of themselves on SNS profiles and via mobile phones ("sexting"), and discussing sexual practices on SNS and blogs. Recent studies (notably, none of which employed a true probability sample) indicate that between one-tenth to one-fifth of teens share "inappropriate" images, references to sexual activity, and/or naked or semi-naked pictures of themselves with others electronically (Moreno et al., 2009a; National Campaign to Prevent Teen & Unplanned Pregnancy, 2009).

Can the act of sharing such sexual content be beneficial for teens in any way? Many would say yes. In fact, it has been repeatedly argued that sexual self-expression on the Internet can be functional for adolescents. The Internet provides a relatively safe space for teens to explore and define themselves

as sexual beings (Stern, 2002). Different forums offer distinct opportunities; for example, SNS allow users to craft themselves as sexual (or not-yet-sexual) people to their friends, compelling reflection on who they are and would like to be, and to initiate and maintain "dating" relationships that can seem more intimidating in the real world (Subrahmanyam, Greenfield, & Tynes, 2004).

Research on gay and lesbian youth, in particular, has demonstrated the value of the Internet as a space for experimentation and self-definition that is often difficult or dangerous in offline spaces. On the Internet, GLBT youth discuss a variety of sexual identities and queer politics, as well as seek partners, navigate the coming out process, and frankly discuss sexual practices, including safer sex (Bond, Hefner, & Drogos, 2008).

The Internet also allows those who have historically been discouraged from exploring or asserting sexual desire (especially adolescent girls) an opportunity to recognize their own agency by expressing such feelings openly. The type of validation they sometimes receive can empower young people to accept and assert agency in their own offline relationships. Communicating with unknown yet similar others can also be invaluable for adolescents in another way: via the Internet, young people with sexual health concerns or problems can find peers in similar circumstances whose empathy and companionship can provide life-saving emotional connection. For example, a teen experiencing emotional trauma who locates others in similar straits may feel less alone and overwhelmed, and thus be more inclined to engage in thoughtful reflection about his or her next steps (Keller & Balter-Reitz, 2007).

There are, however, several legitimate concerns regarding teens' sharing of sexual content in the new media. One concern is that sexual content posted by teens may prompt the perception among teen viewers that sex is normal, even glamorous, and risk-free (Moreno et al., 2009a). Teens who see risky sexual practices that do not indicate negative consequences may be more likely to adopt the behaviors that are referenced. In consequence, Moreno et al. (2009b) suggest, user-generated sexual content may also increase the pressure virginal teens feel to become sexually active.

Another concern is that young people, especially girls, who share provocative or sexual imagery of themselves engage in a form of self-objectification in which young people "learn to think of and treat their own bodies as objects of others' desires." In so doing, young people may "internalize an observer's perspective on their physical selves and learn to treat themselves as objects to be looked at and evaluated for their appearance" (American Psychological Association, 2007, p. 18). The self-objectification involved in "sexting" has received scrutiny

recently. Reputations are harmed, relationships broken, and friendships shattered when receivers of naked images violate senders' trust by sending the images on to others. Despite the growing moral panic surrounding sexting, Goodman (2009) suggested that "there is nothing particularly new about young people taking pictures of themselves. It's as old as the Polaroid. What's different now is that teenagers can be their own paparazzi and be vulnerable to the humiliation once reserved for celebrities" (p. 15). The ease of wide distribution also may increase the intensity and risks of such behavior.

Teens who have poor health literacy are more likely to search for sexual health information using slang terms, which may lead to less credible Web sites.

The kinds of sexual content teens post on SNS may also affect how their friends and potential sexual partners treat them, likely in ways that reinforce the behaviors/identities presented. So, for example, a teen girl who presents herself as very sexual through a provocative picture and content indicating

Table 2 New Media: Illustrative Findings of Adolescents' Use and Effects of Sexual Content

Medium/Channels	Use by Adolescents (12–17 years old)	Sexual Content	Sexual Attitudes/Behavior Implications
Internet	• Average 12.5 hours online per week • Are primarily online for email, IM/SNS, and gaming (Chartier, 2008) • 30% of females, 70% of males view Internet porn (Peter & Valkenburg, 2006)	• Sexual health information available • Sexually explicit images/pornography more accessible than ever before (Brown & L'Engle, 2009)	• 44% report using the Internet to find sexual health information (KFF, 2003) • Exposure to pornography predicts sexual uncertainty, uncommitted sexual exploration, earlier oral sex, and earlier intercourse (Brown & L'Engle, 2009; Peter & Valkenburg, 2008 a, b)
Social Networking Sites	• 38% of tweens (12–14) and 77% of teens (15–17) have a SNS profile • SNS are especially popular among older females: 89% of 15- to 17-year-old girls have SNS (Lenhart, 2009)	• Platform for sexual self-expression and finding like-minded teens (i.e., gay, abstinent) • About 1 in 10 teens are posting sexually suggestive images online (Moreno et al., 2009a)	Little research has yet been reported about the sexual effects of SNS.

Cell Phones	• Have cell phone:
	  52% of 12–13 year olds
	  72% of 14–16 year olds
	  84% of 17 year olds
	• 58% send text messages to friends (38% daily)(Lenhart, 2009)
		• Sexual health information available
		• About 1 in 5 teens are "sexting" (National Campaign, 2009)
			Little research has yet been reported about the sexual effects of cell phones.

interest in sex may find herself labeled a "slut" by some and be more likely to encounter sexual solicitations. A recent study of teen girls who had been abused earlier in life found that those who created provocative avatars (an icon representing a person in cyberspace) were more likely to receive sexual solicitations from strangers (Noll et al., 2009).

Perhaps most worrisome is the possibility that the display of sexual content online increases teens' chances of online victimization. Wolak and colleagues (2008) have conducted a series of national studies that find that teens who send personal information or talk online to strangers about sex are at greatest risk for sexual victimization, since they are most likely to receive sexual solicitations. Other categories of teens who are known to be at greater risk include those with histories of sexual abuse, sexual orientation concerns, and patterns of off- and online risk taking. Teens who respond to sexual solicitations are at risk not only for predation, but also for potential illness. Studies show that sex partners who meet online engage in higher-risk sexual behaviors, and are therefore at higher risk of acquiring sexually transmitted illnesses, than do partners who meet through conventional means (McFarlane, Ross, & Elford, 2004).

New Media as Sexual Health Educators

The newest forms of media also offer a variety of strategies for getting sexual health information to youth. New media can be successful channels for sex education for precisely the same reasons that youth are such avid users. Young people use digital media for exploring and maintaining social, sexual, and romantic relationships because of presumed safety, perceived anonymity, transcendence from adult control, 24/7 availability, and the ability to communicate with peers.

Young audiences are frequent users of new media for sexual health information. Hundreds, if not thousands, of sexual health sites are maintained online, and studies show that about a quarter or more of online teens access the Internet to find information about sex, sexually transmitted diseases, and pregnancy (Lenhart, Madden, & Hitlin, 2005). Sites like www.iwannaknow.org provide interactive games that may foster safe sex negotiation. In one study, 41% of young adults said they had changed their behavior because of health information they found online, and almost half had contacted a health care provider as a result (Ybarra & Suman, 2008).

Most teens (and youth advocates) agree that the Internet is a valuable place to turn for answers to embarrassing sex-related questions, to learn more about uncomfortable topics, to familiarize themselves with intimate body parts, and to gain perspective on conditions and sexual practices. Sexual health Web sites can also provide ideas about how to handle sexual situations, how to use birth control, and how to seek help when needed (Borzekowski & Rickert, 2001). Online sources may offer a sense of anonymity that may encourage teenagers to ask questions they would feel uncomfortable asking in person.

There are two main concerns associated with the use of new media to learn about sex and sexual health. First is the possibility that the information teens access and/or receive is inaccurate or misleading. Since adolescents have shown little proclivity to assess the credibility of Web sites (basing their assessments on how "professional" sites look rather than on who built the site and why) (Fidel, Davies, & Douglass, 1999), it seems reasonable to speculate that teens searching online may receive information that misinforms them, or is misinterpreted by them, potentially to their detriment. This may especially be the case when Web sites created for teens primarily or exclusively use medical terminology to refer to anatomy, sexual practices, and conditions. In particular, teens who have poor health literacy (who are also more likely to be at risk for sexually transmitted diseases), are more likely to search for sexual health information using slang terms, which may lead to less credible Web sites (Cecchino & Morgan, 2009). Furthermore, the several content analyses that have looked at safe sex Web site design have found that sites promote condom use and abstinence, but few discuss other safe sex strategies, such as reducing the number of partners, reducing casual sex, or delaying first intercourse (Keller et al., 2004; Noar et al., 2006).

A second concern associated with the use of new media to learn about sex and sexual health is that teens who turn to the Internet for answers may turn away from real people in their lives. Parents, community members, teachers, and doctors from teens' own communities may better understand the unique needs and situations of individual teens. Moreover, many adults feel a strong desire to communicate certain values about sex to their own teens and dislike the notion that strangers (whether they be Web site creators or senders of sex-ed text messages) might promote or at least not condemn sexual thoughts and activities among teens.

Media Interventions for Sexual Health

Only a handful of small-scale new media interventions for adolescents' sexual health have been systematically evaluated so far. Most of these evaluations have focused on interventions of software administered in classroom settings. Results suggest that computer-based programs may be a cost effective and easily replicable means of providing teens with basic information and skills necessary to prevent pregnancy, STDs, and HIV.

AIDS Interactive, for example, is a program using stories, role models, and demonstrations to provide information about HIV prevention. It was tested with 152 college students, who showed significantly higher HIV knowledge and intentions to practice safe sex with current partners (Evans et al., 2000). Students who interacted with a computer-based curriculum called Reducing the Risk outperformed other students on knowledge, condom self-efficacy, attitudes toward waiting to have sex, and perceived susceptibility to HIV (Roberto et al., 2007). Lightfoot, Comulada & Stover (2007) found that the online version of Project LIGHT ("Living in Good Health Together"), a sexuality education program targeted at high-risk adults and adolescents, was more effective than the in-person version.

Some interventions combine new and old media. A clinic-based approach that used PowerPoint presentations with links to trusted sexual health Web sites on waiting room computers showed that teenagers who viewed the presentation were more likely than others to use two methods of contraception or to use a condom every time they had sex (Howard, 2009). It's Your Sex Life (a.k.a. "Think MTV"), a campaign co-sponsored by MTV and the Kaiser Family Foundation (2003), used TV programming, TV public service announcements, and a comprehensive Web site (www.think.mtv.com). A 2003 survey of MTV viewers (ages 16 to 24) found that those who had seen campaign ads were more likely to use condoms (73%), wait to have sex (60%), and to talk with a partner about safe sex (49%).

Technologies such as cell phones and SNS offer much more interactivity, although evaluations of these approaches are scarce. Some campaigns have been successful in using a SNS component. The National Campaign to Prevent Teen and Unplanned Pregnancy partnered with MySpace to produce the "Stay Teen" PSA contest. In its first month, the contest attracted 100,000 page views and 8,000 friends.

All young people may not like having adults use social networking sites to promote family planning and STD clinics because they see it as "Their Space." A survey of 994 teenagers in San Francisco found that fewer than half (41%) were willing to add a clinic as a friend on their own SNS (Ralph, 2009).

In another study, a physician sent an email to 190 teens she had never met who had posted sexual and other risky content on SNS profiles. The email from "Dr. Meg" indicated concern with the teens' risky posts, provided information about privacy settings, offered a link to a Web site where a free STD kit could be obtained, and encouraged teens with questions to talk to parents, doctors, or to email her back. The results suggested the email accounted for a significant number of the contacted teens removing the risky content from their own pages or changing their privacy settings (Moreno et al., 2009b).

Capitalizing on teens' love affair with cell phones, Internet Sexuality Information Services, Inc. (ISIS), a nonprofit based in Oakland, California, partnered with the San Francisco Department of Public Health to develop a sexual health text messaging service for youth. SexInfo allows teens to use their cell phones in a manner similar to when they vote for their favorite American Idol contestant. The most popular call requests have been: "A1 if ur condom broke," "C3 to find out about STIs," and "B1 if u think ur pregnant." Preliminary data showed that 4,500 callers used the service during the first 25 weeks; 2,500 of the calls led to referrals and requests for more information (Levine et al., 2008).

ISIS also launched a Web site (www.inSPOT.org) that offers information about getting tested and treatment. It also enables people with STDs to send anonymous email warnings to their partners. The site sends e-cards to notify people that they may have been exposed to an infection (e.g., "Sometimes there are strings attached. I got diagnosed with STDs since we were together. Get checked out soon.") (Honan, 2008).

Conclusions

It is clear that both the new and traditional media are being used by adolescents as they learn more about their developing sexuality. Much of existing media content, unfortunately, is not designed to result in healthy sexuality. Both new and older forms of media can be used to promote healthier sexuality among adolescents, however. Certainly we need to know more—both in terms of the types of interventions possible with traditional and new media, and from evaluations to ensure that time and funds are well spent.

Most existing interventions have failed to target messages to specific audiences, such as sexual minorities or adolescents with varying levels of sexual experience. Interventions need to be targeted not only by style and content but also by channel, since different categories of teenagers use new technologies differently. Internet, MP3, and cell phone technologies offer not only more cost-effective dissemination, but also the ability to reach a wider diversity of audiences (including young adolescents) in ways never before possible. Poorer youth, for example, may be reached more effectively with text messages since they are less likely to have access to or use computers, except for schoolwork (Pascoe, 2009).

Table 3 Suggestions and Resources for Adults Working with Adolescents

SUGGESTIONS	RESOURCES
Acknowledge normality and value of using new media to explore sexuality and romantic relationships. Direct teens to the best Web sites.	www.sexetc.org www.iwannaknow.org www.amplifyyourvoice.org www.thenationalcampaign.org
Educate teens about how to assess the credibility of the Web sites they consult for sexual health information.	American Library Association: www.ala.org/ala/mgrps/divs/lita
Encourage teens to use privacy settings on social networking sites. Discourage teens from communicating sexual behavior and preferences, and sending sexual content online, especially to strangers.	Federal Trade Commission: *Social Networking Sites: Safety Tips for Tweens and Teens* www.ftc.gov/bcp/edu/pubs/consumer/tech/tec14.shtm
Educate teens about the pitfalls (e.g., statutory rape laws in most states) of sexual relationships with adults (Wolak et al., 2008).	Statutory Rape Laws by State: www.cga.ct.gov/2003/olrdata/jud/rpt/2003-R-0376.htm

In sum, although adolescents are using digital media to access sexual health information, such media are not yet filling the sexual health gap. Young users need to be taught how to assess the credibility of online information, and parents and others who work with young people need to know about credible sexual health Web sites and content in traditional media that promotes healthier sexual behavior so they can help steer adolescents in the right direction (See Table 3).

References

American Psychological Association (2007). *Report of the APA Task Force on the Sexualization of Girls.* Retrieved Feb. 19, 2007 from www.apa.org/pi/wpo/sexualizationsum.html.

Batchelor, S.A., Kitzinger, J., & Burtney, E. (2004). Representing young people's sexuality in the "youth" media. *Health Education Research, 19,* 669–676.

Bond, B., Hefner, V., & Drogos, K. (2008). Information-seeking practices during the sexual development of lesbian, gay, and bisexual individuals: The influence and effects of coming out in a mediated environment. *Sexuality & Culture,* 13(1), 32–51.

Borzekowski, D., & Rickert (2001). Adolescent cybersurfing for health information: A new resource that crosses barriers. *Archives of Pediatrics & Adolescent Medicine, 155*(7), 813–817.

Botta, R. (2003). For your health? The relationship between magazine reading and adolescents' body image and eating disturbances. *Sex Roles,* 48(9–10), 389–399.

Brown, J.D., Halpern, C.T., & L'Engle, K.L. (2005). Mass media as a sexual super peer for early maturing girls. *Journal of Adolescent Health,* 36(5), 420–427.

Brown, J.D., & L'Engle, K.L. (2009). X-Rated: Sexual attitudes and behaviors associated with U.S. early adolescents' exposure to sexually explicit media. *Communication Research,* 36(1), 129–151.

Brown, J.D., & Pardun, C.J. (2004). Little in common: Racial and gender differences in adolescents' TV diets. *Journal of Broadcasting and Electronic Media,* 48(2), 266–278.

Brown, J.D., & Strasburger, V.C. (2007). From Calvin Klein, to Paris Hilton and MySpace: Adolescents, sex & the media. In M. Blythe & S. Rosenthal (Eds.) *Adolescent Sexuality, Adolescent Medicine: State of the Art Reviews,* 18(3), 484–507.

Cecchino, N., & Morgan, S. (2009). Use of urban adolescent natural language to access sexual health information and education. *Journal of Consumer Health on the Internet,* 13(1), 31–42.

Chandra, A., Martino, S., Collins, R., Elliott, M., Berry, S., Kanouse, D., & Miu, A. (2008). Does watching sex on television predict teen pregnancy? Findings from a national longitudinal survey of youth. *Pediatrics,* 122(5), 1,047–1,054.

Chartier, D. (2008). Study: Teens dropping rags, radio for web, games, and TV. Retrieved June 1, 2009 from http://arstechnica.com/old/content/2008/06/ study-teens-dropping-rags-radio-for-web-games-and-tv.ars.

Collins, R., Elliott, M., Berry, S., Kanouse, D., Kunkel, D., et al. (2004). Watching sex on television predicts adolescent initiation of sexual behavior. *Pediatrics,* 114(3), E280–E289.

Evans, A.E., Edmundson-Drane, E.W., & Harris, K.K. (2000). Computer-assisted instruction: An effective instructional method for HIV prevention education? *Journal of Adolescent Health,* 26, 244–251.

Fidel, R., Davies, R., & Douglass, M. (1999). A visit to the information mall: Web searching behavior of high school students. *Journal of the American Society for Information Science,* 50(1), 24–37.

Goodman, E. (2009, April 24). Is 'sexting' the same as porn? *The Boston Globe,* Opinion, p. 15.

Honan, E. (2008). Website allows anonymous warnings of STD infections. *Reuters,* Feb. 14, 2008.

Howard, M. (2009). *Reducing Teen Health Disparities Through Technology.* Presented at Virtual Sex Ed: Youth, Race, Sex and New Media conference, University of Chicago, June 4.

Hust, S., Brown, J.D., & L'Engle, K. (2008). Boys will be boys and girls better be prepared: An analysis of the rare sexual health messages in young adolescents' media. *Mass Communication and Society,* 11:1–21.

Internet Sexuality Information Service (ISIS). (2008). In brief: What if ur undies had the last word? Retrieved April 24, 2008, from www.undiescon-test.org.

Kaiser Family Foundation (2003). *Reaching the MTV Generation: Recent Research on the Impact of the Kaiser Family Foundation Campaign on Sexual Health.* Menlo Park, CA: Henry J. Kaiser Family Foundation.

Keller, S., & Balter-Reitz, S. (2007). Censoring thinspiration: The debate over pro-anorexic websites. *Free Speech Yearbook,* 42, 79–90.

Keller, S., LaBelle, H., Karimi, N., & Gupta, S. (2004). Talking about STD/HIV prevention: A look at communication online. *AIDS Care,* 16(8), 997–992.

Kunkel, D., Eyal, K., Finnerty, K., Biely, E., & Donnerstein, E. (2005). *Sex on TV 4: A Biennial Report to the Kaiser Family Foundation.* Menlo Park: CA: Kaiser Family Foundation.

L'Engle, K.L., Brown, J.D., Romocki, L.S., & Kenneavy, K. (2007, May). *Adolescents' Sexual Self-Concepts and Media Use Patterns: Implications for Sexual Health Communication.* Paper presented at the International Communication Association (ICA) conference, San Francisco, CA.

Lenhart, A. (2009). *Teens and Social Media: An Overview.* Pew Internet & American Life Project. Retrieved June 1, 2009 from http://pewinternet.org/Presentations/ 2009/17-Teens-andSocial-Media-An-Overview.aspx.

Lenhart, A., Madden, M., & Hitlin, P. (2005). *Teens and Technology.* Washington, D.C.: Pew Internet & American Life Project.

Levine, D., McCright, J., Dobkin, L., Woodruff, A., & Klausner, J. (2008). SexInfo: A sexual health text messaging service for San Francisco youth. *American Journal of Public Health,* 98, 393–395.

Lightfoot, M., Comulada, W.S., & Stover, G. (2007). Computerized HIV preventive intervention for adolescents: Indications of efficacy. *American Journal of Public Health,* 97(6), 1,027–1,031.

McFarlane, M., Ross, M.W., & Elford, J. (2004). The Internet and HIV/STD prevention. *AIDS Care,* 16(8), 929–930.

Moreno, M., Parks, M., Zimmerman, F., Brito, T., & Christakis, D. (2009a). Display of health risk behaviors on MySpace by adolescents. *Archives of Pediatric and Adolescent Medicine,* 163, 27–34.

Moreno, M., VanderStoep, A., Parks, M., Zimmerman, F., Kurth, A., & Christakis, D. (2009b). Reducing at-risk adolescents' display of risk behavior on a social networking web site. *Archives of Pediatric and Adolescent Medicine,* 163, 35–41.

National Campaign to Prevent Teen & Unplanned Pregnancy (2009). Sex and tech: Results from a survey of teens and young adults. Retrieved June 1, 2009 from www.thenationalcampaign.org/sextech/PDF/SexTech_Summary.pdf.

Noar, S., Clark, A., Cole, C., & Lustria, M. (2006). Review of interactive safer sex websites: Practice and potential. *Health Communication*, 20(3), 233–241.

Noll, J., Shenk, C., Barnes, J., & Putnam, F. (2009). Childhood abuse, avatar choices, and other risk factors associated with Internet-initiated victimization of adolescent girls. *Pediatrics*, 123, 1,078–1,083.

NPD Group (March 31, 2009). Always a bellwether for the music industry, teens are changing how they interact with music. Press Release. Retrieved June 1, 2009 from www.npd.com/press/releases/press_090331a.html.

Pascoe, C.J. (2009). *Encouraging Sexual Literacy in a Digital Age: Teens, Sexuality and New Media.* Presented at Virtual Sex Ed: Youth, Race, Sex and New Media conference, University of Chicago, Chicago, IL, June 4.

Peter, J., & Valkenburg, P.M. (2006). Adolescents' exposure to sexually explicit material on the Internet. *Communication Research*, 33, 178–204.

Peter, J., & Valkenburg, P.M. (2008a). Adolescents' exposure to sexually explicit Internet material, sexual uncertainty, and attitudes toward uncommitted sexual exploration: Is there a link? *Communication Research*, 35(5), 579–601.

Peter, J., & Valkenburg, P.M. (2008b). Adolescents' exposure to sexually explicit Internet material and sexual preoccupancy: A three-wave panel study. *Media Psychology*, 11, 207–234.

Primack, B., Douglas, E.L., Fine, M.J., & Dalton, M.A., (2009). Exposure to sexual lyrics and sexual experience among urban adolescents. *American Journal of Preventive Medicine*, 36(4), 317–323.

Primack, B., Gold, M.A., Schwarz, E.B., & Dalton, M.A. (2008). Degrading and non-degrading sex in popular music: A content analysis. *Public Health Reports*, 123, 593–600.

Ralph, L. (2009). *Finding Youth in TheirSpace: Using SNS to Connect Youth to Sexual Health Services.* Presented at Virtual Sex Ed: Youth, Race, Sex and New Media conference, University of Chicago, Chicago, IL, June 4.

Roberto, A., Zimmerman, R., Carlyle, K., Abner, E., Cupp, P., & Hansen, G. (2007). The effects of a computer-based pregnancy, STD, and HIV prevention intervention: A nine-school trial. *Health Communication*, 21(2), 115–124.

Roberts, D., Foehr, U., & Rideout, V. (2005). *Generation M: Media in the Lives of 8–18 Year-olds.* Menlo Park CA: Kaiser Family Foundation.

Stern, S. (2002). Sexual selves on the World Wide Web: Adolescent girls' home pages as sites for sexual self expression. In J.D. Brown, J.R. Steele,. & K. Walsh-Childers (Eds.) *Sexual Teens, Sexual Media*, (pp. 265–286). Mahwah, NJ: Lawrence Erlbaum.

Stern, S. (2005). Self-absorbed, dangerous, and disengaged: What popular films tell us about teenagers. *Mass Communication & Society*, 8, 23–38.

Subrahmanyam, K., Greenfield, P., & Tynes, B. (2004). Constructing sexuality and identity in an online teen chat room. *Journal of Applied Developmental Psychology*, 25(6), 651–666.

Wingood, G., DiClemente, R.J., Harrington, K., Davies, S., Hook, E.W., & Oh, M.K. (2001). Exposure to X-rated movies and adolescents' sexual and contraceptive-related attitudes and behaviors. *Pediatrics*, 107(5), 1,116–1,119.

Wolak, J., Finkelhor, D., Mitchell, K., & Ybarra, M. (2008). Online 'predators' and their victims: Myths, realities, and implications for prevention and treatment. *American Psychologist*, 62(2), 111–128.

Wray, J., & Steele, J. (2002). Girls in print: Figuring out what it means to be a girl. In J.D. Brown, J.R. Steele, & K. Walsh-Childers (Eds.), *Sexual Teens, Sexual Media* (pp. 191–208). Mahwah, NJ: Lawrence Erlbaum.

Ybarra, M.L., & Suman, M. (2008). Reasons, assessments, and actions taken: Sex and age differences in uses of Internet health information. *Health Education Research, Vol.* 23(3), 512–521.

Ypulse: *Youth marketing to teens, tweens & Generation Y* (2009). Retrieved June 1, 2009 from www.ypulse.com/teens-still-watching-tv-tweens-going-green-more.

Critical Thinking

1. How many hours a day do most teenagers spend with some form of media?

2. How are teens using the new media to learn about sex?

3. How can the new media be employed to promote healthier sexual behavior?

4. What specific media was considered in the author's study on media and sexual behavior and attitudes?

JANE D. BROWN, PHD (Jane_Brown@unc.edu) is the James L. Knight Professor in the School of Journalism and Mass Communication at the University of North Carolina in Chapel Hill. She has spent more than 25 years studying how adolescents use and are affected by the media. **SARAH N. KELLER, PHD** Associate Professor of Communication, Montana State University-Billings, is an expert in public health communication and evaluation. **SUSANNAH R. STERN, PHD** is an Associate Professor in Communication Studies at the University of San Diego. Her research investigates how children and teens use and make sense of media, how young people are targeted as media consumers, and how they are affected by electronic media.

Teens, Porn and the Digital Age

From Shame to Social Acceptability

Todd Melby

In the digital age, porn is ubiquitous. Graphic images and video clips—depicting oral sex, anal sex, multiple men engaged in sexual activity with a single woman—are only a computer click away.

One estimate puts the number of sexually explicit web pages at 400 million. And counting. A teenager or pre-teen might see hundreds of such images before talking to a parent or teacher about what constitutes a sexually healthy relationship.

And that worries some observers.

Journalist Eric Spitznagel wrote an article for *Details* magazine titled "How Internet Porn is Changing Teen Sex." The thirty-something reporter frets about the easy accessibility of online sex scenes showing "gang bangs" and other acts not usually described in these pages.

"Any day now," Spitznagel writes, half-joking. "Some poor kid may actually go blind masturbating."

A 2008 study found that 93 percent of boys and 62 percent of girls viewed online pornography prior to age 18. "The Nature and Dynamics of Internet Pornography Exposure for Youth," by Chiara Sabina, PhD, and study co-authors, was published in *CyberPsychology & Behavior.*

Sabina's survey of 594 American college students found very little viewing of Internet porn by 8-, 9- and 10-year-olds boys (less than 2 percent for each age group), but an uptick in first exposure to online porn by age 11 (11 percent), age 12 (16 percent) and age 13 (21 percent). The mean age of first exposure was 14.3 for boys and 14.8 for girls.

The prevalence and frequency of teen porn viewing has been on the mind of Mary Eberstadt, a research fellow at the Hoover Institute. In a *Policy Review* article published earlier this year, she asks, "Is Pornography the New Tobacco?"

"[Porn] is widely seen as cool, especially among younger people," Eberstadt writes. "This coveted social status further reduces the already low incentive for making a public issue of it."

In other words, Eberstadt argues that porn is cool today in the same way cigarettes were in the 1950s, an era when Marlon Brando and James Dean had them dangling from their bad-boy mouths.

Teen Reactions to Pornography

But what do teenagers think about all of this? Are they able to separate the hardcore pornographic images and videos they watch online from reality?

Sven-Axel Mansson, a professor at Malmo University in Sweden who published a study that includes interviews with 73 adolescents, says that in most cases, teenagers are in fact able to separate fantasy sexual play from real-life sexual play.

"The young men stated that they regarded these experiences as something completely different from sexuality experienced in more conventional situations and relationships," Mansson told *Contemporary Sexuality.* "Of course, this presupposes that they have had some real life sex experiences and not all of them had."

"The content of the pornography was usually described as rather violent and rough," he added. "And the discussions we had with them illustrated that pornography as a source of information about sex was critically reviewed by the young people. Sometimes it was perceived as a reliable source; more often, it was judged as exaggerated, distorted or downright false."

Mansson and Lotta Lofgren-Martenson, also a professor at Malmo University, published "Lust, Love and Life: A Qualitative Study of Swedish Adolescents' Perceptions and Experiences with Pornography," in the *Journal of Sex Research* in 2009.

In addition to seeking out pornography as a source of information, participants also viewed it with friends—as a form of social interaction, say the researchers—or as stimulus for sexual arousal.

But especially rough sex was viewed by at least one 18-year-old male as a turn-off. "It is humiliating," the Swedish teen said. "When you see a porn movie with six guys and one woman . . . How fun can that be?"

The adolescents interviewed by Mansson and Lofgren-Martenson also pondered how sexual pleasure, male endurance and female body types are portrayed in porn.

"I don't think it is good looking to have huge silicone breasts," said one 15-year-old girl. "But . . . everyone in the movies has those and they all have shaved bodies . . . so, well . . . they have what is regarded as gorgeous bodies."

Some of the boys didn't find those exaggerated body types attractive either: "Some of the women in porn videos are totally shabby . . . with wave permanents and bodies destroyed by too much plastic surgery," said one male teen.

After listening to adolescents discuss the sexually charged images they've been watching, Mansson and Lofgren-Martenson reached this conclusion: "The results from this study illustrate that the cultural script concerning pornography seems to have changed from having been regarded as shameful and morally reprehensible to something socially acceptable."

Pornography's Affect on Teen Sexual Behavior

In his *Details* magazine article, Spitznagel cites anecdotal evidence suggesting that pornography is influencing the sexual landscape, such as the chatty obsession with porn exhibited by adolescent males in the movie *Superbad* and attributing an increase in oral and anal sex to the popularity of those sexual acts being easily accessible online.

Researchers also wonder whether there's a correlation between increased viewing of pornography by youth and sexual behavior.

In "Early Sexual Experiences: The Role of Internet Access and Sexually Explicit Material," (*CyberPsychology and Behavior,* 2008) by Shane Kraus, MA, and Brenda Russell, PhD, the authors asked 437 American participants to complete an online survey on the topic.

"The primary focus of this study explored whether age of first oral sex, first sexual intercourse, and number of sexual partners would differ by gender, Internet access, and exposure to Xrated movies between the age of 12 to 17," wrote Kraus and Russell. "The results did not support the expected three-way interaction."

However, the study reported that males with Internet access were more likely to have oral sex at a younger age than males without Internet access. In addition, teens with Internet access were more likely to have first intercourse at a younger age than teens without Internet access.

In "Associations between pornography consumption and sexual practices among adolescents in Sweden" (*International Journal of STD & AIDS,* 2005), by Elisabet Haggstrom-Nordin and co-authors, the researchers interviewed 718 students in 47 high school classes on the controversial topic.

"The primary focus of this study explored whether age of first oral sex, first sexual intercourse, and number of sexual partners would differ by gender, Internet access, and exposure to X-rated movies between the age of 12 to 17. The results did not support the expected three-way interaction."

—Shane Kraus and Brenda Russell

When asked whether pornography influenced their sexual behavior, 56 percent of students said it had "no influence," 27 percent said it had "a little influence" and 2 percent said it had "a lot" of influence.

In comparing hours of pornography viewed with actual sexual behavior, Haggstrom-Nordin found little to report. "The only difference found was that more high consumers had had their first sexual intercourse at an earlier age (15 years) than low consumers," she wrote.

Studies like these don't prove cause and effect. "Of course, the question is 'what comes first,'" says Mansson, the Malmo University professor. "These are just correlations and they don't say anything about causality."

Indeed, Sabina and co-authors' 2008 study included this sentence: "On the question of the effects of pornography on adolescents, few youth reported strong effects."

However, some young people completing Sabina's survey also "reported shock, surprise, guilt, shame, and unwanted thoughts about the experience."

How to Talk to Teens about Pornography

Which raises the question of how adults should be engaging adolescents on the subject of pornography.

Irene Peters, PhD, the author of "Pornography: Discussing Sexually Explicit Images," a 2003 book published by a Planned Parenthood affiliate, says it's an especially difficult subject for sexuality educators to address.

"Most educators are not able to go into the classroom and talk about this," says Peters, a lead faculty member at Planned Parenthood University, a certification program for sexuality educators. "It's just not a topic you're allowed to do. It would be too incendiary. If someone asks an anonymous question, you can answer it. But you're not going to develop a lesson plan on watching porn for eighth graders or you would not have a job."

That's why Peters recommends helping parents learn how to talk to their children about pornography. To do that, educators need to understand and address parents' concerns, which may include the following:

- Viewing porn increases sexual activity
- Seeing aggressive images triggers aggressive behavior
- Some images traumatize young viewers
- Teens who watch porn together encourage each other to try what they view
- Women actors are portrayed in unhealthy ways
- Porn actors don't look and act like people do in real life.

Peters believes these fears are largely unwarranted because studies haven't found a link between childhood viewing of pornography and increased sexual behavior. "We have a lot of hysteria and scapegoating around pornography," she says. "It gets blamed for absolutely everything by everybody."

Teenagers most likely to be affected by pornography are ones with poor parental supervision in abusive households, Peters maintains. For the rest of America's youth, viewing pornography isn't harmful.

"It's part of the path of adolescence to experiment with taboo adult behavior," Peters says. "The sexual openness of pornography flies in the face of traditional adult and parental restrictions. It satisfies their curiosity and it challenges their parents' authority."

But that doesn't mean parents and other responsible adults shouldn't talk to teenagers about pornography. They should. By engaging youth in conversation about sexually explicit materials—within the greater context of human sexuality—they can help those adolescents become "sexually resilient."

Peters embraced the term in her 2003 book; Catherine Dukes, PhD, MPH and Rebecca Roberts, BA, are promoting the concept in 2010. Dukes and Roberts led a workshop at the recent AASECT conference titled, "Discussing Pornography with Young People: How Do We Promote 'Sexually Resilient' Youth?"

Dukes, vice president of education and training at Planned Parenthood of Delaware, defines resiliency as "emotional and cognitive flexibility" that allows a person to "bounce back from an obstacle."

In the context of viewing pornography, it works like this: If a teen views surprising or shocking material online, sexual resiliency helps the youth take a step back and think about why that's happening and what he or she can do to cope.

"The key to promoting sexual resilience is for adults to model it themselves," Dukes says. "It involves active coping and not avoiding the obstacle." Parents might ask these questions to teens that have viewed sexually explicit materials: "What happened? How did you feel about that? What are positive and negative things about pornography?"

During the Dukes/Roberts workshop, the pair promoted Peters' book as a guide for tackling this difficult subject.

Another resource that may prove helpful is "Generation P? Youth, Gender and Pornography," edited by Mansson, Lofgren-Martenson and S.V. Knudsen (Copenhagen: Danish School of Education Press); the book has two chapters on how to help teenagers grapple with sexually explicit materials.

"When you live in such a sexualized world that kids live in today, [parents] can take one of two approaches," Peters says. "You can put a bag over their head and hope they don't see anything or you can create a healthy resilience that helps them recover, learn or enjoy, whatever it is that is appropriate. Teenagers are a lot more resilient inherently than we think, we just need to give them the tools to respond."

"When you live in such a sexualized world that kids live in today, [parents] can take one of two approaches. You can put a bag over their head and hope they don't see anything or you can create a healthy resilience that helps them recover, learn or enjoy, whatever it is that is appropriate."

—Irene Peters

Critical Thinking

1. Why do teens use porn sites as described by the author?
2. What was used to come up with the conclusions of how often teens use porn sites?
3. What should parents say in thinking to teens about porn?
4. What additional action might a parent take if he or she wants to curb the use of porn sites by teenagers?

UNIT 4

The Contexts of Adolescents in Society: School, Work, and Diversity

Unit Selections

Learning Outcomes

After reading this unit, you should be able to:

- Explain the reason the NEA reports that many high school graduates are deficient in reading skills.

- Describe why there is a drop in reading among teens.

- Explain why there is an increase of youth taking online classes.

- Contrast the pro and con reasons for students taking online classes.

- Describe the answer the author gives to working with students in trouble.

- Analyze the "army-drill-instructor approach" to working with troubled teens.

- Analyze the controversy surrounding the consequences of adolescent paid work.

- Outline what parents, counselors, and others can do to help youth make sound employment-related decisions.

- Analyze the concept of involving immigrant parents to promote mental health of teens.

- Describe positive adjustment of immigrant youth.

- Explain the two approaches to reduce school violence and school climate.

- Analyze the two approaches to reduce school violence and school climate.

- Explain the reason teenagers find learning a drag.

- Identify possible solutions to correct the problem of students disliking learning.

- Describe the three types of teenage brains.

- Explain how a teen's brain can be shaped to learn.

- Explain the problem of student disengagement in schools.

- Describe the two factors important to solving the problem of disengagement.

While developmentalists in the Piagetian tradition focus on the ways in which the thought processes of children and adolescents differ (as explained in Unit 2), other researchers have taken a different track—a psychometric approach. In this approach, the emphasis is on quantifying cognitive abilities such as verbal ability, mathematical ability, and general intelligence (IQ). The measurement of intelligence, as well as the very definition of intelligence, has been controversial for decades. A classic question is whether intelligence is best conceptualized as a general capacity that underlies many diverse abilities or as a set of specific abilities. Traditional IQ tests focus on abilities that relate to success in school and ignore abilities such as those that tap creativity, mechanical aptitude, or practical intelligence.

© Digital Vision/Getty Images

The role of genetic versus environmental contributions to intelligence have also been controversial. At the turn of the century the predominant view was that intelligence was essentially inherited and was little influenced by experience. Today, the consensus is that an individual's intelligence is very much a product of both nature and nurture. An even greater controversy focuses on the role that heredity versus the environment plays in explaining racial, ethnic, and gender differences in performance on various cognitive tests such as IQ tests.

Adolescents clearly have larger vocabularies, more mathematical knowledge, better spatial ability, etc., than children. Their memories are better because they process information more efficiently and use memory strategies more effectively. Adolescents possess a greater general knowledge base than children, which enables adolescents to link new concepts to existing ideas. Stated another way, psychometric intelligence may well increase with age. On the other hand, because of comparisons to age peers, the relative performance of adolescents on aptitude tests remains fairly stable. A 9-year-old child's outstanding performance on an IQ test, for example, is fairly predictive that the same individual's IQ score at age 15 will be better than the score of most peers.

Performance on standardized tests, IQ or otherwise (e.g. achievement tests), is often used to place junior high and high school students in ability tracts, a practice that is increasingly questioned. Similarly, standardized test results compared across schools are being used to measure a school's educational effectiveness.

School is the place where teens spend much of their time; where their cognitive abilities are encouraged and supported. But schools offer much more than just education. School is also the place where teens acquire new skills and come to grips with the concerns and experiences of adult society. Educational issues of today are many and include greater school choice, students with exceptional abilities and needs, diversity, racial integration, school violence, etc.

School violence by disenchanted youth has peaked in the United States. Only when schools take student concerns into account will they become environments that stimulate attendance, interest, and harmony. Schools need to promote a sense of belonging in order for disaffected and potentially violent students to become productive members of the school community.

In addition to attending school, a majority of American teens work. Younger teens mostly do occasional babysitting or yard work. Those 15 and over are likely to work on a steady basis in offices, restaurants, and stores. Over half of those with jobs work 15 or more hours per week during the school year and more during the summer. A large majority are paid at or close to minimum wage.

The first article in this unit discusses the serious problem of the low reading level of many teens today. Next, Sam Dillon explains that many youth are taking classes online, which has sparked a debate. The New York Times gives one school's answer to working with troubled students, and Jeylan Mortimer provides information on the controversy surrounding the consequences of adolescent paid work.

More than ever there is an increase in immigrant youth. The next article examines the struggles they face, while the following article provides an examination of approaches to reduce school violence, which is on the rise.

Many youth find learning a drag; Jessica Homyelou may have the solution. Jennifer Leigh addresses the question, "can one shape a teen's brain?" And finally, the topic of high schools on college campuses is explained by Terry B. Grier and Kent D. Peterson.

Student Website
www.mhhe.com/cls

Internet References

Afterschool Alliance
www.afterschoolalliance.org

Decision Making/Reasoning Skills
http://cals-cf.calsnet.arizona.edu/fcs/bpy/content.cfm?content=decision_making

National Institute on Out-Of-School Time
www.niost.org

Public Education Network
www.publiceducation.org

Public/Private Ventures
www.ppv.org

What Kids Can Do
www.whatkidscando.org

The 'Alarming' State of Reading in America

CHUCK LEDDY

The National Endowment for the Arts (NEA) recently released a major report about the reading habits of Americans. The report, entitled "To Read or Not to Read" (online at www.nea.gov/research/researchreports_chrono.html), reveals that Americans are reading less and describes how our culture and economy are negatively impacted by the nation's diminishing reading habits.

The NEA report is especially depressing in detailing the severe drop in reading among teenagers and young adults. While this younger demographic may be spending more time reading on the Internet, they are definitely not enthusiastic about reading printed materials such as books, newspapers and magazines. NEA chairman Dana Gioia, who is also a renowned poet and a literary critic, told *The Washington Post* that "this is really alarming data" and bemoaned "a general culture which does not encourage or reinforce reading."

The number of 17-year-olds, for example, who read anything for pleasure each day has dropped from 31 percent in 1984 to a dismal 22 percent today. This is not only bad news for publishers and writers, the report says, but for employers, too. The NEA report notes that 38 percent of employers rate high school graduates as "deficient" in reading skills, while a shocking 72 percent of employers rate such graduates as "deficient" in writing skills. With today's jobs demanding employees skilled at handling and analyzing data, we're in danger of falling short of those needs.

Even among college graduates, supposedly the most literate group of all, the NEA reports, show declines in reading habits. "[B]oth reading ability and the habit of regular reading have greatly declined among college graduates," Gioia notes. In perhaps the most shocking statistic in the entire report, young people between the ages of 15 and 24 spend an average of seven minutes per day reading for pleasure. That's right, seven minutes per day! The so-called "Harry Potter effect," which promised to transform millions of youngsters who began reading the J.K. Rowling series into lifelong readers, has apparently been weaker than expected.

Older people, however, continue to read. Those over 55 spend nearly an hour reading each day for pleasure. This older demographic also makes up nearly half the total book-buying market, with younger people purchasing fewer books and spending more time watching television or using the Internet. Older people also read more newspapers. Daily circulation among newspapers is steadily declining, as younger people either read newspapers online (usually for free) or don't read newspapers at all.

Gioia worries about the economic costs of not reading: "Poor reading skills," he says, "correlate heavily with lack of employment, lower wages, and fewer opportunities for advancement." Those who don't read are also less likely to vote or volunteer, the report notes. Most important, those who miss out on reading miss out on the best form of entertainment and education there is. Books change lives for the better, and have been doing so for centuries.

While the NEA report consciously avoids recommending solutions to the present downslide in reading, preferring to diagnose the problem and allowing others to figure out ways to fix it, there are some things that those of us who care about reading and writing can do.

One is to encourage reading for pleasure among young people, perhaps by asking them what they're reading and discussing it with them. If they're not reading any-thing, you can recommend books or discuss books you've enjoyed reading. You can read to younger children, or take them to the public library. In short, those of us who love books must be more proactive in sharing and pro-moting the pleasures (and importance) of reading with those around us, especially children.

Critical Thinking

1. Why is there a severe drop in reading among teenagers today?
2. How is deficiency in reading defined?
3. What do employers say about reading deficiency in adolescents?
4. What can be done to correct the problem of deficient read-ing in adolescents?

Online Schooling Grows, Setting Off a Debate

SAM DILLON

Milwaukee—Weekday mornings, three of Tracie Weldie's children eat breakfast, make beds and trudge off to public school—in their case, downstairs to their basement in a suburb here, where their mother leads them through math and other lessons outlined by an Internet-based charter school.

Half a million American children take classes online, with a significant group, like the Weldies, getting all their schooling from virtual public schools. The rapid growth of these schools has provoked debates in courtrooms and legislatures over money, as the schools compete with local districts for millions in public dollars, and over issues like whether online learning is appropriate for young children.

One of the sharpest debates has concerned the Weldies' school in Wisconsin, where last week the backers of online education persuaded state lawmakers to keep it and 11 other virtual schools open despite a court ruling against them and the opposition of the teachers union. John Watson, a consultant in Colorado who does an annual survey of education that is based on the Internet, said events in Wisconsin followed the pattern in other states where online schools have proliferated fast.

"Somebody says, 'What's going on, does this make sense?'" Mr. Watson said. "And after some inquiry most states have said, 'Yes, we like online learning, but these are such new ways of teaching children that we'll need to change some regulations and get some more oversight.'"

Two models of online schooling predominate. In Florida, Illinois and half a dozen other states, growth has been driven by a state-led, state-financed virtual school that does not give a diploma but offers courses that supplement regular work at a traditional school. Generally, these schools enroll only middle and high school students.

At the Florida Virtual School, the largest Internet public school in the country, more than 50,000 students are taking courses this year. School authorities in Traverse City, Mich., hope to use online courses provided by the Michigan Virtual School next fall to educate several hundred students in their homes, alleviating a classroom shortage.

The other model is a full-time online charter school like the Wisconsin Virtual Academy. About 90,000 children get their education from one of 185 such schools nationwide. They are publicly financed, mostly elementary and middle schools.

Many parents attracted to online charters have previously home-schooled their children, including Mrs. Weldie. Her children—Isabel, Harry and Eleanor, all in elementary school—download assignments and communicate intermittently with their certified teachers over the Internet, but they also read story books, write in workbooks and do arithmetic at a table in their basement. Legally, they are considered public school students, not home-schoolers, because their online schools are taxpayer-financed and subject to federal testing requirements.

Despite enthusiastic support from parents, the schools have met with opposition from some educators, who say elementary students may be too young for Internet learning, and from teachers, unions and school boards, partly because they divert state payments from the online student's home district.

Other opposition has arisen because many online charters contract with for-profit companies to provide their courses. The Wisconsin academy, for example, is run by the tiny Northern Ozaukee School District, north of Milwaukee, in close partnership with K12 Inc., which works with similar schools in 17 states.

The district receives annual state payments of $6,050 for each of its 800 students, which it uses to pay teachers and buy its online curriculum from K12.

Saying he suspected "corporate profiteering" in online schooling, State Senator John Lehman, a Democrat who is chairman of the education committee, last month proposed cutting the payments to virtual schools to $3,000 per student. But during legislative negotiations that proposal was dropped.

Jeff Kwitowski, a K12 spokesman, said, "We are a vendor and no different from thousands of other companies that provide products and services to districts and schools."

Pennsylvania has also debated the financing of virtual charter schools. Saying such schools were draining them financially, districts filed suit in 2001, portraying online schools as little more than home schooling at taxpayer expense. The districts lost, but the debate has continued.

Last year, the state auditor found that several online charters had received reimbursements from students' home districts that surpassed actual education costs by more than $1 million. Now legislators are considering a bill that would in part standardize the payments at about $5,900 per child, said Michael Race, a spokesman for the State Department of Education.

The state auditor in Kansas last year raised a different concern, finding that the superintendent of a tiny prairie district running an online school had in recent years given 130 students, and with them $106,000 in per-pupil payments, to neighboring districts that used the students' names to pad enrollment counts. The auditor concluded that the superintendent had carried out the subterfuge to compensate the other districts for not opening their own online schools.

"Virtual education is a growing alternative to traditional schooling," Barbara J. Hinton, the Kansas auditor, said in a report. Ms. Hinton found that virtual education had great potential because students did not have to be physically present in a classroom. "Students can go to school at any time and in any place," she said.

But, she added, "this also creates certain risks to both the quality of the student's education and to the integrity of the public school system."

Rural Americans have been attracted to online schooling because it allows students even on remote ranches to enroll in arcane courses like Chinese.

In Colorado, school districts have lost thousands of students to virtual schools, and, in 2006, a state audit found that one school, run by a rural district, was using four licensed teachers to teach 1,500 students across the state. The legislature responded last year by establishing a new division of the Colorado Department of Education to tighten regulation of online schools.

The Wisconsin Virtual Academy has 20 certified, unionized teachers, and 800 students who communicate with one another over the Internet.

The school has consistently met federal testing requirements, and many parents, including Mrs. Weldie, expressed satisfaction with the K12 curriculum, which allows her children to move through lessons at their own pace, unlike traditional

schools, where teachers often pause to take account of slower students. Isabel Weldie, 5, is in kindergarten, "But in math I'm in first grade," she said during a break in her school day recently.

"That's what I love most about this curriculum," Mrs. Weldie said. "There's no reason for Isabel to practice counting if she can already add."

In 2004, the teachers' union filed a lawsuit against the school, challenging the expansive role given to parents, who must spend four to five hours daily leading their children through lesson plans and overseeing their work. Teachers monitor student progress and answer questions in a couple of half-hour telephone conferences per month and in interactive online classes using conferencing software held several times monthly.

A state court dismissed the case, but in December an appeals court said the academy was violating a state law requiring that public school teachers be licensed.

The ruling infuriated parents like Bob Reber, an insurance salesman who lives in Fond du Lac and whose 8-year-old daughter is a student at the academy. "According to this ruling, if I want to teach my daughter to tie her shoes, I'd need a license," Mr. Reber said.

Not so, said Mary Bell, the union president: "The court did not say that parents cannot teach their children—it said parents cannot teach their children at taxpayers' expense."

The Weldies and 1,000 other parents and students from online schools rallied in Madison, the state capital, urging lawmakers to save their schools. Last week, legislators announced that they had agreed on a bipartisan bill that would allow the schools to stay open, while requiring online teachers to keep closely in touch with students and increasing state oversight.

Critical Thinking

1. How many adolescents take online classes?
2. Why have online classes created a debate in courtrooms and legislatures?
3. What is the pro argument to teens taking online classes?
4. What are the reasons some are against online classes?

School's New Rule for Pupils in Trouble: No Fun

WINNIE HU

Like a bouncer at a nightclub, Melissa Gladwell was parked at the main entrance of Cheektowaga Central Middle School on Friday night, with a list of 150 names highlighted in yellow marker, the names of students barred from the after-hours games, crafts and ice cream because of poor grades or bad attitudes.

"You're ineligible," Ms. Gladwell, a sixth-grade teacher, told one boy, who turned around without protest. "That happens. I think they think we're going to forget."

In a far-reaching experiment with disciplinary measures reminiscent of old-style Catholic schools or military academies, the Cheektowaga district this year began essentially grounding middle school students whose grade in any class falls below 65, or who show what educators describe as a lack of effort.

Such students—more than a quarter of the 580 at the school as of last week—are excluded from all aspects of extracurricular life, including athletic contests, academic clubs, dances and plays, unless they demonstrate improvement on weekly progress reports filled out by their teachers.

The policy is far stricter than those at most high schools, which generally have eligibility requirements only for varsity sports teams. It is part of a larger campaign to instill more responsibility in young adolescents in this town of 80,000 on the outskirts of Buffalo. Starting this week, the students also automatically get detention on any day they fail to wear their identification cards; 13 were punished on the first day of the new policy and 14 the second, including several repeaters.

And there are social rules that govern nearly every minute of the day, from riding the bus to using the bathroom, as part of a program known as "positive behavioral interventions and supports." Students are required to keep to the right of the dotted yellow line down the middle of hallways. They are assigned seats in the cafeteria and must wait for a teacher to call them up to get food. If enough students act up or even litter, they all risk a declaration of "silent lunch" in the cafeteria.

"I'd like to go to a normal school," said Anthony Pachetti, 12, a seventh grader who has been barred from activities for failing math, science and social studies. "It's not doing anything for me except taking everything away."

Such harsh regimens are rare, and generally have been found in tough urban schools like Eastside High in Paterson, N.J., where Joe Clark, an Army-drill-instructor-turned-principal, famously expelled dozens of students in a single day in the early 1980s, and inspired the movie "Lean on Me." Now tough policies are spreading to outlying areas like Cheektowaga at a time when they are facing increased pressure to improve academic achievement. Middle schools, in particular, have long struggled with performance slumps and competing theories on how to strike the right balance between structure and independence for students at a transitional, volatile age. But few have gone as far as Cheektowaga has in clamping down on the natural disorder of early adolescence.

Even Joe Clark's Paterson district backed away from requiring that 10th, 11th and 12th graders maintain a 2.5 grade-point average to participate in extracurricular activities in 2006. Instead, it adopted a lower standard—a 2.0 average only for athletes—after community opposition.

Critics of the tough-love approach cite studies showing that students active in extracurricular activities tend to perform better in class, and they worry that without structured activities after school, troubled youngsters will be more apt to find trouble.

"A child who only has detention to look forward to at the end of the day is less likely to come to school," said Laura Rogers, a school psychologist in Harvard, Mass. and the co-author of "Fires in the Middle School Bathroom."

Deborah Meier, a senior scholar at New York University's Steinhardt School of Education and a former New York City principal, said that such "law and order" approaches are counterproductive.

"Sounds like prison," she said of Cheektowaga. "It's such a sad, sad commentary because, in my opinion, the improvements that it can make in behavior are marginal, and it does not begin to touch upon what engages the students in school."

Some similar tactics have been tried recently in places as varied as rural Twin Falls, Idaho, where high school students with grade-point-averages below 2.0 were barred from competing in extracurricular activities and required to attend tutoring starting this year, and in the Pittsburgh suburbs, where the Penn Hills school district set a 1.5 minimum average in 2006 to qualify for activities, raised that to 1.75 this school year, and has bumped it up again, to 2.0, for next fall.

Here in Cheektowaga, the new policy arrived with a new principal, Brian Bridges, who said that over four years as an assistant principal at the school, he saw less and less respect—and more and more attitude—from students growing up in a society that he believes is too permissive.

At the same time, many teachers were not prepared for the new students brought by the demographic changes sweeping the school, he said; its enrollment has gone from overwhelmingly white and working class to 35 percent black and Hispanic in recent years as minority families have moved in from Buffalo. And nearly half the students are poor enough to qualify for free and reduced-price lunches.

Mr. Bridges, 39, is a former social worker who said that he was raised by a strict single mother who smacked him when he so much as gave her a disrespectful look. Teachers here nicknamed him "Joe Clark" and gave him a bullhorn, which he gladly accepted and sometimes uses in the hallways and to direct students to buses. He said that bringing more structure and discipline to the school creates a safer environment and teaches students to be members of a community.

So along with barring failing students from after-school activities, he has added things like pep rallies and hat and pajama days during school hours, and rewarded those who succeed under the new rules with raffle prizes.

On Friday afternoon, Mr. Bridges straddled the yellow line in a hallway to force students passing in both directions to stay on the right side.

"Go back!" he roared at an eighth grader bounding by him.

The boy stopped, protested, went back, then made the trip down the hallway again—at a fast walk.

"I'm the first one in the hallways wanting to have fun with my kids," Mr. Bridges said. "But I know I have to have a stronger hand."

It is too soon to see whether the policies will have an effect on state test scores, since this year's results will not be released until late spring. Last year, 53.8 percent of eighth graders passed the state's standardized math tests and 51 percent language arts, compared with 58.8 percent and 57 percent statewide.

Ms. Gladwell and other teachers said that there has not been an overall improvement in classroom grades, but that they had seen more homework turned in, more class participation, and fewer fights in the hallways and cafeteria. Attendance has stayed steady at about 95 percent.

The new eligibility policy for extracurricular activities drew complaints from more than two dozen parents last October after the school barred 75 students from attending the first dance, Mr. Bridges said.

But Sondra LaMacchia, a stay-at-home mother of five, said that after years of telling her 14-year-old daughter, Cortney, to study harder, the message came through much clearer when Cortney had to watch her friends and younger sister attend school dances from which she was barred.

"It's nobody's fault but hers," said Ms. LaMacchia, 35.

Some teachers have complained that enforcing the policy takes time away from academic instruction and burdens them with paperwork. There have also been concerns that the eligibility policy was keeping students from pursuing academic interests like the math and science clubs.

Ms. Gladwell, who is also the school's volleyball coach, benched one of her top players in October because she forgot to bring her progress report. Afterward, she said, the player's mother came up and thanked her.

"She never forgot again," Ms. Gladwell said. "It's about teaching them responsibility."

Ellen Pieroni, 13, an eighth grader who is co-president of the student council, had considered boycotting a dance in December because her friends could not go, but now says that she supports the policy. "I think they get lazy and don't do the work," she said. But other students said that the school had too many rules.

Having forgotten his identification card for the seventh time this year, Cameron Kaeding, a sixth grader, had to wear a temporary sticker and wait to get his lunch because students without their ID cards are served last. He has also been kept from a pep rally and two dances because of his struggles in math and social studies. "It's horrible," he said. "I think it's going a little too far because kids aren't perfect, and this school thinks that they are."

Critical Thinking

1. What is one answer the author discusses to working with students in trouble?
2. What is meant by "strict rules"?
3. How could an army drill instructor approach teaching?
4. What is your view of this approach working with students in trouble?

The Benefits and Risks of Adolescent Employment

JEYLAN T. MORTIMER, PHD

Having a paying job at some time during high school has become a near-universal adolescent experience (Committee on the Health and Safety Implications of Child Labor, 1998; U.S. Department of Labor, 2000). Many youth start to work informally even earlier, at about the age of 12, most often in their own neighborhoods, babysitting, shoveling snow, cutting grass, or doing various odd jobs. At first, paid work is episodic and generally quite limited. By the age of 16, adolescent workers are more likely to have formal jobs, working in the retail and service sectors of the economy, especially in fast food restaurants, grocery stores, or other retail stores. Employment becomes more regular and more time-consuming during the latter years of high school, with many teens working 20 or more hours per week.

The prevalence of teenage employment has sparked lively debates over whether adolescents should work, for how many hours, and in what kinds of jobs. Most parents like the idea of their children working, as they think that employment instills a whole array of positive traits, including independence, responsibility, interpersonal skills, and a good work ethic (Phillips & Sandstrom, 1990). Parents believe that the jobs that they themselves held during adolescence helped them to acquire these very same attributes. In fact, when asked in very general terms about whether the jobs they held in adolescence had any negative effects, only a small number had anything to report. Their adolescent children also want to work to earn their own spending money to be able to buy the accoutrements of adolescent life and take part in the often expensive leisure activities popular among their peers. While a minority of teenagers give their earnings directly to their parents, earnings from teens' part-time jobs help many families economically insofar as adolescent children are able to purchase themselves items that their parents would otherwise provide. Teens buy clothes, food, gas, and music; some save a portion of their earnings for larger purchases or even to attend college (Shanahan, Elder, Burchinal, & Conger, 1996). Adolescents tend to report high levels of satisfaction with their jobs and hold many of the same beliefs as their parents about the benefits of employment.

On the other side of the debate, some educators complain that working teens put in too many hours on their jobs; they may come to school tired, have little time to see their teachers after school for special help, and avoid extracurricular activities (Bills, Helms & Ozcan, 1995). Some developmental psychologists echo these concerns and warn that employment may cut short, or even deny, youth an essential "adolescent moratorium," a stage of life free from adult-like pursuits, stressors, and responsibilities (Greenberger & Steinberg, 1986; Steinberg & Dornbusch, 1991). They believe adolescence should be a time of exploration—a time to figure out who one is and what path one should follow. According to this point of view, too much work may have severe opportunity costs with respect to healthy identity formation.

This article will address the probable benefits, as well as some potential costs, of teenage employment. Initially, four plausible answers to the general question, "Is working good for teenagers?" are presented. Then it will highlight findings of the Youth Development Study, an ongoing longitudinal study, that bear directly on this question. Finally, implications of the findings that may be of interest to parents, educators, and others with interests in enhancing healthy youth development will be discussed.

Is Working Good for Teenagers?

Researchers across disciplines, including psychologists, sociologists, and economists, have been systematically studying adolescent employment for several decades. As Staff and his colleagues (2009) have noted based on their extensive review of the literature, four basic answers to the question, "Is working good for teenagers?" have emerged. The first is highly affirmative, largely in accord with what youth and their parents believe. Youth themselves think that employment helps them to develop a wide range of beneficial attributes, such as the capacity to take responsibility, develop time-management skills, overcome shyness with adults, and handle money. Furthermore, at least while they are in the work setting, employment makes them feel more like an adult. Employed teens have high rates of job satisfaction (Mortimer, 2003).

The second answer is negative, emphasizing that work carries with it many risks. Critics of adolescent work point out that teens who work long hours tend to have lower grades than teens who work fewer hours; there are similar gradients in a range of academically relevant indicators such as absences from school and dropping out. These critics also report that as hours of work increase, adolescents drink and smoke more, and engage in a wide range of problem behaviors (Steinberg & Cauffman, 1995; Steinberg & Dornbusch, 1991; Steinberg, Fegley, & Dornbusch, 1993).

A third position is that work makes very little difference with respect to healthy development; what pass for "benefits" as well as "costs" of employment are attributable to self-selection. Teens who enter adolescence with strong academic interests and goals may work very little during high school, and when they do have jobs, they limit their hours of employment so as to not jeopardize their grades. Those who choose to work long hours, in contrast, already engage in more problem behavior, are less interested in school, and get lower grades even at the start of high school (Staff et al., 2009). Thus, according to this perspective, problem behavior of adolescent workers is more a function of pre-existing differences than an outcome attributable to their employment.

A fourth answer to this perplexing question has also surfaced: employment has different consequences depending on both the characteristics of the adolescent and the circumstances under which it occurs (Lee & Staff, 2007). To fully understand the consequences of teenage work, we must address the degree of investment in employment and the particular experiences that youth have while working; that is, the quantity as well as the quality of work, as well as adolescents' social backgrounds, academic promise, and motivations to work.

Youth Development Study

The Youth Development Study (YDS) was initiated more than 20 years ago in an attempt to address the controversies surrounding adolescent employment (Mortimer, 2003). Importantly, the YDS is a prospective study, enabling observation of teens' time commitments to their jobs, numerous indicators of the quality of their work, and the adolescents' own self-reports of their subjective experiences of working as they move through high school and into college or the work force. Surveys were initially obtained from 1,000 students, randomly chosen from a list of 9th graders (mostly 14 and 15 years old) attending the St. Paul, Minnesota Public Schools in the fall of 1987. Each spring during the four years of high school (1988-1991), the students filled out surveys containing large batteries of questions about their work experiences, including intrinsic and extrinsic rewards of work, stressors, relationships with supervisors and co-workers, job satisfaction, and commitment

After the students left high school, the YDS continued to survey them near-annually by mail. Currently, the youth are in their mid-30s, and approximately 75% of the original cohort has been retained in the most recent waves of data collection.

There are, of course, both disadvantages and advantages of long-term studies of this kind. The data describe the work experiences of teenagers more than 20 years ago. High school students are less likely to be employed today, especially in the midst of our current recession, and teenagers' attitudes toward work may have changed as a result of their reduced

job prospects. Still, if one is interested not only in immediate correlates and outcomes, but in long-term effects of teenage employment that may not be apparent until many years after high school, then data of this kind are essential. Because of the lengthening transition to adulthood, it takes a long time to ascertain whether early work experience actually influences eventual educational attainments and career establishment. We do have some information, nonetheless, that bears on the question of change over historical time. While the students were in high school, we also asked the students' parents to complete questionnaires to obtain parents' views about their own experiences of employment when they were teenagers and about their attitudes toward their children's work. As noted above, there was general agreement across generations about the benefits of teen employment.

This ongoing panel study has enabled us to understand much about teenage employment, including its short-term consequences as well as its longer-term implications for educational attainment and career establishment. What have we learned from this prospective study?

Patterns of Work Experience Through Time

We find clearly identifiable patterns of teen employment with distinct precursors and likely consequences (Mortimer, 2003). It is insufficient to know merely whether a teen is employed, or even how many hours that teenager works. Instead, it is more fruitful to understand how employment is patterned throughout high school with respect to two temporal dimensions: the duration and intensity of work (see Table 1). The "most invested" workers are employed in most months of observation (22 of 24, in fact, from the 10th through the 12th grades), and during this period they work on average more than 20 hours per week. "Sporadic" workers also put in a lot of hours when they are employed (more than 20), but they only work about half the months of observation. "Steady" workers, like the "most invested," are employed most of the time during high school, but they moderate their hours, working on average 20 hours per week or less. "Occasional" workers are employed relatively few months (similar to the "sporadic" workers), but also limit their hours of work to 20 or fewer per week. Testimony to the ubiquity of adolescent work, only 7% of the panel did not hold any employment when school was in session. Because the debates about teenage employment largely concern the conflicts between work and school, this typology does not reflect summer employment.

The research further revealed that steady and occasional workers came from higher socioeconomic backgrounds and were more intrinsically motivated with respect to school in the 9th grade. They were more likely to enjoy school, to think they were learning things at school that would be important to them in later life, and to have high grades. They also had higher educational aspirations for the future. Not surprisingly, they limited their hours of work and were therefore able to participate in extracurricular activities, spend time with their families and friends, and engage in the highly valued "well-rounded" adolescent lifestyle. When asked about why they obtained their

Table 1   Adolescent Patterns of Employment During the School Year

	Duration (grades 10–12)	
Average Intensity	High (work 22 of 24 monghs)	Low (work 10–12 months of 24)
Work more than 20 hours a week	Most Invested (26%)	Sporadic (18%)
Work 20 hours a week or less	Steady (25%)	Occasional (24%)

first jobs, they were more likely than the other youth to say that they wanted to save money for college.

The most invested workers, in contrast, were distinctive in their interest in gaining work experience. Their parents tended to be less well-educated, and the youth themselves had lower educational aspirations and were less engaged in school. During high school, they described their jobs in ways that seemed more "adult-like"; they not only worked more hours and had higher earnings than their less work-invested peers, they also reported that their jobs gave them more learning opportunities, more supervisory responsibilities, and were more stressful. Sporadic workers were more similar to the most invested than the other youth, but they were the most strongly oriented to their peers upon entry to high school, and reported the most problem behavior.

Clearly the evidence supports processes of selection to work—patterns of employment during high school do not occur randomly but instead are linked to students' socioeconomic backgrounds and their interests in school. The findings suggest that youth may be exercising agency, as their employment experiences during high school reflect their goals, articulated as early as the 9th grade. The steady and occasional workers pursued a line of action that reflected their strong academic motivations; they were building human capital mainly through their high level of engagement in school. For them, work was a "side line," or even an activity that supported their educational goals—through saving for college. The most invested workers, in contrast, were seemingly more reliant on their work experiences than their school experiences to build their human capital.

Furthermore, steady and occasional workers were more likely to attend four-year colleges and obtained highly coveted B.A. and B.S. degrees relatively quickly (Staff & Mortimer, 2007). The most invested workers were more likely to attend community colleges and vocational schools. They moved more rapidly toward "career" jobs, that is, jobs they themselves considered to be their careers (Mortimer, Vuolo, Staff, Wakefield, & Xie, 2008). Sporadic high school workers seemingly fell through the cracks, reflecting their relative lack of investment in work and in school. They were the most likely of all groups to be "idle," neither employed nor in school, during the years immediately after high school.

The Quality of Work

The Youth Development Study also found variability in the quality of adolescent employment. Defying the notion that all teen employment is essentially the same, teenagers generally move from jobs that are more simple to those that are more complex during the four years of high school, obtaining more training, greater supervisory responsibilities, and more opportunities for advancement (Mortimer, 2003). Work quality was found to be significantly related to teen self-concepts and attitudes. That is, those whose work experiences affirm their capacities as workers (e.g., having jobs that "pay well") and give them opportunities to advance develop a stronger sense of self-efficacy over time (Finch, Shanahan, Mortimer, & Ryu, 1991). Stressors at work, in contrast, led to diminished self-esteem and self-efficacy, and appear to foster depressed mood (Shanahan, Finch, Mortimer, & Ryu, 1991). Interestingly, however, these negative consequences are short-lived; work stressors during adolescence may actually increase resilience (Mortimer & Staff, 2004). That is, those who experienced stressors in their jobs during high school were less likely to exhibit declines in self-concept and mental health in response to similar work stressors confronted four years after high school. Those youth, however, who had not had these prior "steeling" experiences responded to the same problems at work in much the same way as their peers had during high school. We conclude that moderate stressors at work during adolescence may teach teens valuable lessons.

In Summary: Is Work Good for Youth?

Based on the findings of the Youth Development Study, we conclude that the first two answers to the question, "Is work good for youth?" are far too simplistic. Employment can have both negative and positive effects, and many of the differences between teenagers who work at high and low levels of intensity may be attributable to self-selection. We find evidence, however, that work experience can promote the healthy development of some young people, especially when it is moderate in intensity and steady in duration—attributes that assure that employment does not interfere with other important elements in a teen's life, and instead foster an appropriate balance between school and work. Steady work may foster the development of time management skills that serve young people well as they move into college, since most college students continue to work to support themselves and to pay tuition, at least partially (Horn, Peter, & Rooney, 2002). In fact, we find remarkable continuity in patterns of working and studying during high school and the years thereafter (Staff & Mortimer, 2007).

High school jobs may also be quite beneficial for those youth who are less interested in college, and do not have the familial or personal resources (high aspirations and engagement in school) to successfully pursue a four-year college degree. Whereas moving quickly into a self-identified "career" job will confer less socioeconomic benefit than pursuing higher education and later career establishment, obtaining steady work with "career prospects" is certainly a positive accomplishment for a young adult.

Much research on substance use, problem behavior, and other so-called negative consequences of employment indicates that these are largely attributable to self-selection rather than to work experience itself (for a review, see Staff et al., 2009). That is, youth who already exhibit problem behavior gravitate toward more intensive work. Employment as well as problem behavior, like early sexuality and the use of alcohol, cigarettes, or drugs, may be seen as "claims to adult status," or indicators of "pseudomaturity." Moreover, earnings from work may be used to purchase alcohol and drugs and to support activities, like cruising around in cars, with like-minded peers. It is noteworthy that, when differences in attitudes and behaviors are appropriately taken into account, the bad consequences of employment often disappear.

Advice for Parents, Teachers and Others Who Work with Youth

In view of these findings, how should parents handle the issue of adolescent work? Our findings suggest that youth work is not a strong matter of contention in most households, since the vast majority of parents and teens seem to be in agreement about the potential value of employment during the adolescent years. Parents, however, can still play an important role in guiding their children toward the kinds of work experiences that will be most beneficial, and helping them to avoid the risks of employment.

Parents . . . play an important role in guiding their children toward the kinds of work experiences that will be most beneficial.

Parents should counsel their children to avoid hazardous workplaces. Though serious injuries in the workplace are relatively rare events, they do happen. From 1992 to 2000 approximately 68 youth died from work-related injuries each year, rates fell between 2000 and 2004 (Windau & Meyer, 2005). Parents and their teenage children should be well informed about the child labor laws in their states, as states vary in their regulations with respect to hours of work on school days, night time employment, and specifically prohibited occupations and tasks for 14-to 18-year-olds. Parents may inform themselves about these laws by checking the Web sites of their State Departments of Labor. For example, Massachusetts has prepared an informative downloadable pamphlet for parents and teens (www.mass.gov/Cago/docs/Workplace/teenguide_final.pdf). The Occupational Safety and Health Administration (OSHA) also maintains a very useful Web site (www.osha.gov/SLTC/teenworkers).

Parents should also monitor their children's employment so that they are aware of the number of hours the adolescents work, the timing of those hours (weekday afternoons or weekends, night time work), and the general patterning of the work throughout high school. These temporal dimensions should be considered in view of the adolescent's long-range goals. If the objective is to graduate from a four-year college, the teenager might benefit from having a steady job, but one that is limited to 20 or fewer hours per week. A "most invested" pattern of employment, is more compatible with the goal to transition more quickly from school to work, and become established in an occupational career. Teens should be encouraged to cut back on employment that "crowds out" other activities that play an important role in adolescent development, such as sports and other extracurricular activities in school, developing friendships, and time with the family. They should also avoid work that is highly stressful and carries with it few learning opportunities.

Teachers, counselors, coaches, and others who work with youth should also be aware of the linkages between patterns of work investments in high school and subsequent educational and career achievements. These adults are in particularly opportune positions to help youth to develop strategies to achieve their higher education and vocational goals. Teachers could take greater advantage of the fact that so many of their students have paid jobs, for example, by encouraging them to reflect on their work and its relation to what they are learning in the classroom in their writing assignments (for example, are they learning things in school that could be helpful in their jobs, presently or in the future? Do experiences on the job help them to better understand ideas what they are learning in school?).

Teachers and counselors might also guide students' job-seeking. Although teens tend to move toward jobs that require more training and involve greater responsibility as they advance through high school, youth who want to work should be encouraged to seek learning opportunities and other experiences that will help them to explore their emerging vocational interests and abilities. To enhance vocational development, jobs in a variety of workplaces may be more useful than settling into a single job during the high school career (Zimmer-Gembeck & Mortimer, 2006). Teachers might present opportunities for students to discuss their work experiences in class—both good and bad—and what they have learned from them, thereby increasing students' collective knowledge of the conditions of work in various workplaces throughout their communities. In this way, students may be able to make more informed decisions about the kinds of jobs that would be most useful to them.

Due to the limited job market for teenage workers, sometimes teens can gain access to a wider range of work settings through volunteering, internships, or various programs sponsored by their schools, including "job shadowing" an experienced worker, or work-study experiences. It is unrealistic to expect teenagers to make firm occupational choices during high school, and relatively few do so in this era of extended higher education and prolonged transitions to adulthood. Nonetheless, it is still worthwhile to begin thinking about work and the kinds of challenges and opportunities that would be most congenial to a teen's nascent interests and capacities. Teens may begin to think about what kinds of rewards at work are most important to them, be they intrinsic (e.g., autonomy, responsibility, opportunities to express creativity, a job that enables them to help other people) or extrinsic (e.g., high income, opportunities for advancement), or some combination of both. It is during high school and the years immediately following that these values crystallize. Much school and major "shopping" as well as occupational "floundering," could possibly be avoided if young people's work values were sufficiently formed to provide a basis for effective educational and career decision making. Some combination of paid jobs, internships, and volunteer jobs might encourage optimal career exploration and long-term benefits.

References

Bills, D.B., Helms, L.B., & Ozcan, M. 1995. The impact of student employment on teachers' attitudes and behaviors toward working students. *Youth and Society,* 27, 169–193.

Committee on the Health and Safety Implications of Child Labor. (1998). *Protecting Youth at Work.* Washington, D.C.: National Academy Press.

Finch, M.D., Shanahan, M., Mortimer, J.T., & Ryu, S. (1991). Work experience and control orientation in adolescence. *American Sociological Review,* 56, 597–611.

Greenberger, E., & Steinberg, L.D. (1986). *When Teenagers Work: The Psychological and Social Costs of Adolescent Employment.* New York: Basic Books.

Horn, L., Peter, K., & Rooney, K. (2002). *Profile of Undergraduates in U. S. Postsecondary Institutions:* 1999–2000. Washington, D. C.: U.S. Department of Education National Center for Education Statistics.

Lee, J.C., & Staff, J. (2007). When Work Matters: The Varying Impact of Adolescent Work Intensity on High School Drop-out. *Sociology of Education,* 80, 158–178.

Mortimer, J.T. (2003). *Working and Growing up in America.* Cambridge: Harvard University Press.

Mortimer, J.T., & Staff, J. (2004). Early work as a source of developmental discontinuity during the transition to adulthood. *Development and Psychopathology,* 16, 1,047–1,070.

Mortimer, J.T., Vuolo, M.C., Staff, J., Wakefield, S., & Xie, W. (2008). Tracing the timing of 'career' acquisition in a contemporary youth cohort. *Work and Occupations,* 35, 44–84.

Phillips, S., & Sandstrom, K. (1990). Parental attitudes toward "youthwork." *Youth and Society,* 22, 160–183.

Shanahan, M., Elder, G.H., Jr., Burchinal, M., & Conger, R.D. (1996). Adolescent earnings and relationships with parents. In

J.T. Mortimer, & M.D. Finch (Eds.), *Adolescents, Work, and Family: An Intergenerational Developmental Analysis,* (pp. 97–128). Newbury Park, CA: Sage.

Shanahan, M., Finch, M.D., Mortimer, J.T., & Ryu, S. (1991). Adolescent work experience and depressive affect. *Social Psychology Quarterly,* 54, 299–317.

Staff, J., Messersmith, E.E., & Schulenberg, J.E. (2009). Adolescents and the World of Work. In R. Lerner, & L. Steinberg (Eds.), *Handbook of Adolescent Psychology,* 3rd ed, (pp. 270–313). New York: John Wiley and Sons.

Staff, J., & Mortimer, J.T. (2007). Educational and work strategies from adolescence to early adulthood: Consequences for educational attainment. *Social Forces,* 85, 1,169–1,194.

Steinberg, L.D., & Cauffman, E. (1995). The impact of employment on adolescent development. *Annals of Child Development,* 11, 131–166.

Steinberg, L.D., & Dornbusch, S.M. (1991). Negative correlates of part-time employment during adolescence: Replication and elaboration. *Developmental Psychology,* 27, 304–313.

Steinberg, L.D., Fegley, S., & Dornbusch, S. M. (1993). Negative impact of part-time work on adolescent development. *Developmental Psychology,* 29, 171–180.

U.S. Department of Labor. (2000). *Report on the Youth Labor Force.* Washington, D.C.: U.S. Government Printing Office.

Windau, J., & Meyer, S. (2005). Occupational injuries among young workers. *Monthly Labor Review,* 128 (10), 11–23.

Zimmer-Gembeck, M., & Mortimer, J.T. (2006). Adolescent work, vocational development, and education. *Review of Educational Research,* 76, 537–566.

Critical Thinking

1. What are the consequences of adolescent paid work?
2. What are the findings from the youth development study?
3. What can parents, counselors, and others do to help youth make sound employment-related decisions?
4. What can be done to improve school-to-work transition?

JEYLAN T. MORTIMER, PHD is Professor in the Department of Sociology and Principal Investigator of the Youth Development Study at the University of Minnesota (morti002@umn.edu).

Acknowledgments—This article summarizes findings from the Youth Development Study, supported by a grant from the National Institute of Child Health and Human Development (HD 44138). It was previously funded by the National Institute of Mental Health (MH 42843). The content is solely the responsibility of the author and does not represent official views of the National Institute of Child Development or the National Institute of Health.

Immigrant Youth in U.S. Schools: Opportunities for Prevention

DINA BIRMAN, PHD, ET AL.

Today 10.6% of children enrolled in kindergarten through 12th grade in the U.S. are foreign born (NCES, 2007), and 1 in 5 are children of immigrants (de Cohen, Deterding, & Clewell, 2005). Historically, immigrants have greatly contributed to the U.S. society and adapted with time. Yet immigrants also face a number of challenges during the initial period of resettlement, adjusting psychologically, socially, and economically to the realities of their new cultural context (Beiser, 2006).

For school-aged children, the most important settings are the family and the school, with the parent-child-school triangle comprising a critical mesosystem within which socialization and development take place (Bronfenbrenner, 1979). Public schools represent the setting where many of the acculturative struggles of immigrant children unfold, having traditionally served as a vehicle of socialization and "assimilation" of immigrants in the U.S. (c.f. Dewey, 1916). Thus school interventions that focus on restructuring educational programming to accommodate immigrants can provide an opportunity to intervene directly with the primary environment that shapes the youth's experience (Trickett & Birman, 1989), providing a more lasting and far-reaching solution than individual interventions. Further, because U.S. schools expect parental involvement, schools can provide an avenue to engage parents in interventions and create a bridge between the worlds of family and school in ways that do not stigmatize the family or the child.

Immigrant students bring a range of diverse experiences, which can be viewed as resources to enrich the school setting. In today's climate of increased accountability, however, schools face many political challenges to addressing the needs of new immigrants who are often perceived as a drain on limited resources. Yet there are a number of possible avenues for intervention that can enhance the success of our immigrant students by engaging existing resources. The remainder of this article first describes today's immigrants, then the stressors and challenges they face, and ends by offering suggestions for prevention and intervention strategies to promote the mental health and positive adjustment of immigrant children.

The Diversity of Today's Immigrants

One of the main features of the current migration wave is its diversity, which presents both challenges and opportunities to school teachers and administrators. While the majority of immigrants enter the U.S.

voluntarily to pursue employment opportunities or to join relatives, refugees and asylum seekers are forced to flee from their homelands because of war or political violence, often coming to the U.S. after extended stays in refugee camps. Many immigrants are well educated (Frey, 2005), however some arrive with little or no prior education, or even literacy in their native language. Further, the migration flow is continually changing, making it difficult to anticipate the needs and characteristics of new arrivals. This places schools in the position of constantly confronting new languages, cultures, and circumstances, and being creative and flexible to meet the needs of such diverse students. In this context, "cultural competence" is not enough, and today's schools need to develop "multicultural competence" to serve the ever-changing student body. Such flexibility and creativity in attention to diversity can benefit all students.

Issues in Adaptation

Immigration is accompanied by dramatic changes in cultural milieu, separation from loved ones, and the need to adapt in the new society. For immigrants who are refugees there is additional stress from traumatic events prior to or during flight from their homeland. Sources of stress for immigrants can be summarized into three inter-related categories: (a) migration stress; (b) acculturative stress; and (c) traumatic stress (Birman, 2002).

Migration Stress

Migration stress involves the difficulties resulting from disruptions in children's everyday lives when removed from a familiar environment. Moving can be very stressful for children (Raviv, Keinan, Abazon, & Raviv, 1990), and moving away from one's native country can additionally be associated with "cultural bereavement" (Eisenbruch, 1992), described as feelings of loss of their past lives, cultural context, surroundings, and friends and family left behind. These feelings of loss may be more acute in children than adults because they were not in control of the decision to immigrate. The disruptions in social networks resulting from migration may also be particularly salient during the early stages of resettlement, and schools can help ensure that immigrant youth have opportunities for social support from ethnic and mainstream adults and peers who can help them cope emotionally and provide orientation to the new culture.

Acculturative Stress

Acculturative stress refers to the challenges that children and their families face in adjusting to the new culture in resettlement.

In addition to learning the new language and culture, children and youth must integrate aspects of the two cultures into their own cultural identity. On one hand, acquiring competence in the new culture is instrumentally useful, and has been found to help immigrants succeed at school (Vedder, Boekaerts, & Seegers, 2005). At the same time, developing a positive ethnic identity is important psychologically (Phinney, 1990).

"Acculturation gaps" emerge in immigrant families when children acculturate to the American culture and language faster than their parents. Because parents are more connected to their native culture, whereas children are often eager to immerse themselves in the new culture, immigrant families may experience conflict and misunderstanding. Additional stress can result from children translating or "culture brokering" for their parents, as such responsibilities may be too difficult to handle at a young age. This stress, however, can be reduced for children who are able to maintain ties to their native culture because this lessens the acculturation gaps and family conflict (Birman, 2006). Schools can help by supporting students' connections to their native cultures and reaching out to their parents.

Traumatic Stress

Many immigrants, particularly refugees, have suffered trauma both before and during migration, in refugee camps, during war, or while crossing borders and hiding from authorities. Symptoms of traumatic stress reactions may manifest themselves at school as academic and behavioral problems, yet are often not recognized or addressed as a mental health concern. Without valid, culturally sensitive assessments available in the immigrant student's native language, it is impossible to determine whether the child's difficulties are due to cultural adjustment or disabilities and to arrive at a definitive diagnosis. At the same time, there is a danger that important problems will go unaddressed for several years before it is possible to rule out cultural adjustment as the main cause. What is needed is a range of strategies that teachers can use to enhance the child's academic and behavioral functioning regardless of diagnosis.

Opportunities for Prevention and Intervention

From an ecological perspective, developing interventions to alleviate the stress of migration, acculturation, and trauma requires identifying existing resources that can be brought to bear on these issues (Trickett & Birman, 1989). With respect to school interventions, potential resources include parents of immigrant children, programs for English Language Learners (ELL), and Special Education services. Suggestions presented below can reduce culture shock, support parents, create bridges between cultures of home and school, lessen the stress for newly arrived immigrant youth, and enrich the school through the talents and diversity of its immigrant students.

Parents as a Resource

When schools form relationships with immigrant parents, they can help reduce acculturative stress for immigrant students. Becoming involved in the school lives of their children can lessen the family acculturation gap. Therefore, it is important to dispel the impression sometimes held by school personnel that immigrant parents are too busy, preoccupied, or disinterested in their child's schooling to get involved (Huss-Keeler, 1997; Crozier & Davies, 2006). Rather, parents may be unaware of the extent to which they are expected to advocate for their children in American public schools and to be able to navigate among a variety of choices about programs their children can enroll in (Birman & RyersonEspino, in press). Many immigrant parents come from societies where such decisions were made solely by schools and they may stay away from contact with schools out of respect and deference to school authorities that is the norm in many immigrant-sending countries (Delgato-Gaitan & Trueba, 1991), or due to lack of knowledge about how and when it is appropriate to contact the school (Birman & Ryerson-Espino, in press).

When schools form relationships with immigrant parents, they can help reduce acculturative stress for immigrant students.

An important component in any strategy to reach out to immigrant parents is the use of bicultural and bilingual liaisons (Huss-Keeler, 1997; Birman & Ryerson-Espino, in press), which can also be an additional way to engage immigrant parents directly in the school. Engaging immigrant parents in this way removes children from culture brokering and helps bridge the worlds of home and school. Other examples of interventions designed to involve immigrant parents in school, such as special after-school events, are presented in Table 1.

ELL Programs as a Resource

English Language Learners (ELL's) in U.S. schools participate in a variety of transitional programs that can be an excellent resource not only for English language instruction but also for providing emotional and social support and cultural orientation to new immigrant students. On one end of the continuum, full-day bilingual programs are designed to educate children in their native language in various subject areas with English as one of their subjects. A more integrative model pulls students out of mainstream classes for two to three periods a day into English as a Second Language (ESL) program. In addition, some school districts have "newcomer" programs (Boyson & Short, 2003) that pull out students with disrupted or no prior education for extensive orientation and academic support (Birman, 2005). Finally, some school districts integrate ELL students into mainstream classrooms by employing "Sheltered Instruction Observational Protocol" (SIOP) programs that are designed to provide "scaffolding" or supportive educational techniques to enable ELL students to catch up (Boyson & Short, 2003).

There are a number of ways that pull-out and newcomer ELL programs can reduce migration and acculturative stress. ELL classes tend to be smaller and often last for several class periods, allowing greater contact with the teacher. ELL teachers tend to have particular interests in helping immigrant students with their cultural adaptation, as many have experienced living abroad or are immigrants themselves. Further, these smaller and longer classes provide opportunities to get to know other students from different countries, which can help normalize students' experience of being different and can help them feel more comfortable about their own blended identity. ELL teachers can also utilize lesson plans and techniques that can simultaneously teach English and also enhance the mental health of the students by providing them with opportunities to share their experiences and receive support from peers (Birman, 2002, 2005).

However, ELL programs can also separate and marginalize both students and teachers from the mainstream of the school. Many teachers of pull-out ELL programs may not have a permanent classroom, and are the first laid off with budget cuts or as the demographics

Table 1 Activities/Interventions to Involve Immigrant Parents in School

Activities/Interventions	Rationale
Designate a bicultural/bilingual liaison between school and parents	A bicultural/bilingual liaison can become a trusted person for immigrant parents who don't know how to communicate with the school. Because many immigrants are used to relying on informal supports of family and friends to get information about schools and their community (Huss-Keeler, 1997), ideally such a liaison would be a member of the immigrant community, perhaps an English-speaking immigrant parent.
Conduct home visits by school teachers and/or administrators	Traditional home visits are rarely used, but visiting immigrant homes can dispel a lot of myths and help the teacher better understand the family situation (Crozier & Davies, 2006). Home visits may not be possible in many cases, but if possible they can facilitate positive teacher-parent communication.
Make interpreters available for parent-teacher conferences	Providing interpreters not only allows parents to communicate with teachers, but also takes children out of the role of "culture broker" and supports parent authority.
Offer special after-school events that incorporate immigrant culture and involve parents. Examples include: • International dinners held at school with parents of all students bringing dishes representing their heritage • School festivals that incorporate displays or activities representing immigrant cultures	Attending or participating in after-school events can help parents become more comfortable with the school and ultimately communicating with the teachers. Activities do not have to involve having parents talk with teachers. For example, watching a performance at a school festival can be less threatening and more comfortable for immigrant parents than more traditional PTA meetings or parent-teacher conferences (Hull-Keeler, 1997).
Provide school orientations for immigrant parents at the school with the help of bicultural liaisons and/or interpreters	Immigrant parents need orientation to the U.S. school system and information about how and when to contact the school. Special events organized for parents at the school reflect an interest in involving immigrant families in the education of their children. Packets of information that the schools send home, even if printed in immigrant languages, are not sufficient to educate immigrant parents about the schools.

of the school shift. They may have been recruited during a sudden immigrant influx and hired provisionally without adequate certification. There are a number of interventions that schools can put into place to make these teachers feel that they are a valued resource in the school and reduce their marginalization (see Table 2).

Most importantly, schools can work to create climates that support the expression of immigrant cultures as they adapt to the school. While acculturation to both the new and the native culture can bring advantages to immigrant youth, some communities and schools believe that an "assimilationist press" to adapt quickly to the host culture is best, yet this results in discrimination experienced by those immigrant students who maintain their native ethnic identity. In a recent multi-national study of immigrant youth, Berry and colleagues (2006) found that adolescents who experienced more discrimination were less likely to be bicultural. Such discrimination forces immigrant adolescents to choose between either assimilating and distancing themselves from their native culture or rejecting the culture of the new society, rather than integrating the two (Birman et al., 2005). Therefore, schools that support immigrant students in exploring their cultural identity, as they are also learning about the new culture, are more likely to endorse a diversity of different acculturative styles and create greater opportunities for successful adaptation. Table 2 provides some examples of how schools can do this.

Special Education as a Resource

Given how much attention is paid in the literature to the mental health needs of immigrant children, it is startling how little discussion there is about Special Education as a potential resource. Special Education services are designed to provide remedial and/or developmental instruction, while also balancing grade level preparation across multiple curriculum areas. There is some concern that referral to Special Education services can impede the adaptation and integration into U.S. schools by stigmatizing and separating immigrant students; but the reality is that immigrant students may require additional supports. For example, refugee students who experience post-traumatic stress and related disorders as a result of trauma may be eligible for and can benefit from Special Education services. Without proper intervention, such mental health needs may manifest in disabilities that are likely to impair their functioning in school. Yet because of the strict laws governing Special Education, assessment and referral of immigrants from diverse countries is extremely challenging because we lack the culturally valid assessments necessary to identify true disabilities.

However, even when arriving at a "definitive" diagnosis is not possible, ELL and mainstream staff can learn from Special Education specialists about useful techniques that can help immigrant students learn, regardless of whether student's learning challenges stem from cultural adjustment, lack of prior exposure to schools and literacy, or mental disorders that are interfering with academic functioning. By utilizing the tools that Special Education specialists have developed through years of working with students with various learning challenges, needs, and strengths, school staff who work with immigrant students can help them benefit from the lessons learned in Special

Table 2 Creating a Hospitable Climate and Reducing Marginalization of Immigrant Students and ELL Teachers

Activities/Interventions	Rationale
Prioritize diversity among school teachers and staff when hiring	Having diverse ethnic and immigrant groups represented among school teachers and staff, particularly in positions of authority, communicates respect for diverse cultures and can serve as a natural bridge/liaison between home and school.
Support ELL teachers by providing avenues to certification when necessary and dedicating physical and human resources	Certification, permanent classrooms, and administrative supports can raise the status of ELL teachers and reduce their marginalization.
Place immigrant students in mainstream classrooms and provide sheltered instruction and scaffolding to the entire classroom	Sheltered Instruction Observational Protocol (SIOP) is an empirically validated program that has been used to allow immigrant students to participate in mainstream lessons rather than pull-out classes while all students benefit from enhanced instruction, group work, and multisensory lesson plans (www.siopinstitute.net/about.shtml)
Create art or information displays around the school about immigrant cultures and languages	Schools can display posters or pictures of immigrant countries or signs, such as a "welcome" sign, in different languages around the halls. One program in Chicago, "Changing Worlds" (www.changingworlds. org), photographed immigrant families and collected their stories. Posters were then created telling the story of migration of each family (with translations into multiple languages), a map of the country of origin, and the family picture. Such displays can help create a climate of hospitality, interest in different cultures, and inclusion of immigrant students in the life of the school.
Hold special school-wide events during the school day that incorporate immigrant cultures (such as school assemblies)	School events and assemblies can incorporate information about the history and culture of the immigrants, inviting the children and parents to contribute (Trickett & Birman, 1989). Topics can include seasonal celebrations from immigrant cultures, or anniversaries of important historical events.
Incorporate immigrant cultures into the curriculum	History and social studies classes can study immigrant cultures, and immigrant parents and students can be invited to classes to talk about their background and experiences.
Peer mentoring programs	Pairing newly arrived students with those who came earlier or were born in the country can help them become more integrated into the peer group and receive support.

Table 3 Adaptation of Special Education Techniques for Immigrant Students

Activities/Interventions	Rationale
Incorporate information specific to individual student backgrounds, including opportunities for students to explore their cultural background, when delivering the general curriculum content to all students.	Because of the diverse learning needs of Special Education students, staff do a great deal of adapting the general education curriculum to the specific learning needs and interests of the students they serve. Therefore, staff working with immigrant students can learn from Special Education staff, who have experience viewing the general curriculum as flexible to make it meaningful for individual students, but delivered to and beneficial for the rest of the students in the class.
Develop multisensory classroom activities that deliver a diversity of curricula.	Multisensory classroom activities may be geared to address the learning styles of a particular student, but can make the lessons more interesting for all students. For example, high school curricula that rely extensively on lectures and written reports can be modified to include hands-on activities, such as art and other media or oral reports, to make the work more accessible for ELL students.
Create individualized plans to enhance the learning needs for individual students. Allow students to be actively involved in the development of these plans.	Because immigrant students have a diversity of learning needs, this approach can ensure that the greatest challenges are identified and progress toward the identified goals can be monitored.
Daily check-in periods with newly immigrated students or immigrant students in the mainstream environment with school staff of their choice.	These strategies can help students feel that they are cared about as a member of the school community, provide continuous feedback about progress, and provide opportunities to make necessary adjustments to facilitate academic progress.

Education. For example, a number of regularly used tools in Special Education could be adapted as preventive activities for use with immigrant students in ELL and mainstream classrooms. Some sample accommodations are listed in Table 3. Therefore, schools need to move past their hesitancy to foster collaborations between Special Education and ELL services and personnel.

Collaboration between ELL and Special Education is especially important, because both are dealing with similar challenges regarding student learning and may be therefore providing similar supports and services for students. As a result of the separate laws and norms governing these two programs, partnership between them is rare. Yet because both of these programs struggle with limited resources, they can only benefit from working together, which could help to streamline the services schools are providing to students with unique learning challenges. This is an important policy direction to pursue because through such collaboration, schools can improve their provision of a range of mental health and educational services to immigrant children.

Conclusions

Immigrant students and their families bring a richness of experience and knowledge that can enrich schooling for all students. Given the large numbers of arrivals and diverse cultures represented among them, schools have a tremendous opportunity to create a climate that views these newcomers as resources and does not constrain the multiple ways in which they can adapt to our society. Immigrant children and parents have much that they need to learn from caring teachers and administrators. At the same time they also have much to offer as we educate our children to function in an increasingly global community.

References

Beiser, M. (2006). Longitudinal research to promote effective refugee resettlement. *Transcultural Psychiatry, 43*, 56–71.

Berry, J., Phinney, J., Sam, D., & Vedder, P. (Eds.) (2006). *Immigrant Youth in Cultural Transition: Acculturation, Identity, and Adaptation Across National Contexts.* Mahwah, NJ: Lawrence Erlbaum Associates Publishers.

Birman, D. (2002) *Refugee Mental Health in the Classroom: A Guide for the ESL Teacher.* Denver, CO: Spring Institute for Intercultural Learning, www.spring-institute.org.

Birman, D. (2005). *Refugee Children With Low Literacy Skills or Interrupted Education: Identifying Challenges and Strategies.* Denver, CO: Spring Institute for Intercultural Learning, 24 pp.

Birman, D. (2006). Acculturation gap and family adjustment: Findings with Soviet Jewish refugees in the U.S. and implications for measurement. *Journal of Cross-Cultural Psychology, 37*(5), 1–22.

Birman, D., & Ryerson-Espino, S. (in press). The relationship of parental practices and knowledge to school adaptation for immigrant and non-immigrant high school students. *Canadian Journal of School Psychology.*

Birman, D., Trickett, E., & Buchanan, R. (2005). A tale of two cities: Replication of a study on the acculturation and adaptation of immigrant adolescents from the former Soviet Union in a different community context. *American Journal of Community Psychology, 35*(1–2), 83–101.

Boyson, B.A., & Short, D.J. (2003). *Secondary School Newcomer Programs in the United States* (Research Report No. 12). Santa Cruz, CA and Washington, D.C.: Center for Research on Education, Diversity & Excellence.

Bronfenbrenner, U. (1979). *The Ecology of Human Development.* Cambridge, MA: Harvard University Press.

Crozier, G., & Davies, J. (2006). Family matters: A discussion of the Bangladeshi and Pakistani extended family and community in supporting the children's education. *Sociological Review, 54*, 678–695.

de Cohen, C., Deterding, N., & Clewell, B. (2005) *Who's Left Behind? Immigrant Children in High and Low LEP Schools.* Urban Institute. Available online at www.urban.org/url.cfm?ID=411231

Delgado-Gaitan, C., & Trueba, H. (1991). *Crossing Cultural Borders: Education for Immigrant Families in America.* Oxford, England: Falmer Press/Taylor & Francis, Inc.

Dewey, J. (1916). *Democracy and Education.* New York, NY: The Free Press.

Eisenbruch, M. (1992). Toward a culturally sensitive DSM: Cultural bereavement in Cambodian refugees and the traditional healer as taxonomist. *Journal of Nervous & Mental Disease, 180*, 8–10.

Frey, W.H. (2005). Second generation rising. *Milken Institute Review*, Second Quarter, 6–9.

Huss-Keeler, R.L. (1997). Teacher perception of ethnic and linguistic minority parental involvement and its relationships to children's language and literacy learning: A case study. *Teaching and Teacher Education, 13*, 171–182

NCES (2007). *Student Effort and Educational Progress.* Retrieved August 4, 2007 from National Center for Education Statistics website: http://nces.ed.gov/programs/coe/2007/section3/table.asp?tableID=700

Phinney, J.S. (1990). Ethnic identity in adolescents and adults: review of research. *Psychological Bulletin, 109*, 499–514.

Raviv, A., Keinan, G., Abazon, Y., & Raviv, A. (1990). Moving as a stressful life event for adolescents. *Journal of Community Psychology, 18*, 130–140.

Trickett, E.J., & Birman, D. (1989). Taking ecology seriously: A community development approach to individually based preventive intervention in schools. In B. Compas & L. Bond (Eds.), *Primary Prevention in the Schools* (pp. 361–390). Newbury Park, CA: Sage.

Vedder, P., Boekaerts, M., & Seegers, G. (2005). Perceived social support and well being in school: The role of students' ethnicity. *Journal of Youth and Adolescence, 34*, 269–278.

Critical Thinking

1. What are the struggles of immigrant youth?
2. How could restructuring educational programming help with the struggles of immigrant youth?

3. How could immigrant parents help promote mental health in schools?

4. How would you define positive adjustment of immigrant children?

DINA BIRMAN is an Assistant Professor of Psychology in the Community and Prevention Research Division at the University of Illinois at Chicago. She is currently partnering with several community-based mental health agencies to study and refine school-based mental health interventions for immigrant and refugee children and youth. **TRACI**

WEINSTEIN is in the Community & Prevention Research doctoral program at the University of Illinois at Chicago. From her experience working as a Special Education teacher with inner-city high school students, her research interests include investigating ways to promote academic achievement for immigrant and minority youth. **WING YI CHAN** is in the Community & Prevention Research doctoral program at UIC. She is interested in the contextual and cultural factors that are related to the resilience of refugees and immigrants. **SARAH BEEHLER** is in the Community & Prevention Research doctoral program at UIC. Her research interests include studying the effects of culturally sensitive mental health interventions for refugee and immigrant groups.

Reducing School Violence

School-Based Curricular Programs and School Climate

MICHAEL B. GREENE, PhD

In this brief review, two different, though interrelated approaches to the reduction of school violence are described and critiqued. The first, and more traditional approach, involves the establishment of classroom-based educational and therapeutic programs that focus on the interpersonal skills, attitudes, emotional literacy, and risk and protective factors that are associated with aggressive behavior and attitudes. These school-based curricular[1] programs (SBCPs) promote pro-soical behavior and endeavor to help students maintain peer relationships and conflicts without resorting to aggressive or violent behavior. The second approach endeavors to improve components of a school's social and interpersonal climate that are associated with aggressive and violent behavior. These components include the quality of relationships among students, staff, and administrators; norms, attitudes, and beliefs among students, staff, and administrators; perceptions and enforcement of disciplinary rules and policies; the organizational structure of schools and their capacity to address school violence; and school connectedness or bonding (Cook, Murphy, &Hunt, 2000; McEvoy & Welker, 2000; Welsh, 2000).

What Is Meant by School Violence?

In terms of a school's jurisdiction and liability, school violence is violence that occurs on school grounds, on school-supported transportation, and at school-sponsored activities. Nevertheless, violence committed on school grounds often derives from conflicts that emerge in the community (as well as vice versa). This phenomenon blurs the distinction between school and community violence and suggests that school personnel need to possess knowledge of the community in which a school is situated and that members of the community should become involved in school-based violence prevention initiatives.

> **Violence committed on school grounds often derives from conflicts that emerge in the community.**

The "what" of school violence is more complicated and multidimensional (Furlong & Morrison, 2000). Violence is generally defined as an intentional form of behavior in which one person threatens, attempts to harm, or does harm another person. Aggression is generally defined as a form of low-level violence that includes verbal, physical, or gestural behavior that is intended to cause minor physical harm, psychological distress, intimidation, or to induce fear in another (Greene, 2005). Aggression can also be indirect or relational, as in instances in which a student is ostracized, isolated, or is the object of nasty rumors. Moreover, students are increasingly disseminating negative, compromising, or humiliating messages through electronic means (cyberbullying, the newest form of adolescent aggression).

Some researchers argue that the disproportionate imposition of negative sanctions upon certain classes of students for the same conduct, as has been found with zero-tolerance policies, is also a form of school violence in that such practices unjustly penalize some students more than others (Skiba, Michael, Nardo, & Peterson, 2002). Similarly, some have argued that institutional forms of racism and sexual oppression (as reflected in behavior, attitudes, curricula, and textbooks), an unwelcoming school atmosphere (often conceptualized as an aspect of school climate), as well as the consequences of unequal distribution of school funding, are structural or systemic forms of school-related violence (Greene, 2006). These forms of violence, however, are rarely tracked, monitored, or addressed by school violence programs.

Some have argued that institutional forms of racism and sexual oppression, an unwelcoming school atmosphere, as well as the consequences of unequal distribution of school funding, are structural or systemic forms of school-related violence.

The "who" of school violence is most frequently conceptualized as student-on-student aggression or violence; ignoring the many other permutations of violence among teachers, staff, administrators, and students; for example, teacher-to-student bullying or coercion (Twemlow & Fonagy, 2005). Most SBCPs are focused on direct forms of aggression among students (fighting, hitting, pushing, verbal intimidation, and threats); excluding the indirect forms of aggression noted above. Correspondingly, as detailed below, these programs are nearly always assessed in terms of the extent to which direct aggressive behavior or known predictors of aggressive behavior (risk factors) are lessened or reduced.

School-Based Curricular Programs

Hundreds of school-based curricular programs are available on the market and described in the professional literature. Programs vary in terms of theoretical foundation, target audience, duration, and intensity, and by the training required to implement them (Fagan & Mihalic, 2003; Greene, 2005). Some programs focus on the ways in which students frame, perceive, or conceptualize the nature and appropriateness of aggressive and violent behavior (cognitive behavioral approaches), some focus on how students learn and unlearn such behaviors (social learning or coaching approaches), some utilize traditional pedagogical methods to teach social skills, some focus on rewarding positive behavior (behavioral programs), some focus on helping students better understand feelings and emotions (social-emotional literacy approaches), and some adopt more traditional therapeutic or counseling approaches.

The vast majority of SBCPs target elementary and middle school students and are designed as universal programs in which all students in a school or grade level participate. One such program is Promoting Alternative Thinking Strategies (PATHS) (Greenberg, Kusche, & Mihalic, 1998). This elementary school program focuses on the promotion of social and emotional competencies. It covers five basic conceptual domains: self-control, emotional understanding, positive self-esteem, relationships, and interpersonal problem solving. One hundred thirty-one sequenced and integrated lesson plans covering each of the five domains are taught during a five-year period. Like many SBCPs, PATHS utilizes a variety of pedagogical approaches including role plays, modeling behavior, student projects, rehearsal strategies, lectures, and classroom discussion and reflection.

Like all classroom curricula, SBCPs require teacher training. Sometimes training is limited to a manual but increasingly programs are requiring face-to-face training and telephone consultation to ensure that the program is implemented as intended and designed. However, this form of teacher training is not generally oriented to helping teachers communicate and build trust and credibility with their students, which are aspects of a school's climate that are clearly associated with peer aggression.

Some programs have additional components such as parent coaching and counseling, home visitation, and individual case management. These programs are targeted to students who exhibit known risk factors (selected programs) or students who have engaged in aggressive or violent behavior (indicated programs). FAST Track is an example of a selected program that includes, in addition to classroom activities, parent training, home visitation, case management, and academic tutoring (Conduct Problems Prevention Research Group, 1999). While FAST Track and other selected and indicated SBCPs generally do not address the quality of teacher-student relationships, they are designed to improve the quality of relationships among students and their parents or guardians.

Evaluations of SBCPs

Over the past two decades, a large body of research has demonstrated that many school-based curricular programs, if implemented properly, significantly reduce aggressive and disruptive behavior among students in the school setting (Hahn et al., 2007; Mytton et al., 2002; Wilson & Lipsey, 2007). Hahn and his colleagues (Hahn et al., 2007), in their review of the evaluation research literature on universal SBCPs, found that 15% fewer students who participate in such programs engage in aggressive behavior in comparison to similar groups of students who do not participate in such programs (an 18% reduction in elementary school programs, a 7% reduction in middle schools, and a 29% reduction in high schools). Wilson and Lipsey's (2007) analysis of the SBCP evaluation literature revealed reductions in aggressive behavior in the 25% range.

No single type of universal SBCP appears to be more effective than others (e.g., cognitive behavioral programs, social skills programs, behavioral, and counseling programs) and generally the programs were equally effective in different types of communities and with different types of populations. However, Wilson and Lipsey (2007) found that SBCPs generally had greater impact in reducing aggressive behavior among low- versus middle-income students.

Wilson and Lipsey (2007) also included selected and indicated programs in their review of the research literature on school-based violence prevention programs. They found that indicated programs were more effective in reducing aggressive behavior than selected programs, in other words, the more aggressive the students the higher the impact of the program. In addition, they found that behavioral learning strategies were significantly more effective than other types of programs for selected and indicated programs, though all types of programs that were subject to rigorous evaluation significantly reduced levels of aggression and disruptive behavior. Mytton and colleagues (2002) reviewed the research literature for SBCPs that were exclusively focused on students at high risk for violent or aggressive behavior. They also found an overall significant positive impact of these programs in reducing aggressive behavior. Their analysis, however, yielded a slightly lower level of aggression and violence reduction than did Wilson and Lipsey's review (2007).

Need for Further Study

Wilson and Lipsey (2007) found that programs that were implemented without the direct involvement of the research team that developed the program were as effective in reducing aggressive behavior as programs that did have direct program developer involvement. While the number of studies without program developer involvement was relatively small, this finding suggests that, with proper training and instruction, school administrators can implement these programs with fidelity and can achieve positive outcomes (see also Fagan & Mihalic, 2003). Nevertheless, Wilson and Lipsey's sample, as indicated above, was confined to programs that were subject to a relatively rigorous program evaluation (in other words, the sample of programs was far from representative of typical situations in which a school implements a program without direct involvement of the program developers).

Indeed, D. Gottfredson and G. Gottfredson (2002), in their examination of implementation fidelity within a national probability sample of schools (without corresponding experimental outcome evaluations), discovered that implementation quality was generally quite low. Given the research literature showing that outcomes of SBCPs are compromised when implemented with poor

fidelity, the question of whether schools can routinely achieve the excellent results revealed in the research literature remains open (D. Gottfredson, 2001).

Another important factor in examining the impact of SBCPs is whether the obtained positive outcomes are sustainable over time. Generally, the follow-up period assessed in published studies is relatively short: the vast majority of studies have used a follow-up period of less than one school year. Consequently, there is no systemic data on the long-term impact of such programs (D. Gottfredson, 2007). This represents a serious gap in our understanding of SBCPs.

In addition, very few of the SBCP evaluations have utilized measures of more serious forms of violence or crimes against persons, such as shootings, aggravated assaults, or robberies (D. Gottfredson, 2007). This is due in part to the relative rarity of such behaviors and thus the requirement of very large sample sizes to detect a program impact on these behaviors. We have long known that early and chronic expression of aggressive behavior, particularly when expressed in multiple domains, predicts subsequent violent behavior. Whether short-term reductions in aggressive behavior lead to long-term reductions in more serious forms of violence remains a compelling theory but lacks direct empirical support.

The Impact of School Climate on School Violence

A robust research literature suggests that many of the components that comprise school climate—cultural norms in the schools, quality of interpersonal relationships, school policies, and student, staff, and administrator feelings and beliefs about their schools—are significantly related to levels of victimization and offending in schools (Furlong & Morrison, 2000). Moreover, because classroom climate often varies within a school, it is important to examine the impact of interpersonal climate at the classroom as well as schoolwide level (Sprott, 2004).

Several researchers have demonstrated that "school connectedness" (feelings of positive attachment to one's school, peers, teachers) is a protective factor for reducing youth violence in general, school violence in particular, and externalizing behavior (Payne, Gottfredson, & Gottfredson, 2003). Furthermore, data from the National Longitudinal Study of Adolescent Health reveal that four aspects of school climate predict school connectedness: positive classroom management, participation in extracurricular activities, tolerant discipline policies, and school size (McNeely, Nonnemaker, & Blum, 2002). These findings suggest that altering these elements will enhance school connectedness. Whether such changes will also result in reductions in peer-to-peer and other forms of school-based aggression and violence remains untested.

With regard to discipline policies, several researchers have found significant associations between the clarity, consistency, and fairness of school rules and violence perpetration and victimization. In schools in which students believe that their school's rules and discipline structure are clear, fair and consistently applied, levels of violence and aggression are generally low (Payne et al., 2003; Welsh, 2000). Similarly, G. Gottfredson and colleagues, in their large scale study of school violence in American schools, found that school climate and discipline practices were the primary distinguishing factors between low and high disorder schools (G. Gottfredson et al., 2000). High disorder schools in which students frequently disrupt classroom activities were characterized by inconsistent use of discipline practices, unclear or low expectations for students, use of zero-tolerance policies, and communication problems among students and staff.

> **In schools in which students believe that their school's rules and discipline structure are clear, fair, and consistently applied, levels of violence and aggression are generally low.**

Battistich and Hom (1997) found that "school belonging," comprised of a combined measure of interpersonal relationships and student autonomy and influence, predicted delinquency and victimization among fifth and sixth grade students. Similarly, Welsh (2000) found that respect for students was associated with lower levels of student aggression for both perpetration and victimization.

Relationships between SBCPs and School Climate

A modest research literature suggests that SBCPs are better implemented in schools that have a relatively positive school climate (Ozer, 2006). That school climate affects the implementation quality of school-based programs is suggested by studies revealing that the implementation of such programs is affected by school organization, key-stakeholder buy-in, expertise implementing programs generally, and staff turnover (Greene, 2005; Hunter, Elias, & Norris, 2001). Given that the quality of SBCP implementation is significantly associated with greater reductions in aggressive behavior, school climate appears to moderate the effectiveness of SBCPs (G. Gottfredson et al., 2000; Wilson & Lipsey, 2007).

School Climate Change Programs

In contrast to the burgeoning experimental literature of SBCPs, few experimental studies have been conducted that directly evaluate the impact of school climate change efforts on aggressive behavior and the few studies that have been conducted reveal modest to moderate effects (Cook et al., 2000; Greene, 2005). The evaluation of Coiner's School Development Program represents the truest experimental test of a climate change program (Cook et al., 2000). This program focuses specifically on changing a school's interpersonal climate through the work of three teams: a School Planning and Management Team, a Social Support Team, and a Parent Team. Each team supports the basic goals of implementing cooperative learning and problem solving and building trust among adults and students in the school. Given the focus on the social environment of the school, climate change from the perspective of staff and students, as well as resultant academic and social outcomes, are assessed. The evaluation of the Comer School Development Program by Cook and colleagues revealed a positive impact on some measures of school climate as well as reductions in acting out behavior (Cook et al., 2000).

Similarly, The Child Development Program is designed to promote caring and supporting relationships among students, staff, and parents. It focuses on the norms of social justice and responsibility, emphasizes a strengths-based approach to students, and engages students with adults in program decision-making (Battistich, Schaps, & Wilson, 2004). The evaluation of this program revealed reductions in student victimization and student misconduct as well as improvements in two aspects of school climate: students' bonding to school and improvements in teacher-student relationships.

Additional programs target multiple domains of the social ecology (teachers, administrators, school policies, family, and community members) but most of these programs focus on unidirectional influences on the child, without significantly addressing bi-directional relationships among students and the adult authorities in the school. For example the Olweus' Bullying Prevention Program (Olweus & Limber, 1999) is often cited as an evidence-based program that adopts a school climate approach. Nevertheless, key components of school climate—including coercive and aggressive behaviors by adults, student connectedness to school, and the inconsistent or unfair administration of discipline policies (though shaming as a discipline policy is discouraged)—are not addressed in this program. Consequently, this program cannot be considered a true school climate change program.

Discussion

Tremendous progress has been made over the past two decades in establishing effective school-based violence prevention programs. Nevertheless, programs designed to stem violence in schools have largely focused on reducing student-to-student aggressive behavior through curricular programs (SBCPs), essentially ignoring interpersonal relationships between students and adults in schools, student bonding to schools, disproportionalities in the application of student discipline, and related organizational factors that comprise school climate. And while selected and indicated school-based curricular programs also include family interventions, their focus has remained on reductions in student-to-student aggression.

In addition, SBCPs implicitly or explicitly adopt a "deficit" model, in that the programs are designed to provide social skills training or related skills because students lack such skills. In contrast, the predominant orientation in neighborhood-based youth programming (and incorporated in The Child Development Project described above) is "positive youth development," in which a student's interests and strengths are pursued and through such pursuits fundamental capacities and skills are developed (Wilson-Simmons, 2007). In these programs, youth are given an active role in the program operations and in some cases even in governance. While SBCPs often include exercises and student projects that rely on the use and discovery of interpersonal skills, an overall enhanced focus on positive skills and interests may yield better results and also may improve the quality of relationships between students and the teachers who oversee such activities. Indeed, the promising results from positive behavioral supports initiatives, supports this shift to an enhanced positive youth development approach (Sprague & Horner, 2006).

We know, as summarized above, that SBCPs must be implemented with fidelity in order to achieve the results attained in efficacy studies. We also know through numerous large scale studies and qualitative case studies that a number of key climate-related factors affect a school's capacity to implement programs effectively. These include strong leadership, political will, prior success in implementing programs, trust among teachers and students, emotional support of students, commitment to the program, participation in training, and ongoing assessment (G. Gottfredson et al., 2000; Greene, 2005; Sprott, 2004). A positive climate improves not only the implementation of SBCPs but such factors should act in a synergistic fashion with SBCPs so that the impact of such programs are more robust. Still, this statement requires experimental verification.

School climate approaches to school violence, in contrast to SBCPs, focus on the quality of interpersonal relationships among multiple stakeholders in the school, including teachers, staff, administrators, parents, sometimes community members, and, of course, students. The focus is on the phenomenological interpersonal world of each stakeholder as well as the organizational structure and policies of the schools. Climate change programs focus on aggressive and respectful behavior among all parties, not just the students. As such, climate approaches have the potential to effect more substantial changes not only in aggressive behavior among students but in reducing direct and indirect forms of aggression and in promoting respectful interpersonal relationships among all key stakeholders, improving the organizational structure of schools, and improving the policies and the enforcement of policies as they affect all stakeholders.

Climate change programs focus on aggressive and respectful behavior among all parties, not just the students.

Increasingly, advocates and academics are signaling the need to focus on broad spectrum climate analyses and actions. SBCPs have their place, but they are only one part of the puzzle. A growing body of research has consistently shown that schools in which students feel welcome, schools to which students feel positively connected and engaged, and schools in which students perceive their school's rules and policies are fair and consistently enforced, are likely to have lower levels of aggression and violence and higher rates of respectful behavior among all key stakeholders. Furthermore, in such schools, SBCPs may well be more effective.

The problem, of course, is that effective strategies have not been developed to change the school climate in ways that are robust and replicable. The task of changing school environments is difficult and daunting (Osher et al., 2004). With respect to strategies to change school climate, we are where we were 20 years ago with respect to SBCPs. Some programs have been developed, but we are really at an early stage in our understanding of how these programs work and in determining how effective they are. A number of ideas have been suggested as frameworks for changing school climates (e.g., a human rights orientation, schoolwide strategic planning processes, positive behavior supports, restorative justice, and reconciliation and nonviolence principles), but these ideas need to be operationalized into testable and replicable programs (Greene, 2006; Skiba, Ritter, Simmons, Peterson, & Miller, 2006).

As Osher and colleagues (2004) have stated: "A focus on individual students alone will not produce safe and successful schools" (p. 22). In short, a significantly enhanced body of research is needed on climate change that will help schools navigate the complex terrain of school climate change as a means to reduce aggressive behavior, increase prosocial and respectful behavior in our schools, and improve the implementation and effectiveness of school-based curricular programs.

Note

1. The term "curricular" is adopted to include instructional guidelines, training manuals, as well as formal curricular guides that proscribe the components of the program and how these components should be implemented.

References

Battistich, V., & Hom, A. (1997). The relationship between students' sense of their school as a community and their involvement in problem behaviors. *American Journal of Public Health, 87*(12), 1997–2,001.

Battistich, V., Schaps, E., & Wilson, N. (2004). Effects of an elementary school intervention on students' "Connectedness" to school and social adjustment during Middle School. *The Journal of Primary Prevention, 24*(3), 243–262.

Conduct Problems Prevention Research Group. (2002). The implementation of the Fast Track Program: An example of a large-scale prevention science efficacy trial. *Journal of Abnormal Child Psychology, 30*(1), 1–17.

Cook, T.D., Murphy, R.F., & Hunt, H.D. (2000). Corner's school development program in Chicago. *American Educational Research Journal, 37*(2), 535–597.

Fagan, A. A., & Mihalic, S. (2003). Strategies for enhancing the adoption of school-based prevention programs: Lessons learned from the blueprints for violence prevention replications of the Life Skills Training program. *Journal of Community Psychology, 31*(3), 235–253.

Furlong, M., & Morrison, G. (2000). The school in school violence: Definitions and facts. *Journal of Emotional and Behavioral Disorders, 8*(2), 71–82.

Gottfredson, D.C. (2001), Schools and Delinquency. New York: Cambridge University Press.

Gottfredson, D.C. (2007). Some thoughts about research on youth violence prevention. *American Journal of Preventive Medicine, 33*(2, Supplement 1), S104–S106.

Gottfredson, D.C., & Gottfredson, G.D. (2002). Quality of school based prevention programs: Results from a national survey. *Journal of Research in Crime and Delinquency, 39*(1), 3–35.

Gottfredson, G.D., Gottfredson, D.C., Czeh, E.R., Cantor, D., Crosse, S.B., & Hantman, 1. (2000). *National Study of Delinquency Prevention in Schools*. Final Report. Ellicott City, MD: Gottfredson Associates, Inc.

Greenberg, M.T., Kusche, C., & Mihalic, S.F. (1998). *Promoting Alternative Thinking Strategies (PATHS)*. Boulder, CO: University of Colorado.

Greene, M.B. (2005). Reducing violence and aggression in schools. *Trauma, Violence, & Abuse, 6*(3), 236–253.

Greene, M.B. (2006). Bullying in schools: A plea for a measure of human rights. *Journal of Social Issues, 62*(1), 63–79.

Hahn, R., Fuqua-Whitley, D., Wethington, H., Lowy, I, Crosby, A., Fullilove, M., et al. (2007). Effectiveness of universal school-based programs to prevent violent and aggressive behavior: A systematic review. *American Journal of Preventive Medicine, 33*(2, Supplement 1) S114–S129.

Hunter, L., Elias, M.J., & Norris, J. (2001). School-based violence prevention: Challenges and lessons learned from an action research project. *Journal of School Psychology, 39*(2), 161–175.

McEvoy, A., & Welker, R. (2000). Antisocial behavior, academic failure, and school climate: A critical review. *Journal of Emotional & Behavioral Disorders, 8*(3), 130.

McNeely, C.A., Nonnemaker, J.M., & Blum, R.W. (2002). Promoting school connectedness: Evidence from the National Longitudinal Study of Adolescent Health. *Journal of School Health, 72*(4), 138–146.

Mytton, J.A., DiGuiseppi, C., Gough, D.A., Taylor, R.S., & Logan, S. (2002). School-based violence prevention programs: Systematic review of secondary prevention trials. *Archives of Pediatric Adolescent Medicine*, 752–762.

Olweus, D., & Limber, S. (1999). *Bullying Prevention Program*. Boulder, CO: Center for the Study and Prevention of Violence.

Osher, D., VanAcker, R., Morrison, G.M., Gable, R., Dwyer, K., & Quinn, M. (2004). Warning signs of problems in schools: Ecological perspectives and effective practices for combating school aggression and violence. *Journal of School Violence*, 3, 13–37.

Ozer, E. (2006). Contextual effects in school-based violence prevention programs: A conceptual framework and empirical review. *The Journal of Primary Prevention, 27*(3), 315–340.

Payne, A.A., Gottfredson, D.C., & Gottfredson, G.D. (2003). Schools as communities: The relationships among communal school organization, student bonding, and school disorder. *Criminology, 41*(3), 749–777.

Skiba, R.J., Michael, R.S., Nardo, A.C., & Peterson, R.L. (2002). The Color of discipline: Sources of racial and gender disproportionality in school punishment. *Urban Review, 34*(4), 317–342.

Skiba, R., Ritter, S., Simmons, A., Peterson, R., & Miller, C. (2006). The Safe and Responsive Schools Project: A school reform model for implementing best practices in violence prevention. In S.R. Jimerson & M. Furlong (Eds.), *Handbook of School Violence and School Safety* (pp. 631–650). Mahwah, NJ: Lawrence Erlbaum.

Sprague, J.R., & Homer, R.H. (2006). School wide positive behavioral supports. In S.R. Jimerson & M. Furlong (Eds.), *Handbook of School Violence and School Safety* (pp. 413–427). Mahwah, NJ: Lawrence Erlbaum.

Sprott, J.B. (2004). The Development of Early Delinquency: Can Classroom and School Climates Make a Difference? *Canadian Journal of Criminology & Criminal Justice, 46*(5), 553–572.

Twemlow, S.W., & Fonagy, P. (2005). The prevalence of teachers who bully students in schools with differing levels of behavioral problems. *American Journal of Psychiatry, 162*(12), 2,387–2,389.

Welsh, W.N. (2000). The effects of school climate on school disorder. *The ANNALS of the American Academy of Political and Social Science, 567*(1), 88–107.

Wilson, S.J., & Lipsey, M.W. (2007). School-based interventions for aggressive and disruptive behavior: Update of a Meta-Analysis. *American Journal of Preventive Medicine, 33*(2), 130–143.

Wilson-Simmons, R. (2007). *Positive Youth Development: An Examination of the Field.* Princeton, NJ: Robert Wood Johnson Foundation.

Critical Thinking

1. What are the two different approaches to reducing school violence?

2. What are the advantages of both approaches?

3. What are the disadvantages of both approaches?

4. What is the relationship between the two approaches?

MICHAEL B. GREENE directs the evaluation of New Jersey's Strategic Planning Framework for alcohol and substance abuse prevention initiatives at Rutgers University, Center for Applied Psychology. He is the director of violence prevention at The Nicholson Foundation, and the sole proprietor of Greene Consulting. Dr. Greene received his doctorate in developmental psychology at Columbia University. He previously established two centers for the study and prevention of violence: the Center for the Prevention of Violence at Youth Consultation Service and the Violence Institute of New Jersey at the University of Medicine and Dentistry of New Jersey. He has published numerous articles and chapters on school and youth violence, including "Bullying in Schools: A Plea for a Measure of Human Rights" and has served as Principal Investigator on federal and state grants. In the mid-1990s he was asked to serve on the American Psychological Association's Cadre of Experts in Youth Violence. Dr. Greene's research interests include bullying and harassment in schools, interventions for high-risk youth, domestic violence, and social justice.

Why Teenagers Find Learning a Drag

JESSICA HAMZELOU

Being a teenager can be a drag. As if dealing with peer pressure and raging hormones weren't hard enough, your ability to learn new things is also reduced. Now the brain molecules behind this learning deficit have been identified in mice—and blocked.

When children hit puberty, their ability to learn a second language drops, they find it harder to learn their way around a new location and they are worse at detecting errors in cognitive tests.

Why is this? Sheryl Smith and her colleagues at the State University of New York now reckon that all of these behavioural changes could be due to a temporary increase in a chemical receptor that inhibits brain activity in an area responsible for learning.

In 2007, Smith's team discovered that the number of these receptors soared in mice when they hit puberty, before falling back in adulthood. In their latest study, Smith's team set about finding out if these receptor changes in mice might lead to impaired learning abilities, rather like those seen in pubescent humans.

Shocking Memory

The group examined the hippocampus—a region known to be involved in learning—in mouse brains. Sure enough, pubertal mice had seven times as many of the receptors as infant mice. In adulthood, the number of these receptors fell back to an intermediate level.

The team was also able to examine individual neurons and could see that the extra receptors were being expressed specifically at "neural projections"—sites within the hippocampus known to be involved in learning. This was further evidence that the increase in receptors might affect learning.

Finally, the group measured spatial learning abilities in the mice. The creatures were placed on a rotating platform, on which a stationary section delivered a mild electric shock. After a single shock, the infant mice learned to dodge the danger zone. The pubertal mice, however, failed to learn to avoid it even after several rounds.

Smith reckons that the same mechanism might underlie the learning deficits teenagers experience. Cheryl Sisk at Michigan State University at East Lansing agrees that "mouse puberty is similar to human puberty, although the timescale is different".

Learning Restored

"The research adds to the growing body of literature indicating that puberty and adolescence are a unique period of nervous system development," says Sisk. "Adolescents aren't just in between children and adults. Their behaviour is different from both."

In a further experiment, Smith found that she could remove the learning deficit by injecting pubertal mice with THP—a stress steroid. In children and adult humans, THP is naturally released in response to stress. It reduces brain activity and calms you down, says Smith. But in pubertal mice, THP has the opposite effect—increasing their stress.

Smith suggests that in her most recent experiment, giving extra THP to pubertal mice similarly increased their brain activity and that this activity may have compensated for their learning deficits.

If similar mechanisms underlie teenage learning deficits in humans, this result might point to ways to deal with them—either through behavioural changes or drugs.

Smith suggests that a synthetic form of THP could be developed for teenagers with learning difficulties, although she acknowledges that care would need to be taken not to create any new problems. "We would have to be careful not to affect their mood," she says.

Sisk cautions that it's too soon to apply the results to humans or to other types of learning outside the spatial type tested in the mice.

Critical Thinking

1. Why do teenagers find learning a drag?
2. How was the research done that determined students find learning a drag?
3. What are the possible solutions to help students with this viewpoint?
4. Do you think the suggested solutions would work?

Thousands Need Teens to Lead Them Back to School

Jennifer A. Leigh

According to the U.S. Department of Education, every single day 60,000 students avoid going to school because they are afraid of being bullied.

Question: How can we help those 60,000 frightened students go to school?

Answer: Teach teens to lead.

Three Types of Teens

There are three types of teens: Bullies, Followers and those who Lead.

Bullies are perpetrators of threats and violence. They have low self-esteem and take out their frustrations on others. They lack a sense of being valued and loved for who they really are.

Followers are afraid to speak or step up for themselves or others who are victimized. Followers go along with whatever is happening in their environment. They do not have a good sense of who they are.

Teens who lead are empathic. They care enough to report and help reduce violence and bullying. They model respectful communication and healthy relationships. They know and live their values. They encourage and lead other teens to make better decisions in their lives.

The Brains of Teen Who Lead, Followers and Bullies

Our brains are either organized or disorganized. An organized brain has a large working neural network that connects to the prefrontal cortex. That is the neural real estate that is responsible for ration, logical, life and love affirming decision making.

A disorganized brain has parts of neural real estate that is locked off from the network. The network does not have as many connections to the prefrontal cortex. Disorganized brains make more decisions using the limbic region, which is responsible for survival: fight or flight. Those decisions are often knee jerk reactions tinged with fear or anger.

Teens who lead have more organized brains while followers and bullies have more disorganized brains.

How Can You Shape Your Teen's Brain to Lead?

1. Answer your teen's Big Brain question with a "Yes!" Social Neuroscientist Dr. Mark Brady reveals all of our brains ask those we care about, "Are you there for me?"
2. Learn about what Stanford neurobiologist Dr. Sapolsky has identified as the four primary destroyers of optimal neural growth.
3. Know how to Look, Listen, Learn and Love.
4. Heal your own wounds.

"YES!" The Needed Answer

You can answer the Big Brain Question by learning True Listening Skills. They are based on the concept of COAL: Curiosity, Openness, Acceptance and Love. When you create a safe relationship so your child trusts you enough to tell you who they really are, you are able to be there for them.

Unsaddling the Four Horsemen of Neuro-Annihilation

Take the saddles away from the four horsemen of neuro-annihilation. Neuro-annihilation comes from four major areas in our lives: 1) lack of control, 2) lack of predictability, 3) having your Big Brain Question answered "No," and 4) stress, especially accumulative stress.

1. Allow your teens to learn age-appropriate autonomy. Let them control things they are ready for physically and emotionally. Teach them how to cope with things they cannot control.
2. Create predictability in their daily lives. That means your teen can rely on ongoing stability to feel safe and secure.
3. Teach teens to lead by answering their Big Brain Question with a resounds "yes!" as often as possible.

4. Stress creates toxic chemicals in the brain and body that stop good brain development. Help your teen learn to manage or reduce stress through exercise, prayer, mediation, talking to a trusted advisor, or any other healthy method.

The Four Ls: Look, Listen, Learn and Love

When you pay attention (look, listen) to your children's actions and words, you start to build a safe and secure relationship. After you look and listen, learn what your children's actions or words mean. What do they want you to know? What do they need? Show love by responding to their needs in a timely fashion.

Heal Your Wounds

The work of every parent who wants to teach their teen to lead is to heal their growing up wounds. Traumatic, or repetitive insults to mind, body or soul, are trapped in our body and brain. These old wounds and memories lock down our neural network. Parents who have unexamined, unhealed wounds have a challenging time raising teens who lead. They may inadvertently be raising followers or bullies.

For those 60,000 students who avoid school due to fear, we as parents and educators need to learn how to teach teens to lead instead of following or bullying. Teens can and do learn how to stop following and bullying when they are shown love and respect by adults and peers.

Critical Thinking

1. How would you describe the three types of teens?
2. How does the author believe a brain can be shaped to lead?
3. Do you think the methods used to shape a leader could work and why?
4. How often should this approach be used?

From *Psychology Today*, February 12, 2010. Copyright © 2010 by Jennifer Austin Leigh. Reprinted by permission of the author.

High School with a College Twist

Terry B. Grier and Kent D. Peterson

Some students just don't fit. They don't like school, dress differently, have no interest in school activities, and are fed up with high school in general. Many are extremely bright and have high potential but do not see the relationship between high school and the real world. Others are behind academically and experience daily failure and rejection at school. Unfortunately, most high schools do not have meaningful strategies to deal with such disengaged students and many of them drop out of school.

That certainly was the case in the Guilford County Schools (GCS) in Greensboro, NC: in 2000, 6% of the district's students dropped out, and the school board demanded action. After considering a variety of options, the district turned to a small-school concept called the "middle college high school" to help reconnect those students and keep them in school. A middle college high school is an alternative school that is housed on a college campus. Students enroll in college classes and take their high school courses in the alternative setting. Eventually, the district created six middle college high schools, each with a different schedule, culture, curriculum, and college context.

Key Factors

Although many unique features of middle college high schools contribute to their success, two factors—small size and the college context—are extremely important.

School Size

Although the number of students enrolled in middle college programs differs site-by-site, keeping enrollments small (100–145 students in each middle college program) is key. In GCS, most middle college high school classes do not exceed 15 students. These small group settings allow the schools to accomplish things that larger, traditional high schools cannot, such as:

- Fostering personal relationships between teacher and student. Teachers get to interact one-on-one with students, picking up on personal issues that might escalate into serious problems.
- Rekindling student academic interest. A low student-teacher ratio encourages direct assistance and immediate feedback.
- Reducing the social drama that exists in larger school settings. Social drama derives from the complex mix

of students' social status, cliques, and search for acceptance.
- Reducing the student-counselor ratio. Each middle college high school has its own counselor who, because he or she serves fewer students, can address more issues, which results in more student time in school, fewer problems, and more academic focus.

In sum, small size makes it possible for a dedicated staff to give students more personalized attention to promote their academic success and improve their opportunities for long-term social and career success.

College Context

Everyone remotely connected to adolescents understands the power of peer pressure. The college campus exerts a similar, positive pressure on middle college students. Enjoying the same freedom as college students and coupling that freedom with self-responsibility is a new experience for students. Almost immediately, they feel pressure to begin acting like, studying like, and looking like college students. Most students welcome the sense that they are being treated like adults with adult rules and responsibilities. For example, they are allowed to take sodas and snacks to class, wear hats in buildings, hang out in the student center, leave the campus for lunch, and enjoy an expanded sense of freedom. In return, they follow the rules and regulations of the colleges they attend.

Although middle college students can attend classes and use the facilities of the higher education institution, they do not participate in evening or social activities. Nonetheless, students report that they feel a part of the greater mission of the school they are in. All of these aspects of the college context have a positive, and often significant, influence on these students, many of whom only returned to school because of the middle college opportunities.

Getting Started

A middle college high school can work almost anywhere in the United States where a need exists. But before any new project is implemented, the community must understand both the concept and the need for it. Data that focus on the negative impact that dropouts have on the local economy and economic development opportunities can help communities understand the need to create alternative placements. Communities will also want to see evidence that the cost of operating a middle college high school over time is no more expensive than a traditional high school—despite the small class size. Existing middle colleges can serve as models and become part of the coalition that navigates the political mine fields of change. They also can offer examples for school officials, elected officials, and community leaders to visit.

Another key element is support and approval from a local postsecondary institution. Middle colleges are located on various types of college campuses, including technical colleges, small liberal arts colleges, and large state universities. Colleges may be interested in hosting a middle college because it generates revenue, builds visibility among potential students, or supports its mission to serve students. Still, colleges view themselves as postsecondary institutions, and seeing the benefit of hosting high school students takes some convincing.

Success can build on success, however. For example, to ensure that GCS's first middle college high school was a success and that the host college understood the concept, Don Cameron, the president of Guilford Technical Community College (GTCC), agreed to fly to Nashville, TN, and tour the middle college Terry Grier helped establish there. The day after GCS's press conference announcing the establishment of a middle college high school on the GTCC campus, Craven Williams, the president of Greensboro College, called the district office and declared that Greensboro College also wanted to host a middle college high school. Both schools opened in fall 2000.

The district and the college must negotiate the use of space, access to labs and classrooms, use of the cafeteria, tuition costs when students take college level courses, and so forth. Formal agreements are necessary regarding the partnership. However, none of the colleges or universities that house GCS middle colleges charge the district fees for facility use, utilities, or maintenance costs.

Convincing college faculty members and administrators to bring in a group of high school students who will work, eat, and interact with their students and staff members also takes considerable negotiation and persuasion. One important thing to remember is that colleges do not mind referring to students as disengaged, but such descriptors as *at risk, troubled, malcontent,* and *discipline problems* should not be used. Not only are these inappropriate descriptions, college and university presidents also have boards of directors and must be politically sensitive to the image of the campus.

Implementation Challenges and Considerations
Design Concept and Proper Fit

Designing a variety of middle colleges that serve different student needs and interests was essential in a district as large as GCS. The district's six middle college high schools have unique focuses, a variety of grade spans, and different schedules. Some are single-sex programs. The programs are housed on large university, small college, and community college campuses.

It is important to consider the history, facilities, and student body of a college or a university before deciding what type of middle college to place on that campus. Every college has a different culture, and districts must give careful thought to the ethos of the host college or university before establishing a middle college.

Staff Selection

Most middle college programs provide a principal, a counselor, and seven or eight high school teachers to serve 125 students. The principal must be the first middle college employee hired and, like a symphony conductor, must understand every player's part. Principals must have the managerial skills to organize school policies and procedures; the political skills to handle the complex interactions of higher education institutions; the interpersonal abilities to work with students with complex needs; the social skills to support teachers working under flexible teaching and relational conditions; and the values and the desire to help students who have faced difficulties in high school, dropped out, and elected to return. Because middle college high school students can take college courses for dual high school and college credit, the principal must be able to communicate and work closely with the college's staff members.

Like good middle college principals, middle college teachers must have high expectations for their students and develop close and supportive relationships with them. They must exhibit unconditional positive regard for others and believe that students possess infinite worth. Successful middle college teachers combine keen insights about their students with creative strategies that help students meet academic expectations. They must be empathetic listeners, have a clear purpose as a facilitator of student learning, and be willing to give students a second chance.

Student Selection

The middle college high school program is not for everyone. It is designed to serve a small percentage of students who do not fit in traditional high schools. Students who have good grades, good school attendance, and a record of good behavior and who like school and participate in school cocurricular activities are not good candidates for the middle college high school. Usually, GCS students who participate in cocurricular activities in their home schools or who simply want to begin college early do not qualify for the program.

The recruitment and selection process should have several components that increase the likelihood of a good fit between the students and the school. Although students can show initiative and apply on their own, staff members and administrators should not passively hope that students will apply. Initially, staff members and administrators should look for students who were once successful but have either dropped out of high school or have been in significant academic trouble. They should actively seek out students by using traditional and nontraditional recruiting techniques. Over time, middle college high school students will nominate and recruit similarly disconnected students to attend their school.

GCS Middle College High Schools

Middle College at Guilford Technical Community College (GTCC)

Established 2001 on the main GTCC campus
Enrollment: 140 students in grades 9–12
Schedule: 11:30 AM–5:20 PM
Twenty-five percent of its students enrolled in 66 college courses; 95% of its seniors graduated, and 94% of those graduates began postsecondary education in 2006.

Greensboro Middle College High School

Established 2001 on the campus of Greensboro College
Enrollment: 110 students in grades 11–12
Schedule: 8:10 AM–3:10 PM
One-hundred percent graduation rate in 2006; made AYP for the last three years.

The Middle College at A&T

Established 2003 on the campus of North Carolina Agricultural & Technical State University
Enrollment: 110 students
Schedule: 9:45 AM–4:15 PM
Only serves male students; 76% of seniors graduated in 2006; the district replaced large percentage of teachers and the principal during the 2006–07 school year.

The Middle College at Bennett College

Established 2003 on the campus of Bennett College
Enrollment: 115 students
Schedule: 11:00 AM–4:30 PM
Only serves female students; 95% of seniors graduated in 2006.

Middle College of Entertainment Technology at GTCC

Established 2005 on a branch campus of GTCC
Enrollment: 120 students
Schedule: 12:00 PM–5:20 PM
School made AYP in 2006.

The GTCC Middle College East

Established 2005 on a branch campus of GTCC
Enrollment: 125 students
Schedule: 12:05 PM–5:30 PM
School made AYP in 2006.

Acceptance is not automatic. Schools may want to use an admissions project team—consisting of the middle college principal, a counselor, and a teacher—to review all applications. The GCS middle colleges have an intensive selection process that requires a formal application in addition to a written statement of interest in returning to school. In-depth interviews are held with each student and his or her parent or guardian. During the interview, students must answer questions that help determine what factors created the largest amount of stress in the student's academic and personal life.

Costs

Although core high school courses are taught by a carefully selected high school faculty, all middle college students have access to the college's facilities. Eligible students can take college courses for both high school and college credit, and most sponsoring school districts are responsible for their tuition payments. Other expenses in the North Carolina middle college high schools include:

- Computers, telephones, and office equipment
- Lower than average student-teacher ratios
- A full-time counselor who serves fewer than 140 students
- Regular school equipment as well as special equipment for special theme middle colleges

- Transportation—door-to-door transportation that is similar to those associated with regular magnet schools
- Access to Plato, a computer-based, self-paced learning program.

Eligible students can take college courses for both high school and college credit, and most sponsoring school districts are responsible for their tuition payments.

A school district must address these and other cost issues when developing and sustaining middle college high schools. Increased state revenues and negotiated cost savings from college faculty use can offset some costs. More important, the social cost of serving and returning disconnected students to school well outweigh these expenses.

Savings and Income

Although there are expenses associated with establishing a middle college high school, the schools do not have many of the high-cost programs that traditional high schools have, such as athletics. Classroom space, laboratories, media centers, cafeteria, auditoriums, athletic weight rooms, and art facilities are also provided by the colleges at no cost to the district.

GCS's middle college high schools serve more than 700 students, the equivalent of a small high school. A new, small high school that could serve these students would cost more than $38 million to build and $455,000 a year to operate. In addition, many of these students had dropped out of school, and returning them to the district's enrollment generated significant revenue to the district. Plus, earning high school diplomas will have a tremendously positive impact on them, their families, and the community.

Lessons Learned

GCS has learned a number of valuable lessons over the years:

- No plan survives initial contact. Expect bumps in the road and be flexible enough to work them out.
- Don't expect immediate support for the establishment of middle college high schools from all quarters. Critics will carefully watch and wait. Be willing to admit mistakes, but move quickly to make corrections.
- Don't underestimate the importance of early success to the survival of a middle college high school. Create and celebrate early victories, such as improved attendance, grades, and student behavior. Invite the press, elected officials, and board members to visit the schools.
- The selection of the principal and the teachers is key to the success of the school.
- A middle college high school must be located on a college campus to benefit from the power of that campus.

Conclusion

Every college and university in the country should partner with school districts and host a middle college high school. Small districts can join together to form middle college consortiums, like the one using Mott Community College in Flint, MI.

In GCS, the grades 9–12 drop-out rate has decreased from 6.34% in 1999–2000 to 3.04% in 2005–06—one of the lowest rates in the nation among metropolitan school systems. The GCS middle college high schools played a major role in that reduction, and their success has not gone unnoticed. North Carolina Governor Mike Easley and his staff members have visited GCS middle colleges on numerous occasions during the past several years. Two years ago, building on what he observed in GCS, Governor Easley developed a "Learn and Earn" Early College model that emulates many of the components of a middle college high school. The governor is partnering with the Gates Foundation to expand his concept across North Carolina.

Middle college high schools help students who were disconnected and disengaged return to school and succeed. Consider visiting a middle college. Although reading this article will better inform you about middle colleges, hearing directly from middle college teachers and students will change your views and beliefs about what can be done to save and serve disengaged high school students.

Critical Thinking

1. How can small high schools on college campuses resolve the problem of disengagement?
2. What two factors contribute to rekindle the interest of disengagement?
3. How would you define disengagement?
4. Do you think the two factors provided would solve the problem of disengagement?

TERRY B. GRIER [griert@gcsnc.com] is the superintendent of Guilford County [NC] Schools. **KENT D. PETERSON** is a professor in the School of Education at the University of Wisconsin—Madison. GCS Middle College High Schools

UNIT 5

Problem Behaviors and Challenges of Adolescents

Unit Selections

Learning Outcomes

After reading this unit, you should be able to:

- Explain the effect of violent video games on youth.

- Provide examples of specific video games that are harmful.

- Discuss the evidence provided to support the effect of violent video games on youth.

- Explain how brain development is affected by violent video games.

- Explain stress, stress reactions, and coping with stress among adolescents.

- Contrast gender differences in stress and stress management.

- Explain health choices of youth as explained by Travis Tygart.

- Discuss the need for coaches, parents, and the media to help guide teens to make healthy decisions.

- Discuss the prevalence of self-cutting in teens.

- Outline prevention and intervention techniques of teen self-injurious behavior.

- Describe dating violence.

- Explain the factors that impact dating violence.

- Describe self-injury behavior and the reason it is increasing among adolescents.

- Identify common risk factors among adolescents for self-injury.

- Outline the factors that contribute to youth's reaction to disasters.

- Discuss both outcomes and predictors in order to prepare professionals who work with youth in post disaster situations.

Student Website
www.mhhe.com

The idea that adolescents can and do engage in high-risk behaviors is not subject to much debate. The statistics on adolescent fatalities demonstrate their risk-taking behavior. The leading causes of death in adolescents are tragic: accidents, suicide, and homicide. Alcohol use is frequently involved, particularly in motor vehicle accidents. About half of the fatal motor vehicle accidents involving an adolescent also involve a drunk, peer driver.

Why adolescents engage in high-risk behaviors is much debated. Some researchers believe that adolescent risk taking is related to cognitive development. They propose that adolescents possess a sense of invulnerability. Adolescents believe they are special and unique; things that could happen to others could not possibly happen to them. Other researchers believe at best this may apply only to young adolescents. By their mid-teens a majority of adolescents are too sophisticated to consider their selves invulnerable. Despite this, however, adolescents still take more risks than do adults.

If older adolescents do not perceive themselves as invulnerable, then why do they take risks? There are several possible explanations. One proposal is that adolescents may not perceive the risk. For example, adults may have a better sense of how fast they can safely drive given differing road conditions. Adolescents, simply because they are inexperienced drivers, may not recognize when road conditions are dangerous and so may not adjust their speed. Adolescents may engage in riskier behaviors than adults simply because they have the time and energy. Many adolescents have free time, money, and a car. Access to these may allow adolescents to put themselves in dangerous situations. Adults may work, do more household chores, and take care of their children. These adults may not have time to drink, take drugs, or joy ride.

Adolescents may also be less adept than adults at extricating themselves from high-risk behavior. For example, adults who attend a party where drugs are consumed may be more comfortable declining offered drugs than adolescents, or they may be able to leave the party without depending on transportation from others. Some researchers indicate that society may be somewhat to blame for adolescents' risk taking. If impoverished adolescents have no chance of obtaining meaningful work, have limited access to recreational activities, and have little encouragement to go to school, then participation in drug-related or violent behavior may be the only options open to them. It may be up to society to provide these adolescents with an increased number of safe choices.

Adolescent risk taking activities can take many forms. The U.S. Public Health Service identifies several categories of

© Jetta Productions/Walter Hodges/Getty Images

behavior related to health risks for adolescents. Included are behaviors that may cause injuries, such as suicide and violence, use of tobacco or illicit drugs (including alcohol), and risky behaviors related to sexuality or eating disorders. All of these can clearly threaten adolescents. Moreover, alcohol use seems to exacerbate many of the other risks, as indicated by the statistics on alcohol use and violent death. Drug use can be related to accidents, health problems, and violence. Violent behaviors are an increasing concern to society. Murder is the second leading cause of death in adolescence; it is the leading cause of death for African American male teenagers. Suicide rates in young people have tripled since the 1950s. Eating disorders are another threat to adolescents. Millions of adolescents suffer from anorexia nervosa or bulimia in the United States.

In this unit problem behaviors and challenges of adolescents are presented. The first article discusses the popularity of video and computer games, raising the issues of obsession and addiction among teens. Emily Sohn reports on the extensive research on violent video games and the harmful effect on teens. An interview with Dr. Craig Anderson continues the important topic of the effect of video games on teens.

The following articles deal with such topics as stress, steroids, cutting, dating violence, and non-suicidal self-injury. Each topic is examined in detail.

The final article addresses youths' reaction to disasters and the factors that influence their response. The article describes both outcomes and predictors in order to prepare those who work with teens.

Internet References

Alcohol: National Center on Addiction and Substance Abuse at Columbia University
www.casacolumbia.org

Anabolic Steroid Abuse
www.steroidabuse.gov

Athlete's Substance Use
www.drugfreesport.com/choices

Center for Change
www.centerforchange.com

CopeCareDeal: A Mental Health Site for Teens
www.copecaredeal.org

Cornell Research Program on Self-injurious Behavior in Adolescents and Young Adults
www.crpsib.com

Depression–Children and Adolescents
www.nimh.nih.gov/publicat/depchildmenu.cfnm

Focus Adolescent Services: Alcohol and Teen Drinking
www.focusas.com/Alcohol.html

Higher Education Center for Alcohol and Other Drug Prevention
www.edc.org/hec

Justice Information Center (NCJRS): Drug Policy Information
www.ncjrs.org/drgswww.html

Mental Health Risk Factors for Adolescents
http://education.indiana.edu/cas/adol/mental.html

MentalHelp.Net
http://eatingdisorders.mentalhelp.net

National Center for Injury Prevention and Control (NCIPC): Sexual Violence
www.cdc.gov/ncipc/factsheets/svoverview.htm

National Center for Missing and Exploited Children
www.ncmec.org

National Clearinghouse for Alcohol and Drug Information
www.health.org

National Sexual Violence Resource Center
www.nsvrc.org

National Youth Violence Prevention Resource Center
www.safeyouth.org

Partnership for a Drug-free America
www.drugfree.org/playhealthy

RAINN
www.rainn.org

S.A.F.E. ALTERNATIVES
www.selfinjury.com

Self-Harm: Recovery, Advice and Support
www.thesite.org/healthandwellbeing/mentalhealth/selfharm

Self-injurious Behavior Webcast
www.albany.edu/sph/coned/t2b2injurious.htm

Suicide Awareness: Voices of Education
www.save.org

Youth Suicide League
www.unicef.org/pon96/insuicid.htm

Video Game Violence

EMILY SOHN

We read every message that readers submit to *Science News for Kids*, and we learn a lot from what you say. Two articles that really got you talking looked at video games. One story argued that video games can be good for you (see *"What Video Games Can Teach Us"*). The other argued that video games are bad for you (see *"The Violent Side of Video Games"*).

These stories ran 3 years ago, and we're still hearing about them, almost weekly. In particular, those of you who enjoy killing people on screen disagree with research suggesting that your game-playing habits inspire you to act out.

"I have played the most violent games available on the market today," writes Matteo, 15. "I don't go killing people or stealing cars because I see it in a game. My parents say that, as long as I remember it's a game, I can play whatever I want."

Dylan, 14, agrees. "I love violent games," he writes. "And I haven't been in a fight since I was 12 years old."

Akemi, now 22, says that he's experienced no long-term effects in 14 years of gaming. "I have been playing the games since I was at least 7," he writes. "I have no criminal record. I have good grades and have often been caught playing well into the night (that is, 4 hours or more)."

Despite what these readers say, many scientific studies clearly show that violent video games make kids more likely to yell, push, and punch, says Brad Bushman. He's a psychologist at the University of Michigan in Ann Arbor.

Bushman and his colleagues recently reviewed more than 300 studies of video media effects. Across the board, he says, the message is clear.

"We included every single study we could find on the topic," Bushman says. "Regardless of what kids say, violent video games are harmful."

TV Watching

TV has been around a lot longer than video games, so researchers have more data on the long-term effects of violent TV shows on people than they do on the effects of violent video games.

In one study, scientists at the University of Michigan recorded the TV-watching habits of hundreds of first and third graders in 1977. Fifteen years later, the researchers looked at what kind of adults these kids had become.

By the time they were in their early twenties, women who had watched violent shows as kids were four times as likely to have punched, choked, or beaten other people as were women who didn't watch such programs as kids. Boys who watched violent TV grew up to be three times as likely to commit crimes as boys who didn't watch such programs.

But that doesn't mean that *everyone* who watched violent programs ended up being violent themselves. It was just more likely to happen for some people.

In Action

Violent playing is even more powerful than violent watching, Bushman says. Maneuvering through a game requires kids to take action, identify with a character, and respond to rewards for rough behavior. Engaging in such activities reinforces effective learning, researchers say.

In the game *Carmageddon,* for example, players get extra points for plowing over elderly or pregnant pedestrians in creative ways. Players hear screams and squishing sounds.

"In a video game, you naturally identify with the violent character, and identification with violent characters increases aggression," Bushman says. "You're the person who pulls the trigger, who stabs, who shoots, who kicks. You must identify with the aggressor because you *are* the aggressor."

Now, I know what some of you are thinking: Maybe people who are already violent to begin with are the ones who seek out violent media.

"Video games may have an influence on human behavior or mentality, but I believe that whoever plays the game already has . . . a violent intent or nature within," writes Jason, 16. "I strongly doubt a nun whom you could somehow get to play *Mortal Kombat* for a while would eventually gain a violent personality or behave as such."

Jake, 15, says, "I think it depends on how the kids were raised more than anything, and if people try to play life like a game then they are IDIOTS."

But the University of Michigan study of TV watching found that people who were more aggressive as kids didn't necessarily watch more violent shows as adults. This finding suggests that watching violence leads to acting violently, not the other way around.

Inflicting Punishment

In some of Bushman's studies, kids are randomly assigned to play either a violent video game, such as *Killzone* or *Doom 3,* or an exciting, but nonviolent, game, such as *MarioKart* or a *Tony Hawk* skateboarding game, for about 20 minutes.

Then, each participant competes with a kid in another room on a task that challenges both players to press a button as quickly as possible. The winner gets to punish the loser with a blast of noise through a pair of headphones. The winner decides how long the noise will last and how loud it will be on a scale from 1 to 10.

In one of these studies, players were told that blasting their partners at level 8 or above would cause permanent hearing damage. (For safety reasons, the invisible competitor in this study was imaginary, but the setup made participants believe that they actually had the power to make another person suffer a hearing loss.)

The results showed that kids who played violent games first, then went to the task, delivered louder noises to their competitors than did kids who played nonviolent games first. Kids who played violent games *and* felt strongly connected to their on-screen characters sometimes delivered enough noise to make their invisible partners go deaf.

Because kids in these studies don't get to choose which games they play, it seems clear that playing violent games directly causes aggressive behavior, Bushman concludes.

And that aggressive behavior may appear not as criminal activity or physical violence but in more subtle ways in the ways people react to or interact with other people in everyday life.

Brain Studies

Some scientists are looking at kids' brains to see how video games might affect their behavior. In one recent study, researchers from the Indiana University (IU) School of Medicine in Indianapolis assigned 22 teenagers to play a violent game for 30 minutes. Another 22 kids played a nonviolent, exciting game.

Brains scans show that the brains of teens playing nonviolent games and those of teens playing violent games have different patterns of activity. Those who played violent games showed greater activity in a region of the brain associated with strong emotions and less activity in a region associated with planning, focus, and self-control.

Indiana University School of Medicine

Then, participants entered a special scanner that measured activity in their brains. For the next hour or so, the teens had to react to mind-bending tasks, such as pressing the "3" button when presented with three pictures of the number "1," or pressing the "blue" button when presented with the word "red" written in blue letters.

The results showed that a part of the brain called the amygdala was especially active in players in the violent-game group, especially when follow-up tasks required them to respond to loaded words, such as "hit" and "kill." The amygdala prepares the body to fight or flee in high-stress situations.

Moreover, among players in the violent-game group, a part of the brain called the frontal lobe was less active. The frontal lobe helps us stop ourselves from hitting, kicking, and performing other aggressive acts.

Frame of Mind

Findings such as these don't mean that every kid who plays *Grand Theft Auto* will end up in jail, researchers say. Nor do they suggest that video games are the single cause of violence in our society. From the brain's point of view, however, playing a violent game puts a kid in a fighting frame of mind.

"Maybe [kids have] figured out ways to control this but maybe they haven't," says IU radiologist Vincent Matthews, who led the brain-scan study.

"If they look at their behavior more closely, they may be more impulsive after they play these games," he adds. "There's a lot of denial in people about what their behavior is like."

Matthews now wants to see how long these brain changes last and whether it's possible to change the brain to its original state.

Brain-scan studies at Michigan State University showed that playing violent video games leads to brain activity associated with aggressive thoughts.

Courtesy of Michigan State University

Danger Zone

It's important that kids understand the risks of violent media, Bushman says. Studies show that virtual fighting is just as likely to make a kid act aggressively as is drug abuse, a troubled home life, or poverty.

"The link between violent media and aggression is stronger than the link between doing homework and getting good grades," Bushman says. "These games are not good for society."

Government agencies and medical organizations have been warning parents and kids about the dangers of violent media for decades. Like smoking and fast food, Bushman says, violent games are a danger we would all be better off without.

Critical Thinking

1. What does research find concerning violent video games?

2. What specific games were studied and cited?

3. How was the study conducted?

4. What did the study find were the effects of violent video games on youth?

Interview with Dr. Craig Anderson
Video Game Violence

Dr. Craig Anderson, a leader in the research on the effects of exposure to violent video games on aggressive behavior, was invited to speak at Nebraska Wesleyan University. A group of Nebraska Wesleyan University students interviewed Dr. Anderson. We explored his interest and experiences in this research area.

SARAH HOWE, JENNIFER STIGGE, AND BROOKE SIXTA

Since 1997, Nebraska Wesleyan University (NE) has held an endowed lecture to honor the 40-year career of Dr. Clifford Fawl. The FAWL Lecture Series brings distinguished psychologists to the Wesleyan campus to present their research and interact with undergraduate psychology students. On March 22, 2007, we welcomed Dr. Craig Anderson as the FAWL lecturer to speak on *Violent Video Games: Theory, Research, and Public Policy*.

Dr. Craig Anderson received his bachelors degree at Butler University (IN) in 1976. He earned a masters degree (1978) and PhD (1980) in psychology at Stanford University (CA). He currently is a distinguished professor of psychology at Iowa State University and is widely regarded as the leader in research on the effects of violent video games and other forms of media violence. He has published widely on depression, loneliness, and shyness; attribution processes; social judgment; and human aggression. He has earned recognition as the second most highly cited scholar in social psychology textbooks. He has testified before the U.S. Senate Committee on Commerce, Science and Transportation's hearing on "The Impact of Interactive Violence on Children" and has served on the Media Violence Expert Panel for the Surgeon General.

Dr. Anderson started his visit by discussing the importance of good methodology to a research methods class. He was then interviewed by a small group of Wesleyan students concerning his work on violence and video games.

Student: What was your motivation for starting research on media violence and video games?

Anderson: It originally had to do with working on the General Aggression Model and learning about the media violence literature. There were literally hundreds of studies, but there were still gaps and unanswered questions. I had some students looking for research topics that were interesting and publishable, and then they identified gaps in the research. That was the initial reason. Later they basically extended the research using video games to test some aspects of the General Aggression Model. Next, my research team looked at priming issues, which prior to our work, had never been used in the context of media violence effects. After talking to some colleagues in cognitive psychology and debating about which method to use, we thought of using some cognitive measures such as a modified Stroop test but we chose a reading reaction time task.

Student: Looking back on many of your articles, we noticed you first did a study on video games in 1987 and another in 1995, but the majority of your studies have been since 1999. Did this more recent increase in research on the effects of video games have anything to do with Columbine and other school shootings?

Anderson: No, it had to do with an internal grant I received about 1996. It funded three graduate students and enabled us to start doing research on the effects of violent video games. I had been writing grant proposals on the topic for some time, but this was the first time I had the opportunity to do some of those studies. Then, Columbine came along.

Student: Were you asked to help with any of the Columbine research?

Anderson: No, although I was asked to testify in the U.S. Senate hearing about violent video games some time after the shooting.

Student: What group of people do you think are the most susceptible to the effects of violent video games, and why?

Anderson: Many researchers in the field of media violence think that people who are high on what you would call trait aggression (especially children and adolescents) are going to be more influenced by exposure to media violence than people who are low on trait aggression. In other words, many scholars believe that highly aggressive people are more susceptible to the harmful effects of media violence than are nonaggressive people. However, I think that the research evidence over the years doesn't bear that out, yet. Some studies show this heightened susceptibility of highly aggressive people, but some studies show the opposite including one of my studies (Anderson, 1997). That study found that people who are lowest on trait aggression showed the biggest effect of a violent movie manipulation. Those data yielded a significant interaction between measures of trait aggression and measures of media violence exposure. The nonaggressive people who watched a violent movie clip displayed more aggressive thoughts than nonaggressive people who saw the nonviolent clip, but highly aggressive people were relatively unaffected by the movie clip manipulation. Other researchers have found the opposite type of interaction. For example, in some studies those who score high on trait aggressiveness and have been exposed to a lot of violent media are the ones who are most likely to have, at some time in their lives, been arrested for assault. Well, is that because the media violence effect only operates on high trait-aggressive people? Perhaps low-trait aggressive people are equally affected, but because their general level of aggression is low, media violence can't increase their willingness to aggress enough to rise to the level of assaulting someone.

Student: From where do you recruit your participants?

Anderson: Well, very often, it's a convenience sample. However, the present grant research that my colleagues/students and I have been doing allows us to pay participants. So we are able to pay kids to play video games, which they think is great (laughter). Some try to come in two or three times, and we have to tell them they cannot. In these situations, we have to select samples to fit the particular research question or issue.

Student: In your experimental research, how do you account for the participants who regularly play video games from those who have little to no experience?

Anderson: We usually give the participants questionnaires that tell us how much the individuals have played and what kinds of games they play. Prior experience with video games can then figure into the data analysis. We seldom find any kind of difference in our experimental studies between those participants with a lot of experience and those without. The one difference we do find is that participants with a lot of gaming experience really like being in the violent video game condition. Typically, we do not find much of a statistically reliable effect of gaming experience on aggressive thought processes and behavior.

Student: Do you feel that your research has or will have an impact on the video game industry? If so, what impact do you think it will have?

Anderson: Our research has probably had a bigger impact in countries other than in the United States. Almost every other modern country has legal restrictions on violent media including video games. Many of them ban some of the games outright and most have age-based restrictions. Certainly the research that my students and I have done over the years has been used by child advocacy groups and others in these countries to make sure that these ratings are enforced. The research certainly has increased the awareness of the issue in the United States. However, there are no U.S. laws regarding violent video games. I have never said publicly whether I support a legislative solution, because my political opinion is not relevant to what I regard as my scientific expertise. Even in the court cases with which I have been involved, I say upfront that I will not comment on what I think about the law under judicial review. I will talk about what the science says or what it cannot say. The work and interviews that we've done concerning violence in video games is used to get the word out to parents about the effect of violent video games. Our research has had a big impact on parents, but not as big as it needs to be. There are still people teaching their 2- or 3-year-olds how to shoot a gun in these video games.

Student: What are some of the stronger arguments against your research? How do you counter those arguments?

Anderson: One of the best arguments, until recently, is that there are no longitudinal studies, but we have now published one (Anderson, Gentile, & Buckley, 2007). Previously in my various talks, I had described the lack of longitudinal data on the effects of video games. The paucity of these studies was due to the lack of government support for longitudinal research. The support for the longitudinal study I just mentioned came from non-governmental sources. More recently, we finally got the funding needed to perform a larger, longer-term longitudinal study after being turned down six or seven times. There really aren't any long-term longitudinal studies, such as when you follow the group of individuals and see where these participants end up after several years. Some participants may end up in jail, juvenile detention facilities, or kicked out of school, which makes this an important field of interest. A response to this criticism about the lack of longitudinal studies on violent video games is that such studies have already been done pertaining to television violence, which is the same phenomenon, but some individuals fail to see the similarities between violence on television and violence in video games. People used this lack of a longitudinal study, focusing on violent video games, as a criticism for the evidence found between increased aggression and exposure to violent video games. Of course, they can no longer do this.

Student: Do you have any plans for the future implementation of your research? How should your research be applied to schools, home, everyday life, etc.?

Anderson: We haven't been thinking much about intervention studies, mainly because I don't do intervention studies. There is a group at Iowa State University that does intervention studies, but most of their work focuses on drug use and intervention to reduce kids' use of alcohol, tobacco, and various illegal substances. There have been some TV/video game interventions done in school systems, but intervention as a whole is done by another group of researchers.

Student: Where do you think video game research will go from here?

Anderson: There are two related issues that are going to be big soon. One is the identification of video game addiction or Internet addiction, including text messaging, as a true addiction in need of clinical intervention for some individuals. The other has to do with attention deficit disorders, executive control, and impulse control. There is potential long-term damage in those brain systems due to extensive viewing of media that flash across the screen and demand constantly shifting attention. Some evidence indicates that extensive use of screening media, whether it is violent or not, leads to attention deficit disorder, especially in very young children who see a lot of TV.

References

Anderson, C. A. (1997). Effects of violent movies and trait irritability on hostile feelings and aggressive thoughts. *Aggressive Behavior, 23,* 161–178.

Anderson, C. A., Gentile, D. A., & Buckley, K. E. (2007). *Violent video game effects on children and adolescents.* New York: Oxford University Press.

Critical Thinking

1. What does the research on video game technology give evidence to support?
2. What increases the influence for youth to behave in a hostile manner?

3. What do studies on brain development reveal concerning violent video games?
4. Is the increased aggression only for a small sample of the population? Why?

SARAH HOWE, a junior at Nebraska Wesleyan University, is a psychology major with a minor in health and human performance. Following graduation, she plans to attend graduate school in counseling. **JENNIFER STIGGE,** also a junior at Nebraska Wesleyan University, is an industrial-organizational psychology (I/O psychology) major with a business administration minor. She plans to begin graduate school in the fall of 2009 in I/O psychology. **BROOKE SIXTA** graduated from Nebraska Wesleyan University in December of 2007 with a bachelor's degree in psychology and a minor in business administration. She is currently working; however, plans to also attend I/O psychology graduate school beginning at the fall of 2008.

Author's note—We would like to thank Dr. Anderson for visiting with Nebraska Wesleyan students and faculty, and presenting his research regarding violence and video games. We would also like to give a special thanks to Dr. Marilyn Petro, Dr. Michael Tagler, Allyson Bell, and Amanda Holmgren for their assistance with the process of this interview.

Adolescents Coping with Stress

Development and Diversity

Approximately 25% of adolescents will experience at least one significant stressor, including the death of a loved one or witnessing a traumatic event.

Melanie J. Zimmer-Gembeck, PhD, and Ellen A. Skinner, PhD

Interventions for adolescents are often aimed at helping them deal constructively with the stressors in their daily lives. Achieving positive outcomes depends on understanding the actual stressors faced by adolescents, the ways they make sense of stressful events, and how adolescents react to and cope with problems. In this article, we summarize some of what is known about stress, stress reactions, and coping among adolescents. Throughout, we focus on typical developmental patterns by highlighting the emerging experiences of adolescents and how they differ from children and adults. We also briefly draw attention to differences between individuals, boys and girls, and racial/ethnic or other diverse groups. Finally, because social partners are sources of stress as well as coping resources, we weave information about the social context and social development throughout this article.

Common Stressors

Stressful life experiences, including major events and common hassles, threaten the well-being of adolescents. Approximately 25% of adolescents will experience at least one significant stressor, including the death of a loved one or witnessing a traumatic event. An even greater number of adolescents experience chronic stressors and daily hassles. The most common of these are related to school (e.g., bullying by peers, problems with teachers, and academic difficulties) and interpersonal relationships (e.g., conflicts or problems with parents, siblings, and peers) (Donaldson et al., 2000; Williamson et al., 2003). Of the many stressors, problems with other people are the most commonly reported and can be significant sources of distress for many adolescents. Compared to children, adolescents encounter many new, potentially threatening or challenging social experiences. These escalate all the way through later adolescence (about ages 20 to 22) when there may be significant social transitions, such as leaving home, finding satisfying educational or career paths, and forming intimate partner relationships.

Outcomes of Stressful Experiences

It is probably not surprising that significant life events and many of the common stressors of adolescence have been linked to mental health and behavioral problems. These problems include depression and anxiety, as well as externalizing behaviors, such as aggression and antisocial acts (Compas et al., 2001). For example, the formation, maintenance, and dissolution of close relationships have been associated with negative affect, sleeplessness, and many other symptoms of depression via experiences of negative interpersonal interactions, rejection, conflict, and related stressors (Monroe, Rohde, Seeley, & Lewinsohn, 1999). Romantic relationships can be one major source of stress, when conflict, jealousy, aggression, and infidelity occur (Gallaty & Zimmer-Gembeck, 2008). Moreover, the dissolution of a romantic relationship can have a significant impact on mental health; breakups have even been linked to the first onset of adolescent clinical depression (Monroe et al., 1999).

Few studies have directly examined the *positive* outcomes of coping with stressful events for adolescents. However, related research has demonstrated that experiences of dealing with just manageable challenges are important to the development of a wide variety of capacities and skills. Researchers point out that mistakes, setbacks, and failures are potential springboards for discovery and learning, offering adolescents the opportunity to build resources for coping with future negative events (Aldwin, 1994). Most researchers also agree that the outcomes of stressful life events and daily hassles will be positive or negative depending on how adolescents respond to them.

Stress Reactions and Appraisals

The impact of stressful events is dependent not only on the objective stressors themselves, but also on adolescents' subjective *appraisals*, defined as an evaluation of an event's potential impact or threat to well-being (Lazarus, 1991). For example, a stressful event can be appraised as a loss, threat, or challenge (Lazarus & Folkman, 1984; Skinner & Wellborn, 1994). Appraisal of loss implies a harm that has already transpired, whereas appraisal of threat implies an anticipation of harm in the future. An appraisal of challenge identifies a stressful event that can potentially result in some positive outcome. These appraisals are linked with emotional reactions to stressors and coping responses. Situations perceived as more threatening prompt certain emotions and coping strategies, such as more fear and more use of escape, withdrawal and support seeking. Situations perceived as more challenging (as opposed to threatening) prompt different emotions and coping strategies, such as more interest and problem solving (Irion & Blanchard-Fields, 1987; Skinner, Edge, Altman, & Sherwood, 2003; Zimmer-Gembeck, Lees, Skinner, & Bradley, under review).

Another important appraisal is the *controllability* of a stressor (Rudolf, Dennig, & Weisz, 1995; Skinner, 1995). Some stressors, such as academic difficulties, are perceived as more open to influence through effort. As a result, adolescents respond to them more instrumentally, using active strategies, persistence, exertion, and problem-solving. When stressors are appraised as lower in controllability or as inescapable, such as for parental conflict or medical events, they are more likely to prompt withdrawal, the use of cognitive distraction, seeking social support, or responses aimed at reducing emotional distress. As would be expected, adolescents' stress appraisals are important correlates of their mental health (Compas et al., 2001). For example, the appraisal of a stressful event as more threatening has been associated with self-reported symptoms of anxiety, depression, and conduct-related problems following parental divorce (Sandler, Kim-Bae, & MacKinnon, 2000).

In our own work, we have focused on how stressful experiences cause distress because they threaten or challenge perceived competence and control, sense of belonging, and autonomy (Skinner & Wellborn, 1994). These are particularly important considerations during adolescence, because these threats parallel three of the major developments during this time of life: the development of self and identity; involvement in groups and the development of close relationships outside the family; and emotional and behavioral autonomy development (Zimmer-Gembeck & Collins, 2003). This implies that adolescence may be a particularly stressful time of life as well as an important time to practice personal coping skills. Although such events are stressful throughout life, a developmental shift occurs between late childhood and early adolescence in stress reactions and coping, based on major biological, cognitive, and social developments. Many younger adolescents are in the midst of the neurochemical changes of puberty and both younger and older adolescents experience structural brain changes; these have been associated with greater stress reactivity and challenges in displaying and interpreting emotional responses when compared to adults (Spear, 2000).

Coping Responses

Coping describes the transactional processes through which people deal with actual problems in their everyday lives (Aldwin, 1994; Skinner & Zimmer-Gembeck, 2007, in press). Coping encompasses a range of emotional regulation strategies, thought processes, and behaviors. This means that coping is founded in an individual's physiological responses to stress, their appraisals of events, their attention, and their goals or the outcomes they desire. Coping also depends on social contexts and interpersonal relationships. Recent conceptualizations of coping have highlighted the importance of two processes: *stress reactions,* which are largely involuntary and might include behavioral and emotional impulses, and *action regulation,* which is purposeful and serves to modulate or boost reactivity to stressful events (Skinner & Zimmer-Gembeck, 2007, in press). Most interventions target intentional ways of coping, but the ability to cope well depends on coordinating all of these systems under conditions of threat, challenge, or loss (Lazarus & Folkman, 1984; Skinner & Zimmer-Gembeck, 2007).

Categories of Coping Responses

In order to describe how people cope in response to different stressors and to identify adaptive means of relieving stress and building resilience, researchers and practitioners need some way of organizing the multitude of coping responses. Yet, there is little consensus about how to do this. In one organizational scheme, coping behaviors have been grouped into those that 1) are more engaged and approach oriented, 2) serve to avoid or minimize stress, 3) depend on seeking others for support, and 4) involve withdrawal or helplessness (Ayers, Sandler, West, & Roosa, 1996; Seiffge-Krenke, 1995; Zimmer-Gembeck & Locke, 2007). The first category, approach-oriented coping, has included direct problem-solving and actions taken to increase understanding of the problem. The second category includes coping strategies that have a common function of avoiding or minimizing the stress, such as trying not to think about the event or distracting oneself. The third category of coping involves other people as resources, either for emotional support or for direct assistance. Finally, the fourth set of strategies includes escaping or becoming helpless and doing nothing.

In our recent work, we have found it helpful to identify more fine-grained "families" of coping. "Families" are multiple ways of coping grouped together because they serve the same core functions (Skinner et al., 2003; Skinner & Zimmer-Gembeck, 2007). For example, ways of coping such as acceptance, distraction, and cognitive restructuring all serve the function of "accommodation" or "going with the flow," that is, fitting in with and adjusting to environmental demands. The idea of "families" helps combine ways of coping which have often been considered separately. At the same time, families identify ways of coping, such as problem solving and support seeking; these are often combined in research studies, but should be considered separately because they serve different sets of functions. We have identified a dozen families of coping (see Table 1). These reflect the main categories of coping that should be considered in research and interventions for adolescents.

Table 1 Twelve Families of Coping, Associated Coping Strategies, and Links to Adaptive Processes and Other Behaviors

Family of Coping	Example Coping Strategies	Function in Adaptive Process	Related Behavior
1. Problem Solving	Strategizing Instrumental action Planning	Adjust thoughts and actions to be effective	Watch and learn Mastery Efficacy
2. Information Seeking	Reading Observation Asking others	Find additional contingencies	Curiosity Interest
3. Helplessness	Confusion Cognitive interference Cognitive exhaustion	Find limits of actions	Guilt Helplessness
4. Escape	Behavioral avoidance Mental withdrawal Denial Wishful thinking	Escape noncontingent environment	Drop and roll Flight Fear
5. Self-reliance	Emotion regulation Behavior regulation Emotional expression Emotion approach	Protect available social resources and attend to goals	Tend and befriend Pride
6. Supports Seeking	Contact seeking Comfort seeking Instrumental aid Social referencing	Make use of available social resources	Proximity-seeking Yearning Other alliance
7. Delegation	Maladaptive help-seeking Complaining Whining Self-pity	Find limits of resources	Self-pity Shame
8. Social Isolation	Social withdrawal Concealment Avoiding others	Withdraw from unsupportive context	Duck and cover Freeze Sadness
9. Accommodation	Distraction Cognitive restructuring Minimization Acceptance	Flexibly adjust preferences or goals to options	Pick and choose Secondary control
10. Negotiation	Bargaining Persuasion Priority-setting	Find new options or select goals	Compromise
11. Submission	Rumination Rigid perseveration Intrusive thoughts	Give up preferences or goals	Disgust Rigid perseverance
12. Opposition	Other-blame Projection Aggression	Remove perceived constraints	Stand and fight Anger Defiance

(See Skinner et al., 2003; Skinner & Zimmer-Gembeck, 2007 for more details.)

Coping Strategies and Mental Health

Some coping families have been found to contribute to healthier functioning, such as problem-solving, taking action to solve the problem, and information-seeking. These active coping behaviors have been most often associated with higher competence, positive functioning, and good health. Other families of coping strategies, such as helplessness, passivity, escape and opposition, have been found to be associated with poorer functioning—less competence and poorer adaptation (see Compas et al., 2001 for a review). Nevertheless, it is difficult to argue that some coping strategies are always preferable and that others should always be avoided. Instead, it may be most important to have access to a sufficient range of strategies and to be able to flexibly employ them when needed. Individuals who use more active coping also tend to use more avoidant strategies (Zimmer-Gembeck & Locke, 2007). Overall, adolescents use a wider range of coping strategies than children, and it is this increasing flexibility and organization of their responses that is likely to be most adaptive (Skinner & Zimmer-Gembeck, 2007). Rigid reliance on a few coping strategies (or a restricted range of strategies) should not be typical during adolescence and is likely to indicate maladaptation and problems in managing stress.

The Development of Commonly Used Coping Strategies During Adolescence

It is clear that there are individual differences in how adolescents respond to stress, but there are also typical patterns of change. Coping experts have concluded that attempts and behaviors aimed at changing the stressful situation (i.e., instrumental coping) are very common, but decrease in use during adolescence, whereas coping that is focused on managing emotions and reducing tension increases (Frydenberg & Lewis, 2000). In a recent review, we focused on specific families of coping and summarized what is known about three families used most often by adolescents—support seeking, problem-solving, and distraction (Skinner & Zimmer-Gembeck, 2007).

Support seeking.

Support seeking includes seeking information, emotional support, and instrumental help. Adolescents' patterns of support seeking differ from those of both children and adults. Compared to children, adolescents are more likely to go to peers for emotional support and help with daily hassles. At the same time there are declines in seeking support from adults. However, these changes are dependent on the type of stressor. When in situations that are appraised as uncontrollable or in which adults are known to have authority, adolescents typically seek support from adults *more* often as they get older. Hence, adolescents, especially those between 10 and 16 years old, still benefit from adult guidance and they typically become better able to identify the best source of support for particular problem domains. At the same time, adults often find it challenging to provide adolescents with developmentally attuned support. Adolescents benefit most from support and guidance when it fits with their needs for autonomy and increasing skills at self-regulation (Zimmer-Gembeck & Locke, 2007).

Adolescents' patterns of support seeking differ from those of both children and adults.

Problem-solving.

When assessed as cognitive rather than behavioral activity to guide mastery over a problem, attempts at problem-solving increase with age. These increases are found throughout adolescence, and between adolescence and young adulthood. This is particularly true for self-reliance in decision-making and use of cognitive decision-making strategies to deal with stress. These increases continue even into early adulthood. As would be expected from recent research on brain development (Spear, 2000), the use of particular cognitive strategies such as strategizing, decision-making, planning, and reflection does not seem to be widespread until late adolescence or even early adulthood. In fact, the pubertal transition marks a time of *less* extensive use of problem-solving than in late childhood. This time-limited decline in problem-solving may correspond to a particular time of heightened stress reactivity that limits a young person's capacity to direct attention to problem-solving coping strategies. At the same time, increases in distraction, rumination, aggression, and avoidance are apparent.

Distraction.

Most people, regardless of their age, rely on distraction to cope with stress as much or more than support seeking and problem-solving. Young children rely on coping strategies like playing with toys, reading or other behavioral distractions. Adolescents continue to rely on behavioral distraction, but the use of cognitive distraction (such as thinking about something positive) is increasingly used. Following a pattern similar to advances in cognitive ability, there are increases in the use of cognitive distraction strategies beginning at about age 6 and continuing to about age 14. Distraction is often used to supplement other coping strategies, and the ability to shift between strategies, for example using both problem-solving and distraction to full advantage, becomes more advanced throughout adolescence and into early adulthood (Skinner & Zimmer-Gembeck, 2007).

Gender

Stressors and Emotional Responses to Stress

Starting at puberty, girls report more stressors in their lives than boys do. These stressors include concerns about physical appearance and body dissatisfaction, interpersonal relationships, school problems, and higher rates of sexual abuse and harassment (Nolen-Hoeksema & Girgus, 1994). One concern that is greater for boys than girls is related to achievement or failure in sports. Moreover, girls show greater general distress, sadness, and fear in response to stress as early as the first years of school and this continues well into adulthood. However, boys report just as much *anger* as girls, especially in response to interpersonal stressors that involve conflict, rejection, or coercion (Zimmer-Gembeck et al., under review).

Rumination and Distraction

The possibility that stressful events will result in mental health problems seems to be compounded when adolescents ruminate about stressors. Rumination involves focusing on the negative and anxiety-provoking aspects of stressful events, which draws attention to and magnifies negative emotions. This is more common among adolescents as compared to preadolescents, and for some adolescents rumination escalates across the teen years (Jose & Brown, 2008). Although there are groups of girls *and* boys who ruminate more than other adolescents, girls are slightly more likely to ruminate than boys. In contrast, boys are somewhat more likely to use distraction to cope. When asked, even adolescents can describe these differences in the use of rumination and distraction between girls and boys (Broderick & Korteland, 2002).

Consistent with the idea that these differences are linked to gender role socialization, both girls and those who ascribe to a feminine gender role engage in more rumination. Unfortunately, rumination has negative implications for the onset and stability of mental health and behavioral problems; it is most strongly linked to depressive symptoms for both girls and boys (Nolen-Hoeksema & Girgus, 1994). Not only does the direct focus on negative feelings exacerbate them, but rumination also increases recall of negative experiences, interferes with direct action to solve problems, and impedes the use of cognitive distraction to relieve distress.

Social Support and Self-Reliance

Another consistent gender difference during childhood and adolescence is girls' greater use of social support to cope with stress. Because girls also use problem-solving and distraction when facing stress, this means that they sometimes use a wider range of coping strategies than boys use. This also implies that boys prefer direct problem-solving, distraction, avoidance or disengaging to seeking social support. Social support can be a positive and adaptive response to stress and should be encouraged among both girls and boys. Yet, it can be maladaptive when used to focus on emotional distress, such as when adolescents co-ruminate with friends about their problems (Rose & Rudolph, 2006).

Contextual Moderators: Poverty and Race/Ethnicity

Many levels of contextual factors can enhance or degrade individuals' coping responses, as well as add to or reduce their experiences of stress. For example, poverty and associated threats may elevate stress in adolescents' lives while undermining their capacities to cope with stress (Tolan, Sherrod, Gorman-Smith, & Henry, 2003). Adolescents living in poverty are more likely to experience severe, chronic, and uncontrollable stressors; to receive less social support; and to have more difficulties coping with such a high number of simultaneous stressful events. Even more challenging to interventionists is the likelihood that the stressors associated with poverty may be particularly uncontrollable or may occur too rapidly to provide adolescents with the time to cope before another is on the horizon. Hence, the multiple disadvantages of poverty may limit opportunities to develop strategies that are needed to successfully overcome stressful events and to build up factors that can assist in resilience (Wyman, Sandler, Wolchik, & Nelson, 2000). For example, in some studies, chronic exposure to uncontrollable stress has been shown to undermine the development of positive expectations of the future, perceptions of competence, and social support (see Tolan & Grant, in press, for a review).

Adolescents living in poverty and those with minority status face many common challenges. However, each deserves an extensive discussion on its own (see other articles in this issue). At the same time, when taken together, studies of those living in poverty and of racial/ethnic minorities alert us to the real possibility that there are circumstances when coping strategies that are typically viewed as "adaptive" may not be available or be the best responses. For example, although in general, direct instrumental action to change external events has been found to be an adaptive coping strategy, adolescents who use this strategy to deal with high levels of neighborhood or school violence and aggression may increase their chances of future victimization. Overall, it is important to emphasize that contextual factors at many levels shape coping strategies and inform considerations of what can be considered *adaptive* coping.

Adolescents increasingly turn to peers for support, but peers are also just developing the skills to provide good advice and help.

Conclusion

Adolescence is a time when youth face a variety of new potentially stressful experiences, but also have strong desires to deal with life events independently. The very events they seek, such as romantic relationships, friendships, and academic challenges, bring new sources of stress. Adolescents increasingly turn to peers for support, but peers are also just developing the skills to provide good advice and help. Youth benefit from adult guidance, but it can be a challenge for adults to adapt their support to adolescent needs for autonomy and self-reliance. At the same time that cognitive strategies for coping are improving, puberty brings biological and neurological changes that can boost reactivity to stress and also interfere with rational problem-solving. Understanding how adolescents experience, react to, think about, and cope with stressful events provides a foundation for preventive intervention services, whether they are aimed at helping adolescents avoid stressful situations, change their appraisals of stress, locate social resources, or improve their own capacity to cope adaptively.

References

Aldwin, C.M. (1994). *Stress, Coping, and Development: An Integrative Perspective.* New York: Guilford Press.

Ayers, T.S., Sandler, I.N., West, S.G., & Roosa, M.W. (1996). A dispositional and situational assessment of children's coping: Testing alternative models of coping. *Journal of Personality, 64,* 923–958.

Broderick, P.C., & Korteland, C. (2002). Coping style and depression in early adolescence: Relationships to gender, gender role, and implicit beliefs. *Sex Roles, 46,* 201–213.

Compas, B.E., Connor-Smith, J.K., Saltzman, H., Thomsen, A.H., & Wadsworth, M.E. (2001). Coping with stress during childhood and adolescence: Problems, progress, and potential in theory and research. *Psychological Bulletin, 127,* 87–127.

Donaldson, D., Prinstein, M.J., Danovsky, M., & Spirito, A. (2000). Patterns of children's coping with life stress: Implications for clinicians. *American Journal of Orthopsychiatry, 70,* 351–359.

Frydenberg, E., & Lewis, R. (2000). Teaching coping to adolescents: When and to whom? *American Educational Research Journal, 37,* 727–745.

Gallaty, K., & Zimmer-Gembeck, M.J. (2008). The social and emotional worlds of adolescents who are psychologically maltreated by their partners, *Journal of Youth and Adolescence, 37,* 310–323.

Irion, J.C., & Blanchard-Fields, F. (1987). A cross-sectional comparison of adaptive coping in adulthood. *Journal of Gerontology, 42,* 502–504.

José, P., & Brown, I. (2008). When does the gender difference in rumination begin? Gender and age differences in the use of rumination by adolescents. *Journal of Youth and Adolescence, 37,* 180–192.

Lazarus, R.S. (1991). Cognition and motivation in emotion. *American Psychologist, 46,* 352–367.

Lazarus, R.S., & Folkman, S. (1984). *Stress, Appraisal, and Coping.* New York: Springer.

Monroe, S.M., Rohde, P., Seeley, J.R., & Lewinsohn, P.M. (1999). Life events in adolescence: Relationship loss as a prospective risk factor for first onset of major depressive disorder. *Journal of Abnormal Psychology, 108,* 606–614.

Nolen-Hoeksema, S., & Girgus, J.S. (1994). The emergence of gender differences in depression during adolescence. *Psychological Bulletin, 115,* 424–443.

Rose, A.J., & Rudolph, K.D. (2006). A review of sex differences in peer relationship processes: Potential trade-offs for the emotional and behavioral development of girls and boys. *Psychological Bulletin, 132,* 98–131.

Rudolph, K.D., Dennig, M.D., & Weisz, J.R. (1995). Determinants and consequences of children's coping in the medical setting: Conceptualization, review, and critique. *Psychological Bulletin, 118,* 328–357.

Sandler, I.N., Kim-Bae, L.S., & MacKinnon, D. (2000). Coping and negative appraisal as mediators between control beliefs and psychological symptoms in children of divorce. *Journal of Clinical Child Psychology, 29,* 336–347.

Seiffge-Krenke, I. (1995). *Stress, Coping, and Relationships in Adolescence.* Hillsdale, NJ: Erlbaum.

Skinner, E.A. (1995). *Perceived Control, Motivation and Coping.* Thousand Oaks, CA: Sage.

Skinner, E.A., Edge, K., Altman, J., & Sherwood, H. (2003). Searching for the structure of coping: A review and critique of category systems for classifying ways of coping. *Psychological Bulletin, 129,* 216–269.

Skinner, E.A., & Wellborn, J.G. (1994). Coping during childhood and adolescence: A motivational perspective. In D. Featherman, R. Lerner, & M. Perlmutter (Eds.) *Life-span Development and Behavior* (Vol. 12, pp. 91–133). Hillsdale, NJ: Erlbaum.

Skinner, E.A., & Zimmer-Gembeck, M.J. (2007). The development of coping. *Annual Review of Psychology, 58,* 119–144.

Skinner, E.A., & Zimmer-Gembeck, M.J. (Eds.). (in press). *Perspective on Children's Coping with Stress as Regulation of Emotion, Cognition and Behavior. New Directions in Child and Adolescent Development Series.* San Francisco: Jossey-Bass.

Spear, L.P. (2000). Neurobehavioral changes in adolescence. *Current Directions in Psychological Science, 9,* 111–114.

Tolan, P., & Grant, K. (in press). How social and cultural contexts shape the development of coping: Youth in the inner-city as an example. In E.A. Skinner & M.J. Zimmer-Gembeck (Eds.), *Perspective on Children's Coping with Stress as Regulation of Emotion, Cognition and Behavior. New Directions in Child and Adolescent Development Series.* San Francisco: Jossey-Bass.

Tolan, P.H., Sherrod, L., Gorman-Smith, D., & Henry, D. (2003). Building protection, support, and opportunity for inner youth and their families. In K. Maton, C. Schellenbach, B. Leadbeater, & A. Solarz (Eds.), *Investing in Children, Youth, Families, and Communities: Strengths-based Research and Policy,* (pp. 193–211). Washington, DC: APA.

Williamson, D.E., Birmaher, B., Ryan, N.D., Shiffrin, T.P., Lusky, J.A., Protopapa, J., et al. (2003). The stressful life events schedule for children and adolescents: Development and validation. *Psychiatry Research, 119,* 225–241.

Wyman, P.A., Sandler, I., Wolchik, S., & Nelson, K. (2000). Resilience as cumulative competence promotion and stress protection: Theory and intervention. In D. Cicchetti, J. Rappaport, I. Sandler, & R.P. Weissberg (Eds.), *The Promotion of Wellness in Children and Adolescents,* (pp. 133–184). Arlington, VA: Child Welfare League of America.

Zimmer-Gembeck, M.J., & Collins, W. A. (2003). Autonomy development during adolescence. In G. R. Adams & M. Berzonsky (Eds.), *Blackwell Handbook of Adolescence,* (pp. 175–204). Oxford: Blackwell Publishers.

Zimmer-Gembeck, M.J., & Locke, E.M. (2007). The socialization of adolescent coping: Relationships at home and school. *Journal of Adolescence, 30,* 1–16.

Zimmer-Gembeck, M.J., Lees, D., Skinner, E.A., & Bradley, G. (under review). *Use of an Analogue Method to Examine Children's Appraisals of Threat and Emotion in Response to Stressful Events,* manuscript submitted for publication.

Critical Thinking

1. How does stress differ in children and adults?

2. What is the main cause of teenage stress?

3. What is the difference between boys and girls in stress?

4. How do teens cope with stress?

Melanie J. Zimmer-Gembeck, PhD (m.zimmer-gembeck@griffith.edu.au) is Associate Professor in the School of Psychology at Griffith University, Australia, and the Deputy Director of the Behavioural Basis of Health Research Centre, Institute of Health and Medical Research. She received training in Developmental Psychology at Portland State University and received her PhD in 1998. She is Deputy Director of the Psychological Health Research Centre and directs The Family Interaction Program, which is a centre for developing and evaluating innovative interventions for children and their families. Ellen A. Skinner, PhD, is Professor in the Department of Psychology at Portland State University. She was trained as a life-span developmental psychologist at the Pennsylvania State University, from which she received her Ph.D. in 1981. She spent the next seven years at the Max Planck Institute for Human Development and Education in Berlin, Germany. In 1988, she moved to the University of Rochester to work with the Motivation Research Group, and in 1992 she moved to Portland State. She is interested in the developmental dynamics of motivation and coping. Her research focuses on developmental changes in how close relationships with parents and teachers, combined with children's own self-system processes (e.g., perceived control, autonomy, relatedness), shape children's ongoing engagement and coping with challenges and failures.

From *The Prevention Researcher,* November 2008, pp. 3–7. Copyright © 2008 by Integrated Research Services, Inc. Reprinted by permission.

Steroids, the Media, and Youth

A Q&A with Travis Tygart

Prevention Researcher

The misconceptions adolescents have about steroids, some of them fueled by the media and influenced by the actual use of performance-enhancing drugs by young people, demonstrate the need for coaches, parents, and other role models to help guide teens to make healthy decisions. This includes understanding the reasons why young men and women choose to use steroids or similar drugs, identifying the immediate and long-term effects of steroid use, and knowing effective prevention methods.

To provide insight into these matters, Mr. Travis T. Tygart, an attorney and sports law expert, answers questions submitted by our readers and board members related to steroids, the media, and youth. As the CEO of the U.S. Anti-Doping Agency (USADA), Mr. Tygart works closely with professional athletes, sports organizations, and educational programs to eradicate the use of performance-enhancing drugs in sport.

Q I currently work with teenage boys, who are very image focused. They seem to believe that the effects of steroids are not long term, and that when one ends using, the side effects subside. In reality, how long do the effects of steroids last? Are some irreversible?

A Depending on the length of use, the side effects of steroids can be irreversible. As steroids are administered in cycles, the side effects from short cycles may subside with time. However, adolescents are at a particular risk as steroids can affect growth throughout puberty, permanently resulting in stunted physical development. Extended use of steroids can lead to a variety of damaging side effects, making any perceived "benefit" not worth the risk (see Table 1).

Q Do performance-enhancing drugs alter athletes' immune systems as they age?

A Depending on the length of drug abuse, there is a chance that the immune system can be damaged. The result: the whole body is more susceptible to a host of diseases and illness. The reality is that for a number of reasons it is nearly impossible to accurately study the impact of the type of steroid abuse that some athletes choose to engage in. As a result, the severity of the long term problems is not completely known. However, some anecdotal evidence is truly horrifying.

Table 1   Risks of Extended Steroid Use

Physiological side effects of anabolic steroid abuse
- Pustular acne on upper black
- Male pattern baldness
- Liver damage
- Premature closure of the growth centers of long bones (in adolescents), which may result in stunted growth

Males
- Breast tissue development
- Testicular atrophy
- Impotence
- Reduction in sperm production

Females
- Lowering of the voice
- Cessation of breast development
- Growth of hair on the face, stomach, and upper black
- Growth of the clitoris
- Serious disruption or cessation of the menstrual cycle

Psychological risks
- Increased aggressiveness and sexual appetite, sometimes resulting in aberrant sexual and criminal behavior, often referred to as "Roid Rage"
- Withdrawal from anabolic steroid use can be associated with depression, and in some cases, suicide

For example, in the 1970s and 1980s East Germany covertly and systematically gave their athletes steroids, telling the young athletes the pills were vitamins. Recently, former East German athletes have sought retribution for such problems as infertility, breast cancer, testicular cancer, and heart problems.

Q Our national media focuses on American athletes who are using steroids. Are other countries also dealing with this? How does America's use of performance-enhancing drugs compare internationally?

A The doping crisis is not just a public image problem for one country, one sport, one group of owners, or certain professional sports. Illicit drug use is a crime that knows no borders and creates an international public health problem that reaches right to the core of our collective values around clean sport, healthy lifestyles, and a level playing field. It adversely affects today's young student-athletes at all age levels.

Unfortunately, there are those throughout the world who would undermine the true meaning of fair play, who are willing to cheat for the sake of winning at all costs. This willingness to put winning above all else erodes our trust in sports. Unfortunately, sports fans worldwide have all witnessed the tragedy of athletes devoting everything to their sport, only to miss their rightful moment on the podium because the competitor in the lane next to them was cheating. We have also seen too many heroes fall from grace and end up compromising their athletic legacy. Some of our heroes have even had to return medals in the wake of scandal.

The fight against drugs in sport is a worldwide effort.

The fight against drugs in sport is a worldwide effort. Anti-doping agencies from around the globe are working hard to protect clean sport and ensure a level playing field. From a statistical perspective, the U.S. falls in the bottom third of Adverse Analytical Findings (AAF)—or cases of proven drug use—with a lower rate of total AAFs as compared with other nations.

Q I recently read an article in Sports Illustrated about a former NFL football player who had taken steroids throughout college and while playing in the NFL. The article described all of the strategies he used to "beat the test." I am concerned that some young people who read this article may not see the real point of it; instead they might only see "How To Beat the Test"

as the main point of the article. I guess my question is how can the media put the message about the dangers of steroid use out there in a way that young athletes can see the drugs' down sides and not just examples of famous athletes who were able to use performance-enhancing drugs and get away with it?

A Those of us in the fight to protect clean sport have a responsibility to effectively communicate the consequences as well as the achievements related to doping, allowing young athletes to learn from the experiences of others—positive and negative—and gain a healthy respect for the significant programs in place that catch and punish cheaters.

The challenge is to get media to engage in the story of anti-doping at a level that truly informs the public about the scope of the problem and the realities of anti-doping efforts and consequences. Unfortunately, the core of the fight against anti-doping is often deemed less newsworthy than sound bites from former cheaters.

An effective anti-doping program employs an integrated collection of tools.

Fortunately, many members of the media have taken the time to dig deeper into the issue. They have come to understand, and have attempted to convey to the public, that it is not enough to simply prohibit performance-enhancing substances and methods and administer testing for the contents of a prohibited list. An effective anti-doping program employs an integrated collection of tools, including an independent agency to conduct the testing and results management, a substantial education program to arm athletes and youth with tools for competing clean and healthy, cooperation and collaboration with law enforcement agencies, and research to advance the science of anti-doping.

On the positive side, much has been achieved already to facilitate success in this movement. In 2000, The U.S. Anti-Doping Agency (USADA) was formed as a truly independent and transparent entity in support of U.S. athletes. The International Olympic Committee externalized its program through the formation of the World Anti-Doping Agency, harmonizing the movement around the globe. In the U.S. we can claim the gold standard in out-of-competition, no-advance-notice testing programs; we have a comprehensive list of prohibited substances and methods for which we test; we have a substantial education program that provides athletes and youth with tools for living and competing healthy and drug-free; we conduct research to advance the anti-doping science; and we have developed effective partnerships with law enforcement agencies to ensure that all parties to doping activity are held accountable.

It is indeed crucial for a balanced perspective to be presented in a public forum. Rather than depicting the "glamour" and sensationalism of doping, it is critical that the media also share the heartache and painful consequences that result from performance-enhancing drug use. Youth need to hear the whole story and comprehend the regret and remorse of athletes who truly wish they had made more ethical, sound decisions.

Q Considering that well-known athletes such as Alex Rodriguez and Roger Clemens, among others, have taken steroids during their starry careers and have either not admitted to it or have only admitted to doing steroids well after the fact, how can we expect our student-athletes not to go the same route to gain the competitive edge for that scholarship, state championship, or professional career? What safeguards do our schools need to put in place to keep the field level for all?

A In the fight against doping at the high school level, education is the key. The doping crisis reaches beyond certain professional athletes or particular sports. Illegal use of steroids poses a public health problem that impacts youth and the way we are approaching good sportsmanship. It adversely affects today's high school, junior high school, and even grade school athletes. The willingness of some to prioritize winning, at the sacrifice of ethics and health, erodes our trust in sport and the notion of fair play. In the U.S., there is no doubt that we face a doping crisis. The question is, to what extent is this but one element of a greater epidemic— an ethical crisis. If we can impact the youth of today, we will be able to affect the athletes—and frankly citizens—of tomorrow.

For its part, USADA is committed to reaching the next generation of student-athletes with impactful, meaningful programs that empower them to make intelligent, ethical, and healthy choices. There are many other parties (e.g., coaches, teachers, mentors) who must contribute to these collective educational efforts. Some states have implemented drug testing at the high school level in an effort to both detect use of drugs, as well as deter young athletes from resorting to this behavior. Much like the anti-doping efforts on the elite level, the educational system's effectiveness in eradicating drug use must rely on comprehensive education to complement testing programs.

Parents, coaches, and other individuals supporting student-athletes must also provide solutions to the grave issues at hand, rather than contributing to the cause. The influence that these support people have can play a crucial role in shaping the future of our youth. Together, we must work to teach the next generation the ethics of sport and emphasize those ethics over a culture that is constantly looking for shortcuts to success. This is not an easy task, but it is an extremely important mission and with the appropriate level of determination and resources it can be achieved.

Q How can athletic codes of conduct and school policies more effectively enforce norms of non use among high school athletes? How can educators/administrators/ preventionists make this issue of greater concern at a policy level?

A Educators and administrators need to grasp the urgency of the situation at hand. Our youth need help and guidance today—not in the future when it may be too late.

As for ensuring instruction on the policy level, funding should be appropriated for an in-school program that would provide a broad-based educational foundation to our children of the importance of healthy living, ethical decision making, and the risks of using dangerous performance-enhancing drugs. Funding also needs to be allocated to gathering additional information on the scope of the problem in our schools and throughout youth sports. I firmly believe that such research will expose that this is a problem spreading its corrupted roots wider and deeper into the heart of youth sports each year.

Q Most of the media attention is on male athletes who have abused steroids, yet we know that female athletes use steroids too, for example, Olympic track star Marion Jones. At the same time, most of the prevention material also appears to be directed at males. What is being done specifically for girls and the coaches who work with them to prevent steroid abuse among our female athletes?

A As a father of three young children all ages 7 and under, I hope that one day they will learn the valuable life lessons that can be obtained by participating in sports played with integrity, honor and without prohibited drugs. I want them, like all of our children, to benefit from the ideal that, in its purest form, true sport builds character and promotes the virtues of selfless teamwork, dedication, and commitment to a greater cause.

As a parent, I have the same hopes for the role of sport in my daughter's life as my sons' lives. I know that sport will have an impact on my daughter's development, and I work each day to make sure that impact is positive. Studies show that there is rising interest on the part of females with respect to performance-enhancing substances, and certainly there is the issue of body image and the desire to cut corners (or take drastic action) for the sake of appearance and acceptance. Young women need to be educated on the dangers of steroid abuse and empowered to make healthy decisions, just as males do. For USADA's part, education efforts are aimed at young people, coaches, educators, and parents, for both the benefit of males and females.

Q We know that many athletes continue to use steroids even though they know steroids are harmful. I am wondering about the dangers of "energy" drinks and supplements, such as Red Bull, "5-Hour Energy," and other caffeine-based energy boosters, some of which are actively promoted by professional athletes. What do we know about these products which are readily available in any supermarket? Are they harmful? Additionally, what is being done to promote healthy eating and healthy exercise so that our youth don't fall prey to the next fad?

A As a society, we are targets for a multi-billion dollar industry promoting the use of dietary supplements, preying on our desire to be thinner, leaner, more energetic, bigger, stronger, faster, younger-looking, etc. There is a huge temptation to pursue shortcuts to these goals, finding the magic panacea that will yield our fountain of youth and the rest of our dreams in an easy-to-take pill, powder, drink, or bar. Like many supplements, energy drinks may seem to be the perfect answer for a quick boost, but they can be laden with sugar, caffeine, and other potentially harmful stimulants.

Just last year, a group of scientists and physicians urged the Food and Drug Administration (FDA) to increase regulations on "energy" drinks. Currently, there is no requirement for the amount of caffeine in such drinks to be listed on the can. The stimulants in these energy drinks, if consumed in abundance and with frequency, can become addictive and cause anxiety, irritability, insomnia, increased risk of stroke, heart attack, cardiac arrhythmia, and possible death.

According to the FDA, energy drinks can also contribute to higher levels of alcohol consumption, involvement with illicit drugs, and non-medical use of prescription drugs—especially in young people. The lesson that you can get a "rush" from a can may start with caffeine at age 14, but that lesson is clearly being extended by our children to harder drugs.

The reality is that the dietary supplement industry as a whole is grossly under-regulated, making it impossible for consumers to guarantee that what they are taking is effective, or even that the products contain the ingredients listed on the label. Education is essential for our youth to become informed and intelligent consumers, and learn how to make healthy and safe choices about what they put in their bodies.

Q Do you think pressure from parents and coaches for good sports performances lead student-athletes to abuse performance-enhancing drugs? If so, what prevention measures are being targeted to parents and coaches?

A In today's society, student-athletes face pressure as never before. In addition to the pressure of competing well for their team and possible scholarships, parents and coaches can also place great pressure on their young athletes. Unfortunately, this pressure may contribute to resorting to performance-enhancing drugs.

What we know for sure is that parents and coaches will shape how our young athletes view sport. For that reason, it is vital that all adults involved in youth sport make a conscious effort to keep the focus on the true values of sport—hard work and perseverance, integrity, respect, and teamwork. If parents and coaches don't uphold these values, the future of sport will surely be compromised.

From USADA's perspective, we are committed to educating parents and coaches on the influence they hold over their athletes. Through presentations at schools, developing athlete events, and the distribution of interactive curriculums, USADA is committed to ensuring that all athlete supporters join the effort against drugs in sport and defend the values of true sport.

Critical Thinking

1. What determines healthy decisions in youth?
2. How can coaches help guide teens in healthy decisions?
3. What part does the media play in helping youth in health decisions?
4. How can parents help guide teens in healthy decisions?

TRAVIS T. TYGART is the CEO of the U.S. Anti-Doping Agency (USADA), which is responsible for steroid education as well as the testing and results management processes for the U.S. Olympic and Paralympic athletes. During the 2008 Olympics, Mr. Tygart was appointed Vice-Chair for the World Anti-Doping Agency's Independent Observer's Team, which focused on testing for the Beijing games. He has testified in several U.S. Senate and House hearings regarding the use of performance-enhancing drugs in sport, while also assisting with several investigations of doping by professional athletes. Prior to his involvement with the USADA, Mr. Tygart was an associate in the sports law practice with Holme, Roberts and Owen, LLP, working with individual athletes and sports entities, such as USOC and USA Basketball. After graduating from the University of North Carolina at Chapel Hill with a Bachelor's degree in Philosophy, Mr. Tygart went on to earn his J.D. from Southern Methodist University, graduating Order of the Coif.

From *The Prevention Researcher*, December 2009, pp. 7–9. Copyright © 2009 by Integrated Research Services, Inc. Reprinted by permission.

Article 33

Understanding Cutting in Adolescents: Prevalence, Prevention, and Intervention

JENNIFER DYL, PhD

Case: Amanda is a 14 year-old girl who just began her first year of high school at a large public school. Prior to starting school, she was excited, but also anxious about making new friends. Now, a couple of months into the school year, even though she says she has made some new friends, she doesn't bring them home to meet her parents. While she previously had been an A/B middle school student, she has difficulty focusing on her schoolwork, is distracted by trying to figure out her new school, and worries about fitting in. Her parents notice she spends a lot more time in her room by herself, and they are not sure what she is doing in there. Her parents are concerned because her mother has struggled with depression and worries Amanda could be too. Amanda recently left her MySpace screen open and her parents saw a message she wrote to one of her friends about cutting herself. When they confronted her, she said "It's not a big deal," and she doesn't know why her parents are so upset about it.

Amanda's presentation is an increasingly common one in inpatient, community, and school settings. Cutting is the most prevalent form of the nonsuicidal self-injurious behaviors (NSSI), defined as purposely damaging bodily tissue without the intent to die. Other NSSI behaviors include burning, sniffing, head banging, bruising. Cutting may involve razors, knives, scissors, glass, paper clips, sharp fingernails, or any other sharp object.

Prevalence

Anecdotally, middle and high school educators are reporting increasing problems with students cutting and seek guidance on how to best address this troubling behavior, while clinicians also observe that cutting has risen in adolescent psychiatric settings in the last decade. Prevalence studies report rates of 5–47% in community adolescent samples,

12–35% among college students, and 4% in general adult populations, underscoring the vulnerability of the adolescent developmental period to this problem. Among adolescent psychiatric inpatients, rates of 39–61% have been reported. Empirical evidence also supports that the prevalence has increased in recent years.

Precipitating Factors
Sociocultural and developmental influences

Hypothesized influences contributing to the prevalence of cutting are multifactorial and include sociocultural factors such as the media and peer group influences, coupled with internal psychological factors and comorbid psychiatric conditions. Identified family factors have included difficulty tolerating the expression of strong or negative emotions, viewing parents as unavailable or disinterested, and parental substance abuse and psychological problems.

With regard to media influences, trends in music and media highlighting violent and self-injurious behaviors have been identified as possible influences. Disturbingly, there are internet web sites and chat rooms dedicated to self-injury, some of which glorify cutting as chic or a source of strength. Some schools have peer subgroups in which cutting is a requirement for becoming a member. There is additional speculation that adolescents are desensitized to self-injury because of the popularity of body piercings and tattoos, with some teens rationalizing that self-injury is an extension of these forms of body art.

Developmentally, adolescence is a time to hone a sense of identity through "trying on" various behaviors, beliefs, and roles through identification with peer groups, music, fashion, etc. While it may be normative for some adolescents to experiment with peer groups with alternative dress or musical interests (i.e., the "Goth" or "Emo" groups), it is not normative when the values of a peer

144

group involve self-injurious behaviors. In psychologically vulnerable individuals (i.e., those with depression, anxiety, or difficulty managing emotions), cutting may begin to take on a life of its own, beyond efforts to fit in. There is also a sizable proportion of adolescents who begin to cut themselves secretively and/or in the absence of direct peer influences.

Psychological functions and vulnerability

Due to increased biological, emotional, social and academic changes, adolescents experience a range of strong emotions and interpersonal challenges and many have not yet learned mature coping skills to manage them. Cutting as a way to regulate emotions or as an attempt to solve interpersonal problems may impede normative socio-emotional problem-solving and the development of healthy coping and self-soothing skills.

Nock and Prinstein (2004) conceptualized contingencies for cutting as either *internal* or *social,* and reinforcement as either *positive* or *negative.* Adolescents most often report cutting for internal negative reinforcement (i.e., "to stop bad feelings" to "relieve feeling numb or empty"), internal positive reinforcement (i.e., "to feel something, even if it is pain," "to punish yourself," "to feel relaxed"), social negative reinforcement (i.e., "to avoid doing something unpleasant you do not want to do," "to avoid being with people") and social positive reinforcement (i.e., "to get attention" to "let others know how desperate you are," to "feel more part of a group"). There is some suggestion that internal factors may be more strongly related to a greater degree of psychiatric impairment, as these reasons for cutting are reported more frequently in inpatient adolescents, while internal and social factors are reported equally in community samples.

Clinically and empirically, cutters frequently report feeling temporary relief from or "blocking out" unpleasant emotional states (i.e., tension, anger, sadness, emptiness). Some report that cutting promotes a "release" of feelings, followed by a rapid reduction in tension and increased perception of psychological equilibrium. Particularly in individuals with comorbid dissociative symptoms or chronic feelings of numbness, cutting may also function to feel in touch with one's body or to "feel pain." Others report feeling temporary "control," followed by a sense of loss of control, shame, alienation, or helplessness. Cutting may also relate to low self-worth and a desire to punish oneself or may function as an inadequately channeled self-care ritual. Cutting may be seen as an alternative form of expression for those with difficulty verbalizing feelings.

Many also describe cutting as "addictive" and there has been some exploration of differences at the neurotransmitter level in self-injurers. Over time, cutting also becomes psychologically and behaviorally habit-forming, and one hypothesis is that with greater exposure to the behavior over time, fears of injury or other negative outcomes decline and the internal reward function increases. Many report needing to cut deeper over time and increasingly employ a wider variety of methods at greater frequency. Severity of cutting (frequency, degree of injury, variety of methods) also correlates with degree of psychopathology and with risk for more serious, life-threatening injuries. Research has found a subset of cutters who do attempt suicide and in those groups the cutting tends to be more frequent and varied in methodology.

In terms of comorbidity, depression and anxiety are consistently found to be related to cutting, while other associated conditions include conduct problems, substance abuse, suicidality, eating disorders, PTSD/dissociative disorders, and a history of abuse or trauma.

Prevention/Intervention

Given the strong association between cutting and psychiatric impairment, along with the possibility that cutting will increase, rather than decrease over time in the absence of treatment, it is imperative that the problem be taken seriously and addressed as early as possible.

It is important to address the problem without reinforcing the behavior. There should be a focus on the underlying feelings and function of the cutting, not on the physical effects of cutting itself. The idea is to help the teen find healthier ways to meet their interpersonal needs (i.e., the need to communicate, the need for attention) and better ways to regulate challenging emotions.

While a variety of treatment models may successfully address cutting, Cognitive Behavioral Therapy (CBT) and Dialectical Behavioral Therapy (DBT) may be particularly effective. Adolescents may be taught DBT skills such as mindfulness, emotional regulation, distress tolerance, and interpersonal effectiveness skills. These include normalizing emotions and helping adolescents "sit with" uncomfortable feelings, emphasizing that feelings are not the problem, but "how you deal with them." Other interventions may involve helping teens to talk about feelings or concerns rather than acting them out, as well as learning skills to self-soothe.

Physical exercises to relieve tension, breathing/relaxation, creative expressions such as journaling or artwork, and temporary distraction techniques may also be taught. Adolescents may be taught to identify triggers such as emotional reactions and cognitive distortions which may precipitate cutting so they can use skills to cope with these thoughts and feelings at an earlier point. Parents and clinicians should encourage positive peer group conformity and the development of feelings of control and self-efficacy through positive channels such as developing a skill or ability. Pharmacological treatment of co-occurring psychiatric disorders may also be helpful.

References

Nock MK, Prinstein MJ: A functional approach to the assessment of self-mutilative behavior. *J Consult Clin Psychol* 2004; 114: 140–146.

Lloyd-Richardson EE, Perrine N, Dierker L, Kelley ML: Characteristics and functions of non-suicidal self-injury in a community sample of adolescents. *Psychol Med* 2007; 37(9):1372.

Swenson LP, Spirito A, Dyl J, Kittler J, Hunt J: Psychological correlates of cutting behaviors in an adolescent inpatient sample. Under Review, *J Child Psychiatr Human Develop.*

Critical Thinking

1. What is the most prevalent form of non-suicidal, self-injurious behavior?

2. What is the prevalence of cutting by youth?

3. What are possible preventive techniques for self-injurious behavior?

4. What are intervention techniques for self-injurious behaviors?

DR. DYL is a staff psychologist at Bradley Hospital in the Adolescent Program and a clinical assistant professor in the Department of Psychiatry and Human Behavior at the Warren Alpert Medical School at Brown University.

Violence in Adolescent Dating Relationships

"The early-to mid-teenage years mark a time in which romantic relationships begin to emerge. From a developmental perspective, these relationships can serve a number of positive functions. However, for many adolescents, there is a darker side: dating violence."

Ernest N. Jouriles, PhD, Cora Platt, BA, and Renee McDonald, PhD

For many, the early- to mid-teenage years mark a time in which romantic relationships begin to emerge. From a developmental perspective, these relationships can serve a number of positive functions. However, for many adolescents, there is a darker side: dating violence. In this article, we discuss the definition and measurement of adolescent dating violence, review epidemiological findings regarding victimization, and describe correlates of victimization experiences. We end with a discussion of prevention and intervention programs designed to address adolescent dating violence and highlight important gaps in our knowledge.

Defining and Measuring Adolescent Dating and Dating Violence

"Dating" among adolescents is complicated to define and measure, in part because the nature of dating changes dramatically over the course of adolescence (Connolly et al., 1999; Feiring, 1996). In early adolescence, dating involves getting together with small groups of friends of both sexes to do things together as a group. From these group experiences, adolescents progress to going out with or dating a single individual. Initial single-dating relationships are typically casual and short-term; more serious, exclusive, and longer-lasting relationships emerge in mid- to late-adolescence.

"Dating" among adolescents is complicated to define and measure.

In research on adolescent dating violence, adolescents are often asked to respond to questions about a "boyfriend" or "girlfriend" or someone with whom they have "been on a date with or gone out with." However, what constitutes a boyfriend or girlfriend or a dating partner is not clear, and these judgments are likely to vary tremendously across adolescents. These judgments are probably also influenced by a number of factors including the amount of time spent with each other, the degree of emotional attachment, and the activities engaged in together (Allen, 2004). They are also likely to change over the course of adolescence, as youth mature and become more experienced with dating.

Most everyone has a general idea about what constitutes "violence" in adolescent dating relationships, but not everyone conceptualizes and defines it the same way. In the empirical literature, multiple types of dating violence have been studied, including physical, sexual, and psychological violence. Definitions for these different types of violence vary from study to study, but each is typically based on adolescents' reports of the occurrence of specific acts. For example, physical violence often refers to adolescents' reports of hits, slaps, or beatings; sexual violence refers to forced kissing, touching, or intercourse; and psychological violence to reports of insults, threats, or the use of control tactics. These different types of violence are sometimes further subdivided. For example, indirect aggression (also referred to as relational or social aggression), which includes spreading hurtful rumors or telling cruel stories about a dating partner, has recently begun to be conceptualized as a form of dating violence that may be distinct from more overt forms of psychological or emotional abuse (Wolfe, Scott, Reitzel-Jaffe et al., 2001). As another example, in a recent prevalence study, sexual assault was distinguished from drug- or alcohol-facilitated rape, with the latter defined as sexual assault that occurred while the victim was "high, drunk, or passed out from drinking or taking drugs" (Wolitzky-Taylor et al., 2008).

In the bulk of studies on adolescent dating violence, the youth are surveyed about the occurrence of specific acts of violence within a particular time period, for example, during the previous 12 months. These surveys are typically administered on a single occasion, in either a questionnaire or interview format. Some include only one or two questions about violence; others include comprehensive scales of relationship violence with excellent psychometric properties (e.g., Wolfe et al., 2001). A handful of investigators have attempted to study adolescent dating violence using other methods, such as laboratory observations (e.g., Capaldi, Kimm, & Shortt, 2007), and repeated interviews over a short, circumscribed period of time (e.g., Jouriles et al., 2005). However, studies using alternatives to one-time, self-report survey assessments are few and far between.

This first section highlights some of the complexities involved in conceptualizing adolescent dating violence and describes how different types of dating violence are often defined and measured, providing a backdrop for understanding and interpreting empirical findings in the literature. As illustrated in the section below, different conceptualizations and definitions of dating violence lead to different research findings and conclusions. Similarly, various data collection methods (such as using more questions and/or repeated questioning) also yield different results. At the present time, there is no gold standard with respect to defining or measuring adolescent dating violence; the field is still developing in this regard.

Prevalence of Adolescent Dating Violence

Over the past decade, data from several different national surveys have been used to estimate the prevalence of the various forms of adolescent dating violence. Surveys conducted by the Centers for Disease Control suggest that 9–10% of students in grades 9–12 indicate that a boyfriend or girlfriend has hit, slapped, or physically hurt them on purpose during the previous 12 months, and approximately 8% report having been physically forced to have sexual intercourse against their wishes (Howard, Wang, & Yan, 2007a, 2007b). The 2005 National Survey of Adolescents (NSA) indicates that 1.6% of adolescents between 12 and 17 years of age have experienced "serious dating violence" (Wolitzky-Taylor et al., 2008). Serious dating violence was defined as experiencing one or more of the following forms of violence from a dating partner: physical violence (badly injured, beaten up, or threatened with a knife or gun), sexual violence (forced anal, vaginal, or oral sex; forced penetration with a digit or an object; forced touching of genitalia), or drug/alcohol-facilitated rape.

Most studies in this area ask about male-to-female and female-to-male violence or include gender-neutral questions without assessing whether a respondent is in an opposite-sex or same-sex relationship. The National Longitudinal Study of Adolescent Health is unique in that it reports data on violence

Table 1 Prevalence of Dating Violence in Same-Sex and Opposite-Sex Romantic Relationships

Data from National Longitudinal Study of Adolescent Health		
In the previous 18 months partner had been:	Opposite-sex relationship	Same-sex relationship
Physically violent	12%	11%
Psychologically violent	29%	21%

Halpern, Oslak, Young, Martin, & Kupper, 2001; Halpern, Young, Waller, Martin, & Kupper, 2004.

in opposite-sex as well as same-sex romantic relationships. As can be seen in Table 1, prevalence rates for both physical and psychological violence are similar in opposite-sex and same-sex romantic relationships among adolescents in grades 7–12.

Prevalence rates for both physical and psychological violence are similar in opposite-sex and same-sex romantic relationships among adolescents in grades 7–12.

The prevalence of physical dating violence appears to be fairly similar across studies of national samples. Variation across estimates most likely reflects differences in how violence is defined, and perhaps differences in the samples from which the estimates were derived (e.g., different age ranges sampled). It should be noted that prevalence estimates based on smaller, less representative, localized samples tend to be higher than those based on national samples. In fact, a number of researchers have reported prevalence estimates for physical dating violence among adolescents (over a one-year period or less) to be over 40% (Hickman, Jaycox, & Aronoff, 2004). These elevated estimates might stem directly from sampling differences, but also perhaps from differences in the conceptualization and measurement of dating violence. For example, in many of the smaller samples, investigators assessed dating violence more extensively (such as using more questions and/or through repeated questioning), which might contribute to higher prevalence estimates.

Taken together, the results across studies yield some general conclusions about the nature and scope of adolescent dating violence. Regardless of how it is defined, it appears that a substantial number of United States youth are affected by dating violence. Even with very conservative definitions, such as the one used in the NSA, it was projected that approximately 400,000 adolescents have been victims, at some point in their lives, of serious dating violence (Wolitzky-Taylor et al., 2008).

Psychological violence appears to be much more common than either physical or sexual violence. Data are mixed on the relative prevalence of physical and sexual violence, but some of the national surveys suggest that they are approximately equal in prevalence.

Onset and Course

Dating violence appears to emerge well before high school. For example, cross-sex teasing and harassment, which involve behaviors often construed as either psychological or sexual violence, is evident among 6th graders and increases in prevalence over time (McMaster et al., 2002). One-third of a sample of 7th graders who indicated that they had started dating also reported that they had committed acts of aggression (physical, sexual, or psychological) toward a dating partner; in over half of these cases, physical or sexual aggression was involved (Sears et al., 2007). In the NSA, serious dating violence victimization was not reported by 12-year-olds, but it was by 13-year-olds (Wolitzky-Taylor et al., 2008).

Longitudinal data on the course of adolescent dating violence are scarce, but there is evidence that psychological aggression predicts subsequent physical aggression (O'Leary & Slep, 2003). In fact, different types of dating violence commonly co-occur within adolescent relationships, with the occurrence of one type of violence (physical, psychological, or sexual) associated with an increased likelihood of other types of violence (Sears, Byers, & Price, 2007). In research on interpersonal victimization in general, victims of violence are known to be at increased risk for subsequent victimization. This appears to be true for victims of adolescent dating violence as well (Smith, White, & Holland, 2003).

Demographics of Adolescent Dating Violence

Certain demographic variables including age, race and ethnicity, geographic location, and sex are associated with increased risk for victimization. Specifically, the risk for dating violence victimization increases with age, at least through the middle and high school years. This trend appears to be true for physical, psychological, and sexual violence (e.g., Halpern et al., 2001; Howard et al., 2007a, 2007b; Wolitzky-Taylor et al., 2008). This might be attributable to a number of things, including the changing nature of dating over the course of adolescence. Some evidence has emerged pointing to racial and ethnic differences in adolescents' experiences of dating violence, but other recent, large-scale studies call these findings into question. For example, a number of investigators have found Black adolescents to be more likely than their White counterparts to experience physical and sexual dating violence (e.g., Howard et al., 2007a, 2007b). However, these differences have sometimes disappeared when other variables, such as prior exposures to violence, are considered (Malik, Sorenson, & Aneshensel, 1997). Moreover, recent, well-designed studies of very large samples have found no evidence of racial or ethnic differences in adolescent victimization

(e.g., O'Leary et al., 2008; Wolitzky-Taylor et al., 2008). There do appear to be regional differences in dating violence, with adolescents in southern states at substantially greater risk for experiencing dating violence than adolescents in other regions of the U.S. (Marquart, et al., 2007). Although the reasons for regional differences are not known, it is interesting to note that the South has a higher prevalence rate of overall violence than other regions in the U.S. In short, there may be factors in the Southern U.S. that facilitate the promotion, acceptance, or tolerance of violent behavior.

When violence is defined broadly, prevalence rates for male and female victimization tend to be similar (e.g., Halpern et al., 2001). However, narrower definitions of violence point to some sex differences in the experience of violence. For example, female adolescents are more likely than males to experience severe physical violence (violent acts that are likely to result, or actually have resulted, in physical injuries) and sexual violence (e.g., Molidor & Tolman, 1998; Wolitzky-Taylor et al., 2008). Females are also more likely than males to experience fear, hurt, and the desire to leave the situation for self-protection (Molidor & Tolman, 1998; Jackson, Cram, & Seymour, 2000). In addition, females are more likely to report physical injuries and more harmful and persistent psychological distress after being victimized (O'Keefe, 1997).

Correlates of Adolescent Dating Violence

Most of the findings on the correlates of adolescent dating violence come from studies in which data were collected at a single point in time. Thus, it is difficult to discern if observed correlates are precursors or consequences of the violence, or if they are simply related to experiencing violence, but not in a cause-and-effect manner. Although it is tempting to interpret some of these associations in a causal, unidirectional manner, more often than not, alternative explanations can also be offered. For example, the documented association between dating violence and psychological distress is typically interpreted to mean that experiencing dating violence causes psychological distress (e.g., Howard et al., 2007a, 2007b; Molidor & Tolman, 1998). However, it is not too difficult to imagine how feelings of psychological distress might influence an adolescent's decision about whom to go out with (i.e., adolescents who are psychologically distressed, compared with those who are not, may make different choices about whom to date) and, perhaps, lead an adolescent to an abusive relationship.

Many adolescents engage in antisocial or illegal activities, but those who do so consistently and frequently are at increased risk of dating violence victimization (e.g., Howard et al., 2007a, 2007b). In addition, simply having antisocial friends increases risk for victimization. For example, females who associate with violent or victimized peers appear to be at increased risk for dating violence victimization (Gagne, Lavoie, & Hebert, 2005). Similarly, male and female adolescents exposed to peer-drinking activities within the past 30 days (e.g., "Hanging out with friends who drank") were victimized more often than their counterparts who were not exposed to such activities (Howard, Qiu, & Boekeloo, 2003).

Many other adolescent experiences have also been associated with dating violence victimization. For example, earlier exposures to violence, both within and outside of the family, are associated with victimization (e.g., Gagne et al., 2005; Malik et al., 1997). Negative parent-child interactions and parent-child boundary violations at age 13 predict victimization at age 21 (Linder & Collins, 2005). Trauma symptoms, which may result from violence exposure and untoward parent-child interactions, are posited to interfere with emotional and cognitive processes important in interpreting abusive behavior, and possibly to heighten tolerance for abuse (Capaldi & Gorman-Smith, 2003). Having had prior sexual relationships with peers increases adolescent females' risk for experiencing relationship violence (e.g., Howard et al., 2007a, 2007b). Also, the likelihood of victimization increases as the number of dating partners increases (Halpern et al., 2001).

Several different dimensions of adolescent relationships have been examined in relation to dating violence. For example, physical violence is often reciprocated within relationships, meaning that when dating violence is reported, both partners are typically violent toward one another (e.g., O'Leary, Slep, Avery-Leaf, Cascardi, 2008). Relationship violence is more likely to happen in serious or special romantic relationships, rather than more casual ones (O'Leary et al., 2008; Roberts, Auinger, & Klein, 2006). It is also more likely to occur in relationships with problems, conflict, and power struggles (Bentley et al., 2007; O'Keefe, 1997).

Relationship violence is more likely to happen in serious or special romantic relationships, rather than more casual ones.

Although there are many risk factors for adolescent dating violence, some protective factors have emerged as well. For instance, having high-quality friendships at age 16 is associated with reduced likelihood of experiencing dating violence in romantic relationships at age 21 (Linder & Collins, 2005). High-quality friendships are characterized by security, disclosure, closeness, low levels of conflict, and the effective resolution of conflict that does occur. Also, adolescents who do well in school and those who attend religious services are at decreased risk for experiencing dating violence (Halpern et al., 2001; Howard et al., 2003).

Prevention and Intervention

Much of the prevention research in this area is directed at an entire population (e.g., 9th grade at a school) with the goal of preventing violence from occurring. However, the prevalence data indicate that a sizable number of adolescents in high school, and even middle school, have already perpetrated and/or experienced dating violence. Thus, in most cases the research

is not technically universal prevention, from the standpoint of preventing violence before it ever occurs. Rather, it is an attempt to reduce dating violence, by preventing its initial occurrence as well as preventing its re-occurrence among those who have already experienced it.

A sizable number of adolescents in high school, and even middle school, have already perpetrated and/or experienced dating violence.

Many of the school-based prevention programs share a number of commonalities, in addition to the joint focus on prevention and intervention (Whitaker et al., 2006). Most are designed to address perpetration and victimization simultaneously. Many are incorporated into mandatory health classes in middle or high school. Most are based on a combination of feminist and social learning principles, and involve didactic methods to increase knowledge and change attitudes regarding dating violence. Despite these similarities, there are potentially important differences in the structure (e.g., duration) and content of these various programs. Unfortunately, most of these school-based programs have not undergone rigorous empirical evaluation to determine whether they actually reduce occurrences of violence.

A notable exception is Safe Dates, a program developed for 8th and 9th grade students (Foshee, Bauman, Arriaga et al., 1998) that has undergone a fairly rigorous evaluation. Safe Dates includes: (a) ten interactive classroom sessions covering topics such as dating violence norms, gender stereotyping, and conflict management skills, (b) group activities such as peer-performed theater productions and a poster contest, and (c) information about community resources for adolescents in abusive relationships. Evaluation results indicate that Safe Dates reduces psychological and physical violence perpetration, but not victimization, among the students who participated in the program. At first glance, this result might be puzzling: How can the perpetration of violence go down, without a commensurate reduction in victimization? This might be explained, in part, by the fact that not all individuals who participated in Safe Dates dated other Safe Date participants. Although the Safe Dates participants were less likely to commit acts of dating violence after completing the program, they were not necessarily less likely to date individuals who commit violent acts.

Evaluations of other school-based programs using techniques similar to those employed in Safe Dates have not had demonstrable effects on violence perpetration or victimization. Some of these evaluations simply did not include measures of perpetration or victimization as outcomes. Others, however, have attempted to measure intervention effects on violent behavior and victimization, but have found no effects (e.g., Avery-Leaf et al., 1997; Hilton et al., 1998). Many of these school-based programs, however, *have* achieved changes in knowledge or attitudes regarding dating violence (e.g., Avery-Leaf et al., 1997; Hilton et al., 1998; Krajewski et al., 1996; Weisz & Black, 2001).

Another program with demonstrated results is The Youth Relationships Project (YRP) (Wolfe et al., 2003). YRP is a community-based intervention designed for 14-16 year olds who were maltreated as children and were thus at increased risk of being in abusive relationships in the future. YRP is an 18-session, group-based program with three primary components: (a) education about abusive relationships and power dynamics within these relationships, (b) skills development, and (c) social action. The skills targeted in this program include communication skills and conflict resolution. The social action portion of the program includes, among other things, allowing program participants the opportunity to become familiar with and to practice utilizing resources for individuals in violent relationships, as well as the chance to develop a project to raise awareness of dating violence within the community. Sessions include skills practice, guest speakers, videos, and visits to relevant community agencies. Evaluation results indicate that YRP reduces physical dating violence perpetration and physical, emotional, and threatening abuse victimization.

It is encouraging that Safe Dates and the YRP have yielded promising results in reducing dating violence among adolescents. However, given the current state of the prevention literature in this area, it would be erroneous to suggest that we know how to prevent adolescent dating violence. Systematic reviews of this literature indicate that the vast majority of studies attempting to evaluate a dating violence prevention program have *not* found intervention effects on behavioral measures, and even though changes in knowledge and attitudes are often documented, it is not really clear if such changes lead to changes in either perpetration or victimization (Hickman et al., 2004; Whitaker et al., 2006). The promising findings of the Safe Dates and YRP programs require replication, and more information is needed on how these programs accomplished their positive effects. Researchers and practitioners can use these programs as a starting point in their own efforts at preventing relationship violence, but it is still important to continue exploring new ideas about prevention in this area.

Concluding Remarks

It is clear that violence in adolescent dating relationships is a prevalent problem with potentially devastating consequences. We also know a great deal about correlates of such violence. On the other hand, there are still important gaps in our knowledge. For example, longitudinal research on this topic is extremely scarce; thus, we know little about the emergence and unfolding of dating violence and victimization over time. This is particularly true for high-risk groups, such as children from violent homes and other groups potentially at risk. In addition, we know very little about how to address the problem of adolescent dating violence effectively. This might be due, in part, to the dearth of well-designed longitudinal studies on this topic, which are necessary to develop a solid knowledge base on the causes of relationship violence and targets for intervention. Although there are promising and notable efforts in the area of understanding and preventing violence in adolescent dating relationships, we still have much to learn.

> Longitudinal research on this topic is extremely scarce; thus, we know little about the emergence and unfolding of dating violence and victimization over time.

References

Allen, L. (2004). "Getting off" and "going out": Young people's conceptions of (hetero) sexual relationships. *Health & Sexuality, 6,* 463–481.

Avery-Leaf, S., Cascardi, M., O'Leary, K.D., & Cano, A. (1997). Efficacy of a dating violence prevention program on attitudes justifying aggression. *Journal of Adolescent Health, 21,* 11–17.

Bentley, C.G., Galliher, R.V., & Ferguson, T.J. (2007). Associations among aspects of interpersonal power and relationship functioning in adolescent romantic couples. *Sex Roles, 57,* 483–495.

Capaldi, D.M., & Gorman-Smith, D. (2003). The development of aggression in young male/female couples. In P. Florsheim (Ed.), *Adolescent Romantic Relations and Sexual Behavior: Theory, Research, and Practical implications* (pp. 243–278). Lawrence Erlbaum Associates, Publishers.

Capaldi, D.M., Kim, H.K., & Shortt, J.W. (2007). Observed initiation and reciprocity of physical aggression in young, at risk couples. *Journal of Family Violence, 22,* 101–111.

Connolly, J., Craig, W., Goldberg, A., & Pepler, D. (1999). Conceptions of cross-sex friendships and romantic relationships in early adolescence. *Journal of Youth and Adolescence, 28,* 481–494.

Feiring, C. (1996). Concept of romance in 15-year-old adolescents. *Journal of Research on Adolescence, 6,* 181–200.

Foshee, V., Bauman, K.E., Arriaga, X.B., Helms, R.W., Koch, G.G., & Linder, G.F. (1998). An evaluation of safe dates, an adolescent dating violence prevention program. *American Journal of Public Health, 88,* 45–50.

Gagne, M., Lavoie, F., & Hebert, M. (2005). Victimization during childhood and revictimization in dating relationships in adolescent girls. *Child Abuse & Neglect, 29,* 1,155–1,172.

Halpern, C.T., Oslak, S.G., Young, M.L., Martin, S.L., & Kupper, L.L. (2001). Partner violence among adolescents in opposite-sex romantic relationships: Findings from the national longitudinal study of adolescent health. *American Journal of Public Health, 91,* 1,679–1,685.

Halpern, C.T., Young, M.L., Wallet, M.W., Martin S.L., & Kupper, L.L. (2004). Prevalence of partner violence in same-sex romantic and sexual relationships in a national sample of adolescents. *Journal of Adolescent Health, 35,* 131.

Hickman, L.J., Jaycox, L.H., & Aranoff, J. (2004). Dating violence among adolescents: Prevalence, gender distribution, and prevention program effectiveness. *Trauma, Violence, and Abuse, 5,* 123–142.

Hilton, N.Z., Harris, G.T., Rice, M.E., Krans, T.S., & Lavigne, S.E. (1998). Antiviolence education in high schools: Implementation and evaluation. *Journal of interpersonal Violence, 13,* 726–742.

Howard, D.E., Qiu, Y., & Boekeloo, B. (2003). Personal and social contextual correlates of adolescent dating violence. *Journal of Adolescent Health, 33,* 9–17.

Howard, D.E., Wang, M. Q., & Yan, F. (2007a). Psychosocial factors associated with reports of physical dating violence among U.S. adolescent females. *Adolescence, 42,* 311–324.

Howard, D.E., Wang, M.Q., & Yan, F. (2007b). Prevalence and psychosocial correlates of forced sexual intercourse among U.S. high school adolescents. *Adolescence, 42,* 629–643.

Jackson, S.M., Cram, F., & Seymour, F.W. (2000). Violence and sexual coercion in high school students' dating relationships. *Journal of Family Violence, 15,* 23–36.

Jouriles, E.N., McDonald, R., Garrido, E., Rosenfield, D., & Brown, A.S. (2005). Assessing aggression in adolescent romantic relationships: Can we do it better? *Psychological Assessment, 17,* 469–475.

Krajewsky, S.S., Rybarik, M.F., Dosch, M.F., & Gilmore, G.D. (1996) Results of a curriculum intervention with seventh graders regarding violence in relationships. *Journal of Family Violence, 11,* 93–112.

Linder, J.R., & Collins, W.A. (2005). Parent and peer predictors of physical aggression and conflict management in romantic relationships in early adulthood. *Journal of Family Psychology, 19,* 252–262.

Malik, S., Sorenson, S.B., & Aneshensel, C.S. (1997). Community and dating violence among adolescents: Perpetration and victimization. *Journal of Adolescent Health, 21,* 291–302.

Marquart, B.S., Nannini, D.K., Edwards, R.W., Stanley, L.R., & Wayman, J.C. (2007). Prevalence of dating violence and victimization: Regional and gender differences. *Adolescence, 42,* 645–657.

McMaster, L.E., Connolly, J., Pepler, D., & Craig, W.M. (2002). Peer to peer sexual harassment in early adolescence: A developmental perspective. *Development and Psychopathology, 14,* 91–105.

Molidor, C., & Tolman, R.M. (1998). Gender and contextual factors in adolescent dating violence. *Violence Against Women, 4,* 180–194.

O'Keefe. M. (1997). Predictors of dating violence among high school students. *Journal of Interpersonal Violence, 12,* 546–568.

O'Leary, K.D., & Slep, A.M.S. (2003). A dyadic longitudinal model of adolescent dating aggression. *Journal of Clinical Child and Adolescent Psychology, 32,* 314–327.

O'Leary, K.D., Slep, A.M., Avery-Leaf, S., & Cascardi, M. (2008). Gender differences in dating aggression among multiethnic high school students. *Journal of Adolescent Health, 42,* 473–479.

Roberts, T.A., Auinger, M.S., & Klein, J.D. (2006). Predictors of partner abuse in a nationally representative sample of adolescents involved in heterosexual dating relationships. *Violence and Victims, 21,* 81–89.

Sears, H.A., Byers, E.S., & Price, E.L. (2007). The co-occurrence of adolescent boys' and girls' use of psychologically, physically, and sexually abusive behaviours in their dating relationships. *Journal of Adolescence, 30,* 487–504.

Smith, P.H., White, J.W., & Holland, L.J. (2003). A longitudinal perspective on dating violence among adolescent and college-age women. *American Journal of Public Health, 93,* 1,104–1,109.

Weisz, A.N., & Black, B.M. (2001). Evaluating a sexual assault and dating violence prevention program for urban youths. *Social Work Research, 25,* 89–102.

Whitaker, D.J., Morrison, S., Lindquist, C., Hawkins, S.R., O'Neil, J.A., Nesius, A.M., Mathew, A., & Reese, L. (2006). A critical review of interventions for the primary prevention of perpetration of partner violence. *Aggression and Violent Behavior, 11,* 151–166.

Wolfe, D.A., Scott, K., Reitzel-Jaffe, D., Wekerle, C., Grasley, C., & Straatman, A.-L. (2001). Development and validation of the conflict in adolescent dating relationships inventory. *Psychological Assessment, 13,* 277–293.

Wolfe, D.A., Wekerle, C., Scott, K., Straatman, A. L., Grasley, C., & Reitzel-Jaffe, D. (2003). Dating violence prevention with at-risk youth: A controlled outcome evaluation. *Journal of Consulting and Clinical Psychology, 71,* 279–291.

Wolitzky-Taylor, M.A., Ruggiero, K.J., Danielson, C.K., Resnick, H.S., Hanson, R.F., Smith, D.W., Saunders, B.E., & Kilpatrick, D.G. (2008). Prevalence and correlates of dating violence in a national sample of adolescents. *Journal of the American Academy of Child and Adolescent Psychiatry, 47,* 755–762.

Critical Thinking

1. How is dating violence defined?
2. What is the prevalence of dating violence?
3. What factors impact dating violence?
4. What are two school-based prevention intervention programs?

ERNEST N. JOURILES, PHD is Professor in the Department of Psychology and Co-Director of the Family Research Center at Southern Methodist University. **CORA PLATT** is a doctoral student in the Department of Psychology at Southern Methodist University. **RENEE MCDONALD, PHD** is Associate Professor in the Department of Psychology and Co-Director of the Family Research Center at Southern Methodist University.

Non-Suicidal Self-Injury in Adolescents

While awareness of non-suicidal self-injury (NSSI) appears to be increasing . . . it remains one of the most difficult behaviors to encounter, with few professionals feeling well equipped to handle these situations.

Elizabeth E. Lloyd-Richardson, PhD

"Amy" was 13 years old when she learned about NSSI from her best friend. She experimented with cutting her first time, although described feeling "dumb" afterwards because it didn't release the tension and emotional pain she was feeling at the time, as she'd hoped it would. About two months later, she scratched herself on purpose with a thumbtack, choosing to repeat this occasionally over the next few months. She stated, "having tried it, it was more on my mind." She described there being mostly no one particular trigger, but an accumulation of small stressors "blown out of proportion." She has been self-injury free for the past two years, describing her self-injury episodes as a "middle-school thing."

"Susan" was 10 years old when she began experimenting with cutting. A victim of sexual abuse, she began to self-injure "because it was something that hurt me physically and made me deal with how I was feeling [physically]." It was a method of distraction. Over the next several years, her cutting began to increase in frequency and severity, leading her to receive medical attention several times. She continued to self-injure whenever she felt "worthless," leading to daily cutting by the time she was 15. Susan attributed the brief periods in which she avoided self-injury to the support provided by her family and friends, which allowed her to "cry it out" instead of cut. She would then return to self-injury when she felt like she became a burden. With the help of a counselor, she has been self-injury free for the past year, attributing this to the social support of her boyfriend and family, stating "I have found better outlets [than NSSI] and more support."

While awareness of non-suicidal self-injury (NSSI) appears to be increasing among school counselors, social workers, nurses, school and program administrators, and others who work with adolescents, it remains one of the most difficult behaviors to encounter, with few professionals feeling well equipped to handle these situations. Long

described in the psychiatric literature, NSSI has received less attention among community samples. There is little formal training in NSSI identification, prevention, and treatment. This introductory article aims to: (1) define NSSI, describe its prevalence, and identify common risk factors among adolescents; (2) distinguish NSSI from suicidal behaviors; and (3) explore the motivations for engaging in NSSI. Unless otherwise specified, the primary focus of this article concerns self-injury among "community" samples of youth, with *community* referring to nonclinical settings in which youth are prevalent, such as high school and college settings.

What Is NSSI?

Non-suicidal self-injury (NSSI; also referred to herein as *self-injury*) consists of a broad class of behaviors defined by direct, deliberate, socially unacceptable destruction of one's own body tissue without intent to die. Also termed self-injurious behavior, self-mutilation, and deliberate self-harm, NSSI spans a wide range of behaviors. These include, but are not limited to, skin cutting, burning, picking or interfering with wound healing, punching oneself or objects, and inserting objects under the skin.

There is a great deal of variation in the frequency and methods of NSSI reported by self-injurers. Among community samples of adolescents, there is wide variability in lifetime NSSI frequency, ranging from single incidents to hundreds of incidents. For instance, among a sample of community youth indicating a history of self-injury, Lloyd-Richardson and colleagues (2007) found an average of nearly 13 past-year self-injury episodes. While cutting is a commonly cited method of NSSI, other common methods include burning skin, hitting self on purpose, and biting self (Laye-Gindhu & Schonert-Reichl, 2005; Lloyd-Richardson et al., 2007), with many self-injurers reporting use of several injury methods. Research also suggests that the majority of self-injuring adolescents engage in NSSI with little forethought, while sober, and report experiencing little to no pain while self-injuring (Jacobson & Gould, 2007).

Among community samples, prevalence estimates suggest approximately 7% of preadolescents (Hilt, Cha, & Nolen-Hoeksema, 2008), between 12% to 40% of adolescents (Ross & Heath, 2003), and between 17% and 35% of college students have engaged in NSSI (Gratz, Conrad, & Roemer, 2002). Rates are higher still among psychiatric and incarcerated populations. While earlier studies of self-injury found higher rates among females than males, more recent studies—and particularly those of community adolescents—show similar occurrence rates among males and females. Few studies have investigated possible racial or ethnic differences, or the role that socioeconomic status plays, in the prevalence of NSSI.

There is general consensus that NSSI most commonly begins in adolescence, typically between 12 and 14 years of age (Jacobson & Gould, 2007). There appears to be some degree of variability, however, with some studies reporting an onset before age 12 (Yates, 2004), and others reporting onset in late adolescence or early adulthood (Whitlock et al., 2006).

Who Is at Risk for NSSI?

Self-injury is listed in the Diagnostic and Statistical Manual of Mental Disorders (DSM-IV-R; American Psychiatric Association, 2000) as a symptom of borderline personality disorder (BPD) *only*. While there is strong support for a relationship between self-injury and BPD (Nock, Joiner, Gordon, Lloyd-Richardson, & Prinstein, 2006), it is important to note that self-injury may occur in the context of a variety of different psychiatric disorders (such as depressive and anxiety disorders, substance abuse, eating disorders, and conduct or oppositional disorders) (Guertin, Lloyd-Richardson, Spirito, Donaldson, & Boergers, 2001; Nock et al., 2006; Ross & Heath, 2003). While in many cases NSSI may precede these disorders, it is also likely to result from psychiatric disorders. With that being said, NSSI may also occur in the *absence* of psychiatric disorders as well.

Emotional dysregulation is a core symptom of Borderline Personality Disorder and may likely contribute significantly to the experience of other psychiatric symptoms, such as anxiety and depression. Linehan (1993) proposed that NSSI is a result of maladaptive emotional regulation strategies, suggesting that individuals who have difficulty regulating their negative emotions are at increased risk of engaging in NSSI. Related to this, research has found that self-injurers are more likely to have altered emotional experiences, such as the experience of dissociation (e.g., describe feeling nothing or unreal), alexithymia (e.g., difficulties identifying their feelings), as well as reporting less awareness of their emotional experiences (Gratz, 2006; Zlotnick et al., 1996).

The Majority of self-injuring adolescents engage in NSSI with little forethought, while sober, and report experiencing little to no pain while self-injuring.

While most of the literature on the psychological traits of self-injurers has focused on adults, several factors have been found to distinguish adolescent self-injurers from non-injurers. Among community adolescents, self-injurers were more likely than non-injurers to report a previous psychiatric history and psychiatric hospitalization, endorse a history of suicide attempt(s), and report elevated current suicide ideation (Lloyd-Richardson et al., 2007).

The role of early childhood environments may also be important to consider. Individuals who self-injure are more likely than non-injurers to describe a poorer family environment, including histories of family violence, separation from parents, and poor relationships with parents. Perhaps most often mentioned in clinical literature is the role of child physical and sexual abuse on development of NSSI. With respect to child sexual abuse, a recent review of 43 studies found that the relationship between child sexual abuse and NSSI was relatively small, suggesting that the association between child sexual abuse and NSSI may be due to risk factors they have in common (Klonsky & Moyer, 2008). The relationship between child physical abuse and NSSI may be stronger, with several studies finding higher rates of child physical abuse among self-injurers than non-injurers (Klonsky & Glenn, 2009).

How Is NSSI Distinguished from Suicide?

NSSI is primarily distinguished from suicidal behaviors (e.g., suicide ideation, threats, and attempts) by whether or not there is a desire to die. This primary distinction is based on the idea that suicide intent is a dichotomous variable—the presence or absence of an individual's wish to terminate his or her life (Prinstein, 2008). NSSI and suicidal behaviors are thought to differ not only with respect to suicidal intent and lethality, but also chronicity and methods used. NSSI is usually engaged in more frequently than are suicidal behaviors, and with more varied methods. Nonetheless, adolescent self-injurers are more likely to have a history of suicide attempt(s) and current suicide ideation than non-injurers (Muehlenkamp & Gutierrez, 2007). While self-injuring adolescents did not differ from those who had made a suicide attempt on their reported depressive symptoms or suicide ideation, self-injurers without a history of suicide attempt(s) reported less "repulsion to life" than those who had made a suicide attempt (Muehlenkamp & Gutierrez, 2004). While there is strong support for the theoretically distinct nature of NSSI and suicidal behaviors, it has nevertheless also been argued that some adolescents, during times of great strain, report feeling uncertain about whether they want to live or die (Rodham, Hawton, & Evans, 2004). Research will continue to explore NSSI and suicidal behaviors for similarities and distinctions that may serve to explain NSSI specifically and self-harm behaviors in general.

What Motivates Adolescents to Engage in NSSI?

The Complex Nature of Motivations for NSSI

The issue of why people self-injure is a complex one for several reasons. First, as Suyemoto (1998) states in her review of functional models of NSSI, "One of the most difficult tasks in attempting to understand any pathological behavior is discerning why this *particular* behavior, at this *particular* time, serves this *particular* function, for this *particular* patient" (p. 537). Thus, an individual portrait of a self-injurer may embody many reasons for NSSI that vary over time and context. Second, NSSI is likely an "overdetermined" behavior, meaning it may serve multiple functions for an individual. For instance, a sample of community adolescents who indicated they had self-injured in the previous year, endorsed an average of five reasons for engaging in NSSI, including such things as "to feel something, even if it was pain"; "to stop bad feelings"; "to try and gain a reaction from someone"; and "to get control of a situation" (Lloyd-Richardson et al., 2007). Third, functions of NSSI may also change across developmental stage and context, such that common functions served by NSSI in pre-adolescence may not be entirely consistent with what is found in young adult or middle-aged self-injurers. As illustrated in the initial case vignettes, many pre-adolescents may begin experimenting with NSSI with a particular expectation in mind (e.g., "This will help me escape from the mental pain I'm experiencing"). Over time, and with greater experience with self-injury, it is possible that adolescents experience and learn more of the "benefits" of their injury episodes, thereby strengthening the cycle of self-injury and its mental rewards.

A Behavioral/Environmental Model of NSSI

Research is relatively consistent across multiple studies of both clinical and community adolescent populations. To date, the strongest empirical support has been found for a behavioral/environmental model of NSSI which focuses on environmental factors that both initiate and maintain self-injury behaviors. Self-injury is reinforced through either internal release or through external environmental gain. These two dimensions are illustrated in Table 1 with common reasons for self-injury cited by adolescents (Lloyd-Richardson et al., 2007). The most commonly cited motivation for NSSI, seeking a release from internal emotions (termed *automatic reinforcement*), refers to an adolescent's use of NSSI to regulate their internal environment: to remove or distract from an undesirable internal state or to generate some desired internal state. Examples of this include "to stop bad feelings" or "to just feel something." It is interesting to note that among a clinical adolescent sample, these motivations were related to diagnoses of post-traumatic stress disorder and also major depressive disorder (Nock & Prinstein, 2005).

In contrast, motivations of external environmental gain (termed *social reinforcement*) serve to regulate an adolescent's external environment by using NSSI to gain attention from others, to access some social resource, or to escape from interpersonal demands or tasks. For instance, this could include motives such as "to let others know how I am feeling" or "to get other people to leave me alone." Among community adolescents, self-injurers—particularly younger adolescents—endorsed social motives nearly as frequently as automatic motives (Lloyd-Richardson et al., 2007). The social functions of NSSI have been theorized by clinicians and families of self-injurers for many years, but until recently have not been examined directly. Developmental theories suggest that youths' behavior may be especially susceptible to interpersonal influence during the transition to adolescence (and perhaps also the transition to emerging adulthood and the college years), thus underscoring the importance of viewing individuals and their self-injury with an eye towards both development and broader context.

From a clinical perspective, teasing apart this multiplicity of functions of self-injury for an individual is incredibly challenging, and yet our understanding of these functions is critical to success in helping to eliminate self-injury and improve the lives of individuals who engage in NSSI. One promising avenue for future research involves studies that have begun to

Table 1　Motivations for Engaging in NSSI

Automatic Reinforcement (Seeking release from internal emotions)
- To stop bad feelings
- To relieve feeling numb or empty
- To feel something, even if it is pain
- To punish yourself
- To feel relaxed

Social Reinforcement (Regulating an adolescent's external environment)
- To avoid school, work, or other activities
- To avoid doing something unpleasant
- To avoid being with people
- To avoid punishment or paying the consequences
- To get attention
- To try and get a reaction from someone, even if it's negative
- To receive more attention from your parents or friends
- To feel more a part of a group
- To get your parents to understand or notice you
- To get control of a situation
- To get other people to act differently or change
- To be like someone you respect
- To let others know how desperate you are
- To give yourself something to do when alone, or with others
- To get help
- To make others angry

investigate whether biological vulnerabilities may mediate the relationship between NSSI and intrapersonal or environmental factors. For instance, Crowell and colleagues (2008) found that adolescents with a history of NSSI had lower levels of peripheral serotonin (5-HT) than those without histories of NSSI, suggesting that self-injury may serve to elevate serotonin levels and thus improve mood. Interestingly, high 5-HT levels were associated with self-injury only in the environmental context of high parent-teen discord, suggesting that biological vulnerabilities may influence behavior in the context of particularly stressful environments.

Exciting new research has begun exploring whether subgroups of self-injurers exist in young adult and adolescent samples.

What Factors Distinguish the Course and Severity of NSSI?

It is clear that variations exist in the profiles of those who self-injure. However, our ability to explain this variability is challenged by the inconsistent presentations noted across various studies of self-injuring samples. These variations in NSSI clinical presentations and functions may be due to the existence of different subgroups of self-injurers.

Exciting new research has begun exploring whether subgroups of self-injurers exist in young adult and adolescent samples. One such study of university students identified three distinct subgroups of self-injurers: The first group consisted largely of women with fewer than 11 lifetime NSSI episodes, using one form of NSSI and causing superficial tissue damage; the second group consisted of more men than women, reporting fewer than 11 lifetime NSSI episodes, but commonly using two to three methods and causing moderate to severe tissue damage; and the third group consisted of mostly women who reported a high frequency of NSSI episodes, using more than three methods of NSSI and usually causing a high degree of tissue damage (Whitlock, Muehlenkamp, & Eckenrode, 2008). Interestingly, young adults in this third group reported the highest levels of comorbid psychiatric conditions and psychiatric treatment history. Despite groups one and two demonstrating less severe NSSI histories than group three, they still exhibited elevated levels of distress relative to their non-injuring peers. Research investigating subgroups of self-injurers has dramatic implications for the development of future treatment strategies that recognize the likelihood of multiple and distinct pathways that lead up to, and continue the cycle of, NSSI.

What Can Be Done about NSSI?

A thorough assessment of the NSSI behavior(s) engaged in and the functions it serves for a particular adolescent is critical to both the clinical assessment and treatment processes. Comprehensive assessment can aid in early detection of NSSI behaviors, early intervention or prevention efforts, as well as aid counselors in better understanding the motives behind engaging in self-injury.

This assessment process should allow for a more detailed review of the antecedents and consequences of self-injury, as well as aid in the continued monitoring of NSSI behaviors and changes that may occur over time in frequency, type, or function. Recent advances in the study of NSSI have yielded better assessment tools, including detailed self-report questionnaires (Lloyd-Richardson et al., 2007) and interviewer-administered interviews (Nock, Holmberg, Photos, & Michel, 2007). Furthermore, these assessment tools allow for a more complete discussion to take place between care provider and adolescents of the behaviors engaged in, their contributing factors, and the resulting outcomes as perceived by the teen.

It is unfortunate that few prevention or intervention approaches targeting NSSI have been developed and empirically supported. According to Nixon and colleagues (2009), the following psychosocial treatments hold promise for adolescents, across the prevention to intervention spectrum: Psychoeducation concerning mental health and NSSI; problem-solving therapy and crisis intervention; cognitive behavioral therapy; and dialectical behavior therapy.

From a prevention perspective, psychoeducational efforts fostering mental health and demystifying self-injury behaviors may aid in teaching young people how to more effectively deal with their emotions, as well as break down barriers to seeking mental health services. At the immediate point of self-injury discovery, crisis intervention and management is critical, as well as the associated problem-solving therapy which serves to assess current level of suicide risk, identify associated stressors, and aiding to diffuse emotionally charged situations. These efforts then serve to facilitate the process of connecting with needed social services or making the way for longer term therapy (Muehlenkamp, 2006).

Cognitive behavioral therapy (CBT) is a well-researched constellation of therapeutic techniques that has proven beneficial across a wide variety of psychiatric disorders (e.g., major depression, social anxiety, post-traumatic stress disorder) and developmental stages (e.g., adolescence, adulthood). Focused around the relationship between thoughts, feelings, and behaviors, CBT aims to assist patients in identifying their maladaptive thoughts, modifying these in order to manage emotions and change negative thinking. Self-injurers who experience significant maladaptive or irrational thoughts may benefit from CBT (Tyrer et al., 2003).

Building upon CBT techniques, Dialectical Behavior Therapy (DBT) has perhaps been investigated the most among self-injuring youth. DBT proposes that emotional dysregulation, an inability to tolerate distress, and the experience of an invalidating environment contribute to both NSSI and suicidal behaviors (Linehan, 1987). It incorporates change-based behavioral, problem-solving, and skills-training skills with acceptance and tolerance strategies from Zen Buddhism. DBT has been used to successfully reduce the incidence of NSSI during hospitalization, as well as in the year following hospitalization (Katz, Cox,

Gunasekara, & Miller, 2004), and has been used successfully with adolescents (Miller, Rathus, & Linehan, 2007). Literature investigating factors that may help to prevent NSSI also provide insight into how DBT might foster recovery. The importance of good communication skills, particularly as they relate to expression of negative emotions, ability to manage negative emotions, and positive family and peer supports are critical to ensuring recovery from NSSI. These protective factors are reiterated as the key ingredients of DBT that contribute to treatment efficacy: an empathic and collaborative client-therapist relationship, as well as development of skills that improve a patient's coping and self-awareness (Muehlenkamp, 2005).

References

American Psychiatric Association (2000). *Diagnostic and Statistical Manual of Mental Disorders,* Fourth Edition, text revision, Washington, D.C. author.

Crowell, S.E., Beauchaine, T.P., McCauley, E., Smith, C.J., Vasilev, C.A., & Stevens, A.L. (2008). Parent-child interactions, peripheral serotonin, and self-inflicted injury in adolescents. *Journal of Consulting and Clinical Psychology, 76,* 15–21.

Gratz, K.L. (2006). Risk factors for deliberate self-harm among female college students: The role and Interaction of childhood maltreatment, emotional in expressivity, and affect intensity/ reactivity. *American Journal of Orthopsychiatry, 76,* 238–250.

Gratz, K.L., Conrad, S.D., & Roemer, L. (2002). Risk factors for deliberate self-harm among college students. *American Journal of Orthopsychiatry, 72*(1), 128–140.

Guertin, T., Lloyd-Richardson, E., Spirito, A., Donaldson, D., & Boergers, J. (2001). Self-mutilative behavior in adolescents who attempt suicide by overdose. *Journal of the American Academy of Child and Adolescent Psychiatry, 40*(9), 1,062–1,069.

Hilt, L.M., Cha, C.B., & Nolen-Hoeksema, S. (2006). Nonsuicidal self-injury in young adolescent girls: Moderators of the distress-function relationship. *Journal of Consulting and Clinical Psychology, 76,* 63–71.

Jacobson, C.M., & Gould, M. (2007). The epidemiology and phenomenology of non-suicidal self-injurious behavior among adolescents: A critical review of the literature. *Archives of Suicide Research, 11,* 129–147.

Katz, L.Y., Cox, B.J., Gunasekara, S., & Miller, A.L. (2004). Feasibility of dialectical behavior therapy for suicidal adolescent inpatients. *Journal of the American Academy of Child and Adolescent Psychiatry, 43*(3), 276–282.

Klonsky, E.D., & Glenn, C.P. (2009). Psychosocial risk and protective factors. In M.K. Nixon & N.L. Heath (Eds.) *Self-Injury in Youth: The Essential Guide to Assessment and Intervention* (pp. 45–58). Routledge Press: New York.

Klonsky, E.D., & Moyer, A. (2008). Childhood sexual abuse and non-suicidal self-injury: A meta-analysis. *British Journal of Psychiatry, 192,* 166–170.

Laye-Gindhu, A., & Schonert-Reichl, K.A. (2005). Nonsuicldal self-harm among community adolescents: understanding the 'whats' and 'whys' of self-harm. *Journal of Youth and Adolescence, 34,* 447–457.

Linehan, M.M. (1987). Dialectical behavior therapy: A cognitive behavioral approach to parasuicides. *Journal of Personality Disorders, 1,* 328–333.

Linehan, M.M. (1993). *Cognitive-behavioral Treatment of Borderline Personality Disorder.* New York: Guilford Press.

Lloyd-Richardson, E.E., Perrine, N., Dierker, L., & Kelley, M.L. (2007). Characteristics and functions of non-suicidal self-injury in a community sample of adolescents. *Psychological Medicine, 37*(8), 1,183–1,192.

Miller, A. L., Rathus, J.H.,& Linehan, M.M. (2007). *Dialectical Behavior Therapy with Suicidal Adolescents.* Guilford Press: New York.

Muehlenkamp, J.J. (2005). Self-injurious behavior as a separate clinical syndrome. American Journal of Orthopsychiatry, 75(2), 324–333.

Muehlenkamp, J.J. (2006). Empirically supported treatments and general therapy guidelines for non-suicidal self-injury. *Journal of Mental Health Counseling, 28*(2), 166–185.

Muehlenkamp, J.J., & Gutierrez, P.M. (2004). An Investigation of differences between self-injurious behavior and suicide attempts in a sample of adolescents. *Suicide & Life Threatening Behavior, 34*(1), 12–23.

Muehlenkamp, J.J., & Gutierrez, P.M. (2007). Risk for suicide attempts among adolescents who engage in non-suicidal self-injury. *Archives of Suicide Research, 11*(1), 69–82.

Nixon, M.K., Aulakh, H., Townsend, L., & Atherton, M. (2009). Psychosocial interventions for adolescents. In M.K. Nixon &. N.L. Heath (Eds.), *Self-Injury in Youth: The Essential Guide to Assessment and Intervention* (pp. 217–236), Routledge Press: New York.

Nock, M.K., Holmberg, E.B., Photos, V.I., & Michel, B.D. (2007). Self-Injurious Thoughts and Behaviors Interview: development, reliability, and validity in an adolescent sample. *Psychological Assessment, 19*(3), 309–317.

Nock, M.K., Joiner, T.E., Gordon, K.H., Lloyd-Richardson, E., & Prinstein, M.J. (2006). Non-suicidal self-injury among adolescents: diagnostic correlates and relation to suicide attempts. *Psychiatry Research, 144*(1), 65–72.

Nock, M.K., & Prinstein, M.J. (2005). Clinical features and behavioral functions of adolescent self-mutilation. *Journal of Abnormal Psychology, 114*(1), 140–146.

Prinstein, M. (2008). Introduction to the special section on suicide and nonsuicidal self-injury: A review of unique challenges and important directions for self-Injury science. *Journal of Consulting and Clinical Psychology, 76*(1), 1–8.

Rodham, K., Hawton, K., & Evans, E. (2004). Reasons for deliberate self-harm: Comparison of self-poisoners and self-cutters in a community sample of adolescents. *Journal of the American Academy of Child and Adolescent Psychiatry, 43*(1), 80–87.

Ross, S., & Heath, N.L. (2003). Two models of adolescent self-mutilation. *Suicide & life Threatening Behavior, 33*(3), 277–287.

Suyemoto, K.L. (1998). The functions of self-mutilation. *Clinical Psychology Review, 18*(5), 531–554.

Tyrer, P., Thompson, S., Schmidt, U., Jones, V., Knapp, M., Davidson, K., et al., (2003). Randomized controlled trial of brief cognitive behavior therapy versus treatment as usual in recurrent deliberate self-harm: The POPMACT study. *Psychological Medicine, 33,* 969–976.

Whitlock, J.L, Muehlenkamp, J.J., & Eckenrode, J. (2008). Variation in nonsuicidal self-injury: Identification and features of latent classes in a college population of emerging adults. *Journal of Clinical Child and Adolescent Psychology, 37*(4), 725–735.

Whitlock, J.L., Powers, J., & Eckenrode, J. (2006). The virtual cutting edge: The Internet and adolescent self-Injury. *Developmental Psychology, 42*(3), 407–417.

Yates, T.M. (2004). The developmental psychopathology of self-injurious behavior: Compensatory regulation in posttraumatic adaptation. *Clinical Psychology Review, 24,* 35–74.

Zlotnick, C., Shea, M.T., Pearlstein, T., Simpson, E., Costello, E., & Begin, A. (1996). The relationship between dissociative symptoms, alexithymia, impulsivity, sexual abuse, and self-mutilation. *Comprehensive Psychiatry, 37,* 12–16.

Critical Thinking

1. Why do professionals not feel equipped to handle non-suidal self-injury?

2. What are the common risk factors among adolescents who self-injure?

3. What are the motivations for engaging in non-suicidal self-injury?

4. Why is awareness of non-suicidal self-injury increasing?

ELIZABETH E. LLOYD-RICHARDSON, PHD is Assistant Professor in the Department of Psychology at the University of Massachusetts, Dartmouth and Assistant Professor (Adjunct) in the Department of Psychiatry and Human Behavior at Brown Medical School. Her research aims to better understand adolescent and young adult health risk and protective behaviors and to develop effective Treatment strategies for improving the lives of youth.

Youth's Reactions to Disasters and the Factors That Influence Their Response

While most individuals are resilient even in the face of catastrophe, the chaos, confusion, and destruction as well as the human morbidity and mortality associated with disasters can create collective trauma.

BETTY PFEFFERBAUM, MD, JD, ET AL.

An apparent increase in disasters in recent years has garnered the attention of both professionals and the public resulting in an expanded knowledge base about these events and their effects. Disasters can damage and overwhelm the infrastructure needed for response. As we saw with Hurricane Katrina, inadequacies in response can engender enduring mistrust, demoralization, and social disarray. While most individuals are resilient even in the face of catastrophe, the chaos, confusion, and destruction as well as the human morbidity and mortality associated with disasters can create collective trauma (McFarlane & Norris, 2006). Youth are especially vulnerable to the effects of disasters. Their reactions span the continuum from distress and transient emotional and behavioral changes to impaired functioning and enduring psychopathology (Norris et al., 2002).

Disaster mental health is a burgeoning field with opportunities for general practitioners as well as specialists. In fact, disaster management encourages, and indeed depends on, professional and lay volunteers from the community where an event occurs. Fortunately, events do not occur often, but they are commonly unpredictable. Thus, some level of professional readiness is essential. This article addresses the need for preparedness by providing a basic primer on youth's disaster reactions and the factors that influence their reactions. Rather than providing a comprehensive critique of the literature, we review exemplary research to summarize pertinent findings and also present additional studies to highlight other issues of interest.

Disaster management encourages, and indeed depends on, professional and lay volunteers from the community where an event occurs.

Outcomes Associated with Disasters

Numerous studies have contributed to the knowledge base about child disaster mental health. The outcomes most commonly examined in relation to disasters are posttraumatic stress disorder (PTSD) and stress symptoms, depressive and anxiety disorders, disturbed behavior, grief, and impaired functioning.

In a comprehensive study of youth's reactions to disasters, William Yule and colleagues (2000) assessed a survivor group of over 200 young adults five to eight years after being exposed to a shipping disaster during their adolescence. This sample was compared to a group of sex- and age-matched friends and acquaintances attending the same school. Approximately one-half of the survivors developed incident-related PTSD, which endured for over five years in one-fourth of the survivors who developed the disorder (Yule et al., 2000). Rates of any new post-disaster anxiety or mood disorder among survivors who developed PTSD were higher than rates of these disorders among the unexposed participants. Survivors who did not develop PTSD did not have higher rates of anxiety and mood disorders than unexposed participants (Bolton et al., 2000). This suggests that the occurrence of other post-disaster disorders was more tied to vulnerability to PTSD rather than comprising an independent response to disaster exposure per se.

Some studies have investigated outcomes in terms of emotional and behavioral responses rather than diagnoses. For example, Shaw and colleagues (1995; 1996) examined a host of internalizing and externalizing symptoms in a longitudinal study of elementary school children (6–11 years of age) exposed to Hurricane Andrew. Participants in this study were enrolled in both high- and low-impact schools. The high impact school was directly in the path of the hurricane, while the low-impact school was north of Miami and not in the hurricane's direct path. Most children in both high- and low-impact schools exhibited at least moderate levels of symptoms. Two months after the event, children in the high-impact school had significantly higher posttraumatic symptom frequency scores than those in the low-impact school (Shaw et al., 1995). Posttraumatic stress symptoms decreased over time. At 21 months, 70% of all of the children from the high-impact school still exhibited moderate to severe symptoms (Shaw et al., 1996).

The findings related to externalizing behaviors are of particular interest. There was an initial marked decrease in school-reported externalizing behaviors in children in the high-impact school during the first two grading periods post-hurricane which was followed by a return to levels of the previous year. By contrast, in the low-impact school, there was a temporary increase in disruptive behavior, which the authors suggested may have resulted from increased demand and limited resources in the low-impact school due to the influx of students transferring from directly affected areas coupled with a shift of resources to directly affected areas (Shaw et al., 1995).

Traumatic grief, which may occur with loss of a loved one in traumatic events such as disasters, is conceptualized as intrusion of trauma symptoms into the bereavement process. Youth do not typically experience persistent trauma symptoms as part of the grief process even if the loss is traumatic (Cohen et al., 2002). With traumatic grief, thoughts and images can be so terrifying and anxiety-provoking that the child avoids or suppresses other thoughts and images of the deceased that might serve as comforting reminders of the person (Brown & Goodman, 2005). Preliminary evidence suggests that traumatic grief can be distinguished from normal grief. Brown and Goodman (2005) studied children (8–18 years of age) of uniformed service personnel killed in the 2001 World Trade Center attack. Factor analysis identified three distinct child response factors. The first, a traumatic grief factor, included PTSD symptoms (intrusive reexperiencing, avoidance/ numbing, hyperarousal), revenge, yearning, and impaired functioning. Two other factors, positive memory and ongoing presence, delineated normal grief responses. Positive memory appeared to capture the process of memory construction needed for the child to maintain an inner representation of the deceased. Ongoing presence of the deceased may provide comfort to the bereaved child.

Factors Affecting Outcome

Many factors can influence how youth respond to disasters. These can include the characteristics of the disaster and youth's exposure to it, individual characteristics, family factors, and the social environment—both pre- and post-disaster. See Table 1.

Disaster Characteristics and Exposure

The literature identifies disaster characteristics, and characteristics of the environment in which the disaster occurs, as predictors of outcome. These characteristics include, for example, predictability, duration, morbidity and mortality, property loss and destruction, disruption and chaos, and later secondary disaster-related adversities (e.g., unemployment and lost income) (Institute of Medicine, 2004). Predictability of a disaster is likely to influence preparedness activities. Duration may influence

Table 1 Factors Affecting Outcomes in Youth Exposed to Disasters

Disaster Characteristics
- Predictability of the disaster
- Duration of the disaster
- Morbidity and morality caused by the disaster
- Property loss and destruction due to the disaster
- Disruption and chaos created by the disaster
- Secondary adversities

Exposure
- Physical presence
- Close relationship to victims and survivors
- Subjective appraisal of danger and life threat
- Media coverage

Individual Characteristics
- Demographics (age, gender, ethnicity, socioeconomic status)
- Preexisting conditions

Family Factors
- Parental reactions
- Family interactions

Social Factors
- Social support

perceived life threat, loss, and secondary adversities. The extent of victimization and property damage may determine response and recovery efforts.

Youth may be exposed to disasters in many ways. For example, they may be physically present at the disaster site or their close family members and/or friends may be directly exposed. We know little about the relative importance of these exposures or about confounding effects among them. While not representing disaster exposure per se, youth may also lose cherished possessions in disasters, and they may watch extensive and graphic television coverage of the event, which can also be distressing and further confound exposure effects. Secondary adversities in the recovery environment may further stress children by creating hardship that precipitates, maintains, or increases negative reactions. Shaw and colleagues (1996) attributed increased psychopathology and high levels of enduring posttraumatic stress and behavioral disruption 21 months after Hurricane Andrew to experiences of persistent secondary adversities, ongoing traumatic reminders, and pervasive demoralization.

The youth's subjective appraisal of danger and life threat in association with an event is a key aspect of the traumatic experience. The diagnosis of PTSD requires a subjective reaction of "intense fear, helplessness, or horror" as part of exposure (American Psychiatric Association, 2000, p. 463). Numerous studies document the association between subjective appraisal of danger and life threat with adverse outcomes (Silverman & La Greca, 2002).

The youth's subjective appraisal of danger and life threat in association with an event is a key aspect of the traumatic experience.

For example, with the young adults exposed to the shipping disaster, subjective appraisal of life threat, along with the degree of exposure and level of anxiety measured five months post-disaster, were the best predictors of PTSD (Udwin et al., 2000).

Individual Characteristics

A number of individual characteristics have been linked to disaster outcomes. These include demographic features such as age, gender, and racial/ethnic heritage; preexisting disorders; and exposure to prior trauma.

Demographics: Of the demographic factors thought to be important in youth outcomes, only gender has been well studied and the results are inconsistent. The influence of age on trauma is complex (Silverman & La Greca, 2002). Immature cognitive and verbal ability may limit or alter the expression of distress in very young children, but that does not mean young children are unaffected. Greater cognitive capacities of older children and adolescents enable them to conceptualize the dangers that accompany disasters. Older children and adolescents also should have better developed coping skills to deal with these events. Studies suggest that ethnic minority youth may be at greater risk for maladaptation in the context of disasters than youth from the majority population (Silverman & La Greca, 2002). It is unclear, however, to what extent poorer outcome reflects differences in socioeconomic status, different disaster experiences, exposure to other traumatic events, and/or family or other social influences rather than ethnicity.

Greater cognitive capacities of older children and adolescents enable them to conceptualize the dangers that accompany disasters.

In the final analysis, demographic characteristics of youth exposed to disasters may prove less important than exposure and other variables in predicting disaster outcome. These other variables include preexisting conditions, exposure to other trauma, and family and social variables, as described in more detail below.

Preexisting Conditions: Disaster studies have identified the importance of preexisting conditions, especially anxiety symptoms and disorders, in disaster outcomes. For example, preexisting anxiety symptoms, attention problems, and academic difficulties predicted PTSD symptoms associated with Hurricane Andrew three months after the disaster while preexisting anxiety symptoms predicted PTSD symptoms seven months after the disaster (La Greca et al., 1998). Similarly, one year after the Northridge earthquake, youth (8–18 years of age)

with pre-event anxiety disorders had significantly more post-traumatic stress symptoms than did those without pre-event anxiety disorders. Neither pre-event depressive disorders nor disruptive behavior disorder were associated with PTSD symptoms (Asarnow et al., 1999).

Other Trauma: Exposure to other trauma also contributes to disaster outcome. In a study of children six months after Hurricane Andrew, lifetime trauma and post-hurricane events were among a number of variables that predicted PTSD (Garrison et al., 1995). Pfefferbaum and colleagues (2003) found that posttraumatic stress reactions related to other trauma contributed significantly to disaster-related posttraumatic stress in Nairobi school children (9–17 years of age) 8 to 14 months after the 1998 bombing of the U.S. Embassy.

Family Factors

While children's disaster reactions reflect their developmental status and thus may differ from those of adults, children's reactions generally parallel those of their parents in degree (Silverman & La Greca, 2002). Children may respond to parental distress, and they take cues from their parents about danger and safety. Decreasing strength in the relationship between parent and child reactions as children age may reflect increasing autonomy as youth develop and mature (Laor et al., 2001).

Children's reactions generally parallel those of their parents in degree.

The quality of interactions within the family also influences the child's adjustment (Laor et al., 2001; McFarlane, 1987). For example, McFarlane (1987) found emotional and behavioral problems in children from families characterized by parental irritable distress, over-involvement or enmeshment, and overprotection. Neither parental overprotection nor irritable distress alone was a problem, but together they did constitute problems for children, perhaps because parents in these families conveyed the potential for danger. High involvement and high parental irritable distress also created problems (McFarlane, 1987). A five-year longitudinal study of Israeli families displaced because of damage to their homes by SCUD missile attacks during the first Persian Gulf War found that family cohesion—the emotional bonds among family members—was a predictor of preschool-aged child adjustment. Both disengaged and enmeshed families created risk for displaced children. Disengaged families may not help the child process traumatic experiences while enmeshed families may spread unmodified negative emotions from one family member to another (Laor et al., 2001).

Social Factors

Social factors have not been well examined as predictors of child adjustment to disasters. Udwin and colleagues (2000) found that self-reported perceived and received social support just after a shipping disaster and at follow-up were associated with the development and duration of PTSD. Among adolescents with PTSD, those who reported receiving little or no help from their schools following the disaster had more PTSD symptoms (Udwin et al., 2000). Similarly, La Greca and colleagues (1996) found that children reporting high levels of social support from significant others during the three months immediately after Hurricane Andrew had fewer posttraumatic stress symptoms at ten months.

Among adolescents with PTSD, those who reported receiving little or no help from their schools following the disaster had more PTSD symptoms.

Conclusions and Implications for Providers

Research has documented stress reactions, PTSD, and comorbid conditions in youth exposed to disasters. As many as one-half of those directly exposed to severe events may develop diagnosable psychopathology which may endure for years. PTSD appears to be the most prevalent post-disaster disorder and to be associated with vulnerability to other disorders. Thus, providers working with youth in post-disaster environments should anticipate PTSD symptoms but must not be so focused on PTSD that they miss other treatable symptoms and conditions. In some youth, preexisting externalizing behavior problems may decrease initially, but these behaviors appear to resume later. Follow-up is essential to understanding the full course of youth's reactions and recovery.

Research has also elucidated a number of factors that contribute to youth outcomes including event characteristics and exposure, and individual, family, and social predictors. These factors help providers identify high-risk groups and they suggest service delivery strategies. For example, youth with the greatest exposure and those with preexisting conditions are likely to suffer the most. In addition, since youth in the disaster setting tend to respond to parental distress, interventions aimed at helping parents should benefit youth as well.

Additional research is essential to address numerous gaps in our knowledge. For example, more precision is necessary in exploring trauma exposure and its differential effects on outcome. Further research is also necessary to clarify the potential interactive risks created by socioeconomic disadvantage, preexisting conditions, and exposure to other trauma as well as to better delineate the contributions of family and various social factors. Moreover, our appreciation of outcomes and the factors that predispose and protect youth would be enhanced by systematic exploration of resilience, coping, and the factors that promote healthy adaptation.

While many youth are resilient in the face of disaster, distress in many and suffering in some requires professional attention. Disasters are often unpredictable, and they have the capacity to damage social and professional infrastructures, sometimes overwhelming response systems. The disaster mental health field is advancing, with apparent increased interest in the field. Providers who serve youth must prepare for disasters by learning about the effects of these events and about the factors that influence their effects.

References

American Psychiatric Association (2000). *Diagnostic and Statistical Manual of Mental Disorders* (4th ed., text rev.). Washington, DC: Author.

Asarnow, J., Glynn, S., Pynoos, R.S., Nahum, J., Guthrie, D., Cantwell, D.P., & Franklin, B. (1999). When the Earth stops shaking: Earthquake sequelae among children diagnosed for pre-earthquake psychopathology. *Journal of the American Academy of Child and Adolescent Psychiatry, 38*(8), 1,016–1,023.

Bolton, D., O'Ryan, D., Udwin, O., Boyle, S., & Yule, W. (2000). The long-term psychological effects of a disaster experienced in adolescence: II: General psychopathology. *Journal of Child Psychology and Psychiatry, 41*(4), 513–523.

Brown, E.J., & Goodman, R.F. (2005). Childhood traumatic grief: An exploration of the construct in children bereaved on September 11. *Journal of Clinical Child and Adolescent Psychology, 34*(2), 248–259.

Cohen, J.A., Mannarino, A.P., Greenberg, T., Padlo, S., & Shipley, C. (2002). Childhood traumatic grief: Concepts and controversies. *Trauma, Violence, & Abuse, 3*(4), 307–327.

Garrison, C.Z., Bryant, E.S., Addy, C.L., Spurrier, P.G., Freedy, J.R., & Kilpatrick, D.G. (1995). Posttraumatic stress disorder in adolescents after Hurricane Andrew. *Journal of the American Academy of Child and Adolescent Psychiatry, 34*(9), 1,193–1,201.

Institute of Medicine (2004). *Preparing for the Psychological Consequences of Terrorism: A Public Health Strategy.* Washington, DC: The National Academies Press.

La Greca, A.M., Silverman, W.K., Vernberg, E.M., & Prinstein, M.J. (1996). Symptoms of posttraumatic stress in children after Hurricane Andrew: A prospective study. *Journal of Consulting and Clinical Psychology, 64*(4), 712–723.

La Greca, A.M., Silverman, W.K., & Wasserstein, S.B. (1998). Children's predisaster functioning as a predictor of posttraumatic stress following Hurricane Andrew. *Journal of Consulting and Clinical Psychology, 66*(6), 883–892.

Laor, N., Wolmer, L., & Cohen, D.J. (2001). Mothers' functioning and children's symptoms 5 years after a SCUD missile attack. *American Journal of Psychiatry, 158*(7), 1,020–1,026.

McFarlane, A.C. (1987). The relationship between patterns of family interaction and psychiatric disorder in children. *Australian and New Zealand Journal of Psychiatry, 21,* 383–390.

McFarlane, A.C., & Norris, F.H. (2006). Definitions and concepts in disaster research. In F.H. Norris, S. Galea, M.J. Friedman, & P.J. Watson (Eds.), *Methods for disaster mental health research* (pp. 3–19). New York: Guilford Press.

Norris, F.H., Friedman, M.J., Watson, P.J., Byrne, C.M., Diaz, E., & Kaniasty, K. (2002). 60,000 disaster victims speak: Part I. An empirical review of the empirical literature, 1981–2001. *Psychiatry, 65*(3), 207–239.

Pfefferbaum, B., & North, C.S. (in press). Children and families in the context of disasters: Implications for preparedness and response. *The Family Psychologist.*

Pfefferbaum, B., North, C.S., Doughty, D.E., Gurwitch, R.H., Fullerton, C.S., & Kyula, J. (2003). Posttraumatic stress and functional impairment in Kenyan children following the 1998 American Embassy bombing. *American Journal of Orthopsychiatry, 73*(2), 133–140.

Shaw, J.A., Applegate, B., & Schorr, C. (1996). Twenty-one-month follow-up study of school-age children exposed to Hurricane Andrew. *Journal of the American Academy of Child and Adolescent Psychiatry, 35*(3), 359–364.

Shaw, J.A., Applegate, B., Tanner, S., Perez, D., Rothe, E., Campo-Bowen, A.E., & Lahey, B.L. (1995). Psychological effects of Hurricane Andrew on an elementary school population. *Journal of the American Academy of Child and Adolescent Psychiatry, 34*(9), 1,185–1,192.

Silverman, W.K., & La Greca, A.M. (2002). Children experiencing disasters: Definitions, reactions, and predictors of outcomes. In A.M. La Greca, W.K. Silverman, E.M. Vernberg, & M.C. Roberts (Eds.), *Helping children cope with disasters and terrorism* (pp. 11–33). Washington, DC: American Psychological Association.

Udwin, O., Boyle, S., Yule, W., Bolton, D., & O'Ryan, D. (2000). Risk factors for long-term psychological effects of a disaster experienced in adolescence: Predictors of post traumatic stress disorder. *Journal of Child Psychology and Psychiatry, 41*(8), 969–979.

Yule, W., Bolton, D., Udwin, O., Boyle, S., O'Ryan, D., & Nurrish, J. (2000). The long-term psychological effects of a disaster experienced in adolescence: I: The incidence and course of PTSD. *Journal of Child Psychology and Psychiatry, 41*(4), 503–511.

Critical Thinking

1. What factors contribute to youth's reactions to disasters?
2. What outcomes help prepare professionals who work with youth in post-disaster situations?
3. What predictors help prepare professionals to work with youth in the area of post-disaster situations?
4. How does the nature of youth's exposure to disaster contribute to their reactions?

BETTY PFEFFERBAUM, MD, JD (betty-pfefferbaum@ouhsc.edu) is the Paul and Ruth Jonas Chair in the Department of Psychiatry and Behavioral Sciences at the University of Oklahoma Health Sciences Center, Oklahoma City, Oklahoma. **J. BRIAN HOUSTON, PHD,** is Assistant Professor of Research in the Department of Psychiatry and Behavioral Sciences at the University of Oklahoma Health Sciences Center, Oklahoma City, Oklahoma. **CAROL S. NORTH, MD, MPE,** is the **NANCY** and **RAY L. HUNT CHAIR** in Crisis Psychiatry and Professor of Psychiatry and Surgery at the University of Texas Southwestern Medical Center, Dallas, Texas. **JAMES L. REGENS, PHD,** is Presidential Professor and Director of the Center for Biosecurity Research at the University of Oklahoma Health Sciences Center, Oklahoma City, Oklahoma.

Acknowledgment—This work was supported in part by the Substance Abuse and Mental Health Services Administration (SAMHSA) grant 5 U79 SM057278-03 and the National Institute of Mental Health (NIMH), National Institute of Nursing Research (NINR), and SAMHSA grant 5R25 MH070569-04 to Betty Pfefferbaum; the NIMH grant RO1 MH068853-06 to Carol S. North; and the Defense Threat Reduction Agency (DTRA) and the Air Force Research Laboratory under Cooperative Agreement FA8650-05-2-6523 to James L. Regens. Points of view expressed in this article are those of the authors and do not represent the official position of SAMHSA, NIMH, NINR, DTRA, or the Air Force Research Laboratory.

Test-Your-Knowledge Form

We encourage you to photocopy and use this page as a tool to assess how the articles in *Annual Editions* expand on the information in your textbook. By reflecting on the articles you will gain enhanced text information. You can also access this useful form on a product's book support website at www.mhhe.com/cls.

NAME: _____   DATE: _____

TITLE AND NUMBER OF ARTICLE:
_____

BRIEFLY STATE THE MAIN IDEA OF THIS ARTICLE:
_____
_____

LIST THREE IMPORTANT FACTS THAT THE AUTHOR USES TO SUPPORT THE MAIN IDEA:
_____
_____
_____
_____

WHAT INFORMATION OR IDEAS DISCUSSED IN THIS ARTICLE ARE ALSO DISCUSSED IN YOUR TEXTBOOK OR OTHER READINGS THAT YOU HAVE DONE? LIST THE TEXTBOOK CHAPTERS AND PAGE NUMBERS:
_____
_____
_____
_____
_____

LIST ANY EXAMPLES OF BIAS OR FAULTY REASONING THAT YOU FOUND IN THE ARTICLE:
_____
_____
_____
_____
_____

LIST ANY NEW TERMS/CONCEPTS THAT WERE DISCUSSED IN THE ARTICLE, AND WRITE A SHORT DEFINITION:

We Want Your Advice

ANNUAL EDITIONS revisions depend on two major opinion sources: one is our Advisory Board, listed in the front of this volume, which works with us in scanning the thousands of articles published in the public press each year; the other is you—the person actually using the book. Please help us and the users of the next edition by completing the prepaid article rating form on this page and returning it to us. Thank you for your help!

ANNUAL EDITIONS: Adolescent Psychology 8/e

ARTICLE RATING FORM

Here is an opportunity for you to have direct input into the next revision of this volume.
We would like you to rate each of the articles listed below, using the following scale:

1. **Excellent: should definitely be retained**
2. **Above average: should probably be retained**
3. **Below average: should probably be deleted**
4. **Poor: should definitely be deleted**

Your ratings will play a vital part in the next revision.
Please mail this prepaid form to us as soon as possible.
Thanks for your help!

RATING	ARTICLE	RATING	ARTICLE
	1. Passage to Adulthood		19. Teens, Porn and the Digital Age: From Shame to Social Acceptability
	2. The Independence of Young Adults, in Historical Perspective		20. The 'Alarming' State of Reading in America
	3. Adolescent Decision Making: An Overview		21. Online Schooling Grows, Setting Off a Debate
	4. Something to Talk About		22. School's New Rule for Pupils in Trouble: No Fun
	5. Intuitive Risk Taking during Adolescence		23. The Benefits and Risks of Adolescent Employment
	6. Healthier Students, Better Learners		24. Immigrant Youth in U.S. Schools: Opportunities for Prevention
	7. Mental Assessment Test		25. Reducing School Violence: School-Based Curricular Programs and School Climate
	8. Body Dissatisfaction in Adolescent Females and Males: Risk and Resilience		26. Why Teenagers Find Learning a Drag
	9. Goodbye to Girlhood		27. Thousands Need Teens to Lead Them Back to School
	10. The Teenage Brain: Why Adolescents Sleep in, Take Risks, and Won't Listen to Reason		28. High School with a College Twist
	11. Adolescent Stress: The Relationship between Stress and Mental Health Problems		29. Video Game Violence
	12. I'm Just Tired: How Sleep Affects Your Preteen		30. Interview with Dr. Craig Anderson: Video Game Violence
	13. Supporting Youth during Parental Deployment: Strategies for Professionals and Families		31. Adolescents Coping with Stress: Development and Diversity
	14. When Play Turns to Trouble: Many Parents Are Now Wondering: How Much Is Too Much?		32. Steroids, the Media, and Youth: A Q&A with Travis Tygart
	15. Aggression in Adolescent Dating Relationships: Predictors and Prevention		33. Understanding Cutting in Adolescents: Prevalence, Prevention, and Intervention
	16. A Host of Trouble		34. Violence in Adolescent Dating Relationships
	17. Adolescent Sexual Attitudes and Behaviors: A Developmental Perspective		35. Non-Suicidal Self-Injury in Adolescents
	18. Sex, Sexuality, Sexting, and SexEd: Adolescents and the Media		36. Youth's Reactions to Disasters and the Factors That Influence Their Response

‖‖‖

NO POSTAGE
NECESSARY
IF MAILED
IN THE
UNITED STATES

BUSINESS REPLY MAIL
FIRST CLASS MAIL PERMIT NO. 551 DUBUQUE IA

POSTAGE WILL BE PAID BY ADDRESSEE

McGraw-Hill Contemporary Learning Series
501 BELL STREET
DUBUQUE, IA 52001

ABOUT YOU

Name _____   Date _____

Are you a teacher? ☐ A student? ☐
Your school's name

_____

Department

_____

Address _____   City _____   State _____   Zip _____

School telephone # _____

YOUR COMMENTS ARE IMPORTANT TO US!

Please fill in the following information:
For which course did you use this book?

_____

Did you use a text with this ANNUAL EDITION? ☐ yes ☐ no
What was the title of the text?

_____

What are your general reactions to the Annual Editions concept?

_____

Have you read any pertinent articles recently that you think should be included in the next edition? Explain.

_____

Are there any articles that you feel should be replaced in the next edition? Why?

_____

Are there any World Wide Websites that you feel should be included in the next edition? Please annotate.

_____

May we contact you for editorial input? ☐ yes ☐ no
May we quote your comments? ☐ yes ☐ no

NOTES

NOTES

NOTES

NOTES

NOTES

NOTES

NOTES

NOTES